Acts of Faith in a Secular World: The Sermons of Beverly Asbury

Acts of Faith in a Secular World: The Sermons of Beverly Asbury

Fifty two weeks of thoughts and meditations
as delivered in the sermons of
Rev. Beverly A. Asbury
at the
College of Wooster
Wooster, Ohio

Between December 30, 1962 and December 4, 1966

With relevance to the 21st Century

Introductions by Douglas J. Eder, Ph.D.
College of Wooster, Centennial Class of 1966

Published by Douglas J. Eder and the College of Wooster Class of 1966
2016

First Printing: 2016

ISBN 978-1-329-78196-2

Douglas J. Eder
1111 Franklin
Edwardsville, Illinois 62025

www.siue.edu/~deder/

Ordering Information:

U.S. trade bookstores and wholesalers: Please contact: (618) 530-0562; email   deder@siue.edu.

Dedication

This book is dedicated to:

The memories of Addie Mae Collins, Carole Robertson, Cynthia Wesley, and Denise McNair, ages 11-14, who suffered from the oppression of race when they died on September 15, 1963 in the bombing of Birmingham's 16th Street Baptist Church.

The memory of Aylan Kurdi, age 3, who suffered from the oppression of war when he died on September 2, 2015 in the waters off the coast of Turkish Bodrum while fleeing with his family from Syria to Greece.

The work of Malala Yousafzai, age 18, the Pakastani activist who suffered from the oppression of women when she was shot in the head for advocating education for girls and women around the world. She received the Nobel Peace Prize in 2014.

We have much to do.

Contents

Acknowledgments

I wish to acknowledge gratefully the kindness of Karol Crosbie, editor of *Wooster Magazine*, who helped initiate the collecting of sermons that comprise this book. Thanks go to Lib (Westhafer) O'Brien, Ginny (Keim) Brooks, Kathy (Rowland) Matsushima, Stephen Hills, and Suzanne (Lohrey) Eder, who responded to the call for Rev. Asbury's printed sermons and together supplied a total of 146 sermons, of which 75 are unique. The Special Collections division of Andrews Library at the College of Wooster supplied an additional nine sermons and the lead photograph. I am grateful to Elaine Smith Snyder of Andrews Library for her many preparations both seen and unseen by me, her arrangements for my on-campus parking and working desk space, and her excellent assistance in accessing the Andrews Library Special Collections, its historical material, and photographs. Prof. Gordon Tait, Professor Emeritus of Religious Studies, receives thanks for guiding me specifically to the sermon of Sept. 13, 1964, entitled "Poisoning the Student Mind." It is this core sermon – the one that became the lead sermon for this book – that led me to Wooster's Special Collections. Finally, I thank Beverly Asbury for allowing us the honor and enjoyment of reliving his sermons and, once again, finding meaning in the Word he conveyed to us some 50 years ago.

--Douglas Eder

Foreword

Thank you for remembering so well and for thinking that sermons are more than "one time things." I never expected to see these sermons ever again. I am deeply moved that you and others have kept copies and still find them relevant and meaningful. To my surprise, I look forward to reading them again and engaging with others who read or re-read them. If it puts me in my old age – approaching 85 – with people I know – and loved – all those years ago, it will be a blessing indeed.

Beverly A. Asbury
Albuquerque, NM
August 6, 2013

Preface

Among the items my mother kept beside her bed was a thick book written in Old German. When we emptied her apartment after her death in 2010, several relatives in the room examined the family inscriptions in the book going back to 1819. They guessed the book to be a Bible. My mom could read Old German with difficulty, and I am no better at it than she was. It took patient study to reveal the book to be a collection of sermons by the German Pietist, Immanuel Gottlob Brastberger (1716-1764). Brastberger ended his career as pastor to the Lutheran church in Nürtingen, which is a town a dozen miles or so southeast of Stuttgart. The book was published in 1758. In terms of German chronology, that's the era of Immanual Kant. In France and the American Colonies, it's the era of the Enlightenment and Benjamin Franklin. This is certainly the oldest book I own.

The book's title (from the German) is lengthy. It translates roughly as: *Evangelical Testimonies of Truth to cheer in true Christianity, partly from ordinary Sundays and holiday Gospels, partly from the History of the Our Savior's Passions, and all delivered in the Cycle of a Full Year together with some casual Notes.* Indeed! The sermons – 52 in all – follow a liturgical year beginning with Advent and ending with the following Advent. Each sermon is accompanied by Brastberger's lengthy "casual notes" (obviously the author's modest understatement) making for a book of over 1000 pages! For those people in the 18th century who could read, these sermons provided a thought-for-the-week, plus commentary. The book is reported to have been popular among German-reading people at the time – which it had to be for them to lug around such a heavy volume. Whether these sermons were "The Best of Brastberger" or a gathering of 52 sermons into several special themes, I don't know. I do know that, as a group, they provide insight into social and spiritual conditions in southern Germany of the time. They also provide insight into the thoughts and actions of Rev. Brastberger himself – sort of a *Festschrift* (celebration in writing) of his life.

In early spring, 2011, while visiting Albuquerque to give a university seminar, I reunited with College of Wooster Class of '66 secretary Elizabeth (Westhafer) O'Brien, who informed me that Rev. Beverly Asbury had recently moved to Albuquerque from Gainesville, Florida, with his wife, and wouldn't it be nice if we could all have dinner together. Rev. Asbury was pastor to Westminster Church on the College of Wooster campus during 1962-1966. I hadn't seen him for more than 40 years. I agreed with enthusiasm because not only had I spent four years as a member of the choir listening to Rev. Asbury's sermons, I had also interviewed him as part of my Senior Independent Study.

I majored in religion at Wooster before turning to medical physiology and biophysics as a graduate student at Florida State and onward to a faculty career in research and teaching. As a member of Wooster's Centennial Class of 1966, I remember the attention bestowed on us by the College. I also recall the turbulence roiling through the College and the nation at the same time. In my student idealism, I recognized Rev. Asbury's sermons about the law, civil disobedience, freedom, responsibility, consequences, and positive deeds as intellectually well founded and balanced. It was also plain to us students that Rev. Asbury's ruminations on war, racism, social injustice, poverty, and suffering were not to be received as simple academic musings from an ivory tower pulpit. No, his messages contained calls to action. Nevertheless, we students were aware that those exhortations were received with less than jovial agreement by several members of the College's administration and Board of Trustees.

I wondered, how could Rev. Asbury do this? How could he encourage from the pulpit our youthful energies, point out injustices and insincerities in society, serve as sympathetic and non-judgmental chaplain to individuals in need, and do this while retaining the enduring support of the College? Amidst the turbulence of the 1960s, how could *any* college chaplain do this? Thus, my Senior Independent Study was an examination of the college chaplaincy among the (then) 46 Presbyterian colleges in the United States. I surveyed most of the colleges by mail and telephone, but Rev. Asbury was someone I could interview in person...and so I did. Among the revelations of that interview, two things stand out – one revealed back then and one revealed within the last two years. (1) Rev. Asbury was *not* chaplain to the College of Wooster. He was Pastor to Westminster Presbyterian Church located on the Wooster campus, a position that was officially independent of the College of Wooster. Because he was independent and did not receive pay as a College employee, he was free to take positions at odds with College pronouncements. This was intentional on his part. Among the 46 Presbyterian colleges in the United States, he was the *only* college pastor to establish this kind of independence. It was a separation he continued during his subsequent career at Vanderbilt University. (2) Rev. Asbury closely overlapped our time as the Centennial Class of '66 at Wooster. He arrived on Sept. 5, 1962, gave his first sermon on Sept. 30, was installed on Oct. 21, and preached his last Wooster sermon on Dec. 4, 1966.

During the Albuquerque dinner with Beverly and Vicky Asbury and Lib O'Brien, we replayed these musings. We recalled how we appreciated the written copies of his sermons that were placed at the back of the chapel each Sunday. Those of us in the choir had the benefit of the recessional, which put us at the back of the church, first to sing the final "Amen," and then to scarf up copies of the sermon before anyone else could. Also during the Albuquerque dinner, the subject of my mom's copy of *Evangelical Testimonies* by Brastberger came up, and it was followed by a comment and question to Bev Asbury: "It might be interesting to assemble the Asbury sermons into a similar book. Lib and I have only a few copies between us...do you by chance have a set of your Wooster sermons?" "No," he and Vicky replied in unison, "We cleaned them out a month ago before moving from Gainesville to Albuquerque."

Arrrgh. What to do next? Ideas cascaded quickly toward contacting Karol Crosbie, editor of *Wooster Magazine*, the alumni quarterly, in order to put out a call for print copies of Asbury's sermons. Coincidentally, the *Magazine* had scheduled to run an article by Prof. Gordon Tait about his manuscript, *Personal Reflections on the History of Religion at The College of Wooster*. The manuscript included a discussion of the role of

Rev. Asbury. So, in the Summer, 2011 issue, Karol Crosbie ran excerpts from Gordon Tait's manuscript (p. 36) plus an accompanying call for Asbury sermons (inside back cover). Prof. Tait's manuscript contains the following paragraph:

"What did [College of Wooster] President Lowry think of Bev and his influences? In public, he supported the preacher; after all, he was truly engaging the students and making religion very relevant. In private, he must have had moments when he wished Bev would turn down the volume, for Bev couldn't help being a factor in the change taking place in the 1960s – change that Howard Lowry tried to resist."

A few weeks before Rev. Asbury's departure from Wooster to Vanderbilt, President Lowry handwrote to him a letter of thanks, encouragement, and farewell. The letter reveals that Lowry saw large changes on the horizon and sensed their arrival as probably inevitable. Prof. Tait's conclusion above is bang-on target. Lowry's letter reveals that he did not wish Asbury to turn the volume *off*. It does acknowledge that he (Asbury) had exerted strong spiritual guidance during unsettled circumstances and that, regardless of any divergent viewpoints between the two of them, Lowry knew that the College community was undoubtedly the better for Asbury's guidance. Indeed we are!

Douglas J. Eder, Ph.D.
Edwardsville, Illinois
July 23, 2013

Introduction

The Cycle of Sermons appearing in this book is arranged in themes for weekly meditation. The sermons as presented here do not follow chronological order, although for continuity of thought, some sermons do appear in their original sequence. A "Cycle of Sermons" classically follows the liturgical year from Advent to Advent. Because these sermons occurred on a college campus, the schedule for this book follows an academic year. In the 1960s, when Beverly Asbury was at Wooster, the collegiate year generally began in early September. At the time of this writing, the year 2015, college classes commonly begin in late August, so the Cycle is timed to current custom. The Cycle embraces Thanksgiving, Christmas, Palm Sunday, Easter, and Wooster's Color Day at their appropriate times, and finishes 52 sermons later in late August of the following year. Because some special days (*e.g.,* Thanksgiving, the first Sunday of Advent, and Easter) vary with the calendar from year to year, the schedule is approximate. Approximate end-of-semester markers appear in the Contents and end-of-month markers appear in the Introductions to guide a reader's weekly progress through the Cycle.

The sermons have been chosen, and are intentionally arranged, to fulfill three goals: (1) to present themes that unify Rev. Asbury's sermons across the four years he was at Wooster, (2) to reflect the sociopolitical environment of the mid-60s, as the themes of Asbury's sermons point to lessons for today, 50 years later, and (3) to reveal the man, Beverly Asbury. All three goals are intended to be achieved within the format of the year-long Cycle of Sermons. The reader must decide whether achievement of these goals in this format has been successful.

The reader will undoubtedly notice that the sermons are reproductions of manuscripts. The manuscripts are those that were collected at the back of the church by students on the day they were delivered, exactly as Rev. Asbury typed them. A couple of sermons have handwritten underlinings that students placed to highlight a passage or two. Removal of these modifications was not attempted. In addition, the language of the early- and mid-60s used the masculine pronouns "he" and "his" and the masculine nouns "man" and "mankind" to refer to both genders and to humanity in general. There is no evidence that gender discrimination was ever intended by Rev. Asbury, and so the original language remains as typed in the original manuscripts.

Rev. Brastberger's work in German, his *Evangelical Testimonies*, is a collection of his own sermons, edited by himself, and accompanied by his own "casual notes." The collection of Rev. Asbury's work in this book is different. It was not collected by Rev. Asbury himself. Hence, the sermons have not been edited, and there are no accompanying interpretive "casual notes" to annotate the text. The separate introductions that accompany each sermon aim at setting the context, making relevant the sociopolitical environment of the 1960s, strengthening connections between the sermons, and providing some background for the Biblical passages themselves. None of these efforts is intended to be analytical. They may somewhat explicate the texts of the sermons but, in the main, they are intended to be descriptive summaries and illustrations rather than interpretations.

The Cycle of Sermons

Two sermons begin this collection as well as the cycle of the academic year. They were delivered about a year apart at the beginning of the school years. Together they focus on the changes and challenges of being a student.

1. **9/13/64** **Poisoning the Student Mind** <u>Begin last week of August</u>

Two themes that occupied the years 1962-66 were the civil rights movement and the war in Vietnam. This first sermon opened an academic year of college by challenging students to recognize that doubt is a symptom of becoming educated…and that hope is a countervailing and appropriate response. This sermon is prophetic in recognizing that collegiate years in the mid-60s would be filled with challenges to traditional thought, behaviors, and beliefs.

This sermon is the one referred to by Prof. Tait in his manuscript (see the Preface). The beginning of the school year in 1964, which was the setting for this particular sermon, was surrounded by unusually large changes, doubts, and unrests. Internally, US society faced the visible onset of the civil rights movement. With Lyndon Johnson as President of the US, the summer of 1964 was to become known as the *Mississippi Summer* because it was the summer when volunteers, many of them students, went to Mississippi to assist with voter registration. The effort cost three civil rights volunteers their lives when they were murdered…this event following the assassination of President Kennedy seven months previously. During the summer of '64, the Warren Commission was just finishing its work and was about to issue its report that Lee Harvey Oswald acted alone in the assassination of President Kennedy. Externally, North Vietnamese torpedo boats were reported to have attacked US destroyers, and that led Congress to pass the Gulf of Tonkin resolution…the official beginning of the war in Vietnam.

In light of a summer of unrest, the scripture readings that accompany this sermon express doubt, futility – and, yes, hope:
> "I consider the sufferings of this present time are not worth comparing with the glory that is to be revealed to us" (Romans 8:18).

Moreover,
> "We know that the whole creation has been groaning in travail together until now; and not only the creation, but we ourselves...groan inwardly…" (Romans 8:22-23).

Nevertheless,
> "…we hope for what we do not see, we wait for it with patience" (Romans 8:25).

And,
> "Now faith is the assurance of things hoped for, the conviction of things not seen." (Herbrews 11:1).

Rev. Asbury offers faith and patience as worthy tools for overcoming doubt and discontent, even though complete overcoming of doubt is unlikely ever to occur. Such is the life of an educated person.

The sermon opens a school year by showing, in Prof. Tait's words, that religion is a source of challenge as well as a source of comfort. Doubts are uncomfortable, but doubt is what gets you an education. This sermon also establishes Rev. Asbury's frequent pattern of drawing a lesson from literature, in this case, John Updike's 1960 novel, *Rabbit, Run*.

Westminster Presbyterian Church
Wooster, Ohio
Rev. Beverly Asbury, Minister
September 13, 1964

"POISONING THE STUDENT MIND"
(What to look for in theology)
Romans 8: 18-25
Hebrews 11: 1-3

A graduate of this College, now dean of the Mount Holyoke College Chapel, wrote an article this summer called "The Time Has Come". Deane Ferm's words were printed in The Christian Century, (July 15, 1964) and they expressed forthrightly what he feels should happen ecclesiastically and theologically in the years ahead. He stated bluntly that too much present-day theology deals with trivial concerns in a world hanging on the rim of disaster. The Church, he says, must escape triviality, concern for ecclesiastical organization and sectarian tradition, and deal with far weightier matters. Then Deane Ferm goes on to give radical reinterpretation to major historical doctrines; to declare the interdependence of the human race; and to assert a "healthy optimism" that the problems of our generation are capable of solution.

Deane Ferm always manages to stimulate. The form of stimulation depends on whom you are. Louis Cassels happens to be the religion editor of UPI, and he was stimulated to give a vigorous answer to Deane Ferm's article. However, Cassels' vigor did not hide the fact that he was giving the "same old answers" to Ferm's argument. The UPI religion editor wanted it clearly understood that the time would never come when he --and other religious literalists--could accept radical reinterpretations. And he felt that men who proposed them were dangerous beyond compare. So, again, the cry was raised, "Beware, the modernists".

All this reminded me of nothing so much as the response of Canadian students of a generation or more ago to charges of "modernism" against their leaders in the Student Christian Movement. I really don't know all the history of this very well, but I do know that the literalists of another day charged that the SCM leaders were poisoning the student mind. You know, the kind of thing that Cassel thinks Ferm is doing today. Well, anyway, the students in the SCM thought this a ridiculous charge; they were looking for new answers to old questions; and so they wrote a song, a parody, on the charge that the leaders were poisoning their minds. The words go like this:

> The SCM has found its true vocation
> It is poisoning the student mind.
> Its leaders by astute manipulation are poisoning the student mind
> And there are some that say that we will go
> To toast our toes below
> If we pay heed to leaders that we know
> Are poisoning the student mind.
>
> Bad men, bold men, villains double-eyed
> 'Neath their smiling countenances hide
> Spiritual arsenic and moral cyanide
> For poisoning the student mind.

It is likely that those who work in academic communities will think that the time has come to rethink theology, and it is likely that those who raise no questions will feel that minds are being poisoned. Parents and religious leaders of a certain bent always express concern over what happens to the student mind in college, and students after a short while wonder why nothing ever happened to the minds of their

9-13-64

parents and religious leaders. However, laying all charges aside, we must face the fact that students of all generations raise questions of religion and seek new and more relevant beliefs by which to live. In this generation, particularly, with its rapid scientific and technological change, its urbanization, automation, and industrialization, its population explosion--there are even greater arguments for the revision of outworn dogmas. Students who are new to this place and are worshipping here today for the first time will soon be more disturbed religiously than they are now. Some will feel that their minds are being poisoned, but a greater number will be searching for something more than the religious luggage they brought with them.

In short, all of us (not just students) endure doubt. Deane Ferm is not alone in feeling that we Christians are trying to believe in God in a time when the pictures we have had of God are inadequate or even downright false. All men who search for God find Him to be elusive and even wonder if He is not completely absent. Part of living in our times seems to be the lack of power to affirm the traditional images of God. The supports on which we have always depended seem to be gone, knocked from under us, and so we wonder if God has gone. Perhaps that is why we feel most comfortable during Lent, which is marked by Jesus'cry of dereliction from the cross-- "my God, my God, why hast thou forsaken me?" If Jesus can wonder, are we to be blamed? Is it enough to say that our minds have been poisoned?

No, we have not had our minds contaminated. But that does not mean that we can or should stay where we are--or will shortly find ourselves to be. In fact, we cannot live as Christians for long with the suspicion that God himself has withdrawn from our lives. We must seek a way to turn the corner and move away from the fading of traditional images to a new sense of the presence of God. Yet, as we seek to move to a new faith, let us recognize that we shall never go back exactly to what we have left. Doubt will have become necessary to our faith. Faith never overcomes doubt completely. Indeed, a lively faith can bear a good deal of doubt around the edges, and benefit from it. Nevertheless, faith and doubt are not the same, and we must make a choice between them. Ultimately, every one of us, who seeks to be a Christian, has to move to an affirmation of God's presence even if that affirmation comes in bold reinterpretations. In other words, those of us who are seeking to be Christians curiously find it possible to pray for God's return to our lives even when we are most keenly aware of his absence.

John Updike's novel, Rabbit, Run, has some surprising light to shed on this aspect of our lives, without God but desperately in need of Him. The novel is the story of a conceited and yet strangely fascinating young man called Rabbit, who has never lived up to the glory of his high school days. Leaving his wife and child, he goes to live with a prostitute. Rabbit is temporarily brought back to his wife through the efforts of a young Episcopal clergyman, Jack Eccles, but he runs away again. The wife, in a drunken stupor, accidentally drowns her child in the bathtub, and again Eccles brings about a reconciliation.

At the funeral, as the dirt covers the casket, Rabbit turns to the people there and says: "You all keep acting as if I did it. I wasn't anywhere near. She's the one." This crude remark evoked hostility from the crowd, and not even Rabbit's thick hide of insensitivity could hide it from himself. Still in character, the Rabbit turns tail and runs.

What, you say, makes it worthwhile to read or hear of such a person? What does this tell us about theology and what to look for? Just this, Rabbit personifies man living unto himself and attempting to be true to that alone. Updike shows us the result of a shallow, truncated humanism that elevates the individual to the level of God. Updike shows us the kind of human produced by a society that believes we are to seek first our own good and the kingdom of heaven will be given unto us. In short,

Rabbit's moral emptiness points us to the need of theology.

What then of the Church? What _are_ we to look for in theology in this kind of society? Well, here's a hint. Rabbit's parents belonged to a Lutheran Church, and their pastor delivers a scathing denunciation of Eccles' role in the whole affair. He rudely rebukes Eccles for getting involved as no pastor should. He admonishes Eccles to pray instead and wait for God to bring the kingdom.

While some of this may be deserved, there is much more to be said for Eccles. Never forget that Rabbit presented a prodigious undertaking. He had an ego of pathological proportions. To be sure, Eccles failed in his attempt to redeem Rabbit, and it is certain that the Lutheran pastor did not fail. The very best insurance against failure is never to get involved. Play it safe and cool. The agonizing, ambiguous mess that Jesus came into, where He got involved and failed as often as not, is a world that "Christians" strive to avoid.

Considering the seeming absence of God in Rabbit's life and the condition of Rabbit's heart, it's a wonder that Eccles accomplished as much as he did. At the very last Rabbit thinks of Eccles as one of the three significant people in his life. Eccles evokes the only unselfish thing that Rabbit ever does. He attempts to phone Eccles so that he wouldn't be discouraged.

Perhaps we ought to conclude that a special burden of our time is the situation of being without God. We have not, most of us anyway, reached Rabbit's extreme, but we share his condition. For some reason, there is no possession of God for us, but only a hope, a waiting. Part of the truth of being a Christian today is to stand, somehow, as a man with hope. We know, or will know, too much to take "God" as portrayed in our childhood. We know too little to know God now as He is. But we do know enough to be able to say that he will come in our involvement in the world. God will come, that we know, to the broken and contrite heart, if we continue to offer Him that by identifying with suffering humanity. Faith is, for many of us, a kind of trust that one day God will no longer be absent from us. "Now faith is the assurance of things hoped for, the conviction of things not seen....what is seen was made out of things which do not appear."

We, Christians, live in hope, As Deane Ferm put it, "we need a declaration of healthy optimism holding that the tremendous problems of our generation can be solved ...the Judeo-Christian faith has always declared that there is no human being and no human situation beyond the possibility of redemption....The distinguished psychiatrist, Viktor Frankl, has written of three years in concentration camps in the midst of conditions of indescribable brutality and human degradation. Yet despite all this suffering and destruction of human values Dr.Frankl found a new and deeper meaning to life:

> For the first time in my life I saw the truth as it is set into song by so many poets, proclaimed as the final wisdom by so many writers. The truth--that love is the ultimate and highest goal to which man can aspire...that the salvation of man is through love and in love.. For the first time in my life I was able to understand the meaning of the words,"The angels are lost in perpetual contemplation of an infinite glory."...I sensed my spirit piercing through the enveloping gloom. I felt it transcend that hopeless, meaningless world,and from somewhere I heard a victorious "Yes" in answer to my questions of the existence of an ultimate purpose."(_From Death Camp to Existentialism_,pp 36-39,Beacon Press

So it is that we "consider that the sufferings of this present time are not worth comparing with the glory that is revealed to us". We wait with hope. We hope for what we do not yet see. We wait with patience. We love with zeal. In the midst of the uncertainty that some will call "poisoned minds", we look for the time when we can declare a victorious yes in which we affirm the reality of light over darkness,of life over death. This is what we look for in theology. What we look for is that abiding conviction that man's life has meaning and that his problem can be solved. In this hope were we saved.

2. 9/26/65 **A Teaching Ministry**

This sermon accompanied the dedication of the Church House on campus.

College is a place to learn, and so is the church. Jesus was a teacher, and people learned in his presence. The process of learning some things can be uncomfortable, disturbing, difficult, and even revolutionary. Rev. Asbury chose as a reading for this sermon the story known as the parable of the sower.

> "A sower went out to sow. … Some seeds fell along the path, and the birds came and devoured them. Other seeds fell on rocky ground…. Other seeds fell upon thorns…. Other seeds fell on good soil and brought forth grain…. He who has ears, let him hear" (Matthew 13:3-9).

Rev. Asbury used the reading – and the parable itself – as a metaphor for the student mind as fertile ground. Indeed, the Church House was to be cultivated as a hospitable place for the nurture and growth of ideas.

This sermon, which was given at the beginning of a school year, encouraged students to be open to new ideas, even if those ideas initially appeared to be uncomfortable. Learning from Jesus can be uncomfortable, disturbing, and revolutionary, because he broke barriers.

> "Truly, I say to you, many prophets and righteous men longed to see what you see, and did not see it, and to hear what you hear, and did not hear it" (Matthew 13:17).

9/26/65

Westminster Presbyterian Church
Wooster, Ohio
Rev. Beverly Asbury, Minister
September 26, 1965

A TEACHING MINISTRY
Matthew 13: 1-17

The popular teaching of the Church and its corporate behavior in worship, often
and perhaps normally, has been inhibited by a thousand conventions. And most of them
have little or nothing to do with the gospel. Church-patterns have a quaint tendency
to select certain details but ignore others. It is obligatory to open meetings with
prayer but not obligatory either to compose meaningful prayers or listen to the prayer
itself. We find an insistence that we follow certain liturgical forms but we do not
insist that those forms express anything of contemporary life. The meeting on Tuesday night at 8 must be absolutely counted on; but we don't ask whether the hymns used
there make any tolerable sense or that the Bible study make contact with the real
facts of our lives.

Church life to the ordinary man, unless he has been innoculated against such
things, seems a queer mixture of the inhibited and eccentric. You know, there are
many things that you must not do in church; and there are some things you wouldn't be
caught dead doing unless you were in church. That's the way it is for a growing number of men. And anybody who sees church life that way is not going to listen to the
Church's teaching on so urgent and immediate a subject as sex--or even money. The
objective effect of most church teaching and behavior is to make many folks say:
"We believe in religion; we want our children educated in moral and spiritual values.
But that doesn't stand any real concern of mine. It's the place that I would go if
I really wanted a question of mine answered."

The Church cannot survive in a meaningful form unless this changes. To be sure,
the Church may reach those who make use of its services, but that is a smaller proportion of our people, even in this "Christian land", each year. And the corporate
life of the Church cannot reach those who stay outside, who never even dream that they
have questions, much less that the Church could have answers for them. Those who are
more-or-less outside the Church are going to be reached only through the individual,
personal lives of Church members; they, and they alone will carry the burden of the
teaching ministry of the Church outside. They, and they alone--the laity--can and
will transcend and transform the old conventions in order to meet the real questions
of our day.

Yet, this possibility and hope has frequently been thwarted by people such as
the professional pastors, the educators, and administrators of the conventional church.
We have insisted almost that the laity is equipped to do its job only when it knows
what we know--only when it has command of a body of theological knowledge. We have
not stopped really to ask what the laymen is prepared to learn. And we are not entirely clear what it is we have to teach. In our emphasis on basic beliefs and knowledge, we have not led either ourselves or our laity in the task of _thinking_ theologically. We make "churchmen" conscious of their church-institution self, but we fail
to meet those same men in the normative structures of _their_ life. If we did, we would
discover a desperation to be faithful, a desire to learn, an unspken need to rethink
or re-conceptualize faith.

The missing element lies in our ability and willingness to think theologically--
to look at the events of our history and at our lives; to ask what they mean; to in-
quire into their implications for our lives. The teaching ministry begins with learning from each other; with understanding that the professionals can help in the task
of reconceptualizing faith once they understand the structures of lay life. The

teaching ministry begins when the laity can be with those outside the Church in such a way that they can talk freely, share burdens, and offer comfort. Persons individually can become centers of reconciliation, and thus disciples. In their presence others can raise questions or discover that there are questions to raise. In their presence, others come to see that the world is "the Father's house", and that the freedoms of that house are more truly liberating than freedoms of nihilistic living.

Thus, the function of a Church House, such as we dedicate this day, lies in pointing laity to the world, to the "Father's house." The function of the Church House is to equip men and women to engage in a teaching ministry, by helping them learn to think theologically. The Church House then is a basis, a fundamental need, but its operation is not our central concern. Rather, our primary task lies in our service to the world.

In this task we can turn directly to the New Testament and learn from the teaching ministry of Jesus. This is the right and proper course if Jesus is the paradigm of true humanity and of the mission of the Church. In fact, what we discover in and from him shatters the patterns and conventions of Church life. We discover in him that freedom to be unreligious, impious, open-if- you-will, to thinking theologically in new terms. Jesus himself ministered in a time in which conditions were such that people in general were unresponsive. Nevertheless, he made every effort to communicate effectively, and we can learn here even today some important considerations for a teaching ministry for laity in the world.

Jesus spoke in a simple, direct, vivid way. He appealed to familiar experiences --he dared to deal with experiences which we might politely ignore even though we live with them daily. Jesus talked frankly about evil, death, money--the subjects we treat so gently and discreetly. We fail to consider the real face of evil and so fail to detect it in ourselves. We cosmetize death and, as a society, continue a delusion of bodily immortality. We speak of it in hushed funeral tones and disguise it in funeral homes. We secretly worship money and accept it as the sign of where we stand in our culture. But we don't talk about its influence on important ethical decisions in our lives. Jesus did! He used those experiences to point to profound truth. And if we would today speak with or to modern man, we will need to discover a new language. We cannot assume that the old words of orthodox Protestant theology will do, for often enough we do not understand these words ourselves. We see Jesus asking questions to help those around him understand the meaning of his teaching and the needs of their lives. He was willing to create new words; new, powerful, original ways of speaking. His creative parables broke down barriers in the way people thought and understood themselves, in the light of a transcending reality. And this is precisely what it means to think theologically. If we seek to follow Jesus in our teaching ministry, we must dare to do this.

However, such a dare must also take account of Jesus' great sensitivity to the persons whom he taught. Jesus shows an amazing flexibility in his response to different persons. This surely means that we cannot canonize one way of speaking and one way of acting for all Christians at all times. To the smug, self-assured Pharisees, Jesus spoke directly and in a brutally frank way. He seemed to feel that was the only way to break through a tough crust. With a sensitive person, who had been preached at and condemned and knew how bad he was, Jesus spoke with encouragement and hope. Jesus had an uncanny ability to meet each individual situation. We cannot expect to have that ability ourselves, but we at least ought to be aware of what our ability is and is not, where it should be used and where it should not. At the very least, we ought to learn how to recognize different motives, and how we can accept and learn from them. Whatever our teaching ministry may be--in class, dormitory, community--our goal must be the same. We can learn to avoid saying the wrong word at the wrong time; we can avoid the shabby tactic of winning a victory with doctrinaire teaching; we can seek rather to relate to the person in our presence.

If we learn these things from Jesus' methodology, we can learn something as well from his content. (Here we limit ourselves to certain broad conclusions). For one thing, Jesus constantly emphasized that true life was more than the accummulation of things. He pictured man's great temptation to lose himself in the side issues of life, to make of _things_ an end, a god, rather than using them to direct his life to greater end. Now, we live in a day of unprecedented prosperity. The latest figures indicate that personal debt stands at an all-time high. We're so convinced of a prosperous future that we're unafraid of violating every one of Ben Franklin's sayings. Our society has been built on obsolescence and covetousness. Consciously and unconsciously, we have become accummulators, and we have lost some of our dignity and integrity in the process. We scramble for "savings", "bonuses", "discounts". We enter contests to get "something for nothing". We demolish every notch of "man's dignity" by our behavior on "Dollar Day". We secretly yearn to win from Sohio but hesitate to be open about it. We buy what we don't need and often "need" what we don't really want.

Must we not learn to ask again what it means to gain the whole world and lose our soul? The content of Jesus' teaching may well indicate that the manner of thinking theologically today will be economics, the use of leisure, etc. Jesus does not ask us to deny the world, but he does ask us to consider what makes life worth living. It is important to think theologically about our wealth, how we invest it--our time and how we use it --our possessions and how they influence our relations with other men. To think about these things in a positive, creative manner becomes an urgent matter for contemporary Christians if they would teach other men how to live in any qualitative sense.

Another thing which we must relearn from Jesus lies in our empty practice of religion. This is important in our teaching ministry, because a new Church House offers great possibilities of more empty practices. Many people in this day still believe that man's relationship with God centers in such things as opening meetings with prayer, keeping the Sabbath, etc. But Jesus taught us that a right relationship with God comes along with a right relationship to one's neighbor. The healing and helping of one's neighbor in need constitutes a more religious act by far than scrupulously keeping the Sabbath. You cannot live in a right relationship with God and remain alienated from the sons of men. This must surely mean that our teaching ministry in the life of the Church must concentrate on the life of man, on the rights and responsibilities of being human, on the need for love and justice and peace among men.

Jesus' teaching was directed toward the end that man might live in a totally different pattern than that which prevailed and was accepted in that day. And our teaching must also challenge men to break out of their neat, legalistic patterns. If we are dedicating a Church House to a teaching ministry in the world, let us make sure that it does not reinforce the things that enslave but that it seeks to follow Jesus in teaching men to live as free sons of God. Jesus' teaching was revolutionary in his day, and it still can be in ours. He dared men to be different, and as long as the teaching ministry does that, we cannot expect the church to be less than controversial. Jesus did not seek only to be admired and respected, and neither must we. Jesus called men to decision about their lives and so must we. Jesus was unwilling merely to be tolerated and so must we. Jesus was prepared to bear a cross for the sake of witness and so must we.

The passage of time and the conventionality of religion have dulled our sensitivities to these facts. In our day, as Martin Luther King has said, the Church is too often the taillight on the caboose, rather than the headlight pointing the way. A teaching ministry for us means surrendering the status quo, acting despite our fears, and facing the problems of the modern world.

We now have a Church House. Will our lives in it be dedicated to a teaching ministry so that our lives outside it will be centers of reconciliation? Will we use it to discuss frankly and freely how to become free and living? Will we learn here how to share burdens, to discover meaning, to think theologically? The answer depends on our resolve. On what we will be; on what we will do as men of faith; on the laity in the world—the Father's House.

The next 13 sermons recorded the social and political environment in which we found ourselves during the early-mid-60s. To what extent are similar circumstances recognizable today? This group of sermons also builds the foundation of a Christian stance for dealing with these conditions. The stance embraces patience, involvement, engagement, and action.

3.   10/17/65   Tares and Dilemmas

This is a sermon about politics. Like the sermons that follow, it urges maturity, restraint, and good judgment. The sermon takes a Biblical parable about weeds and extends the metaphor to cover modern politics.

> "[A] man…sowed good seed in his field; but while men were sleeping, his enemy came and sowed weeds among the wheat, and went away. So when the plants came up and bore grain, then the weeds appeared also" (Matthew 13:24-26).

Because the roots of the grain plants and the weeds are so intertwined, the farmer in the parable urges the reapers not to pull out the weeds because the act of doing so will likely destroy the grain plants as well.

Issues of politics are usually deeply intertwined with each other and are not subject to superficial, simple yes-we're-right-no-they're-wrong interventions. Rev. Asbury uses the parable of the sower to point out that in the debate over the war the US was fighting at the time in Vietnam, neither the hawks nor the doves entirely owned righteousness. Moreover, attempts of either side in the discussion to annihilate the other would likely bring ruin to both. Thus, the theme of the sermon is patience and reflection; each side should attempt to understand the perspective of the other.

In addition to patience, the sermon advocates acceptance of imperfections. There is a gap between what one may wish for and what one may realistically attain. In a conversation retold by former Senator Robert Dole (R - Kansas) during his farewell visit to Kansas during the spring of 2014, Dole recalled informing President Reagan that the Democrat-controlled Senate would not give him 100% of what he wanted. "How much can you get?" asked Reagan. "Maybe 70%," replied Dole. "Then let's go for 70%," said Reagan, "and we'll try for the rest later." This is Rev. Asbury's message: The mature student examines viewpoints with which s/he disagrees. The mature student is patient with those who do not agree with his or her own position. Lack of immediate agreement does not entitle the mature student to stomp angrily out of the room. Not surprisingly, this sermon speaks directly to today's divided and grid-locked partisan politics. The mature Christian role is to recognize imperfections and to work patiently to fix them. When they cannot be fixed 100% immediately, one should work realistically and patiently to fix them perhaps 70% of the way, and then fix them the rest of the way later.

Westminster Presbyterian Church
Wooster, Ohio
Rev. Beverly Asbury, Minister
October 17, 1965

TARES AND DILEMMAS *
Matthew 13: 24-30, 36b-43

We turn today to the Parables of the Kingdom found in the first 52 verses of the 13th chapter of the Gospel according to Matthew. We have selected a parable which can be found only in this Gospel account. The parable itself comes in verses 24-30 and an interpretation is given in verses 36-43. The interpretation may well be the later creation of the Church, and, at least, has been sharpened by the early Church to express its particular concern.

This parable does not concern itself with the soils into which seeds fall; rather it is concerned with the seeds themselves. The tare is a name for a weed called darnel, which grows in Palestine to this day. In its early stages this useless weed somewhat resembles wheat. Once it reaches maturity the difference is obvious. However, by that time the roots have hopeless entangled themselves with the roots of the wheat, and one cannot be removed without removing the other. Therefore, the general rule was to leave the tares and separate them from the wheat after the threshing.

The parable makes it clear that the poisonous weed was planted with malicious intent. While the men slept, the enemy came. Interestingly, here men are not blamed for sleeping, because the point is that the enemy acts in secrecy. The wrong becomes apparent only as the plants grow. This story implies the actual fact of the ancient world--that men were at least as vindictive then as they are now. And one of the commonest ways of "getting even" with a man was to sow bad seed in his field. Such an act could really be damaging where, as in Palestine, you could only eke out a bare existence from the land.

The servants, when they notice. the darnel, ask a natural question; surely the farmer sowed good seed; how then did the darnel get into the field? Evidently, the field had been well cared for or else the darnel could have come from previous crops. But that is not the point. The farmer knows that this could only have come from an enemy's work. He is used to remind us that evil is a real force in human history. There is a malevolent force which workd against wha t we have apprehended to be the purposes of God for human life. Whatever name we give, we cannot doubt the presence and reality of evil. In this Century we have seen it in wars of incredible inhumanity, and we still see today--albeit on a lesser scale. The threat of total annihilation cannot be explained solely on the basis of human maladjustment. Genocide and racism reveal the nature of evil in plain, ordinary men. We begin to suspect that there is a saboteur behind our conscious lines, sowing seeds of discord, planting the poison of suspicion, choking the growth of better understanding. When we look today at South Africa and Red China; at India and Pakistan; at Los Angeles, Gleveland, and Crawfordsville, Ga.; when we contemplate the astronomical sums of money we spend to develop weapons of devilish destruction, we can only say, "an enemy has done this." Surely, Berdyaev was correct when he claimed that modern history has a demonic ele - ment. To recognize that reveals how powerfully this parable can speak to our condition.

It speaks to the dilemma of politics. All of us, whatever our party labels, are concerned with what we have come to call the Cold War. The clash between East and

----

*(With an acknowledged debt to a sermon of some years back by Dr. Murdo E. MacDonald, notes of which I have kept until now, waiting to appropriate.)

West is not an academic problem. In the most literal sense, it is a matter of life and death---economically and militarily. Think of the terrible sums this nation now spends to develop weapons which are out of date before they can be mass produced. Were this practice ever to disappear, the repercussions would be far reaching. Money would be available for every educational need and to develop the backward nations of the earth.

Now what is the sane approach toward Communism? To put it another way, what is the Christian attitude? Are we to regard it as a deadly weed which has malevolently sprung up? Are the men who lead it to be seen as the sworn enemies of Christ? Do they think only in terms of world domination? Are they dedicated not only to the destruction of the Christian Church, but also to doing away with every institution which protects the freedom of the individual person?

There are some in the midst of the Church today who look upon Communism as something which is unqualifiably and absolutely evil. America has its Billy James Hargis; its John Birch Society, its Christian Anti-Communist Crusade, its Carl McIntyres and Paul Harveys, its Lifelines and all the numerous followers. The arguments presented are unambiguous, to say the least that can be said. They regard coexistence as a downright betrayal of "God, country, and Yale", of Christianity and all it stands for. Why compromise with evil---wipe it out? Why enter diplomatic relations with the Devil: better to act as though China doesn't exist! Take the risk of war; tear out this satanic growth by the roots.

Yet such an attitude has two overwhelming weaknesses. First, the oversimplification is obvious. It is guilty of seeing things only in terms of opposites, in terms of polarities. It assumes that Communism is on the Devil's side and Western Democracy is on God's side. Such a belief simply doesn't do justice to the facts; the Christian simply cannot accept such a belief as self-evident. Democracy as we have known it is far from perfect. It can be shockingly corrupt. And how can we say that Communism with all its disregard of liberty and its contempt for individual persons is not a mixture of good and evil?

Nevertheless, let us admit that many view the matter just that oversimply. This leads to the second weakness---a willingness to declare war on the Communists in a determined attempt to eradicate them from the nations of men. Such a program would involve the use of atomic weapons and would approach something like total annihilation. To root out Communism involves a willingness to destroy Western civilization along with it. The roots of good and evil in the complex patterns of human relationships which we call society are so inextricably intertwined that in practice they cannot be separated. If we take the parable of the tares seriously, it leads us to understand the necessity of coexistence. We see that as a Christian direction for society. We must be prepared to let two diverging political systems coexist in the world. The ultimate judgment does not belong to us; it belongs to God. Thus, in one of the great dilemmas of our time, the parable of the tares speaks to us of ultimate trust and a willingness to live with our enemies, to resist them, to love them, to pray for them, and to work that they might have life abundantly and the peace which passes understanding.

Secondly, this parable of the tares speaks to the dilemma of religion. Jesus used this parable originally as an answer to the criticisms levelled against his tolerance of unbelievers. Jesus welcomed all sorts and conditions of men. Some of them, socially speaking, were far from reputable. Morally speaking, some of them left much to be desired.

This puzzled the disciples but it shocked the Pharisees. The religious leaders felt a sense of outrage that he ate with sinners, prostitutes, and the like. How could they take him seriously when Jesus questioned the credentials of the holy community? How could they accept him when he seemed to prefer the company of social and moral outcasts?

This has always been the dilemma of religion. Religiously-minded folks have always been concerned about their "purity" and "righteousness" and the great tendency on their part through history has been to separate themselves from these who would contaminate them. It has been considered wise to keep outside the Church any who deviate from the requirements laid down, no matter how slightly. And then the "good Guys" think of themselves as "God's squad", the elite corps, the faithful nucleus.

The parable of the tares shows such a view to be untenable. This attitude of religion forgets why the Church was placed in the midst of the world. It forgets that the Church in a sinful world can never be pure this side of the end of time. The roots of good and evil in history are inextricably intertwined. Even the most religious person and institution is tainted with evil. The more he or it tries to separate itself from the world, the more impotent it becomes and the less influence it exerts on a society it wants to save.

However, the chief count against exclusiveness in religion lies in the fact that it sets man up as judge. Man arrogates to himself the power which belongs only to God. Man doesn't have the ability to look within the hearts of men, and when we try to do so in an air of moral superiority we become obnoxious and malicious. If we gave into the temptation to drive the awkward people out of the church, the chronic whiner, the mentally unbalanced, the pious and/ or critical spectator, the incurably complacent--we would be left with the priggish elect--an abomination in the sight of the Lord. The truth is that those Christians who make exclusive claims for themselves are generally worse than those whom they condemn.

Now, in the day of growing explorations between denominations and Churches, this parable has a profound and salutary message. Good and evil have always existed in the life of the Church and will continue to do so to the end of time. No one church has the monopoly on what is right and good. If we today engage in denominational backbiting, if we today enter a war to separate the wheat of orthodoxy from the tares of secularism, if we carry it to its logical conclusion, it would tear Christianity up by its roots.

Thirdly, this parable speaks to the <u>dilemma of personality.</u> Even the most innocent among us has probably experienced the chasm which exists between what we ideally seek and what we in fact attain. Paul put it well: "The good that I would, I do not, and the evil that I would not, I do." This is running through the whole human nature =a radical split--if not a split, a twist. And toward this split, we can take various attitudes.

One attitude of growing prevalence today scorns discipline and is at the beck and call of every w him, fancy, or passion. This attitude does not seek to deal with the tough problems of ethics in our day; it accepts moral anarchy as a mode of personal life. It knows no norm for the "good that I would do"; its norm is the capriciousness of impulse. Naturally, this attitude leads its adherents to stand outside community life, because community by its very nature demands a measure of coherence. And for the purpose of self-preservation, community needs an element of ethical restraint.

At the other end of the moral spectrum,(and it is this primarily with which I wish to deal here), we find the perfectionist with his exaggerated and even pathological sense of guilt. He cannot tolerate or accept weakness in any form. It is anathema to him, and he is prepared to go to any extremes to eradicate it. Psychologist inform us that perfectionists populate their offices and are difficult to help.

10-17-65 -4-

Therapy is difficult when the patient projects an impossible ideal. They make heroic and herculean efforts to attain it, and this explains why moral perfectionists have a high incidence of nervous breakdowns.

Perfectionism is born of egotism. It refuses to accept the self with all its warts on, with its tensions, frustrations, and temptations. Perfectionism is the secret wish to be God himself, perfect and without blemish. Psychological health makes it imperative that we come to terms with such deadly pride by recognizing that sin or evil is an integral part of our human nature. It can never be completely eradicated. The attempt to remove the tares of inner conflicts and complexes from the soil of our personalities succeeds only in ripping up the wheat of sanity and stability.

The Christian answer is very different. It accepts sin and evil but not in a docile and acquiescent spirit. A Christian recognizes the tares in his life. And he can have psychological health because he knows that his acceptance as a person does not depend upon his perfection. Parents do not wait until their children are angels to condescend to give them love. If so, some of us would still be waiting. No, we love despite imperfections, and we know that God does so in Jesus. This parable emphasizes the positive. Despite the tares, the wheat will grow and proliferate. A harvest will be reaped. So must we work for the defeat of the strategies of organized evil. So must we labor for reconciliation among men. We shall never get rid of pride and self-posturing and vain ambitions. But these never have the last word. There is a new quality of life we find in Jesus Christ. There is a new humanity in following the pattern of his life. In short, the Christian is the man who accepts himself as he is, a creature of circumstance and a new man in Jesus Christ, for whom old things have passed away and all things have become new.

4. 10/24/65 Strangers and Sojourners

New students in college are sojourners in an environment that is new and different for them. Part of this is because early in students' college careers, they discover that their roommates and classmates did not have the same upbringing. Hence, they do not have the same ideas, values, goals, and faiths. Students discover that many people are not like "us." To use Quaker terminology, some people are running dogs (they companionably share our pathway for a short time), others are fellow travelers (they share our path, our meals, and our conversations), and others are kindred spirits (they share our ideals). How do we treat people who differ from us in terms of race? Do we invite them to become fellow travelers? How about those who differ in their country of origin? In attitude toward government? In system of belief?

Events in the summer that preceded this sermon included President Lyndon Johnson's signing of the Voting Rights Act, the racial anger and six days of riots and rebellion in Watts, California, and the arrival on US shores of the first officially acknowledged Cuban refugees. These events followed earlier in the year the assassination of Malcolm X and Bloody Sunday, with its subsequent racial clashes that culminated in Martin Luther King, Jr.'s march from Selma to the state capitol in Montgomery, Alabama. It is difficult to portray adequately the nation's wounds, the disarray, and the rancor to people who weren't there to live through it. The country not only seemed to be – it actually was – estranged from itself as if it, too, were a sojourner entering an unfamiliar place.

How should one deal with new, different, perhaps upsetting, and even disturbing people and ideas, whether they are in our residence halls, our cities, our states, or our nation? Rev. Asbury draws on three Biblical passages for guidance, reminding us that even the experienced students among us were once newcomers and novices. From Exodus 22:21 he advises that

> "You shall not wrong a stranger or oppress him, for you [too] were strangers...."

He continues through Ephesians 2:17-19 to remind us that Jesus

> "...preached peace to you who were far off and peace to those who were near; for through him we both have access in one spirit.... So then you are no longer strangers and sojourners, but you are fellow citizens...."

And finally, Leviticus 23:22:

> "And when you reap the harvest of your land, you shall not reap your field to its very border, nor shall you gather the gleanings after your harvest; you shall leave them for the poor and for the stranger...."

In the autumn of 1965, the response of many Americans to people of a different race, a different language, or a different cultural history was rejection and violence. The same response is recognizable in the year 2015 as this is being written. Is the American dream only about advancing the self? Rev. Asbury suggests that citizens with experience, privilege, and talent have a duty to share resources and ideas with those strangers and sojourners who have need of them and will use them for benefit. The Christian response is to invite them to become kindred spirits. After all, we ourselves were once strangers and sojourners. This sermon invokes Martin Luther King's "I have a dream" speech 2½ years before his death.

Westminster Presbyterian Church
Wooster, Ohio
Rev. Beverly Asbury, Minister
October 24, 1965

STRANGERS AND SOJOURNERS
Exod. 22: 21-24; Lev. 23: 22
Ephesians 2: 11-22

The Hebrew term ger refers to "the strangers who sojourn among you". It can be taken to mean "alien", but "stranger" and "sojourner" more completely express the meaning.

A sojourner occupies a position between that of the native-born and the foreigner. He has come from another people, has settled for a time, but lacks the protection and benefits ordinarily provided by kin and birthplace. He lives in a place, then, that is not inherently his own. If he has any status at all, it must be bestowed on him as an act of hospitality. He lives according to whatever rules govern a guest.

Israelite law expressed the principle of sympathy and consideration for the weak, the stranger, the sojourner with astonishing variety. On the whole, the law had a rather phenomenal gentleness of spirit. The well-known and repeated law on gleaning is a case in point---"you shall not reap the field to the very border, nor shall you gather the gleanings....you shall leave them for the poor and for the stranger...." And this stranger and sojourner who happens into the community on a peaceful, friendly and legitimate errand gets a break that the foreigner doesn't get: "You(the Jew) shall not eat anything that dies of itself; you may give it to the ger...or you may sell it to the foreigner." (Deut. 14: 21)

Old Testament laws in their totality are not consistently on a high moral plain. Their social ethics is sometimes intolerably unjust. Nevertheless, the various codes' predominant motivation and prevailing spirit is one of compassion. In Exodus 23: 9, we read: "You shall not oppress a ger; you know the heart of a ger, you were strangers (gerim) in the land of Egypt." Here it is implicit that one must love another as he loves himself, and in Leviticus 19:34, it is made explicit: "you shall love him as yourself."

From the hundreds of examples relative to the stranger and sojourner, we can draw three underlying perspectives and motivations. First, Israel was to remember that she was a sojourner in Egypt and that God saw her oppressed, delivered her, and established her in a new land. Secondly, the God who saved Israel from bondage is himself the One who protects the poor, the weak, the disinherited. Israel's economy exists to supply need, and special attention goes to those who need help ---"The Lord your God.. ...is not partial and takes no bribe. He executes justice for the fatherless and the widow, and loves the sojourner, giving him food and clothing. Love the sojourner therefore; for you were sojourners in the land of Egypt."(Deut. 10:14-19) Thirdly, the covenant between God and Israel depends upon the participation of all members of the community in its requirements and benefits. So, even the Ger is entitled to almost all the rights and responsibilities of the community.

To put it bluntly, the stranger and sojourner received preferential treatment. The Jew understood that such treatment was right because Israel herself lived by God's invitation. The treatment of strangers and sojourners was derived from the conviction that God acts in history. This faith in the Lord's presence and activity in the movement of time and history lends to Israelite law a unique compulsion---as you have known God in your own history, so shall you be.

The treatment of strangers and sojourners arose then from what can only be called a theological base or perspective. It is important for us to remember that when we face the problem of strnagers and sojourners among us today. Otherwise, we who claim

to be followers of the Judeo-Christian tradition may be deciding attitudes and courses
of action on quite different grounds; yes, even grounds which contradict the theological insights of our faith.

And we are today faced with a time of testing of our theological insights and our
faithful commitments. Strangers and sojourners are in our midst today in large numbers
and their presence places upon us the need to sift through our attitudes and arrive at
a decision about where we shall stand, what we shall do. Lest you begin to think otherwise and no matter how this sounds, this sermon is not concerned with race per se. It
is not "here we go, civil rights again" day! There are other, albeit related, matters
demanding our attention as a faithful people. What this sermon is concerned with is
our attitude toward strangers and sojourners.

A column in The Cleveland Plain Dealer of August 18, 1965, by Novak and Evans concerned itself with the treatment of strangers and sojourners in America today. The
strangers fall into four groups today--the Cubans, the Southern White mountaineer, the
Negroes.* In a previous generation they were the Italians and Jews and Poles. But Novak and Evans make vividly clear that a vast difference now exists in the plight of
our strangers and sojourners. For example, when the Jew finally was able to abolish
discrimination against his economic and social progress, he was ready to move up the
social ladder of American Culture. He had the education, the skin color, the richness
of tradition in Western Civilization on his side. Perhaps, the Cuban sojourner today
matches the Jew of a previous generation, because the refugee from Castro is essentially educated, middle-class, skilled. He can be readily placed in American Society and
absorbed within it. This is not equally true for Southern White, despite skin color,
nor does this situation hold for either Negro or Puerto Rican.*(and Puerto Ricans)

Novak and Evans contend that confidential studies have shown that if all discrimination were abolished tomorrow, the Negro, unlike the Jew, would not be ready to move
up the social ladder. He does not have the education, the cultural background, the
skin color to move out into middle class life. As a matter of fact, the Negro has
been systematically excluded from the training which would have made this possible.
Mountaineers huddled in the city; Negroes and Puerto Ricans in the Ghetto--all are
strangers and sojourners. They are "lost in the crowd". They are a "lonely crowd"
who have been more or less isolated until recently from cultural progress, and they
have not been given(have not attained) the skills necessary to participate in it.
Then Evans and Novak note that the proposed solution for the predicament of the strangers and sojourners in American culture lies in preferential treatment. Nat Hentoff
has written in The New Equality that suddenly to offer these people "equal opportunity"
to compete for the largess of the 20th Century is much like offering "a man who has
one leg the 'right' to enter a race with a man who has two." Obviously such a man
needs help, preferential treatment.

Then the article points out that government officials, industrialists and soci-
ologists are pessimistic about the prospects for such preferential treatment because
it is "against the American dream". It won't be accepted, they say, because every
man should be responsible for himself. And right here we get back to the major concern before us: our attitude as Christians to the strangers and sojourners. It is not
the role or function of this sermon to deal with the ins and outs, the details if you
will, of preferential treatment. It is the role to raise the issue of what determines
our attitudes, to examine if there is a "Christian dream" that places men of faith
over against the "American dream", or at least puts it in perspective.

Israel understood her economy to exist in order to supply need. For what does
our economy exist? How do we Christians understand our economy? Is it only to function to satisfy the needs of those individual persons who can afford what it offers?
Do we Christians understand both government and industry also to have a social responsibility ? Do men exist to serve society, to consume the benefits of the economy, or
do society and its economy exist to serve the needs and purposes of men? Why always

ask about failure of the poor and never about the failure of the economy? These questions should not be taken to imply that Christians cannot or should not be involved in business; cannot or should not be making profits; cannot or should not own stocks in major corporations. The real implication of these questions is that in doing these things Christians should understand what they are doing and how they can use their wealth and power to direct the economy toward desirable ends. The real implication lies in our Christian commitment to seeing that the benefits of the economy are so equitably distributed that we do not "always have the poor among us", that the strangers and sojourners in American culture are treated with mercy.

Of course, the stubborn problems cannot be solved with money alone. Saturday Review of October 16, 1965, published an article entitled "Is There a Future for Yesterday's People?" and it made abundantly clear that money alone would not help Appalachia's mountaineers. Yesterday's People are part of our strangers and sojourners, and the article confesses the fear that we Americans shall grow weary of our well-doing in Appalachia before we solve the problems. It calls for the investment of energy for a generation, and that in turn requires a patient attitude on our part; compassion, preferential treatment, special attention.

The "American Dream", if it is one merely of every man caring for himself, simply will not do here and now in relation to the stranger and sojourner. We Christians must have a dream, a vision of what our land can be, of what it can do. If I ever feel callous or insensitive, I think that my emotions can be restored by pulling out a recording of a speech given at the "March""on Washington. On that August day of 1963, Martin Luther King stirred us all with his cry, "I've got a dream". And we need a dream, a Christian dream, a vision of what God in Christ calls us to be and do.

The attitude that we shall have toward the stranger and sojourner depends upon our dream. Paul reminds us that once we Gentiles were strangers and sojourners. We were goyim, a term of derision. We stood outside the covenant of promise, without hope of being inside it—Godless in the world. Then we who were far off were brought inside by Jesus. He broke down the dividing wall of hostility. He abolished the difference between Jews and Gentiles. Strangers and sojourners were to be no more. Whatever minute differences which once existed in Ancient Israel in the treatment of strangers and sojourners can exist no longer. We have been reconciled. The Cross brings hostility to an end. We who were strangers and sojourners are no longer so, but fellow citizens.with the saints and members of the household of God. To us has been given the work of reconciliation. To us has been given the task of taking up the Cross of Jesus which breaks down the barriers of hostility. Jesus gave us preferential treatment; of that there can be no doubt. He did for us what we could not do for ourselves. And he commissions us for preferential treatment to others, doing for them what they cannot do for themselves—enabling them in turn to do for others what...
......

The real problem for the stranger and sojourner today can be found in our attitude. Some feel that other's gaining their rights deprives them of theirs. Not so! His future depends on our willingness to go on untiringly doing him well. He has no legal claim on our charity. He too has citizenship in the nation. He will not beg for our forbearance. But theologically and morally speaking, charity, mercy, love, forbearance, patience become us —for we live by grace ourselves. Both the Old and New Testaments insist upon mercy, not for mercy's sake, nor alone because God is merciful, but much more because we have ourselves received mercy. Mercy it must be to the stranger and sojourner because we know God's mercy.

10-24-65

Love the Negro, the Puerto Rican, the Southern White, not because you ought to love him, not because that is the way to prevent future riots in the cities. Love the Negro, the Jew, the Cuban, the lonely, friendless, etc., not because you were once a stranger and sojourner yourself, but much more because as a stranger you were loved by God, befriended by Jesus who broke down the barriers for you. As you know God to be out of your own personal experience, out of your own days of loneliness, estrangement, and unacceptance, so shall you be. Remember so to put yourself in the place of the stranger and sojourner that your attitude can be a part of a national consensus that will lead to preferential treatment. Dream a dream. Have a vision. If we can do no more, we can at least as Christians manifest such an attitude that will allow and compel professions, government, and industry to act preferentially to create the conditions in which strangers and sojourners can become fellow citizens. Christians can dare to dream and then act to fulfill it, for we too were once strangers and sojourners.

5. 5/2/65 Poverty, Pride, and Perversity

In his January, 1965 inauguration speech, President Lyndon Johnson proclaimed that the establishment of his Great Society "rests on an abundance of liberty for all. It demands an end to poverty and racial injustice to which we are totally committed in our time." Johnson had used the "Great Society" nomenclature earlier in 1964 in his speeches, first at Ohio University and then, more famously, for graduation at the University of Michigan on May 22. In its reach, the Great Society echoed Roosevelt's earlier New Deal and Four Freedoms, and it resulted in Congress passing – and Johnson signing in July – the law that established Medicaid and Medicare. The number of poor people was staggering 50 years ago, amounting to approximately 19% of the US population. Early in the 21st century, the gap between the haves and the have nots has grown such that, according to recent US census data (cited by CBS News, Dec. 11, 2011), roughly one half of the US population qualifies as low income or poor. With approximately 20% of its children living in poverty, the US ranks second in the developed world in terms of childhood poverty (UNICEF, 2013). Circumstances and behaviors that precipitated the Great Recession that began in 2008 have amplified these divergent conditions.

This sermon argues that poverty is a fatal malignancy of pride and of living only for the self. That is, poverty is not a simple external ailment of circumstance; it is an internal infection of the heart and soul. In his Great Society graduation speech, Johnson said that elimination of racial and economic injustices would require efforts of the heart as well as of the body:

"There are those timid souls that say this battle cannot be won; that we are condemned to a soulless wealth. I do not agree. We have the power to shape the civilization that we want. But we need your will, and your labor, and your hearts, if we are to build that kind of society."

Indeed – and ignoring the gender-limited language of the time – the Great Society required a shift of internal values. As an effort and process, it was a difficult journey toward a worthy reward:

"It is a place where men are more concerned with the quality of their goals than the quantity of their goods. But most of all, the Great Society is not a safe harbor, a resting place, a final objective, a finished work. It is challenge constantly renewed, beckoning us toward a destiny where the meaning of our lives matches the marvelous products of our labor."

Isaiah was even more impatient with superficial deeds in the absence of a deep commitment of the heart. Isaiah spoke what he heard from the voice of Yahweh:

"I have had enough of your burnt offerings of rams and the fat of fed beasts…. Your new moons and your appointed feasts my soul hates; they have become a burden to me…. Wash yourselves; make yourselves clean; remove the evil of your doings from before my eyes; cease to do evil, learn to do good; seek justice, correct oppressions; defend the fatherless, plead for the widow" (from Isaiah 1:11-17).

"…Because this people draw near with their mouth and honor me with their lips, while their hearts are far from me, and their fear of me is a commandment of men learned by rote…" (Isaiah 29:13).

Rev. Asbury cites dire statistics and bewails the circumstances, as did Isaiah and Johnson, in order to capture our attention. And, like Isaiah and Johnson, he offers constructive alternatives.

Westminster Presbyterian Church
Wooster, Ohio
Rev. Beverly Asbury, Minister
May 2, 1965

POVERTY, PRIDE, AND PERVERSITY
Isaiah 1:1-6, 10-20; 29:13-16; 30:1-5

The problem of poverty was the concern of the Christian Church before it became a matter of national debate. In terms of "before" and "after", sermons on poverty were preached here and elsewhere "before" LBJ proposed his "poverty package". So the "Great Society's program came "after". But this not to claim either a direct or indirect relation between sermons, LBJ, Adam Clayton Powell, Sargeant Shriver, and over- t.. paid politicians. It is to claim that poverty cannot be seen as a simple one-dimensional matter. That is, poverty poses problems for the social, political, and religious communities of our world, and it is not susceptible of simple solution.

The statistics themselves do not give an adequate picture of the human factors involved. Three years ago, (and these are the latest figures we have), over 9.3 million families had incomes below the level of severe poverty($3000). More than 1.1 million of these families contained 4 or more children. More than 17 million people had incomes below $2000 (5.4 million families). More than 1 million children were being raised in families with 6 or more children and incomes of less than $3000. Add to these statistics the fact of low-income individuals living alone. Three years ago, there were 5 million such persons who had incomes under $1500 a year and an additional 3 million lived on less than $1000 annually.

This means that 35 million Americans were living in poverty in 1962--one=fifth of the families of our land and nearly one-fifth of the total population. They have no choice about being poor. That's what they are. It is a rigid way of life, handed down from one generation to another in a cycle of inadequate education, inadequate homes, inadequate jobs and stunted ambitions. Eleven million children are among them, and that means nearly one third of the poor are under 18 years of age. (and some of you who say that I can never preach without a mention of race can now relax.) Eight million Negroes--between one-third and one-half of the total Negro population--lives below the line of severe poverty.

Today, we live in an economy of abundance, not one of scarcity. We have the technical means by which to make minimum subsistence available to millions. There is enough to go around; it just is not getting around. And most of the time, we don't know it. The poor are hidden from our sight; they have no political power of representa tion. They sadly lack the opportunity for educational and vocational training, and, consequently, they lack opportunity for employment in a time requiring increasing skills. This vicious circle more and more defeats them.

The costs of poverty are staggering. How can you measure the human cost? How would you measure the cost to a child born into a rat-infested slum? How would you measure the cost of growing up without adequate medical and dental care? How do you measure the cost to the dignity of one who can find no useful employment of his undeveloped abilities? The experts estimate that it costs $40,000 to keep a person alive at the lowest subsistence level for his lifetime. Those same persons now receiving "benefits" from the society could be adding $13 to 18 billion annually to the Gross National Product. We now pay $6 billion each year for public assistance alone, a minimum program. Ohio pays only 70% of what is the recommended figure for personal assistance where children are involved. And the cost in crime and delinquency alone far exceeds these figures.

5-2-65

You will have to excuse this. One could get even more carried away with the awful facts of poverty. But enough. This is not a factual matter. It is a moral issue. As the National Council of Churches said: "because poverty is no longer necessary, it is ethically intolerable." When something as awful as poverty cannot be considered as a necessary fact of human life, then it can only be termed immoral to allow it to continue.

Yet, the most perplexing thing is the indifference of Christian churchmen to this and other pressing social issues. The relatively affluent persons of most of our churches simply cannot or do not wish to see the reality of poverty. Moreover, churchmen often hold naive and self-righteous notions about the poor. You hear churchmen saying: "If a man wants to succeed bably enough, he can do it." Others say: "Anybody can get a job and support his family today if he tries. The poor are mostly lazy, shiftless, or dishonest men who would rather be on relief than do an honest day's work." Still, others: "Why get excited about our poor in a world in which most men are poor? If we helped them, we'd end up poor ourselves."

Well, these attitudes and assumptions are in fact the concern of the sermon today, for they are not unlike the pride and perversity of Judah in the day of Isaiah. The holiness of the Lord(YHWH) involves the demand for justice and righteousness. And Isaiah, no less than Amos, categorically condemns social sins, especially the "grinding the face of the poor." Isaiah quite literally damns the total structure of the religious community of his day—not because it is religious, but because its ceremony and practice are accompanied by a corporate life of injustice, violence, and oppression. Isaiah sees this as the grossest hypocrisy. So does he say, "I cannot endure inquity and solemn assembly." The two form the unholiest of alliances. In 29: 13, he says:

> This people draw near with their mouth
> and honor me with their lips,
> While their hearts are far from me,
> And their fear of me is a commandment of
> men learned by fote.....

Nevertheless, Isaiah clearly understood that social iniquity can be perceived as only a symptom. Social evil symptomizes the deep and fatal malignancy of man living only for himself. Isaiah sees in Judah a willful and total rebellion of covenant men against the covenant with God. He sees these men of Judah as living in an unmitigated, uncompromised, unrelieved way solely for themselves. In 1:5,6a he says:

> Why will you still be smitten that you continue
> to rebel? The whole head is sick, and the
> whole heart faint. From the sole of the foot
> even to the head, there is no soundness in it....

In a word, the malignancy of Judah is pride. Isaiah repeatedly and almost relentlessly pursues and probes it out. He uses a variety of approaches:

> You turn things upside down!
> Shall the potter be regarded as the clay;
> that the thing made should say of its maker,
> "He did not make me";
> or the thing formed say of him who formed it,
> "He has no understanding"?   29:16

5-2-65

> Their land is filled with silver and gold,
>   and there is no end to their treasures;
> their land is filled with horses,
>   and there is no end to their chariots.
> Their land is filled with idols;
>   they bow down to the work of their hands,
>   to what their own fingers have made. 2: 7,8

All this is about covenant man, about churchmen, if you will. All this is about men of faith who live unto themselves alone and have thereby and therein created their own gods. They really trust themselves alone, and in one of Isaiah's oracles his prophetic ire lays it on the line:

> Hear the word of the Lord..........
>
> "What to me is the multitude of your sacrifices?.....
> I have had enough of burnt offerings...
>
> "When you come to appear before me,
>   who requires of you this trampling of my courts?
> Bring no more vain offerings;
>   incense is an abomination to me." 1: 10ff
>
> "Wash yourselves; make yourselves clean;
> remove the evil of your doings from before my eyes
> cease to do evil,
>   learn to do good;
> seek justice,
>   correct oppression;
> defend the fatherless,
>   plead for the widow." 1:16,17

In a word, does not Isaiah come close to saying "Live for others." Isaiah does come very close here to what we today would call a "doctrine of man." Pride and perversity render man sick. Isaiah did not say "live for others" but he approaches it in his condemnation of human pride, his judgment upon the perversity of men who have no sensitivity to the suffering of others, no compassion upon the poor. Isaiah spares not in his indictment of the deep, firmly established pride of Judah. Nevertheless, the final prophetic word is not one of judgment but of redemption. The wrath of the Lord (YHWH) has a constructive purpose:

> "Come now, let us reason together, says the Lord(YHWH),
> Though your sins are like scarlet,
>   they shall be as white as snow;
> though they are red like crimson,
>   they shall become like wool." 1:18

Judgment is the extremity to make redemption possible. The hoped-for result is a change of heart, a change of attitude and so of direction. God's purpose in history lies in reconciling man to Himself and to all men.

So it is today with us. We are relatively affluent persons living in a land of plenty and all too often unaware of and indifferent to the poor who live in the midst of our plenty. We too stand under the judgment and admonition of God to live for others and offer ourselves for the relief of those in need. We too stand in need of a change in attitude, We need to examine our assumptions about the poor. We need to see clearly if we assume that the poor are merely failures in our society. Do we simply

5-2-65

then write them off? What about the children? Are they to blame? What can they do?

It is bad enough that we do so little for the poor; do so little to restructure society so that all men can live above the poverty line. But it is worse yet to be churchmen whose attitudes of piety and righteousness prevent them from knowing and caring about the severe conditions of want and deprivation. It takes an effort of the intellect and the will to move beyond our self-concern to concern for the poor. We need a change in attitude. But that change may come only as we move outside the church and get to know those who are struggling with poverty.

The editor of The Christian Century (3/25/64) put it this way: "We cannot see and hear them until we stand in the presence of one or more of them, talk with them, sense something of the emotional strain from which they are never free. Until we lower the barriers which are so easy for the comfortable to raise and justify...We fail in simple humanity.... All government action will amount to nothing unless we act through the churches to renew and strengthen an attitude of simple humanity." This attitude, says The Century, is not sentimentality nor an emotional substitute for justice. "It is the attitude of the good man who sees and hears his neighbor's need."

Our pride and perversity must be overcome so that the nature and cost of poverty may sink in on us. Poverty is not somewhere else. It is local. It is in Wooster. And its solution lies in the local community in which it exists. It lies where there is the simple humanity which expresses a willingness to become personally involved and to support through taxes and out of increasing incomes greatly needed expansion of public services. This state advertises: "'Profit' is not a dirty word in Ohio" Well, is 'poverty' a dirty word? It ought to be. Are we willing to give enough of ourselves to abolish it? The solution lies with those who seek to humanize income maintenance programs and seek full and adequate help for those in need.

The question for us is not "what does the law require?" Rather, it is "What does the Lord require?" and he surely requires a change in attitude. He requires more than commandment learned by rote; more than solemn assemblies. He requires that we cease to do evil and learn to do good. Most of all he requires of us a simple humanity in our acts to bring a new humanity to those in need. The answer to poverty in its human dimensions can be found only when our pride and perversity yield.

Surely, Paul was fully consistent with Isaiah and the Lord's purpose when he instructed us:

> "Let each of you look not only to his own interests, but also to the
> interests of others. Have this mind among yourselves, which you
> have in Christ Jesus, who, though he was in the form of God, did not
> count equality with God a thing to be grasped, but emptied himself,
> taking the form of a servant, being born in the likeness of men.
> And being found in human form, he humbled himself and became obedi-
> ent unto death, even death on a cross."
>
> Phil 2: 4ff

6. 3/24/63 **The Forgotten Poor**   <u>End of September</u>

This sermon actually preceded by two years the prior one (Sermon #5), but it seems to read better in reverse chronological order because that one makes observations and this one calls to action. The topic, as before, is wealth, arrogant affluence, consumptive society, and charity. Rev. Asbury discusses the Big Rock Candy Mountain, which is a hobo's utopia expressed in a folk song recorded first by Harry McClintock in 1928. The song has been reprised several times, including by Dorsey Burnette in 1960. A fanciful wish for hobo riches is expressed in this stanza:

> In the Big Rock Candy Mountains there's a land that's fair and bright,
> Where the handouts grow on bushes and you sleep out every night,
> Where the boxcars are all empty and the sun shines every day
> On the birds and the bees and the cigarette trees,
> Where the lemonade springs, where the bluebird sings,
> In the Big Rock Candy Mountains.

Rev. Asbury gave this sermon mere months after resolution of the Cuban Missile Crisis. The nation was full of itself, unaware of how President Kennedy had negotiated a settlement and what he had given away. A naïve nation sighed relief over a presumed return to the normalcy of post-WWII 1950s and early 1960s. John and Jacqueline Kennedy presided over Camelot. The apparent bliss of post-war consumption seemed about to return. However, "normalcy" was a white normalcy. Under the cover of returning to the way things were, a stewpot of poverty and racial strife simmered.

The theme of the sermon is to make the poor visible, and for his sermon title, Rev. Asbury draws upon Psalm 19:17. To reinforce his message, Asbury invokes two of the most beloved and widely cited Biblical passages: The Beatitudes from the Sermon on the Mount, found in Luke 6 (and also Matthew 5), and Paul's short discourse on faith, hope, and love – used in countless weddings – that begins, "If I speak in the tongues of men and of angels, but have not love, I am a noisy gong or a clanging cymbal."** Asbury spotlights the plight of the poor by invoking Jesus's exhortation to Christian action when he called the poor – not the rich and powerful – "blessed." The reason that the rich are not blessed is because they have become insensitive to the needs of others and have done nothing to alleviate the obvious sufferings of the less fortunate. With half of the US population living at low income or poverty levels, the sermon makes obvious parallels to contemporary US society.

Asbury builds his picture of Christian duty in front of a backdrop provided by the 1958 book on post-war wealth disparity, *The Affluent Society*, written by economist John Kenneth Galbraith. Galbraith maintained that the differences between socioeconomic groups in the acquisition of goods, the accumulation of debt, and the caloric intake of food are evident enough to cause embarrassing divisions in society. Unchecked, they have expanded to become the conditions of today.

It is characteristic of Rev. Asbury's sermons – and this will become apparent in the ones yet to come – that most of them contain a call to action. The historical Jesus was a person of action. Yes, he spoke and preached, but he also taught, healed, led protests, visited slums, confronted authority, and traveled widely in his world. These traits of engagement with society appear throughout Asbury's sermons, including this one. Asbury says in his sermon, "Let the conditions [of the poor] make you wince."

The sermon closes with a non-traditional translation of the word *love*:
> "So faith, hope, love abide, these three; but the greatest of these is love" (I Corinthians 13:13).

The Greek word for love that is used throughout Paul's passage is *agape*, which is complicated to translate into English. *Agape* love recognizes a relationship with a *person* rather than with an object. *Agape* love acknowledges dignity, respect, and independence. *Agape* gives rise to Martin Buber's concept of *I and Thou* rather than *I and It*. *Agape* love is not love of an object (*It*) and, accordingly, it is not dominating, analytical, formulaic, or possessive (see I Corinthians 13:4-7). In line with this, Rev. Asbury chooses an alternative translation for *agape* to close his sermon: *Charity*. The word *charity* implies a relationship with a living being, a recognition that the other being in the relationship is not an object but, rather, a *person* with dignity, rights, and needs. Charitable love aims to fulfill the needs.

A bit more than two years before Rev. Asbury wrote this sermon, John Kennedy issued his own admonition about the forgotten poor in his Presidential Inaugural, January 20, 1961: "If a free society cannot help the many who are poor, it cannot save the few who are rich."

**Rev. Asbury also uses Paul's poetic words from I Corinthians 13 in his Chapel talk found in the Epilog, *Item A*.

March 24, 1963

THE FORGOTTEN POOR
Psalm 9: 17-20
Luke 6: 17-26
I Corinthians 13

It is the promise of the Judaic-Christian tradition that the needy shall not be forgotten. The arrogance and pride of men and nations are judged harshly by the psalmist and the prophets. There is the promise of a moral outcome for God's world. We are told that those who forget God are destined for Sheol—for life in an unreal world, for God will not forget His people, and neither must the people of God forget the needy. The expectation of the poor shall not perish. Such is the promise of the Old Testament.

The promise of the New Testament is even greater: Blessed are you poor....Blessed are you that hunger now....Blessed are you that weep now.... And note that Luke did not give the later Hebrew meaning of "saintly" or "pious" to the word poor. Luke retains the meaning of "poor in money and possessions." Matthew took the teachings of Jesus and softened them or "spiritualized" them. Matthew makes these verses read "hunger and thirst after righteousness" and he substitutes the word "mourn" for "weep". But not so Luke. When you contrast 6:20, "Blessed are you that hunger now, for you shall be satisfied," with 6:24, "But woe to you that are rich, for you have received your consolation," you know what Luke means by "poor." He retains the sense of that famous teaching of Jesus that riches constitute an almost insuperable barrier to the Kingdom of God (18: 24-25). Again, there is the definite implication that, while wealth per se is not wrong, with wealth comes the inevitable danger of being insensitive to other values and the danger that we shall find complete satisfaction in the goods of this world. This is why one of the leading contemporary Christian leaders recently said that any Christian who knows any luxury whatever ought to be concerned about the state of his soul. Jesus himself warned us of the great spiritual perils of wealth: "Woe to you rich", and there is the antithesis, "Blessed are you poor."

But look who we are! We live on "The Big Rock Candy Mountain." Nearly everyone here today is rich. Ours is an affluent economy of abundance. We are a people of plenty, a nation with more than enough. Our big rick candy mountain is an incredible, unprecedented fantasyland. Our consumer commodities challange the stars in number and glitter. We are the boast of statesmen, the pride of businessmen, the envy of foreigners, the lure of immigrants. Our Gross National Product exceeds $500 billion, and some are predicting one of $750 billion by 1970—a 50% increase over 1960. The Big Rock Candy Mountain gets BIGGER.

We eat so well we have to diet. The average one of us takes in 3100 calories in a day. Now men can sell products by advertising that theirs have less food value. We have it so good on our mountain that advertisers seek new ways to stimulate our consumption, and industries must build obsolescense into their

2

wares to keep men and machines busy. All this means that we are so rich that our mountain is cluttered with expensive junk, most of it never used--but kept handy in case it might be. Everyone on our mountain, it seems, is well-fed, well-dressed, well-wheeled, well-housed. Jesus must have been wrong; the blessing has been to us and to our children: Blessed are you, rich Americans.

But our Big Rock Candy Mountain has its problems. In spite of so much there are some mountain-dwellers, if not mountain-climbers, who are becoming discontent. Even the moderately wealthy--which includes most of us--wonder if we have not become slaves to our possessions, if a moral and spiritual deterioration has not set in. We buy things to liberate us from our chores, but we still complain that we "don't have enough time". We spend our time operating or repairing the labor-saving devices, and we discover that the freedom we thought we were purchasing is only a new form of slavery. Yet, we pile invention on invention, possession on possession, until like the famous existentialist, we also could describe life as "Just one damned thing after another." Who possesses whom? Small wonder that Jesus taught that it was easier for a camel to pass through the eye of a needle than for a rich man to enter the Kingdom. And those of us who live on the Big Rock Candy Mountain are probably far richer than the man Jesus had in mind.

We've never had it so good. We have made consuming a way of life. The closest we come to a religious experience in our day is the gasp we let out in a store when we see the splendor of what is offered for sale. We wallow in debt. We offer our motives to researches, even when we do not wish to do so. We join in the affirmation that the key to the good life lies in having good things, and our Bible is the Sears catalogue.

The needy shall not be forgotten and the expectation, the hope of the poor shall not perish: God may not forget, and He may not disappoint. But whom are We kidding? We have forgotten. On our Big Rock Candy Mountain it is easy and convenient to be blind to the fact that an incredible number of our brothers in America, to say nothing of the world, are still on the plains and in the foot-hills--with longing eyes and empty pockets. God may keep his promise, but God's people have surely forgotten theirs.

Herman P. Miller, in the January 26 issue of the Nation, says that this might be the year when America rediscovers poverty. If we do not, it shall be our fault. In the January 19 issue of The New Yorker, Dwight MacDonald has a long review article of several new books concerning the invisible and forgotten poor of the world's wealthiest nation. Even if you never read the books themselves, MacDonald says enough to shatter the illusion of the Big Rock Candy Mountain. Moreover, he takes J. K. Galbriath and his book, The Affluent Society, to task. He contends that Galbriath's phrase enabled prosperous men to erase their awareness of poverty's "massive affliction."

The very idea of an affluent society builds our egos and ab-
sovles our conscience of social guilt and responsibility.
Galbraith implied that such poverty as remains can be largely
credited to the incapacities of the poor rather than to the
inequities and inefficiencies of the economic system. It is
pointed out that Galbraith did not, in 1958, see poverty as a
"massive affliction," because he defined "poverty" in terms of
those making less than $1000 a year--a figure first used by
Congress in 1949. That was low then. Today such a figure is
fantastic. No one can live on the big rock candy mountain for
that.

A recent Conference on Economic Progress defined poverty as
families having less than $4000 a year (3½ members per family)
and "unattached individuals" having less than $2000 a year.
Using those terms there are 38 million AMERICANS who are POOR.
FDR spoke once of one third of the nation being "ill housed,
ill clad, ill nourished." Today it is "only" 1/5 of the nation,
but that 1/5 means just as many persons now as did the 1/3 then--
almost 40 million. Beyond the poverty-stricken, there is another
case of underprivilege which we can call "deprivation." Into
this classification go all those families, many of them "Senior
Citizens," who make between $4000 and $5999 and individuals who
receive $2000 to $2999. These people are described as those
"above poverty but short of minimum requirements for a modestly
comfortable level of living." Add their number to the poor and
then we have 77 million, or ALMOST HALF THE POPULATION.

Yet, the poor have been forgotten, and their expectations go
unrealized. Their condition, to quote MacDonald, "is not vivid
to those who run things--the 31% whose incomes are between $7500
and $14,000 and the 7% of the top most top dogs, who get $15,000
or more. These two minorities, sizable enough to feel they are
the nation, have been...unaware of the continued existence of
mass poverty...."

Haven't we all been unaware? Haven't we all forgotten? We need
not be defensive, as such. As a matter of fact, it is becoming
harder and harder to see the poor and deprived. One of the
recent authors argues that they are slipping from the very
experience and consciousness of the nation. They live in the
inner city, isolated from the suburbs and smaller towns in which
we live. Furthermore, it is true that even the poor dress better
in America than elsewhere, but it is easier to be well-dressed
than it is to be well-housed, fed, or even doctored. The poor
are not only forgotten; they are also invisible. They are often
very old or very young and outside our experience. They have no
lobby in Congress or in the state legislatures. (One could go on
endlessly giving facts, presenting statistics, shattering il-
lusions, shocking hearts, angering minds. But you read the
books or articles.)

Don't be defensive. Just recognize where you live--on The
Big Rock Candy Mountain, where Liz Taylor spends $150 a day
for food and $450 a week for liquor, and where you and I eat
well and sleep deeply. Let the conditions make you wince. Look

4

at the rest of the world which is even less nice to see. Don't turn your well-clad back by invoking the old explanation that the poor are lazy and that candy is on the mountain for any who would climb. And don't be so modern in spirit that you ignore your brother's plight by asking for more government agencies to do what you don't want to pay taxes to have done.

Look again to the Authorized Version of I Corinthians 13. Here is where Paul sets forth the best way of all---the way of love. But I suggest the Authorized, the King James, Version, in order that we might not spiritualize what is meant. "Charity" may not be the best translation, but at least it reminds us that love is an act, that the love of God in Jesus Christ is shed on us, the undeserving, that we are to act in love toward even those we may judge to be undeserving. Yes, simply because we do judge others undeserving, we need to restore charity to our lives. Those of us who live on the Big Rock Candy Mountain can afford to be charitable. Most urgently, for the welfare of our own souls, for the fulfillment of the promise of God, we must be charitable. If we, of all people, do not have charity, we are noisy gongs and clanging cymbals. If we, who spend so much on ourselves, who have no place for our old, do not have charity, then God ought to cast us out for we shall have lost our lives to the subtle temptations of the affluent society. How can we pray "Give us this day our daily bread" and have no charity for the migrants, the Negroes, the Puerto Ricans, the idle miners and steel workers, the poor white share croppers, the skid-row derelicts, the elderly isolated in one-room homes?

Much has been given to us on the Big Rock Candy Mountain. From us, much is expected. Faith, Hope, Charity abide. But the greatest of these is charity.

7. 1/13/63 A Pilgrim People: Catholic and Apostolic – first of a 4-part series.

The next four sermons develop the concept of the church as a community. The community is dynamic…and not just in terms of the turnover of people moving in and out. It is dynamic in the sense that a moving wagon train of pilgrims is dynamic. The concept of sojourners was introduced back in Sermon #4 and that theme is developed extensively here. Because Sermon #4 was delivered chronologically two and a half years after these four, its ideas are denser and more fully developed; hence, it seemed to serve its purpose better as a separate foundation and prelude to this series of four rather than a summary afterwards.

The Biblical reading for this sermon, I Peter 2:4-10, offers a pun on the Greek word *petra*, which means *massive rock* or a *solid foundation*. Both the name *Peter* and the saying, *"On this rock will I build my church"* come from the same word. The English word *petrify* also comes from this Greek word. The reading in I Peter also fittingly introduces the theme of the next four sermons: the organized church.

The Christian connection to issues of politics and race has been established through previous sermons. That connection will reappear as a major theme in subsequent sermons. This sermon urges that before taking action on either of these connections, it is useful to ponder what kinds of action we wish to take. That action, whatever it is going to be, is likely to be effective as a steady, perhaps intermittent, and slow progress of the sort that pilgrims often undertake. This kind of progress is usually not flashy. And because it takes place in the confused, messy, and inconvenient "real world," it is also not likely to be "churchy." Thus, Christian pilgrims act out of humility and harmony – if not unanimity. But most of all, they *act*. Neither their work nor their faith is ever finished.

Westminster Presbyterian Church
Wooster, Ohio

January 13, 1963

A PILGRIM PEOPLE: CATHOLIC AND APOSTOLIC
I Peter 2:4-10

Three years or so ago, a minister showed several of his friends a letter from a 16 year old girl who was president of her Senior High Fellowship. She wrote that while God had been real to her at one time, He was real no longer. She confessed that she would like nothing better than to believe in God, but somehow found it impossible to do so. Finally, the letter stated: "I might find it easier to believe in God if God had nothing to do with the church."

She is not unique in that feeling. The Church is today under attack more from its friends than from its enemies. Peter Berger's devastating sociological analysis, The Noise of Solemn Assemblies, is addressed to Christians, and it was written by a profoundly concerned believer. Numerous students in this College have expressed the view that the contemporary church has outlived its usefulness. And while I do not know it for sure, I can make an educated guess that the community of Wooster has a large share of people whose real lives are untouched by the messages from pulpits and who might find it easier to believe in God if all preachers were silent this morning.

Who can deny that the Church often evades or ignores the truly great issues of human existence? Have we not all heard the "good news" presented in the dullest and most inapplicable manner possible? Does not the very atmosphere of pious and self-righteous goodness discourage or even prevent expression of doubt, estrangement, anxiety, and suffering?

Ben Bradford and Frank Weiskel expressed much of this in their "Litany of the Apathetic":

Minister: Our Church has stood on the same spot for over two hundred years.
Congregation: Isn't that nice!
Minister: I preach sermons that the people like and never disturb anybody.
Congregation: We enjoy your sermons so much.
Minister: Our Women's Association has more money in the bank than any other women's association in the Presbytery.
Congregation: Isn't that nice.
Minister: We don't believe the church should mix in politics, social issues or economics.
Congregation: It is so nice to be a churchy church.

2

Minister: Our church school teaches the Bible from
cover to cover.
Congregation: Little children are so sweet.
Minister: We believe charity begins at home.
Congregation: And ends there.
Minister: We believe that theology just mixes people
up.
Congregation: It is so nice to have our religion
make us feel good.
Minister: Our elders are the most popular men in
the church.
Congregation: It's so nice to have such spiritual
looking men.
Minister: Our trustees never waste money on any new
fangled ideas.
Congregation: Isn't that nice.
Minister: Our church is typically small town.
Congregation: We thank God we are not as other
people are.
Minister: Our church had to close because there
was nobody as good as we are to continue it.
Congregation: Isn't it a shame!

Of course this is a caricature, but it is a
caricature. Small wonder that one can feel that God
would be more of a reality if He had no connection
with the Church. Yet, there is another side to this.

It is reported that Reinhold Niebuhr was once
asked how he could remain in the life of the Church,
given all its corruption and irrelevance to society.
It is said that Neibuhr replied that the Church is
like Noah's Ark. On the inside there were two animals
of each species on the earth. They were together for
forty days and forty nights without ventilation or
sanitation. The stench can be imagined by anyone who
has ever lived near a stockyard or a barnyard. Neibuhr
says that the only reason that one does not desert
the Ark is that the storm outside is worse than the
stench inside.

This may be a negative view of the Church, but
it explains the efforts of contemporary Christians to
cleanse it, restore it, reform it, renew it. The
Church for all its faults cannot be separated from
the Christian faith nor can the Christian faith be
separated from the Church. P. T. Forsyth has said
in The Church and the Sacraments: "The same act which
sets us in Christ sets us also in the society of Christ...
To be in Christ is in the same act to be in the Church."
This kind of positive affirmation is carried farther
and deepened by a Confession of Faith prepared by the
World Presbyterian Alliance in 1960. After this

3

Confession acknowledged our faithlessness and irresponsibility, it went like this:

> We are forgiven sinners and, by the gift
> of Thy own Holy Spirit, a new
> humanity, committed to the service
> of Christ. In grateful obedience
> we accept our calling to participate
> in His mission to the world.

> We are Thy pilgrim people, bound together
> in one, holy, universal Church of
> Christ, through whom we are nurtured
> in faith and disciplined in courage
> to bear witness to Thy healing love
> and righteous judgment.

This is what I believe the Church to be: God's pilgrim people. To belong to God is to belong to His faithful people who have a mission to the world. To hear the call of God, to enter into the new life in Jesus Christ is to be called into the Church. I must confess my own conformity with the New Testament view that the Church is the concrete embodiment of the new life of faith into which Jesus Christ brings men. In other words, the Church is necessary to the Gospel, and because I believe that I can give my life to it-- in conservation, in criticism, and in reconstruction.

The important thing to remember is that the Pilgrim People have not arrived. Quite obviously, we live in the 20th century. We cannot recapture the first blush of the church in the 1st century. Jesus Christ is the same Lord, but we have him under vastly changed circumstances. Even the boldness of Luther and Calvin can no longer be said to characterize Protestant Christianity. Our journey is incomplete. We must be true to New Testament faith, and yet be relevant to 20th century living. We must hold to the truth, and yet entertain every doubt, face every question. We must be God's people, and yet never deny our human nature.

What we need desperately now is to redefine the Church in a culture which, by its very nature, makes it essential that we know who we are. Gayraud Wilmore of Pittsburgh Seminary, who will preach here next month, has written a book on The Secular Relevance of the Church in which he reminds us that our culture knows nothing of unity and holiness and so much less of catholicity and apostolicity. He argues cogently that these concepts have an urgency about them if we are to understand our role as God's pilgrim people.

The key concept is that of apostolicity. What does it mean to stand in the "Apostolic Succession?" The laying on of hands? Apostolicity means that the

4

Church is sent not only to preach what the Apostles preached, but also to demonstrate, as they did, the power given to the church. To stand in the apostolic succession means a demonstration of the power to cast out demonic powers as they reappear in our time and with the trappings of a culturally totalitarian, technilogical civilization. Such a demonstration would make it possible for a 16 year old who wondered how God could have to do with the church believe that God had indeed done something with His church. And I suspect that it is this apostolicity for which many are waiting--the demonstration of the power of love. Surely, the sit-ins, as an example, lead us to see that the Church's ministry does not belong to the professional ministers but to all the pilgrim people. Any lesser understanding of apostolicity indulges in the luxury of orders and prerogatives which we can no longer afford.

Yet the Church must not only be apostolic; it must also be catholic. Again, Wilmore's book helps us to see that catholicity needs to be spelled out in terms of the wholeness of Christian truth which comprehends not only religious knowledge but also scientific and cultural knowledge. All too often the church sounds religious and acts religious to the exclusion of catholicity. For example, it speaks only to those who know and share its language; who agree with it; who are either already saved or act as though they were. In this sense, as well as in others, religion has become the greatest enemy of the Christian faith. If we are to be catholic as we profess to be, the church can no longer ignore the wholeness of truth-- and this church less than most. The pilgrim people of this church in particular can do great service in rediscovering the catholicity of the church.

Of course, a sermon can do no more than hint at the kind of reinterpretation that must take place in a church trying to understand itself in the 20th century. In the next few sermons, some particular items will be examined more closely, but, as in most matters concerning the Church, action must take place in the fellowship of believers or it does not take place at all. Neither the pastor nor the members must expect the pilgrimage to be over soon and for all answers to be in hand, for even the apostolic and catholic church is a piece of earth. We need to recall Bonhoeffer's reminder that holiness implies a holy worldliness--a worldliness that discovers its own ultimate meaning and concern in its own terms and not in terms of some vague "spiritual reality." God's pilgrim people have to discover and rediscover their apostolicity and

5

catholicity in the world in which they live. Wilmore
says the same thing in other words: "The Church is
a followship of secular men and women who are responding to the Gospel and are being constituted by the
Holy Spirit as a servant to this world.".....They
are called to discern and announce what the living
God is doing in this world and to express a way of
thinking and acting that constantly reminds this
world of costly grace by which Christ has freed it
from false gods that rob it of its humanity--until
Christ comes again.

8. 1/20/63   The Gathered Church: Its Integrity

This is a communion sermon. It asks the question, if we are indeed pilgrims, what kind of pilgrims are we? A family, perhaps?

The Biblical reading for this sermon is Paul's letter to the Ephesians 4:1-16. The port of Ephesus lies in what is now the Turkish city of Selcuk, about 500 miles west-northwest across the Mediterranean Sea from Israel. It is much closer to Athens than it is to Jerusalem. Paul spent perhaps three years there cultivating the church. As a port, Ephesus had visitors and residents of all kinds, and Paul had a big job making sense of it all. In this public letter, or epistle, perhaps written while imprisoned in Rome, Paul urged the Ephesians to accept the diversity of characters, beliefs, talents, and roles and to gather them together into a unity of faith and purpose. To use a modern aphorism, "The Main Thing is to keep the Main Thing the Main Thing." And in Paul's time, the Main Thing was for them

> "to lead a life worthy of the calling to which you have been called, with forbearing one another in love, eager to maintain the unity of the Spirit in the bond of peace" (Ephesians 4:1:3).

Paul urged the Ephesian church to do this as a
> "whole body, joined and knit together by every joint with which it supplied, when each part is working properly, makes bodily growth and upbuilds itself in love (Ephesians 4:16).

In unity, there is integrity.

In his sermon, Rev. Asbury reflects on the role (his role?) of a preacher. He lays a foundation for dialog between preacher and members of the gathered church. He also provides for engagement with "the sword of the Spirit," and eventual action. He suggests that integrity of action arises from dialog around the communion table, that is, the sort of wresting with ideas around a meal place that family members do. Accordingly, the communion table should be familiar and available rather than eccentric and remote. It is a family place. Thus, the communion meal itself becomes a common basis for gathering pilgrims of all kinds together for common purpose. In diversity, there is unity.

Westminster Presbyterian Church
Wooster, Ohio
Mr. Beverly Asbury, Minister

January 20, 1963

THE GATHERED CHURCH: ITS INTEGRITY
Ephesians 4: 1-16

The failures and frustrations of Protestant Christianity as it faces modern American culture pose a unique
opportunity for a church such as this one to serve the
whole church. Here, on a college campus, owning no
building, striving for a deep quality of fellowship,
and with a constituency of all ages, from all areas,
races, and denominations, we are in a good position to
meet head-on with the facts of modern life. However,
we ought to know, if we do not already know, that current patterns of church life, largely carried over from
the past, are almost totally unable to meet the challenges of our urban culture. While some Christians may
mourn the passing of the rural culture, other Christians are reminded that faithful men always look for
God's patterns for new days in the very life we now
live. The fact that our present life as Christians is
frustrated by the irrelevance of traditional patterns
of church life does not mean that the church is doomed
to failure. It may mean instead that our calling is
not to spend time making old patterns work but to be
concerned with new relationships, with faith and love
and witness in new forms.

The fourth chapter of the Letter to the Ephesians
begins: "I therefore, a prisoner for the Lord, beg
you to lead a life worthy of the calling to which you
have been called...." That, I would submit, is what
the Christian and his Church must be about--leading a
life worthy of the calling to be God's pilgrim people
in contemporary culture. The Chruch's integrity is
to be about its business, being true to its purposes
both in its gathered life as Christians and in its life
as dispersed Christians in the world. The Church's
integrity lies in its life and mission of being Christ's
Body; His realm of redemption in, to, and among men.

The Church cannot have that integrity unless, on
one hand, it is true to its own life as a worshipping
community of faithful people, and, on the other, unless
that worshipping community scatters itself relevantly
and effectively in the world which God loves. This
Sunday and next we shall look at the gathered nature
of the Chruch's life before turning the following week
to the life of the scattered church. While we shall
look specifically next week at the church's liturgy,
our concern now must be the very integrity of the
church at worship. " I therefore, a prisoner for the

2

Lord, beg you to lead a life worthy of the calling to which you have been called..." Unless there is integrity in what happens inside the Church, we can hardly expect to have any success in finding new patterns for relationships, new patterns of faith, love, and action.

For us Protestants one of the most pressing needs is the recovery of integrity in preaching. Nearly everyone hearing my voice today has a Bible, but for nearly everyone hearing my voice it is a closed book. Even those who take courses in the Bible read more pages about the Bible than they read in the Bible. Preaching can no longer assume biblical knowledge on the part of the congregation, and yet Protestants continue to assert the claim that the Bible is their source of authority. We do not know its content well, or its meaning. We are largely unfamiliar with its concepts or its applications. We substitute warm piety and vague religiosity for biblical understanding. But to preach the word with integrity and relevance presupposes a congregation which is studying the Bible, wrestling with its issues, searching for the Word of God here and now in this campus situation.

Real integrity in this pulpit does not come by filling it with famous men. Integrity of preaching comes when the congregation listens to God's Word and seeks to accept God's direction in its life long before Sunday morning arrives. When the laity has commited itself to Bible study--takes seriously its importance for Christian life--then preaching takes on a new character. The preacher becomes more of a teacher; he is more involved in give-and-take--in genuine dialogue where both preacher and congregation are confronted by God's Word, standing under its judgement and encouragement. When this happens, the Bible becomes exciting and relevant, preaching improves, and we learn to defend ourselves in the world by "the sword of the Spirit, which is the Word of God."

No less important for the gathered church is the recovery of integrity in Holy Communion, for this sacrament has become less meaningful to the common life of Christians. Even the symbols are wrong in most contrmporary Protestant Churches. The Table is far removed from the congregation, or inconspicuous,(as here), or has become an alter--all of which tend to suggest that the service of holy communion is rather special, esoteric, peculiar. Thus, in most churches, communion is celebrated infrequently, and that suggests that it is not central and normative in worship. Moreover, the Lord's Supper has taken on a rather personal and private character--as distinguished from a corporate and family character.

3

Some of these things are probably inevitable when we gather as Christians who do not know each other. In this respect, Westminster Church has much in common with the urban and suburban churches of our land. How can men come to a family meal when they do not know each other as brothers? When men and women do not know each other as persons, there is little reality in the symbol of the Table where we gather in fellowship with God and celebrate his mighty acts. In brief, integrity in communion means that those who gather at the Table must be a family--not just as a theological fact, but as a reality--as people who care for one another. Camus' indictment of collectivized compassion is based on the idea that individuals simply follow the crowd in feelings toward others. Integrity in compassion demands that men realize individually what they feel and how they act. Just as truly, integrity in communion demands that those who come to the Table know what they are doing and in very truth are re-enacting the meaning of the Lord's Supper.

This integrity cannot come unless the family of the Church spends enough time together to discover the reality of the unity in Christ and learn what it is that sustains our life together. Family Night Dinners, in this respect, cannot replace Bible study where men come to know each other as brothers. If it is important for the student members of this church to know one another, it is no less important to remember that "there is one body and one Spirit" and that other members too were called "to the one hope that belongs to your call." All must learn the joy of speaking the truth in love, and harder yet, of accepting the truth, spoken to us in love. When we have learned this, we shall find then that the Holy Spirit is really able to speak to us with power.

Still more important, when we gather for Holy Communion we shall come as a family. Perhaps we ought then to gather in large circles around the communion Table, looking at each other not as strangers, but as those who know one another in love. Then there will be true fellowship, true communion, and a handshake under those conditions will mean a shared calling more than a friendly greeting. I suspect that we would also rediscover the power of community and find the strength and courage to embark on a vigorous mission.

As a church comes to know itself as God's pilgrim people, then baptism begins to take on a new reality as a symbol of entrance to that family of people. When a child is baptized, he is surrounded with all kinds of relatives who are concerned about his nature. The "Christian Name" then takes on meaning. But integrity in baptism depends very much again on the Church being

4

a family. Even more it depends on the church becoming
a fellowship of people who have experienced a new
birth, new beginning, new creation. The integrity of
baptism arises out of lives which express the meaning
of baptism as rebirth. These are the lives that are
lived by the grace of insecurity, by and through the
Holy Spirit, if you will. The very meaning of baptism is that we cannot be satisfied to judge by institutional terms but by daring to look and see if
men in the church have discovered any new life in
Christ.

Now, all that we've said this morning about the
integrity of the gathered church in preaching, communion, and baptism may lead you to the conclusion
that all church members should be saints. Well,
that conclusion is both wrong and right. It is wrong
if you take saint to mean 'holy joe', otherworldly,
and smugly pious. But the conclusion is correct if
you take 'saint' to mean ordinary men and women--by
worldly standards--who are learning to live by God's
grace alone.

Without hesitation or apology, I admit that the
integrity of the church depends upon people whose lives
are burdened by mistakes and guilt but who have rejected self-deception and despair and face their problems
before God with honesty and courage. By their very
understanding of their own sin and their need for continued grace, they become the best ministers to men
and women in the world. A saint is not one who is perfect, but one who knows himself as a sinner still to
be in need of grace. Such a saint restores the
church's integrity because he has ceased to desire importance and symbols of success and prestige. Such
saints are able to give and not count the cost. Such
saints insist that the church be about its business,
because they need its preaching, its communion, its
baptism.

Integrity depends upon the presence of those who
are learning to live by the grace of God. And in a day
when old patterns fail, must we not all learn so to
live? In the face of the threat of utter depersonal-
ization, must we not learn again to become a family?
In the midst of so much inhumanity, must not preaching,
communion, and baptism be channels of restoring and
preserving genuine humanity?

Our struggle to achieve integrity can at least
point us to the reality of God's Church. And perhaps
we shall see half-dead symbols live again, shall hear
the Wrod preached with power, shall feel the presence
of Christ at his table and shall share in the miracle
of rebirth.

9. 1/27/63 The Gathered Church: Its Liturgy

If the first step is to understand and accept what it means to be a Pilgrim People, the second step is to comprehend what binds a Pilgrim People together. The pilgrims pictured in these sermons don't just *be* together as spectators. They *participate* together as doers. The foundation for participation is found in – and explained here as – the liturgy of service.

The letter to Timothy that is used as a Biblical reading for this sermon was written to Timothy, who was Paul's assistant and delegate at Ephesus. Whether it was written by Paul himself is in doubt. Whoever wrote it exhorted Timothy to stick to Main Things, as outlined in the previous sermon, and to establish practices for maintaining a strong community. Likewise, the Acts reference for this sermon also advocates establishing a community, especially around the fellowship of mealtime.

Similarly, Rev. Asbury explains that the contemporary church liturgy is a means for gathering Pilgrim People together. The gathering is not organizational for the purpose of doing mindless committee work. Instead, it is for the purpose of reinforcing the Main Thing. Being a member of the Pilgrim People is not a spectator sport. It requires participation and, accordingly, the liturgy is designed to promote active participation. It is a preparation for Christian action.

Jan.27,1963

THE GATHERED CHURCH: ITS LITURGY
Acts 2: 41-47
I Timothy 2: 1-8

The Church, God's Pilgrim People, lives visibly in two dimensions. Because Christians are a pilgrim people who share faith and mission in common, they gather together to worship. They are brought together from all peoples, occupations, and groups for worship. Yet, their real pilgrimage in the world begins when they leave worship and scatter themselves in the world. Indeed, unless the Church disperses in the world, it can never understand its catholicity or its apostolicity. The gathering is not the end. The end of the Church's life is in its scattered life in the world. The gathering is the means by which the Church is prepared to scatter.

Thus, the church lives by a process of gathering and scattering, and such a process is not accidental but essential to its life. God's people gather in worship that they may also be God's people in the world. It is inconceivable that we can worship God without serving him or serve him without worshiping him. Our life in the world as God's people depends on the fact of being God's people in devotion and having been prepared in and through his Word.

Since the earliest time, the Pilgrim People have gathered to worship. We are reminded by the New Testament that the Church is the Church of the Word of God. The Church does not gather, in the first instance, for organization and activity. That is greatly misunderstood in our day. Much organization and activity is marginal, impersonal, non-involving, and distracting. The first and most important business of the Church is worship through the Word of God. The center of Church life, the fountain source of its vitality, should be worship. Out of this everything else grows and is judged, for worship is not so much a reaching out for the unknown as it is a response to the God who has reached out to us in Jesus Christ. The purpose of gathering to worship is not to mold moods or create impressions but to proclaim the Word by which we seek to live in the secular structures of society. Nothing we do as a gathered Church has as much significance. If it has become merely routine, lacking in profundity, and vaguely comfortable, it only acknowledges the death of God within the Church.

When God's people gather for worship, they do not gather as spectators. Worship depends on confrontation. You will recall that John Calvin defined the Church as that place where the Word of God is purely preached and <u>heard</u> and the sacraments duly administered and <u>received</u>. Obviously, participation is essential. God's people, like any people, cannot hear unless they are prepared to hear. The story of salvation means nothing until and unless it has become the personal story of the worshipping congregation. One cannot really participate by hearing and receiving unless he can <u>recall</u> in worship the mighty acts of God and unless these acts have become living realities, contemporary and compelling. As we gather, there should be a certain expectancy, a sense of being prepared to participate in a family, a community of shared faith and experiences.

But in what does one participate? Too easily the answer comes: in the order of worship, in the ceremony. And that answer has a truthful ring about it. But its ring is also hollow, because it falls short of the heritage of our reformed tradition. Actually, we participate in the liturgy. Now, liturgy is a dirty word to a good many Protestant Christians of the Puritan strain. One wing of the Puritan movement opposed all set liturgies. They argue, as many of you do, that the Spirit bloweth where it listeth and so true worship must be spontaneous, without form. These Puritans were convinced that any liturgical form quenched the Spirit. Yet, even they succeeded in making a formality out of informality. Today, the so-called informal services of worship are so formal that their patterns do not change week-by-week or year-by-year. However, we must give heed to the objection that worship is impoverished when freedom is banished.

On the other hand, the New Testament teaches us that the Spirit also constrains us and that the early Church did indeed have certain set acts which the members performed (as illustrated in today's Scripture lessons.) Along with freedom, there must be order. The Christian is not set free to do as he pleases-- but to serve Christ. The Spirit of God both evokes and restrains worship. Liturgy, then, is not just ritual or ceremony. It is not just formality, not formality for the sake of formality. The root meaning of "liturgy" is "work." It means the work of the pilgrim people of God.

A liturgy is good only if it reminds us who we are--God's pilgrim people. A liturgy is good only if it calls us to what we should be doing. A liturgy is good only if it sends us forth into the world as apostles. This is why some churches have "services" of worship. The Church has been called to service. That is the Christian's work in the world; the service of God. His life as God's man is a liturgy. Liturgy means recall, reenactment, participation -- in worship and in the world. Indeed, it would sometime seem that those who sit as spectators in worship would prefer to sit as spectators in the world. The cries against "standing up too much" or "kneeling too much" or "responding too much" seem also to be cries for a prone Christianity --flat on its back in the world. It might be that those who do not prefer to have acts of worship are those who prefer not to act as Christians in daily life. We dare not let them or ourselves forget that we have a liturgy -- a work to do under God.

If the scattered church has a liturgy, a work, a service in response to God in Christ, what is the liturgy of the gathered church? What should the service of worship be --for recalling who we are and calling for reenactment in the world?

We know from Scripture that certain elements should be included: the singing of hymns and psalms, prayer, the reading of the Word, the making of the offerings, and the celebration of the sacraments. However, the Bible does not prescribe an unbreakable sequence for the acts of worship. The one guiding principle ought to be this: AN ORDER OF WORSHIP IS ORGANIZED AROUND THE MOVEMENT OF GOD TO MAN IN THE WORD, AND THE MOVEMENT OF MAN TO GOD IN RESPONSE TO THE WORD. Again, the worship first reminds us of what God has done for us; of who we are; and then it calls for our response, our work, our service which does not stop with a benediction. Rather, our response only brings in the gathered church and finds its real fulfillment in the dispersed life in the world.

All this, in other words, is said in the Directory of Worship of our Church. And now that we are at the point where we can speak directly about the order, the liturgy, of the worship service itself, the Directory speaks an important word: ".... the Church is obliged to remember both that men are to stand fast in the liberty with which Christ has set them free, and that all things are to be decently and in order. Public worship thus need not follow prescribed forms, but careless public worship may be both an offense to God and a stumbling block to His people." Let me submit to you a progression of worship which seems to be both true and meaningful,--a progression that confronts us with who we are, with God's Words, and calls to respond by working out our salvation in the world.

1-27--3

The _first_ general heading of a liturgy is _Preparation for the Word._ It presupposes expectancy on the part of the gathering. Preparation takes the form of PRAISE, ADORATION, CONFESSION. Divine worship always begins on this note of praise to God who became flesh in Jesus Christ. Since God revealed himself in Christ as holy and redeeming love, men may dare to approach him in confidence and repentance, confessing their sins, asking for forgiveness and the gift of newness of life, and receiving by faith that which they have asked. Thus, it is appropriate that a confession of sins be made by all the people together, followed by an assurance of the reality of divine mercy. In the people's response of thanksgiving, their gratitude to God for the gift of forgiveness may be expressed by the reading or singing of a psalm, a hymn, an anthem, or a corporate prayer of thanksgiving.

The _second_ part of the liturgy centers around the movement of God to man in the Word; we can call it the _Ministry of the Word._ This includes the READING and PREACHING of the Word of God. Public worship always includes the reading and hearing of the written Word of God. The Scripture is the record of God's mighty acts in making himself known to men, and is also a means by which, through the power of the Holy Spirit, God makes himself known to men today. It is appropriate to read from both the Old and New Testaments that all may understand the New as the fulfillment of the Old, to the end that the unity and completeness of God's revelation may continually be set before us.

After the Scripture is read, its message is proclaimed and expounded to the people. The preacher is the instrument through whom the Word of God incarnate in Jesus Christ, and witnessed to in all of Scripture, may be heard as the living Word of God in the life of the Church and in the lives of all present. The preacher is called upon to relate the eternal gospel of the living God set forth in the Scriptures to the life of the particular congregation. Actually to signify the close relationship between the written and the preached Word, the sermon should follow immediately upon the reading of Scripture.

Then should begin the _real liturgy_, the service of God's people: the _Response to the Word._ This is man's movement to God in faith, and it includes: CREED, PRAYER, OFFERING. The Affirmation of Faith commences the people's response of faith to God's revelation. It is the "yes" of faith to the Word which has been heard. The prayers arise out of faith. We could not pray to God unless we believed first in His presence and His power to answer prayer. Following the reception of the Word, prayer takes the form of supplication and intercession. Because of God's grace, we can present our needs before Him and intercede before Him for others--for all sorts and conditions of men, especially for the sick, suffering, and bereaved, and for those that are in authority.

After the response of prayer, we respond by the offering of gifts. This offering is an Act of Thanksgiving, and it is also an act which shows(perhaps more clearly than any other) how seriously we take the Word of God. The offering comes after the sermon, because divine worship should end on the theme of doing, not on the note of hearing only: "Whosoever heareth my words and doeth them." The offering, then, is a symbolic offering of ourselves in God's service.

The people having come to praise God, they now depart with the singing of a hymn of praise; the minister pronouncing a benediction in the words of Scripture. The service then ends on a note of joy in the Lord.

1-27--4

Upon occasion of the celebration of Baptism and the Lord's Supper, a liturgy also includes the Ministry of the Sacrament. Indeed, even when Communion is not being celebrated, it should be implied in the offering -- an Act of Thanksgiving -- and in the prayers. We cannot neglect God's communion with us or ours with Him.

Now, if you will permit me a few comments, some loose ends can be drawn into this picture.

The Choir has not been mentioned, and the Choir is important--especially so in this church. However, a worshipper should never forget that in any Christian liturgy the congregation is the true choir. When the "chancel choir" sings, it sings for the congregation, acting in its stead to glorify God. Thus, the words of anthems are printed not merely that you may know them in case the choir does not enunciate clearly, but rather that you may make them your own, offering them to God. Again, we are called to participate in the music.

In a similar manner, the morning prayers by the minister are said by him for the congregation. It is entirely proper that the congregation join in saying "Amen" at the end of all prayers. We must make the prayers our own, participating in them instead of using a period of prayer as a time to rest from the Saturday night activity.

Lastly, I remind you that worship in a Presbyterian Church is "ordered" by the Session together with the Pastor. The minister does not decide alone. Both the Teaching Elder and Ruling Elders determine the order of service in the light of Scripture, the Directory for Worship, our Reformed Heritage, and the Book of Common Worship. However, I propose to you that the entire church should participate in the discussion of worship. If "liturgy" means "the work of the people", that works may well include the development of a meaningful, effective, and faithful liturgy. The liturgy should in every sense be the work of the people, the response of a Pilgrim People to the Word of God, an indication of what God and man might expect from us as we disperse into the world.

Sermon preached by
Beverly A. Asbury
Westminster Presbyterian Church
January 27, 1963

10. 2/3/63   **The Scattered Church: Its Secular Life**   <u>End of October</u>

This fourth and last sermon of this short series of four contains the directive to act. The church is a group of pilgrims who gather together for common purpose and refreshment. Thus, the first sermon of the series described the Pilgrim People. The second and third described church structure and liturgy – the bonding together of the Pilgrim People and their preparation to act on a unified ideal. The fourth outlines why acting on the ideal is a responsibility.

So what happens when pilgrims scatter? This fourth sermon expresses a theme found throughout this entire collection: the secular church. After gathering, after finding renewal through common liturgy, a Christian life takes place boldly outside the walls of the church. Not everyone has the temperament to do this…and that's understandable. Nevertheless, an appropriately active life does not spend its time in a stained glass foxhole. Instead, the responsible Christian leads an involved secular life "out there" in the secular world, and that includes the out-there world of hunger, poverty, and racism.

The Biblical reference for this sermon is from the Sermon on the Mount and includes the familiar passages, "You are the salt of the earth…" (Matthew 5:13) and "You are the light of the world….[Do not] put it under a bushel" (Matthew 5:14-15). The directive instead is to "let your light shine," to lead a life on the frontiers of the secular world that is worthy of the calling that you perceive in your soul. In Rev. Asbury's words from this sermon, learn to "uproot and plant, to burn and heal, to build and transform."

Westminster Presbyterian Church
Wooster, Ohio
Mr. Beverly Asbury, Minister

February 3, 1963

THE SCATTERED CHURCH: ITS SECULAR LIFE
Matthew 5: 13-16

A service of worship has to do with man's service in the world. Worship is an act--the act of the people of God. At least since the time of Kierkegaard, Protestant Christians have been aware that the worshippers are the actors. Kierkegaard reminded us that the minister and choir are more like the prompters. They remind the actors of their lines, of their places, of their movements. The play would not come off if the actors merely listened to the prompters. The role of the minister and choir is to enable the people, the actors as it were, to act. The liturgy is the play: it reminds us of who we are, and it calls us to participate in the work of God in the world. But if 'liturgy' means 'work', then it only begins in the service of worship. The actors, the worshippers, are being prompted to leave the sanctuary and the acts of worship there to act out their worship in the world. Those who recall that they are the Pilgrim People of God are called to go forth as a catholic and apostolic people.

When we go into the world, then the real liturgy begins--if it has any meaning at all. The light must shine if men are to believe in the importance of what we do in worship. The salt must result in flavor or else it is useless. The gathered church must scatter--dispersing itself in the world or else it has not learned to be the church. The process of gathering and scattering is essential to its life, and it can never forget that its mission lies in service to the secular world.

Yet, from the outset, it must be allowed that not all Christians will assume a witness of active engagement with the world. Familiar institutional patterns will continue. The main direction for what is done in church building will be the same. Indeed, some people are called of God to Housekeeping--to keeping the House of the Lord--and they provide the continuity and stability necessary for the institution if it is to provide a base for scattering into the world. Thus, the sermon today assumes the value of and need for those Christians who give their lives and services to the Church as an institution. This means then that this sermon is not so much addressed to them as to those who are called to a radical new relationship to the world. Its intention is to prompt those who stand ready to live on the frontiers of the secular, where they will have to learn new ways to declare the Gospel and to give expression to its power to uproot and plant, to burn and heal, to build and transform.

The World Council of Churches, meeting in Evanston in
1954, saw clearly that the whole Church shares Christ's
ministry in the world and that the effective exercise of
this ministry must largely be by church members, when they
are dispersed in the world. The World Council of Churches
said this: "The real battles of faith today are being fought
in factories, shops, offices, and farms, in political parties
and government agencies, in countless homes, in the press,
radio, and television, in the relationship of nations. Very
often it is said that the Church should 'go into these
spheres', but the fact is that the Church is already in
those spheres in the persons of its laity." (Section IV,
Page 11 .

We have to recognize immediately then that the minister
is not and cannot be the scattered church. The minister is
not in the world in the same way as most of the members.
He is protected by the institution, and, inevitably, much
of his life is given to the institutional role of prompter.
Therefore, even in subtle ways, he should not stand at the
forefront of the Chruch's activity in the world, for he will
inhibit, discourage, and even prevent the scattered Chruch
from fulfilling its legitimate functions. It also requires
that this minister not be presumptuous in this sermon by
attempting to provide a blueprint for action. I am more
in the position of stating guidelines from which the ar-
chitects will proceed and the builders construct. Even
saying that, however, I do not underestimate guidelines of
prompting.

Nevertheless, the World Council of Churches was correct: The Church is already in the world in the persons
of the laity. It could have added that the Protestant
Christian has nowhere to stand except in the world. We
have no other alternative to seeing the secular realm as
an instrument of divine providence and as a partner of the
Church in the work of reconciliation. Precisely because
Jesus Christ is Lord, the secular is within his domain.

Of course, this doesn't mean that the Church and the
world are at peace with one another. That isn't so. At
points there is real conflict. But the great problem of
our day does not lie in the combat between Church and world
so much as it lies in the fact that the world has invaded
the Church and encourages the Church itself to be falsely
secular. The world looks upon religion as a "good thing"--
just so long as it is favorable to the status quo, just
so long as it manifests the same standards of the world and
occasionally shows its religious credentials. But let the
Church really get involved in secular life--in the struggle
for freedom and justice--and the world objects. The Church
is so sensitive to such objections and to threats of withdrawal of money and members that it quickly retreats into
approbation of the powerful elements of society. Thus,

3

there should be small wonder that many men who know very
well what the Lordship of Christ means find themselves
unable to accept the bland Christianity which the Church
represents to them.

Sam Williams, a Harvard PHD, a Baptist minister, and
a professor at Morehouse College in Atlanta, has said of
the Church: "It is asking too much of the Church as an
institution to take any forthright stand on any issue,
especially if it is controversial. The very nature of the
ecclesiastical organization is such that it will never
rise to the occasion when decisions are called for...."
Williams goes on to say that most statements about society
made by church groups are too tame to come from Christians.
He adds: "The Church will wait, as it always has, until
the time is safe. Once the political and social institutions announce the 'all clear' signal, the churches will
speak out and speak out fervently. The Church follows, it
does not lead. It can come along after a decision and
hallow that decision and make it holy, but it cannot or
will not make the decision and lead others to follow it."

If that is true, and it often seems to be, it means
that the Church has abandoned the secular realm and that
most sensitive Christians will seek to act outside the
Church. Apart from the action of the Holy Spirit, the
Word of God through the Church to the secular order will
not be heard unless we recapture a sober this-worldliness.
Christians must not fear being empirical about the world.
The faith of our fathers calls us to a serious concern
about the ordinary, the commonplace, the self-evident.
The true this-worldliness, the true secularity of the
Church, means to follow Christ into an acceptance of the
vitalities and realities of world existence of the tragedy
and creaturely joy that human freedom means. It is the
business of the Church not to fit Sam Williams' description
by seeking a true secularism and fighting for it—resisting
the false secularism the world encourages the Church to
embrace. That is, the Church must resist the secularism
which expects and desires the Church to be sentimental,
mystical, and middle-of-the-road.

Anyone who has ever engaged in the struggle against
hunger, poverty, and racial segregation knows that authentic
secularism is opposed by the very churches which might be
expected to give aid. The ones who talk most of "religious
value" are often the most opposed to the amelioration and
correction of social ills. They see nothing very wrong
with society anyway, and when they do, they think the
battle ought to be fought from stained-glass foxholes.
The truly secular Christian knows better. He knows that
he must yet bear a cross. He knows the world well enough
to realize that it will object to relevance, and he also
knows that when this world is its true self, when it is
genuinely human, there is a glory that shines in it. Thus,

4

the authentically secular Christian has a passion for life. He has a passion to perfect the world as man's world under God who commands him to be free.

But the false secularism of the world is more afraid of passion than anything else. It desires "all quiet" on every front. Preserve the status quo at all costs. Don't be radical. Be enlightened. Don't fight city hall. Think of your future. The false secular man places propriety above every other value, and he beseeches the truly secular Christian not to affront the memory of Gentle Jesus. Most churches heed the request and become happy and comfortable. The truly secular Christian cannot give in, for he has too deep a passion for truth, justice, and freedom. He continues his fight, and he finds that his allies come from the most unexpected places. He discovers that God moves in hidden ways and encounters him in the midst of secular activity. The Christian who scatters into the world discovers that he has not been left alone. From the lonely and marginal people of society, from the dispossessed and disillusioned, from the tired liberals and hopeful intellectuals will come companionship and support. At that point, the Christian finds himself in that wierd position of witnessing to his friends as well as to his enemies. He can, indeed must, explain both his apostolicity and catholicty to both—— why he is where he is and what he hopes to accomplish.

Much can and must be said about corporate action of the scattered Church, but that will wait for another day, another series of sermons. Now, it is important to recognize the mission of the scattered Church in terms of its membership. Christians must be sufficiently interested and trained to be involved in secular life. It is in that life that funds are invested, agreements made, pronouncements delivered, projects executed. It is not the function of the Christian to seek power over these matters. Rather, he seeks with savvy, skill, and faithfulness to use power to promote the ends of justice, to serve human need, to humanize life. This Christian is so confident that God is at work that he is able to make decisions about "what is going on" even when this is not clear. He fights even when most of his fellow Christians have gone fishing. He says 'no' when others say 'yes' and 'yes' when everyone else says 'no'. He also seeks to use the structures and institutions of secular society in such a way that they function as true creatures of God. The task, then, of the scattered Church is the faithful use of power——sometimes to bless, sometimes to oppose.

An immense opportunity is open for Christian witness. This opportunity can only be realized when the climate and emphasis of churches such as ours change and seek renewal under God. No one fully understands the scattered life in it, and that if we can——at this moment——do nothing else, we can listen to it——listen to the trials and difficulties,

hopes and fears, opportunities and needs. When the gathered
Church listens, it may hear more clearly how it shall
scatter, how it shall meet actual conditions, and discern
where it must, in obedience to God, fight for justice,
mercy, freedom, and truth.

11. **11/10/63** **The Silence of God I** – first of a series of 4 sermons on "The Secular Meaning of the Christian Faith."

The next five sermons –four of them planned as a series– took place late in 1963, the year that CBS News described as "The Year Everything Happened." That year began with newly-elected Alabama Governor George Wallace announcing "Segregation now, segregation tomorrow, segregation forever" in his inaugural address and it continued in June with his "Stand in the Schoolhouse Door" at the University of Alabama. After getting arrested in Birmingham in April, Martin Luther King, Jr. wrote his "Letters from a Birmingham Jail" and made his "I Have A Dream" speech in Washington DC at the end of August. Meanwhile that summer, Medgar Evers, civil rights activist, was assassinated in Jackson, Mississippi, President Kennedy made his *"Ich bin ein Berliner"* speech in the divided city of Berlin, and the US and Soviet Union signed the nuclear test ban treaty. In September, the 16th Street Baptist Church in Birmingham, Alabama, was bombed, killing four young girls and injuring 22 other people (see Sermon #26). President Diem of Vietnam was overthrown and executed a few days before Rev. Asbury gave this sermon and, of course, chaos ensued in Vietnam shortly thereafter. President Kennedy would live to see only one more Sunday after this one.

It is difficult to impart to someone who wasn't there what it was like to live through 1963 and 1964. Wooster was called – as were many colleges – an ivory tower by its students and faculty members alike. The world outside was jangling and students inside the nation's colleges were calling for relevance in education. In counterpoint, Wooster's President Howard Lowry was urging measured self-control. A collegiate ivory tower that provided a citadel for composed and reflective thought, he maintained, wasn't such a bad place to be. In the middle of this was sojourner Rev. Asbury with his Pilgrim People.

This sermon continues to develop the theme of secular Christian responsibilities and actions that were outlined in the previous series of four sermons. This sermon also begins a series of four that examines the foundation for secular activism as expressed in the Apostle's Creed. It raises activism above merely doing "anything" and asks, "What is the meaning behind my action? What is the meaning of my life in this action? If I do not see meaning clearly, how do I find it? And when I ask for answers, why do I hear only silence?" For students in 1963 and 1964, these were – and are again today – powerful and even necessary questions to confront.

With answers not on the horizon, the choice of Biblical verses for this sermon is understandable. The references are two: Proverbs 22, which begins, "My God, my God, why hast thou forsaken me?" and Ecclesiastes 9, which contains, "…the race is not to the swift, nor the battle to the strong." In the absence of swift or powerful answers, the secular Christian should stay true to the calling perceived in the soul. This encouragement seems to have been what Bob Dylan later summarized in his 1975 song, *Tangled Up In Blue*: "Keep on keepin' on."

Close reading of this sermon – especially the second paragraph and again on the second page – reveals evidence that perhaps Rev. Asbury was making his own pilgrim's progress along with us.

No.1 in a series

Westminster Presbyterian Church
Wooster, Ohio
Rev. Beverly Asbury, Minister
10 November 1963

THE SILENCE OF GOD
Psalm 22: 1-11
Ecclesiastes 8: 14-9:6

Some weeks ago, I formulated an intention about today's sermon. I fully intended to relate the Biblical word to The Crucible, the play by Arthur Miller appearing on campus this week. I shall not do so even though I have re-read the play and found myself just as moved as when I saw it on Broadway over a decade ago.

For reasons too many to mention and for some which are very personal, I shall get on instead with the first sermon in an open-ended, but not "never-ending;" series on the theme "The Secular Meaning of the Christian Faith." One, but only one, of the reasons for this series lies in the recurring request to preach about the Apostles' Creed, or some aspect of it. However, as one person has said,—my wife in fact, "Why, that's silly. All your sermon's are about the Apostles' Creed." Even allowing for her biases, she is correct--the Creed is not static. It does not lie apart from the Biblical faith, the preaching of the Word, or from our lives as Christians. The Creed is a confession. It confesses faith. It has been used for centuries by Christians to affirm what it is that has happened and what they hold to be true.

Yet, today many find that it does not confess their faith, or at least not the way they want to confess it. A good many Christians assume that it is just a matter of language. They hold that if it is explained to them, then it can be said. But that does not necessarily hold. After all, the problem of truth is not with the Creed but with the truth it confesses. That is, even with clear, unambiguous language, a person might say, "well, I don't believe that." So, the object cannot be mere clarity, to remove objections--from the series of propositions.

Others say that the problem can be solved for the believer by singing the Creed. They would hold that the Creed is a mythical or symbolic expression that must not be taken literally. Thus, they say: "sing it". That implies that what is sung does not have to be taken seriously--a position shared by many others, but not one held by this church. In any case, it does not really face the seriousness of the problem of belief by modern man, for it says that poetic belief is 'ok' but rational belief is 'out'. You can believe with your heart and body, but not with your mind.

The time has come to put aside all suggestions that skirt the problem and begin directly with where we think we are and with what we think we are. And where do we think we are? If we take our clue from artistic and literary expressions of our age---and from our own deepest experience--we answer that we are cosmically alone. In the face of war and the constant threat of war, modern man feels forsaken, at the mercy of a blind fate that robs life of any meaning. Because of our cosmic alienation we find ourselves alienated from society and from our own best selves. We proclaim that we and our lives are absurd, and to those who doubt that life is so void of meaning we point to death as the proof of absurdity. Life ends before we know who we are and what life is.

Ruth McKee Gordon has expressed the contemporary problem of belief in a poem entitled "Dark Glass".

-2-

Man cannot imagine God
So man imagines man,
Holds his mind as mirror to
Deeps he cannot span,
Lifts a loveless heart to love,
A prayerless soul to prayer,
Reads his hunger and cries out,
"No one--no one is there!"

To his recent film, Winter Light, Ingmar Bergman has examined the same theme of man's inability to believe. Bergman focuses on a pastor in remote northern Sweden, a man who has lost his hold on faith. God is completely unreal to this pastor, who lacks not only the capacity to believe but also the capacity to love. The minister obviously has concluded that he must proceed nevertheless with the functions of his office--preaching, communion, counselling--as though God does exist. While some of the qualities of the film are subject to criticism, they do not stand in the way of our understanding Bergman's message.

The pastor is brought face-to-face with a parishoner who is depressed and at the point of taking his own life. The dilemma is that the pastor is called on to provide a man with a faith to live when he himself has no faith. The pastor speaks not of hope but of his own despair. He shares the condition of the man who needs his help, but to share hell offers no relief from hell. The pastor can give no comfort or hope in this godless world and seems to feel nothing when the man takes his own life.

The p astor's inability to love is dramatized in furtive affair with a drab schoolmistress. He cannot love. Eczema, sniffles, and memory of his dead wife stand in the way. The p astor has no sensitivity evento the love of this woman who would accept him anyway.

The only understanding of God and the Gospel in this movie comes from the mouth of the church custodian--a crippled man who suffers pain constantly. He says much the same thing Mr. Stringfellow said last Sunday about Palm Sunday. The sexton says that the greatest suffering is not physical, not the cross of physical pain, but the cross of desertion, of the silence of God. "My God, My God, why hast thou forsaken me?" These words represent Jesus' greatest suffering. If the pastor can understand this, he can understand his own suffering--and perhaps find meaning. But he doesn't recognize the Gospel, and the movie ends on the stark note of futility. At evensong, the pastor holds a service at which only his mistress and sexton are present. He presides over the devotions nonetheless. The movie ends as the pastor joylessly and faithlessly intones: "Holy, H oly, Holy, Lord God Almighty. The Whole earth is full of thy glory."

The problem is not in man himself. It transcends man. The problem is not social, with hope of correction. The problem is not psychological, with the possibility of therapy. Not even Physics, Chemistry, and Biology offer answers to the cosmic mean-ingless-ness, we face. Our problem is the threat of total meaninglessness, and that problem has no solution in the wistful hope that we shall leave something good behind us in the form of our works or of our children. Pascal came closer to stating the truth: "When I consider the brief span of my life, swallowed up in eternity past and to come, the little space that I occupy, lost in the immensity of space of which I know nothing and which knows nothing of me--- I am terrified."

The silence of God, our cosmic alienation, shakes us to the core. With the psalmist, forsaken and afflicted, we lift our cry of loneliness. God, Where are you?

Why don't you understand? Why can't we find help? Physical suffering we can bear, but the distress of our souls.....We have heard that you have helped others. We know that our forefathers trusted and were saved. God, don't you see? We want to believe. We yearn to believe. But the fear of death is not enough. Come to us with freedom from the threat of total meaninglessness.

If this be our cry, than let us see that the silence of God has cut through our notions of self-sufficiency. To cry out: "Be not far from me, for trouble is near and there is none to help,"is to recognize that we are T. S. Eliot's "The Hollow Man":

> We are the hollow men
> We are the stuffed men
> Leaning together
> Headpiece filled with straw. Alas!
> Our dried voices, when
> We whisper together
> Are quiet and meaningless
> As wind in dry grass
> Or rats's feet over broken glass
> In our dry cellar.
>
> Shape without form, shade without colour,
> Paralysed force, gesture without motion;
>
> Those who have crossed
> With direct eyes, to death's other Kingdom
> Remember us--if at all--not as lost
> Violent souls, but only
> As the hollow men
> The stuffed men.

Even though we continue to move in the same weary motions as before, oriented to split-level living around the values of money, success, and popularity, we know that we are unsatisfied. The preacher in Ecclesiastes speaks of life's lack of purpose. He reckons rightly that man cannot count on good fortune as the reward of good character. The preacher knows that it is dangerous self-deception to hold that all is well with those who fear God. He concludes then that all is vanity and that man might just as well live by the shallow philosophy of eat, drink, and be merry--if you can. Modern man, at least, finds that the preacher has seen the enigma of life correctly. Ecclesiastes is the most modern, then, of the Biblical books, simply because it faces--as we have to--death as the common fate of man. This book could furnish a text to every contemporary novelist of absurdity, because the preacher grants that existence does not permit of any glimpse of a plan which might yield a clue to the meaning of life. Look for God and you will find Silence, Nothing, Death.

Yet, we cannot stop there. The very riddle of our lives lies in the fact that we choose to go on living. To say that there are no certainties has not ended the matter. Ultimately, we move away from the purely rational level where we are wont to keep things in an academic community. We move because we must--because we have the capacity to think and reflect on our universe; because we have the passion to love and to be loved; because we are aware of human compassion and loyalty and courage and responsibility. Death, suffering, and deaf-mute universe do not constitute the whole of our experience.

Perha ps the silence of God, the absence of God, drives us to see that. To live is to act. And one cannot act without presupposing that there is some answer to life's meaning. God's silence drives us to examine the grounds on which we act, by which we live. God's silence tears away cheap assertions. It demolishes the barren assumptions of religion, rationalism, scientism, and humanism. God's silence exposes the hollowness of those who find meaning in their cry that there is no meaning. God's silence forces us to see that personal man in an impersonal universe constitutes an agonizing riddle. God's silence leaves us standing naked--without defenses to clothe us. God's very silence compells men who sleep night after night to arise day after day to repeat the same weary routine time after time to cry forth,"My God, Why?" Without the silence of God we might never have wondered how life can be distinguished from death. But for the silence of God we might have gone one thinking that our problem lay in rational assent to a set of rational propositions set forth in a Creed.

However, what the very silence of God forces us to see is that we modern men in the present world are godless. God's absence drives us to see that all men--including Christians--are basically without God in the world. And in so seeing our conditions, we then sta nd ready to explore with seriousness the Christian faith. For it is precisely for those "without God in the world" whom the Christian faith claims God sent his Son. Indeed, the Gospel has nothing to say except to those who know that they are without God. It speaks only to those who are in some sense without God, who face life as an agonizing riddle. The Gospels can be considered"good news" only to those who have found all other news to be no news.

By the grace of God's astounding silence, modern man may yet see that there are no answers without God's answers; no hope without God's hope. The miracle of God's silence may foster the humility in us to pray for the capacity to see what God is doing in our world and the willingness to let him do it his way instead of ours. Then we can say again "I Believe."

12. 11/17/63   **The Silence of God II** – second of a series of four sermons on "The Secular Meaning of the Christian Faith."

The Epistle to the Romans, verses from which are used in this sermon's message, was almost certainly written by Paul while he was in Greece. This letter is regarded as his theological legacy. Paul wrote it while planning a visit to Jerusalem and anticipating subsequent visits to Rome and onward west to Spain. The letter is filled with encouragement and hope.

In contrast, nearly two millennia later, the American author Stephen Crane wrote,

> A man said to the universe:
> "Sir, I exist!"
> "However," replied the universe,
> "The fact has not created in me a sense of obligation."

There is an account in science that physicists searched for the origin of the universe by scanning the skies across the visible and invisible spectrum, crashing particles into each other in nuclear accelerators, computing theoretical histories and prophecies, and arguing pointedly with each other. Finally, they settled on the Big Bang as responsible for the creation of the universe. When they looked up from their journey of experimentation and calculation, they found theologians already there waiting for them.

As abandoned as humankind may feel in a vast, uncaring, and, to our ears, uncommunicative universe, the meaning of life is *not* what remains after the cacophonies of science and business and the residual echoes of the Big Bang have explained everything else. Meaningfulness is *not* found in the silence that is left over. As Rev. Asbury suggests through a faint echo of Paul's Letter to the Romans that reverberates in the sermon's last paragraph, meaning exists in a place called hope.

II in a Series

Westminster Presbyterian Church
Wooster, Ohio
Rev. Beverly Asbury, Minister
November 17, 1963

THE SILENCE OF GOD II
Romans 8: 18-25

Every affirmation of the Christian faith has come out of a confrontation with some threat to what it considered basic. Christian theology has never been static. It was not devised by scholars sitting up late in their studies. Rather, every credal affirmation made by Christians has arisen because some heresy has threatened to alter what was considered essential. Every expression of Christian faith has grown out of some immediate condition of life. Indeed, one can hardly understand Karl Barth and his system of theology apart from the changing conditions of the Twentieth Century which have brought it forth. The same thing is true of the Apostles' Creed.

This Creedal expression was produced in Rome between the years of 150 and 175. Undoubtedly, it was used as a form of instruction before baptism into the Church, and it only later came to be used as a part of the liturgy. The occasion for writing this Creed was the threat of the Gnostics. The name Gnostic comes from the Greek gnosis, which means knowledge. The Gnostics were concerned with mystical forms of knowledge. They were philosophers who wanted to bring about a unity of religions by taking the best of each of them. As they came into the Church, their aim was to change Christianity to fit their ideas.

This created a crisis for the early Church. The Gnostics were in accord with much Greek philosophy. They held to a dualism, to the view that there were two worlds--the world of matter and the world of spirit. Following Greek thought, they held that the world of matter was evil. Therefore, they rejected the OT and its Creator God, for any God who would create a material world must be an evil God. The Gnostics sought salvation from the material world. The soul must be freed from the body and from the world by denying the flesh and living by knowledge.

Naturally, there were aspects of Christianity which the Gnostics liked. Since Christ was sent by God, he could free men from flesh and matter. That also meant, however, that Jesus could not have been truly a man. He could not have been born of woman, even a virgin, without being contaminated. He could not have grown weary, suffered and died. With variations, the Gnostics held that Jesus was not a true human being.

The Apostles' Creed arose, then, as a refutation of this heresy. It came during the same period in which the NT Canon was being put together. Both the Creed and the NT stood as authorities that God is creator and both retained a firm hold on the humanity of Jesus. Tp put it bluntly and perhaps to make it too simple: The Apostles' Creed was formulated in a day when the world of the "Spirit" was very real and when the philosophers of the time stood ready to deny the world of matter. It served its purpose well.

On the other hand, our difficulty with the Apostles' Creed and with similar formulations of the Christian Faith may well arise out of the fact that we live in a day when the world of matter is very real and when both the philosopher and common men of our time stand ready to deny the world of the "Spirit". What the sermon last week on "The Silence of God" attempted to say is that modern man often concludes that man is an accidental by-product of a huge, mindless, purposeless, mathematical machine.

-2-

Modern man has accepted materialism so completely that he feels a cosmic alienation---that is, that man has no meaning and is only an insignificant* cog in an unending process that is going nowhere.

Obviously, than, what we believe about the world today is quite different from what men believed about it when the Apostles' Creed was formulated. Our minds have been thrown wide open to the impact of the new dimensions of time and space revealed by the astronomers, quantum physicists, geologists, and biologists. And, if we are intellectually honest, we cannot help asking such questions as "What is God?", "What is That behind everything?"; "What is the Ultimate Reality?"; "Can the completely insignificant dot in the immensities of time and space think of this Reality as a Father, as a Personal God?" "If this incredible claim of the Christian faith is true, what is the nature of this revelation or disclosure of God?"

These are the questions of modern man made necessary by our experience and by science. They reflect the spirit of an age that cannot imagine the "world of the Spirit". However, we need to face head-on the fact the the questions made necessary by science cannot be answered if we assume, as modern man is likely to do, that what is not disclosed by science cannot be true. This common assumption is unfounded. Science in the mid-Twentieth Century seems to have reached a new self-understanding where it no longer absolutizes the scientific method and no longer makes a totally materialistic world-view necessary.

Science now sees that her job is one of description. Her final court of appeal is experimentation. The scientific view of reality in terms of the smallest discernable quantitative parts must be understood as one method for understanding one dimension or level of reality. To convert that method into an all encompassing philosophy is not required or supported by the scientific method. As a matter of fact, it is quite unscientific to assume that the whole of life can be understood through an understanding of its parts. Whenever a scientist says that science has disproved or displaced God or religion, he speaks not as a scientist but as a "theologian". His science may lead him to raise the question. It cannot give the answer.

This summer, a scientist for whom I have great respect told me that he looked upon "God" in terms of one of the laws of thermodynamics. He explained his position clearly, and both you and he will have to forgive my inability to explain it correctly. Anyway, he said that "God" was, to him, what thermodynamics calls "entrapy"--- that which is left over when energy has been ex pended. I understood him then to mean that "God" was the unexplained "disorder", the "left over". In conversation he admitted that he did not speak here as a scientist, but he spoke with the assumption that "God" has to lie in what science cannot explain. I answered that such an assumtion was not warranted by science. He finally agreed that we have to conclude that science can in no way eliminate or decide these questions of God, of meaning. It has helped to put them as keenly as they are put, but science as science is an important type of investigation that does not require or defend any particular conclusion concerning the meaning or meaninglessness of reality. To put it another way, the findings of modern science have brought upon us the necessity of asking "What is God?" but modern science cannot find the answer. It has led us to wonder if there is meaning in the universe, but it cannot give us the answer. It has caused us to reject familiar notions of God as "up there" or "out there", but it offers no clues (because it cannot) to what and where God is.

Thus, modern man has been left. In a void, without the older and more familiar images of God. In a state of doubt, with all the unanswered questions. In an agonizing dilemma, with personal man in an impersonal universe. What ought now be clear is that man cannot be moved from where he has been left either by "rational proofs" or by scientific findings. The answers lie on a different level or dimension of reality, and we don't know how to get them.

Therefore, we feel, as the sermon last Sunday tried to state, that God is hidden or silent. Men are tired and weary unto death of searching. We hear no voice. We receive no revelation breaking through the doubts. We only see men swept along in the ordinary and cruel events of our time. We live in distress and shock but hear no hound of heaven baying after us. We are loaded with information b ut have no knowledge of God. We have no certainties, and that is reflected in art, literature, drama, movies, and television. We find ourselves ever in deeper mires of meaning-lessness. But this is no academic matter. We have a living awareness of the NEED for God. We WANT to believe. We HOPE to find meaning. But HOW? God's silence has thrust us into the agonizing search for meaning. How do we find an answer?

One thing is certain, in intellectual honesty we cannot and should not return to the simplicities of childhood, but strive for what Bonhoeffer has called "ultimate honesty." Such honesty, in Bonhoeffer's opinion, leads us to recognize that "God is teaching us that we must live as men who can get along very well without Him." Bonhoeffer holds that God makes us live in this world without using Him as a working hypothesis. Bonhoeffer goes on: "God allows himself to be edged out of this world and onto the cross." What we must understand is that man has learned to cope with all questions of importance without recourse to God as a working hypothesis. Everything gets along and just as well. In science and human affairs what we have called "God" has been edged more and more out of life. What we have called "God" loses more and more ground. What we called "God" has forsaken man, removed Himself from man, left man in a void in order to shatter man's self-sufficiency and vaunted arrogance. Man would look in his distress to the power of "God", but he sees nothing.

We must proclaim then to the current human queries about how to find God that we do not know, and we must insist upon that to the Christian dogmatists who think they do. Ironically, the greatest Christian dogmatist of this century, Karl Barth, has done the most insistent job of asserting that no institution or man has the answers. Barth says: "God is known through God, and through God alone." Barth then sees faith first of all as a confession of the hiddenness and silence of God—as a judgment on our need and impotence, as a sign of the fact that man actually knows God only when God is ready to be known. God's silence shows the futility of man seeking his own ways to God, for the "God" man has sought really is not needed in our world.

The world of spirit, so real 2000 years ago, has no reality for us. The "God" so present in a Creed that confesses him "Maker of Heaven and Earth" is no longer assumed by us. An elder in a church I formerly served was a successful business man. He once said in a Session meeting: "I don't think of God all day long, and, if I did, I'd be neglecting my business. I don't need God in my business; I get along fine." At the time, I was dismayed, but later on I understood that the man was telling me that no working hypothesis called "God" was helpful or necessary in his business. Yet, later, it was this same businessman whom I came to know as a sensitive person, who was asking why he worked so hard, what his money meant, who he was, what his security amounted to. He didn't need a working hypothesis, but he needed a God. This is true of doctors, engineers, teachers, and politicians. They have no working hypothesis called "God". Yet, the very absence of that 'God' and the failure of science to answer our questions of WHO we are; WHY we are here; HOW personal man in an impersonal universe, drive us to desire A GOD. Now, more than ever we have learned that every moment of life is a sheer gift over which he has no control. We see our existence as a mystery. This very fact of coming into being and remaining in being is what drives man beyond himself to see the mystery of existence.

-4-

According to both Bonhoeffer and Barth, none of the awareness to which we are forced by God's silence can be interpreted as a revelation of God. To become aware of our dependency, to find ourselves "without God as a working hypothesis", to learn that we are impotent to find God requires no special act of revelation. Rather, they assert that men perceive this truth by the mere fact of their existence. In other words, this is the relation to God in which one already stands, whether one knows it or not. To face death as the one fact or event to which man cannot say NO is to face that we neither create or sustain life. We exist only because there is a mysterious depth in the Ground of our being. Even Barth recognizes in man a mysterious determination that belongs to his nature. This is not revelation, but human awareness, an understanding of the God-dependence in which one stands. But one is not here dealing with the clear, the easily analyzed and understood. It is something apprehended rather than comprehended. It falls short of the knowledge of God. We still wait for our adoption as sons. We still wait for our redemption, if this is all we know and can know.

Barth is right. To know this much is not enough. God's silence forces us to see that "God is known through God, and through God alone." In Bonhoeffer's words, the fact that "we live without God" compels the conclusion that we hope for what we do not see, and what we hope for requires a Divine Act of Self-Disclosure. For the Christian Bonhoeffer is undoubtedly right: God remains silent to make man look to the powerlessness and suffering of God in Jesus Christ.

13. 11/24/63   In Memoriam: John Fitzgerald Kennedy

The event of November 22, 1963 interrupted life as we knew it. It punctuated the end of Camelot, which was already occurring, and changed the course of future history. The Biblical references for this sermon cite, first, Matthew's description of Jesus' examination by Pontius Pilate and, second, Paul's message of salvation to the Romans. This sermon is an important interruption of the series on "The Secular Meaning of the Christian Faith."

Westminster Presbyterian Church

Wooster, Ohio
Rev. Beverly Asbury, Minister
November 24, 1963

IN MEMORIAM: JOHN FITZGERALD KENNEDY

Romans: 6-11
Matthew 27: 1,2,11-26

During those hours on Friday when it was so difficult to comprehend the incredible and devastating news about President Kennedy's death, my children were asleep--"safe and secure from life's alarm." Still in a trauma from this stunning blow, it was nevertheless clear that, when they wakened, I had to tell them of their President's death. And I knew that their young age would make this even more inconceivable than it was to me at my age. The first response was an inquiry about the President's "little girl", a natural question from little girls. Hard on the heels of that question came: "How could anyone do that to our President?" Such a question belongs not to children alone. We too have asked how such a thing could happen to him, to his family, to the nation, to us! A complete answer may lie beyond our ability to answer, but we are not thereby delivered from trying to give some answer or answers.

For someone to murder the President of the United States requires a tremendous capacity for evil. The grotesque horror of John F. Kennedy's assassination drives home to us the incarnation of the possibility of evil resident within man's capacity for freedom. In the Biblical world-view, this evil is seen as Satanic, as demonic. In the last forty-eight hours we have heard it oft expressed that the murderer must be insane, a demoniac. We have in two days found our belief in Satan restored, for we have seen evil--senseless evil, unmitigated evil. We have witnessed the demonic power of mortal man using his freedom to take the life of another mortal man, and remind us all of our mortality.

But let us understand that the evil lies not only in the life of the man who fired that rifle in Dallas. It also resides in us. The demonic is in us. We are involved in what has happened and we share the guilt.

Every time we have hears a "nigger joke" and laughed, we have implicated ourselves. Everytime we have kept silent in the face of bigotry, we have given support to the forces of evil. Every time we have gone beyond the bounds of fair-play in politics, or allowed our party leaders to do so by saying that "that man" was ruining the country, that we could not survive another term as a nation under him, that he was selling us out, we have given encouragement to fanatics and murderers. Whether from the right or from the left, demonic men have gained strength from our own evil, for our words and our silence, our action and our complacency have led them to believe that they could be heroes by killing the real "demon".

We have not meant it that way. We have not wanted murder. We despise it now. But we are part of a culture that has cultivated a demonology, and we become its victim. "If Hitler were killed, Naziism would die." "When Stalin dies, then Communism will collapse," "If Khrushchev were deposed, then peace with Russia would be easier." "Get rid of Castro, and the Cuban problem will vanish." We think in terms of simplicities and over-seimplicities. Trusting in ourselves, and not in God, we cannot tolerate the ambiguities of history. We seek our explanations in terms of demons and we seek our solutions in the overthrow and murder of demons.

-2-

John F. Kennedy had become a demon to those on the far right and those on the far left. Ross Barnett placed the blame of Ole Miss at the foot of the President. Castro carried on a diatribe for hours about the evil of our President. George Wallace blamed the blood of Birmingham Negroes on Mr. Kennedy. Men of affairs blamed him for all wrongs and credited him for no progress. And some of us went beyond the bounds of humor, telling dirty, vulgar, malicous stories of which we would today be ashamed.

When Pontius Pilate offered the crowd the choice between Jesus and Barabbas, and saw that it was hopeless, he resigned himself and shouted to the crowd: "I am innocent of the blood of this just man. You must see it." And the people: "Let the responsibility for his blood be on us and on our children." The man who murdered John F. Kennedy is as guilty as Pontius Pilate. And we cannot proclaim our innocence any more than the crowd that demanded Barabbas. We share in the bloodguiltiness of mankind. Our very freedom carries with it the capacity for evil. Indeed, the Biblical allusions to the struggle between God and Satan remind us in very real terms that we have the freedom to forsake God; that the freedom to idolatry is the freedom to do evil; that God acts to restore true freedom by reconciling us again to Himself.

The Christian message is that God suffered and died in Jesus Christ to redeem us, to buy us back from evil, to save us from the perversion of our freedom, from our demonology. God in Jesus Christ died for Pontius Pilate. He died for John F. Kennedy, and for his murderer. He died, then, for me and for you. What I see in the Cross is the most profound portrait of God. I do not see just a Creator, a Ground of Being. In the Incarnate Figure of Christ, I see the Suffering God, the God who wills to undergo all the horrors of finite evil, the God who acts with infinite compassion and ultimate concern about man. This is not God "The Unmoved Mover" but the most "moved" of Movers. My confession of faith this day is that Jesus Christ died for us as the ultimate demonstration of God's love. He died for the demonic to show unlimited love. He died to cast out our demons.

The wonder of Jesus Christ is that he died for us when we are evil men, in a state of enmity and hostility to God and one another. Love can go no further than that to give up life to end our demonic choice of death. In seeing in the act of the crucifixion the most powerful portrait of divine love, the man of faith can believe that love undergirds suffering and evil. Through the resurrection comes the certainty that love has the last word, that death is overcome and infinite good is brought out of evil. God in Christ has identified with man's incredible power of disintegration and degradation, there to bear man's alienation and death in order to lead men into the life of God.

Unless this is so; unless we can see God himself active within the evil of life, unless we see hypothesis transcended by divine fact, then we are left with traumatic shock, with despair, with the gnawing anxiety of our own mortality. Unless there is a new relation of forgiveness brought into being for us and all men, we are left only with desolate explanation of "how" this tragic murder could take place--without salvation.

But the last word in the death of President John F. Kennedy, as in the death of all men and as in our death, is not word of the dead, the dying, or the assassin. Man stands guilty before God, but the last word is not sentence of our guilt.

-3-

Epitomized in the cross, the believer sees God accepting him despite his unacceptability. Man kills the very Incarnation of God's love with the same evil which killed our President, with the same evil which made it possible. And yet from the very threshold of death God loves and forgives. This is divine love. This is God's special act which establishes for one who believes a new relationship. Now one can love because he has already been loved. Now one can love because Christ died for us while we were godless. We have nothing more to gain, because here we receive everything: total acceptance, total love, total forgiveness.

"In the beginning was the Word, and the Word was with God, and the Word was God. He was in the beginning with God; all things were made through Him, and without Him was not anything made that was made. In Him was life, and the life was the light of men. The light shines in darkness, and the darkness has not overcome it."

14. 12/1/63 The Springboard of Reflection – third of a series of 4 sermons on "The Secular Meaning of the Christian Faith."   End of November

The silence of God, identified in the first two sermons of this series, is reflected in the unspeakable name, YHWH. The sermon's metaphor is that the unspoken name of God is part of the silence of God, which can lead to a faith that is also silent through inaction. To make Christian belief actionable, faith must be taken out of the church to be spoken aloud and reflected on thoughtfully (see I Corinthians used as a reference for this sermon) in a secular world. Matthew's version of Jesus walking on water (also used as a reference for this sermon, and described in Mark 6:45-52 and John 6:16-21) begins with the disciples departing from Jesus by boat after the Feeding of the 5000 near the Sea of Galilee, present day Israel's largest freshwater lake. The metaphor continues: When the disciples next encounter Jesus, he is walking toward them on the wind-whipped waters of the lake. Matthew's version adds Peter's own endeavor to walk toward Jesus. That Peter succeeds, if only partially, points to the prospect that faith is to be *practiced*, even in a tempest. It should not be left inactive inside the boat…or inside the church.

III in a Series

Westminster Presbyterian Church
Wooster, Ohio
Rev. Beverly Asbury, Minister
December 1, 1963

THE SPRINGBOARD OF REFLECTION
I Corinthians 4: 1-5
Matthew 14: 22-36

The dialogue concerning this series of sermons does not end with the formal dialogue each Sunday following worship. All week long one hears echoes of the dialogue continuing and that carries with it a powerful satisfaction--even when the echoes show distortion and perversion of what the preacher thought he was saying. The continuing c onversation has indicated how very difficult it is to communicate and to understand sermons which have been aimed at a non-religious interpretation of the Biblical categories.

The first two sermons have put an 'ok' upon Bonhoeffer's insistent demand to give new interpretations to the concepts of Biblical thought. They have not rejected the Biblical categories. On the contrary, they are attempting to take them seriously by seeing that "God" cannot be a "working hypothesis", only a living, acting God. At this point the ancient Hebrews could teach us a great deal in their refusal to speak the name of God. YHWH, which with vowels, we pronounce Yahweh, was an unspoken name. To speak it was thought to be blasphemy. However, it is more nearly correct to say that it is unspeakable. Perhaps if we ceased to use the word "God", we could be more expressive of the Reality for which the word stands. Perhaps we could catch the sense of wonder and awe which the Hebrews possessed. It may well be that in our "Godology", we have lost the meaning of the words. We say "Jesus Christ" as if that were a first name-last name instead of a confession of faith. In our talk we have lost even a sense of what "Christ" means. In so much of our talk about "God", he is a working hypothesis, and there is the absence of awe and mystery. As long as we fail to reinterpret the Biblical faith, we are bound to have a matter-of-fact attitude which robs us of the sense of wonder. As long as God is merely a convenient explanation of what we do not understand, then we cannot move beyond the fixed and formal doctrines that do not give life to Christian faith.

Theology, our thinking about God, our reasoning about our faith, must begin with the situation at hand. "Modern man" is not "out there", not in the world apart from the Church. "Modern man" is within the being of every Christian trying to understand his faith. We are not apart from "modern man"; we know him as a real part of ourselves. Our situation is personal--it is we who are reasoning about our faith. Our situation is communal--we do our thinking about God in community with others who have done so before and are doing so now. We are not along, for we stand in a community of faith. The Bible has been produced by the community of faith, and it speaks to those who are in the community of faith. But, if we have to read ourselves into the world of the Bible in order to understand it, we still have to remember that it is we who have to live ourselves into it. Barth is correct, then, in insisting that theology is done by the Church, takes place in the Church, and is for the Church. However, that position must not blind us to the fact that theology begins with and is involved with men--men in their loyalties, sufferings, doubts, failures, and hopes. Theology for such men does not, for it cannot, arise as a defense of what men already believe. Rather, the task of theology within our personal and communal situation is to seek the truth that will be greater than anything we have yet conceived. And, if it shakes what one has held to be true, it has only the purpose of building something more meaningful and formidable in its place. Too many "orthodox" Christians assume that what Christians say about their faith can be considered apart from how they say it. The "liberals" protest that the most important matter is how theology is stated. I should not go so far as to say that it is the "most important" concern, but I do consider it a valid point. That is, how we say what we say is important if our witness to Jesus as Christ is not to be considered literally nonsense by "modern man".

The theological task, undertaken in these sermons, does not require a suspension of belief. Contrary to what some people seem to think, I have not stopped believing in order to preach this series. My faith has not been left behind or "checked" at the door. It remains what and where it was. It constantly informs what I am trying to say. I am simply trying to begin with our situation, with where we are, in a quest to reinterpret the Biblical categories. I am starting with us, for it is we who have to read ourselves into the Bible. And as I do so, I am acutely conscious of the community of faith in which I am doing it. I am doing so from a pulpit, from behind a Table, in the presence of God's people. That is what makes this talk possible. The question, then, is one of how the Christian can preach the Gospel to "modern man" so that he will be able to hear, understand, and become a Christian. Again, this assumes that "modern man" is not "outside" the Church, but that he is more or less inside the Church--wondering what in the world he's doing there.

Since we are more or less in the Church, we can be relieved of the sin of defensiveness. In the community of faith, we know that we don't have to be right if God is right. The task of the Church is not to protect its thoughts as if they were themselves the thoughts of God. The world has grown sick of Christian defensiveness, and we should be sick of it ourselves. It has grown out of dogmatism, the love of our own voices, the security of hearing others say what we like, the fear of hearing anything else, and from thin pietism that equates other words with a lack of faith. Surely, the Church, which exists not for its own sake but for the sake of God's world, must tell the world what it believes in terms the world can grasp. The Church must make clear that only the man of faith can radically question his faith--and that it is the man of faith who should do so.

To raise the critical questions often seems a burden; actually, it is a gift of grace. (Parenthetically, I must say that these questions often have seemed burdensome to me. I have not asked for them or courted them. It would be a more peaceful existence if they went away and left me alone. But they will not! And I now accept them as givens, part of what God has brought into my life.) For the Christian to entertain the questions out of his own existence without fear, repression, or guilt means that he has come to believe in salvation by grace, rather than salvation by theology or by convictions. While the Christian may not be completely free of defensiveness about his faith, he stands ready to expose his own defensiveness--his own pockets of uncertainty and insecurity, his own points of pride.

The Christian learns, with Paul, that he may well be judged by men, and the judgment of men may be instinctively right. However, he also learns that he need not be defensive about the judgment of men, even when he cannot disregard it. He cannot answer the criticisms of others by resorting or retreating to his own judgment of himself. The Christian learns, with Paul, that he can't look at himself with anything resembling complete transcendence. Therefore, he knows that the only important judgment is that of God, for only God knows all the circumstances and motives.

This means, to me, that the minister should lead people to live by grace by learning to do so himself. He cannot justify what he says. He has not been set apart as a superior authority to hand down truth. Rather, he is to be a man of faith,

-3-

radically questioning, not pronouncing judgment before the time, avoiding the false
security of absolutized theological analyses-- learning thereby to live by grace. And
unless he d oes so, he cannot invite questioning man to come to the Table, or to bring
his children to be baptized.

In saying all these things, have we ruled out what is so often called a "simple
faith"? Frequently, those who ask this question are being quite defensive, because
they feel a lack of education. THEOLOGY TODAY (Oct. 1963) recently helped to answer
the question: "Of course fa ith, if it is truly self-surrendering trust, has simplicity in it; the simplicity of grasping a hand, or layihg down a burden; but any human
being who thus entrusts himself is complex, regardless of his background, his education, his knowledge. And if his faith is truly trust, and not simply credulity, there
is also something thoughtful about it."(page 340) There are those, then, who have the
"gift of faith", who are never plagued with doubt or troubled with questions. They
are truly blessed of God in a way that many of us are not. They may well feel that
these sermons are not directed at them. They are partly right--but partly wrong. For
even those blessed with a gift, must reflect on the gift and what it means to them.
Faith may not, then, require education, but it does require reflection. Reflection ,
not education, is necessary to move into the depths of life. The long springboard
of reflection must be built to connect our faith with our knowledge, with our lives,
with our situation. The job of the preacher is not to hand out ready-made spring-
boards that members can tote home with them. There is always the personal necessity
of doing this oneself. A basic decision is involved here for the Christian. Either
being a "Christian" is something "religious"(in the sense of"religiosity") and distinct from the rest of our affairs, or Christian faith is a human posture possible
for a man who is a part of his "secular" culture. These sermons assume that the decision is in favor of the latter, and that assumption is grounded in the conviction
that if one separates faith and culture, he is rejecting the very heart of the Gospel
--the Incarnation.

Unless one reflects on who he is and what he knows, he cannot possibly know what
it is that God in Jesus has to say to him. Until one engages in reflection on the
dilemma of human life, he cannot know a God who is anything more than a working hypothesis. Yet, we forever hear that all we need is faith; that it doesn't really matter
what you believe as long as you believe; that people think too much. People who talk
like that and believe like that deny the need for reflection. They should be reminded
that even NT faith was not so simple and unreflective. When Peter stepped out onto
the water when Jesus said"Come", we see that faith itself fails. "Faith in faith"
fails. Faith is not worthy of trust. The only thing that saved Peter is the hand
of Jesus, not Peter's faith in Jesus.

God does not ask that we blindly trust in blind faith. When Jesus calls "Come",
when we enter into the depth of life, we find that the only faith worth having is that
in mysterious depths of God's love. This is a faith that cannot be proved and so
requires reflection. This faith is not a faith-in-faith that refuses the insights
of knowledge out of a fear that knowledge will destroy it and lead to atheism. Rather,
this faith loves knowledge that can lead to awe and wonder, to sharp awareness of
God's sovereignty, and to true worship. Through reflection on the complexity of
human life we can understand why Jesus always insisted that a man should look at a
situation in all its bleak grimness before he acted. (Luke 9:57f; Matthew 16:24f)
Jesus was always honest with men. He always told them to assess how difficult it
was to follow before attempting to do so. Surely, we can only learn from this that
we should not act without reflection, without first counting the cost.

-4-

The distinguishing mark of deep Christian faith is a thorough and complete reliance on grace of God that allows him the freedom and the joy to reflect on what he believes. That reflection is a sign of the grace in the Christian's life as he sharpens the issues, and lets the God of existence work his way patiently, insistently, dramatically through the crevices of life. All the reflections,then, of this series which holds that Christian faith does not deny our involvement in the world and its way of thinking, are based on the conviction that "Jesus is Lord".

15. 12/8/63   **In the Place of God** – fourth of a series of 4 sermons on "The Secular Meaning of the Christian Faith."

The theme here is freedom of action in a secular world. Jesus exhibited freedom of action because he drew from a set of principles. As described in the Biblical reading for this sermon (Mark 2:1-12 – the same story appears in Matthew 9:1-8 and Luke 5:17-26), he acted as a human being "in the place of God" and, therefore, did not have to consult books of laws in order to figure out the right thing to do. Finding ourselves in similar positions of stress where we must lead, act, manage, or decide, we frequently find ourselves leading, acting, managing, or deciding in isolation. We sense that we are alone, estranged from God and from others by silence. Within this sermon is the message that the silence of God is allayed through the words and principles of Jesus.

Incidentally, this sermon mentions a question that was popular 50 years ago to explain the apparent silence of God, namely, "Is God dead?" (*see Item D in the* Epilog). This question will be developed in a subsequent sermon (#45). Moreover, we will return to the series on The Secular Meaning of the Christian Faith in sermon #21 after Advent.

IV in a series

Westminster Presbyterian Church
Wooster, Ohio
The Rev. Beverly Asbury, Minister
December 8, 1963

IN THE PLACE OF GOD
Mark 2: 1-12

The first sermons in this series have been concerned with the first two words
of the Creed, "I Believe", with the difficulty of saying them at all, with the reflection that is necessarily involved in doing so. Today we make our first move
beyond, and we move to that portion of the Creed that has to do with Jesus. Why
do that? Why not go simply to the next part of the Creed-- "God, the Father Almighty, Maker of Heaven and Earth"? You may think that the decision to "skip" that
phrase, even for now, has to do with Advent, with the requirements of the Tradition
of the Church. That really is not the case. Rather, as the Rationale for these
sermons states, we "skip" because it is so odd to speak of "God". We don't know
what to do with the word "God", Even Nietzche's cry that "God is dead" is not
understandable. If "God " were dead, how would we know? If God is "silent", who
would tell us so? Our problem, then, is that the word "God" is dead. So much the
better. That helps us to see again that the real issue of the Christian faith is
not theology but Christology, not "Godology" but "Christ-ology".

Acts (2:2) declares that the first proclamation of the Gospel was a message
about "Jesus of Nazareth, a man attested to you by God with mighty works and wonders and signs which God did through Him in your midst, as you yourselves know."
Paul asserts in the opening verses of his letter to the Romans that the Gospel concerning Jesus, a man "descended from David." Whatever else it may say or is, the
Gospel has to do with Jesus of Nazareth. His name is central to confessions of
faith by Christians from the earliest times. The Gospel in its barest form has
always had to do with a particular man who lived and died in Palestine.

No reasonable historical doubt ex ists that a man named Jesus died in Palestine in the first third of the First Century. He has been the concern of the
Christian faith ever since. What Christians are able or unable to say about "God"
relates directly to what they are able or unable to say about Jesus of Nazareth.
But what do we and can we know about this man Jesus?

We know, for one thing, what has been underscored since Albert Schweitzer's
book in the early part of this century: that there is a radical difference between
the outlook and attitude of Jesus and ourselves, which all but blocks penetration
into Jesus' own perspective. There is the further difficulty, that the Gospels
are not records or original sources about Jesus. The accounts of the Gospels
express the viewpoint of the early Church as well as that of the authors. They
express the early preaching of the Church. They are radically colored by faith
in the resurrection of Jesus. They are not written to answer an inquiry but to
ex press a faith.

In any event, the Gospels leave us with a choice. We can either accept
Schweitzer's view that the historical Jesus was completely oriented toward Jewish
apocalyptic thinking and so beyond our understanding today, or that we can know
the preaching of the New Testament Church but almost nothing about the historical
Jesus. Both Bultmann and Barth take the skeptical end of the choice. They agree
that the documents at our disposal do not provide the careful historian with the
material for a biography of Jesus. Almost every fact we have about him, from the

birth stories to his arrest and death, has come to us through the preaching of the early church. These so-called "facts" were not meant to be documentary facts.

Bultmann and Barth are both pleased about this, but, of course, for opposite reasons. Bultmann's concern lies in the meaning of the cross, and he looks upon Jesus' teaching and preaching as only the starting point of a new self-understanding offered to man. Bultmann's Christology is man-centered in orientation. Barth, however, holds that all that matters for faith is that God has acted, has raised Jesus from the dead and has commissioned the Apostles as witnesses to this. Nothing more need be sought. The history behind the texts, in Barth's view, is what the texts say: namely, the history of God's gracious act in and for this world. This, to Barth, is the only history that matters, and to know more about Jesus, biologically or psychologically, would not help us to acknowledge God's act. Barth's Christology is completely God-centered in orientation.

Nevertheless, there are others—students of both Barth and Bultmann—who say the choice is not as na rrow as it has been put. They recognize that all the reports concerning Jesus were colored and shaped by the Easter faith. They even grant that many of the reports were produced by that faith. However, scholars like Bornkamm recognize that faith and the elaborations of the tradition about Jesus were responses to the whole person and mission of Jesus. They hold that even later additions and interpretations are indirect sources for our knowledge of Jesus. They agree that we cannot know Jesus from the inside, as it were, but they hold that there are many incidents which allow us insights into the man. That is, we may not have the making of a biography but we do have enough by which to catch meaningful glimpses of Jesus of Nazareth.

From the many little episodes of the Gospel tradition, we gain glimpses. We may not be able to say when or where certain things took place, but we see a central figure stand out boldly. In these glimpses we see the originality and the distinctiveness of this man, Jesus of Nazareth.

On the basis of these glimpses, what can we say about him? Well, it depends on the glimpse, on what you bring to it. You may be impressed with the authority and immediacy with which Jesus met every person and situation. You may be more impressed by his conduct, by a man who dared to act as God's son. You may be impressed primarily by the question of faith he posed for every man he confronted. However we may be impressed, we can agree that Jesus is a singular individual.

In the Biblical record he stands out as a remarkably free man. The New Testament writers have many ways of indicating his freedom. They speak of his "openness" to others, friend and foe. He is faithful to his parents but free from the ordinary claims of a family. He follows religious customs and obligations, but he felt free to disregard them. In the miracle stories Jesus is presented, symbolically, as being free from the limitations of natural forces. He has authority to say "You have heard it said of old.....but I say to you....." He made no attempt to justify his his assertations or actions; he felt free to assert and act. He even evaded the questions, both hostile and friendly, as to the basis for his authority. His was a singular freedom that gave him a memorable authority.

The most radical expression of the freedom of Jesus comes in the story where Jesus forgives the sins of a sick man. Immediately, he was questioned: "How can this fellow speak like this?" "He is insulting God". "This is blasphemy." "Who besides God can forgive sins?" In the face of these questions, Jesus demonstrated

his right to forgive sins by healing the man. Here we see the freedom and authority to act IN THE PLACE OF GOD. Jesus did not leave it to "God" to forgive men
their sins. He forgave them. Jesus acts for "God", and in his teachings he reveals
this same freedom. When he calls men to live without anxiety about the future, he
shows them by his own conduct that he is free from anxiety. Again, we see this
singular freedom in the fact that he makes no claims for himself. He cites no
authority. He seems freed of every need for status, and he resists all attempts
to bestow it upon him.

Yet, this freedom cannot be fully appreciated by us unless we see that Jesus
was not only free from anxiety and status but also was free to live for other men.
This is the point so emphasized by Bonhoeffer in his Letters and Papers From Prison
and picked up with equal emphasis in J.A.T. Robinson's Honest to God. He was free
to love his neighbor, no matter who that neighbor may be. He was free to live for
others without regard to himself. He was open to all others. He was willing to
be with those whom others avoided. The New Testament reports that he taught that
freedom lies in service, and we see his freedom expressed in humble service to
others. Apparently, he could give himself freely, and that is what the story of
his washing the disciples' feet represents. The glimpseswe get show us that he
lived this way. They show us that he was put to death for being this kind of man
in the presence of defensive, insecure, fearful men.

All the characteristics of Jesus seem to center around his remarkable freedom.
You may prefer instead to talk about his faith, but "freedom! is a word that has
more meaning for the "modern man" in us. "Modern man" can understand what it means
to have freedom from fear and the freedom to love another. Those who have this
freedom can assert that they believe, because the "modern man" in us can say at
least this much about other men. We can go this far in defining Jesus, but is it
far enough?

We can know without "believing" that he acted in place of God. An historical
knowledge of Jesus is not the same thing as faith. Indeed, the historical glimpses
may not even be an adequate explanation of the origin of faith in Jesus.
To be sure, there were not any Christians prior to Easter. Not one of the disciples was loyal to Jesus at the point of his arrest. Whatever they had seen and
felt of his freedom, they did not have enough freedom themselves to remain true during the last events of his life. They turned, ran away. They lost hope. They were
discouraged and in despair. The record of the New Testament admits this without
qualification. As teacher and example, one can only conclude that Jesus failed. One
can only conclude that Christian faith does not result directly from seeing the
historical Jesus. His disciples did not share in his remarkable freedom, and our
glimpses into Jesus of Nazareth do not lead us to do so automatically. That is, one
can read and understand the New Testament and yet not believe. Something else must
happen before a man stands ready to test his understanding of, and response to,
every concrete situation in life by reflecting on Jesus of Nazareth. Christmas,
the symbolic beginning of the story of the manJesus, is not an end in itself. It
does not provide its own explanation or a basis for believing.
In fact, between the historical Jesus and the New Testament witness to him
stands Easter. It also stands between historical Jesus and us, who believe but are
only more or less in the church. What happened on Easter is described in the New
Testament as a radically new event but inseparably related to Jesus of Nazareth.
This fact indicates to us that our faith is not based simply on the historical
Jesus but that the historical Jesus is indispensable for faith. To understand the
man who acts in the place of God, we at Christmas, every Christmas, must turn to
Easter.

(I am profoundly endebted, consciously and unconsciously, in this sermon to Paul
van Buren's "The Secular Meaning of the Gospel, The Macmillan Co., N.Y., 1963)

A series of four sermons focuses on Advent, and does so by demonstrating that the rules for action in a secular world derive from faith. Preceding sermons have established this foundation. However, faith as explained in the sermons that follow, is not blindly abstract. Instead, it is expressed in concrete human terms, and the focus of faith-derived action is on our neighbor.

16. 11/29/64 Beginning with Faith

The year 1964, in which the next four sermons are set, was punctuated with discord. Rev. Asbury's preceding sermon ends at the beginning of Advent. This next sermon begins the four weeks of Advent that lead into Christmas. The sermon starts by listing several disturbing events of the year. *Not* mentioned specifically in Rev. Asbury's list are the additional events of the stabbing murder of Kitty Genovese in Queens, New York, while several nearby apartment dwellers either dismissed the disturbance or failed to investigate it; kidnapping and beating deaths by the Ku Klux Klan of two hitchhikers in Meadville, Mississippi; the murder of three civil rights workers near Philadelphia, Mississippi; the Gulf of Tonkin incident and Congressional Resolution; the Philadelphia, Pennsylvania race riot; release of the Warren Commission report on the assassination of President Kennedy; and the confrontational US Presidential election between Lyndon Johnson and Barry Goldwater. The year will end with the violent Berkeley sit-ins and the Free Speech Movement, and the escalation of the war in Vietnam.

Not all influences in the early-mid-'60s are identifiable as specific events. Some influences were cultural and transcended a decade. As the '50s receded and the '60s proceeded, stage music, folk music, and rock-n-roll music all evolved, intertwined, and emerged transformed. Stage music reverberated with *West Side Story* (Arthur Laurents book, 1957, Leonard Bernstein - Stephen Sondheim - Jerome Robbins stage musical 1957, movie 1961), which retells Shakespeare's *Romeo and Juliet* romantic tragedy as the stylized but still agonizing outcome of racial prejudice and territorial conflict between two rival New York City gangs. [Rev. Asbury used *West Side Story* lyrics for Sermon #38.]

On the folk music side, Bob Dylan's *Oxford Town* swiped at the University of Mississippi's resistance to admitting its first black student, James Meredith (1962). Dylan recognized that *The Times They Are a-Changin',* Peter, Paul, and Mary wondered *Where Have All the Flowers Gone?* (written and sung by Pete Seeger, also recorded by The Kingston Trio, Joan Baez, and others), and Arlo Guthrie experienced a 1965 Thanksgiving dinner event that later became the war protest song, *Alice's Restaurant*. On the rock-n-roll side of music, the 1964 invasion of British bands, especially the Beatles (*I Want To Hold Your Hand*) and the Rolling Stones (*I Can't Get No Satisfaction*) midwifed the birth of pop/rock out of rock-n-roll, introduced more sexually suggestive lyrics, and solidified the use of the electric guitar as an instrument of change. Bob Dylan shifted from the acoustic folk guitar in 1965 to the electric guitar, a metaphor for the seismic social shifts taking place culturally and musically – abetted by Wolfman Jack – and setting the stage for the end-of-the-decade California Sound of Brian Wilson and the Beach Boys.

Where and when, many people asked, would the social upheaval of the '60s end? Bob Dylan answered enigmatically, "The answer, my friend, is *Blowin' In The Wind.*"

The Biblical reading for this sermon begins with Jesus, saying, "Now my soul is troubled." The events he foresees on his horizon are overwhelming. The events of 1964 proved distressing to those who faced them, and the numerous reactions and counter reactions to them produced troubled souls throughout the country for the remainder of that decade and beyond. Deeply troubled souls that struggle with deeply troubling issues have often turned to solutions of last resort. Such a choice, contends Rev. Asbury, does not solve the problem but, rather contributes to its severity. Options of last resort become gap fillers because they try to fill in the empty spaces rather than address the whole issue. Correspondingly, God becomes a God of the gap. Such a God is relegated to the periphery to explain what can't be explained and help what can't be helped – to become a God of last resort. In such a condition, faith is also relegated to the gap where evidence and reason leave off.

Issues that are overwhelming can lead to paralysis of action. Rev. Asbury recommends avoiding the unreasoned rules of gap faith for dealing with overwhelming issues, because those kinds of issues are not gap issues. Instead, Asbury urges in this sermon to adopt a new *Blik*, a German word that translates roughly as "view." However, *Blik* connotes something bigger than simply a "view" of something. *Blik* implies *stance, orientation, approach*, and even *conviction* and *commitment.* Asbury advocates making decisions, committing to action, and living a life with conviction – Christian conviction. In a life of conviction, faith and evidence are both central; neither is peripheral. In this *Blik*, God becomes a God of first resort. Thus, even in troubled times, we will "lead a life worthy of the calling to which [we] have been called" (Sermon #8).

This theme appears multiple times in subsequent sermons.

Westminster Presbyterian Church
Wooster, Ohio
Rev. Beverly Asbury, Minister
November 29, 1964

BEGINNING WITH FAITH
John 12: 27-36

Advent is the season of the Christian year in which we give special and particular consideration to the significance and meaning of the coming of Jesus Christ
into the world. Advent presents us with an opportunity to reflect not only on the
New Testament interpretation of Jesus' coming but also on what his life means in
our lifetime. We do not look to Advent as simply past event. If we do that, we
bind ourselves to a primitive picture of the world that is irrelevant to a scientif-
ically-oriented, urban, industrialized society. We look then to Advent as present
event, as a time to understand, hopefully in a new way in the newness of our times,
what the coming of Jesus Christ means to us.

To look at Advent in this way does not change the Good News of the New Testament, but it does give us a changed understanding of what that Good News is. Indeed,
our understanding must change, because of the changed and changing nature of our
world.

Look at the catalogue of recent events across the world: Anti-nuclear riots in
Japan.... a protest against atomic submarines.....a bomb explosion in remote regions
of China....the John Birch Society condemning the United Nations and accusing the
government of being soft on communism.... Carl McIntyre accusing ‑ the National
Council of Churches of communist infiltration.....sensational reports in TIME and
NEWSWEEK on campus morals......Hugh Heffner and the PLAYBOY philosophy.....The "new
morality" of Bishop Robinson....the sex symbols of Madison Avenue.... Elizabeth
Taylor takes a fifth husband.....Cigarettes sales rise after temporary loss...Report
on the effect of smoking on incidence of lung cancer........increase of crime in the
nation....Civil rights bill passed by Congress.....renewal of demonstrations.......
massacre in the Congo....repression in South Africa....an endless mire in South
Vietnam.

What a world to come into! Christians suffer great agony in explaining the
evil of the world, facing its reality, and reconciling it to the Goodness of God.
Christians at Advent turn to one who brings "peace on earth, good will to men." But
they are hard-pressed to say what it means to a world in which peace is tenuous at
best and in which good will distinguishes itself by its rare appearance. Not a few
Christians feel that the present state of the world confronts the Christian faith
with its greatest challenge in centuries, and perhaps with its most serious threat
in 2000 years. Lay and professional theologians alike are attempting to resist the
Church's tendency to avoid the agony of the modern world. They advocate that we
get out from behind the barricades of our protective ideologies, that we leave behind the musty odors of irrelevant formulations and enter into the world's agony.
Our most creative theological voices cry for us to be willing to lose our Christian
life in the uncertainties and confusions and battles of the present-day in order to
have that life given back anew. I heard just yesterday about a city in our state
where there is tension between whites and Negroes but no conversation is going on
to ease it. A group of churchmen proposed an on-going dialogue, a continuing conversation between men of good will in both races. The group went to their ministers--
all Presbyterian -- and no encouragement was offered. The ministers considered so
tame a proposal as dialogue to be too controversial. They felt it would hurt finances
and membership rolls. This was the wrong season--the season of every member canvasses
and statistics compilations. The ministers felt that the dialogue would kill several
organizations. They were unwilling to risk or lose anything. They haven't heard or

11-29-64

heeded the theological sages.

That theological counsel sounds to many as advice to die, and that is what it is. But death is not easily or pleasantly faced, not even institutional death. We do not let old doctrinal formulations die without a struggle, even for the sake of understanding afresh the Advent of Jesus Christ into the world. But precisely here we have something to learn about facing death from the One whose coming we seek to understand.

Jesus faced death. "Now is my soul troubled. And what shall I say? 'Father, save me from this hour?' No, for this purpose I have come to this hour......"

The obedience of Jesus and his disciples unto death is no easy and passionless obedience to the will of God. Jesus knew agony too in facing death; his soul was troubled, as a person, as the soul of the Christian is troubled in the world of today. Only by accepting his dea th, only by obedience to the will of the Father does he overcome the trembling in the face of death. Jesus' acceptance of death constitutes the foundation of the Christian faith. He did not come to this hour to escape. He crushes the desire to flee the trouble by giving himself to death. He seemingly understands his death as necessary--as precisely that which fulfills his purpose of coming into and being in the world. "For this cause I came into the world." Are we better than our Master?

This surely is what Bonhoeffer meant by telling us to look for God in the suffering of Jesus at the hands of a godless world. This simply means what the New Testament tells us: "God chose what is foolish in the world to shame the wise; God chose what is weak in the world to shame the strong." (I Corinthians 1: 27). The concrete obedience of Jesus unto death reveals the nature of the One for whom we use the word "God". H e gives himself to death to bring to nothing the things that are, the things that tyrannize man. This suffering at the hands of a godless world out of love for that world discloses the nature of the Love which has come into the world. His acceptance of his agony and death tell us, do they not, something about the faith necessary for this hour of the world, this world of doubt, uncertainty, ambiguity, and struggle.

We learn from Jesus that faith means the response of the whole man who commits himself in trust. An old notion holds that "faith" takes up where evidence leaves off. This view teaches that faith "explains" what can't otherwise be explained. Some of our contemporary theologians speak of this as "faith in the God of the gap." The gap refers to what lies between what we know and what we would like to know. "Faith" here refers to positing a "God" "to explain" what "cannot be explained." The trouble lies in the fact that modern knowledge keeps narrowing the gap. Science, technology, etcetera, keep pushing the frontier back. And so "God" keeps getting pushed on to narrower ground, until there is no gap left for "God". Such a "faith in a God-of=the-gap" must forever be on the defensive as it is forever edged out of the true center of our lives. This is not faith as the New Testament understands faith. It is never "Faith in faith." Rather, faith is convictional. The Reformers spoke of faith as a gift. The response of faith is not comparable to assessing a body of facts and making a rational judgment about certain probabilities. Rather,in faith we are "grasped" or overwhelmed by the facts. Faith implies a commitment. It is a "blik." As the Reformers declared,, faith is trust. It comes for us, as for Jesus, as we put our lives into the hands of God. It is a conviction of knowing that it is related to a Convictor that comes from beyond ourselves, grasps us, over-whelms us-----convicts, convinces us. Faith is being gripped by a reality.

Faith consists then of the convictions by which one lives and dies. Faith decides what in life is supremely worthwhile, what is real, what is good, what we can ultimately depend upon, what we can hope for, what we are willing to die for, what or to whom we can say: "Not my will but thine be done."

The reason that Jesus did not flee death lies in his conviction about the purpose and cause of his life. His cause and meaning could only be fulfilled by facing this hour. His death was necessary if he was to be true to his faith and to show the way to those who would follow. A man would not be persuaded to be a Christian unless he saw Jesus as a man of conviction who lived those convictions and who died for them. Jesus said, "the light is with you for a little longer. Walk while you have the light, lest the darkness overtake you; he who walks in the darkness does not know where he goes. While you have the light, believe in the light, that you may become sons of light." He thereby invites men to come and live with him in the confidence that what has convinced him will convince them.

This is our clue for a day when the world threatens so much of our Christian heritage with extinction. Here may be the clue for the fresh understanding of Advent. When the Christian today points to his Convictor, he points to the totality of the Christian way of life. He tells the "old, old story". He stands in the continum of Christian history. I stand here as a Christian because parents and friends told me the Christian story. I stand here because Sunday School teachers taught me the Biblical story of God's acts. Today, I may differ with what they taught me. I may find their interpretations naive or uninformed, but the story they told "grasped" me. It grasped me through the lives of Christians whom I have encountered. This "story" is not merely one of words but of a total way of life, and it reaches out from the life of another to us. It "caught" me as it has "caught" others. So, do we learn that the Christian exposes himself in candor to any other person who will look and listen, and he has the confidence that what has grasped him may well grasp the other person. Faith in Jesus as Lord is the conviction that we have the power of evidence that persuades men of the meaning and purpose of life. For this purpose we have come to this hour. ".....and I, when I am lifted up from the earth, will draw all men to myself."

The Christian today, then, begins with faith. He admits that he is convicted. He seeks to proclaim and live the message that has grasped him in the confidence that others will be grasped. He accepts the present conditions of the world's life; he enters its agony and struggles; he suffers with it and for it. He may even die for it. Rolf Hochhuth in the The Deputy had Father Fontana identify with the Jews facing the death camp of the Nazi regime. Fontana explained his moving action by saying that any Christian in this era who is consistent with his faith cannot survive. The consistent Christian may have to face death in its full reality before learning to live his convictions. Then the Christian will know that he must use every resource of his reason to show the meaning and reasonableness of the Christian "blik". In short, the Christian understands the struggles of the world in the light of his faith, and he attempts to "make sense" out of that world. In order to make sense, he may have to die to cherished notions in order to find new expressions. He may have to die to old formulations of the "good news" to discover bold and radical reformulations of it. The world of confusion does not call for us to surrender our faith. It calls us to begin with our faith. Beginning with faith, move on to reason things out. Bring out the grounds for the convictions we have and commend the ground of the convictions of others. Declare the "blik" to be ultimately important to us and hence to give it the evidence of our lives. Beginning with faith, we can turn to Advent and find new meaning in the face of a godless world.

Into this world Jesus came and comes. In this world Jesus grasped and overwhelmed men—and still does. "and now is my soul troubled. And what shall I say? 'Father, save me from this hour? No, for this purpose have I come to this hour."

So have we. Let us begin with faith.

17. 12/6/64 Honest About God

The preceding sermon argues against a God of the periphery. This sermon continues the argument. When humans have faced overwhelming problems or deep mysteries, there has been a historical tendency to invoke God to explain things that are "beyond understanding." Does this mean that God is a magician who occupies time/space where rational explanations of overwhelming events and deep questions are inadequate? When science does uncover a new rational explanation for how the universe works, does that explanation push God further to the edge? How does the language we use to describe *faith* contribute to this marginalization and sense of magic? And an especially important question to ask around Christmas is, What is the relationship between God and Jesus?

Rev. Asbury uses his Biblical references (also found fragmented in Mark and Luke) to remind us that children ask clear, central questions about God, to which adults tend to provide marginal answers. Asbury proposes that instead of using the language of marginalization, we should think and speak using the language of core conviction. To paraphrase three key sentences from the sermon,

> All we need to offer is a means whereby humankind is enabled to live life with a sense of purpose, direction, and integrity. Christian faith, that is, Christian conviction, centers on life, meaning, and redemption. Therefore, our thinking about God must speak to us centrally – about life's meaning and mystery.

This, Rev. Asbury advises, is the message of Jesus, who is the one who showed us how to be honest about God.

Westminster Presbyterian Church
Wooster, Ohio
Rev. Beverly Asbury, Minister
December 6, 1964

HONEST ABOUT "GOD"
Matthew 16: 1-4; 18: 1-3

A few years ago, the most popular slogan in some church circles was "God is the answer." Those of us who belonged to another circle in the life of the Church wanted to know, "but what is the question?" We know, of course, that "God" is not the answer to every question. You do not answer the question about the elements of water by saying "God." That is, you don't if you care to pass the Chemistry course. To say that theology cannot answer biological and astronomical questions does not mean that theology has no relation to those disciplines, but it does mean that we have to understand the kind of questions that are being raised. Furthermore, to say that "God is the answer" ignores the questions about "God," about the language we use and what it means. Quite often, those who say that "God is the answer" attempt to close off conversation and inquiry rather than try to communicate meaningfully about who or what it is that answers what questions. Yet, the heart of the Christian task lies in communicating what is said to be "good news". It would seem, then, rather important to face the question of how we can use human means to speak about ultimate or transcendent reality.

One of the things every parent discovers is that children raise profound theological questions. Despite the naivete of the expression, their questions are in essence the same questions raised by theologians who are attempting to analyze theological language. Children ask about "where" God is "up there", and if you have any theological sophistication at all, you are hard pressed to give an honest answer. As a matter of fact, Bishop Robinson's book, Honest To God, begins with the questions which are asked even by children, and he takes those questions seriously. He confesses that a notion of God "up there" is incomprehensible to modern man. If we teach that to our children now, no wonder they reject "God" later. And because we have such antiquated "pictures" of God, Robinson suggests that we may have to discard the word "God" and find another word with more significance.

This is our problem of communication, and I am inclined to agree with Robinson's judgment. A recent experience at another college taught me that the key obstacle lies in the conception of a personified and spatially oriented deity. In a long evening bull session, we ran head-on into the limitations of human imagination. Both the "literalists" and their opposite numbers, the self-styled "atheists", were bound up in these limitations: either "God is there or not there, and if there, then somewhere; and, if "God " is meaningful at all, must be exerting force. Now, you don't settle this matter by replacing the picture of a "supernatural God" with Tillich's non-picture of "Ground of Being". Analogical thinking is fundamental to the human mind. We have to perceive "to picture" things. The human imagination requires new "pictures", new analogies to replace the "God out there" pictures. One puts down Robinson's book without a clear picture of what is being proposed. Yet, the questions which he has raised have expressed the problems we find in the language of the Christian faith. Robinson's confusion probably commends him all the more because our language itself is so confused.

How do we use the word "God"? A large majority of those who say they believe in "God", a deity, simply don't know what they're talking about. "I don't believe in Jesus Christ, but I believe there's a God." How nice! Exactly, what is believed

12-6-64

If we use it to point to a Creator and not a creature, to the Lord over all things and not to a thing in the world, can we use the same words to talk about Him and still use these words to talk about creaturely things? And vice versa? Here we see the real confusion of our language. To use a noncontroversial example, we confess that "he descended into hell", but we know that such terms are quaint, faintly humorous, and even ridiculous in the modern world. So we use one set of phrases in church and another in our other affairs. We ask our ministers if they really believe the words they use, and they reply that they use the words "symbolically" —whatever that means. And then we wonder why they have to be used at all. Even when we understand that the language of the church has its assets, as well as its liabilities, we wonder if the words still do not represent a way of crossing one's fingers while telling a lie? This is not the first age to face the question about the truth of theological language. However, it may be the first one to confront the claim that theological language is neither true nor false—just meaningless. That it just doesn't make sense. We know too much to speak cosmologically as we once did and not enough to conceive and speak cosmologically in another way.

Let's face it, as children must and do —the word "God" is a strange word. Let us be honest about "God". It looks as though it were the proper name of an individual, but who is the individual? We cannot introduce another to "God" as we would to our friend. We cannot point to any work that is "God's alone, for everything to which we point can be described without any reference to "god". This is what Bonhoeffer meant when he said that we needed no "God-hypothesis" to explain a "world come of age." If you insist on saying that "God" can be found in all that is, then it becomes impossible to identify "God" with anything in particular. To be honest about "God" leads us to the conclusion that the word "God" does not point to an individual. The word "God" is not a proper name in the way in which proper names are meant to function.

We have reached a critical point in our concepts of "God". Can we really honestly claim meaning for our language? Can we speak meaningfully of a "Creator" when even our theologians admit that so to speak does not imply a hypothesis about the beginnings of the universe? What kind of statement is "God created the world"? A theology that takes seriously its task to proclaim "good news" to the whole world cannot sidestep these questions anymore than a parent can ignore the questions of a child. It becomes clear very quickly why you cannot simply say "God is the answer." Such language has more problems than it can possibly solve. Furthermore, you cannot even turn to a new language unless you know what it is you are trying to express. You cannot secape the strangeness of "God-talk" unless you know the purpose of theological language.

Very simply, the purpose of theological language is to speak about one's faith. And this is an important way to speak, for it expresses the problem of the meaning of human existence. I take that to be the greatest problem now facing us. So, theological language attempts to speak, to tell a story about one's convictions, about the purpose and meaning of human life. As we said last Sunday, an old notion holds that "faith" takes up where evidence leaves off. This view teaches that faith "explains" what can't otherwise be explained. Some of our contemporary theologians speak of this as "faith in God-of-the-gap." The gap refers to what lies between what we know and what we would like to know. "Faith" here refers to positing a "God" "to explain" what "cannot be explained." The trouble lies in the fact that modern knowledge keeps narrowing the gap. Science, technology, etcetera, keep pushing the frontier back. And so "God" keeps getting pushed on to narrower ground, until there is no gap left for "God". Such a "faith in a God-of-the-gap" must forever be on the defensive as it is forever edged out of the true center of our lives. This is not faith as the New Testament understands faith. It is never "Faith in faith." Rather, faith is convictional. The reformers spoke of faith as a gift. The response of faith is not comparable to assessing a body of facts and making a rational judgment about certain probabilities. Rather, in faith we are "grasped" or overwhelmed by the facts. It is a conviction of knowing that it is related to a Convictor that comes from beyond ourselves, grasps us, overwhelms us---convicts, convinces us. Faith is being gripped by a reality. Christian faith is misunderstood even by Christians when it is seen as concerned about proving the existence of "God" "out there". Christian faith is convictional. It has to do what one holds to be the purposes of life. Theology and its language seeks to express the convictions which have grasped Christians. For example, we have met remarkable people who are able to love those who hate them; who do not grow bitter in the face of long suffering. When these remarkable people are Christian, they tell us a story. Their story marks the source of their love in Jesus Christ. Their story relates their suffering to him. He has set them free for this. That is their conviction. You may say that their story is "false". But, to be sure, it is not meaningless. There is full meaning for the man convicted of the "good news".

This points to the framework of convictions in which one interprets all the other areas of knowledge. Theology does not set itself apart from the rest of life and thought. It deals with a believer's total conviction. Theological language attempts to give integration and direction to life. It has used words such as "God" to do that, and now it must use other words to express convictions about the meaning of life.

Let's put it another way. To be honest about "God" means that we stop pretending to offer a systematic explanation of the universe. Let's stop using "God" to supply answers to all the questions left unanswered by science. All we need to offer is a means whereby man is enabled to live his life with a sense of purpose, direction, and integrity. The Christian faith centers on life, meaning, and redemption of man. Theology must speak to a man in his total life--about the meaning and mystery of human life.

In the November 7, issue of Saturday Review, the noted British cosmologist, Fred Hoyle, asked, "Can we learn from other planets?" He maintained that man is still in the grip of natural processes and that we are not in charge of our own destiny. Then says Dr. Hoyle: "I am going to make one big hypothesis--a religious hypothesis----that the emergence of intelligent life is not a meaningless accident. But I am not going to follow orthodox religions by presuming that I know what the meaning is." This astronomer speaks of intelligent life as a "remarkable phenomenon to emerge out of the basic physical laws."

In the light of what we have said today, we can surely agree with him if he means that a "God-hypothesis" is not the answer to the emergence of intelligent life. We can agree that the emergence of life is not accidental or meaningless. We can, because we are honest about "God". We do not claim that "God" is the supreme manipulator of the universe, the hypothesis used to explain it. Yet, Hoyle makes a religious assumption of meaning. As a man, he knows that science has not satisfied the questions of human life. As a man, he seeks meaning. As a man, he possesses a deep sense of mystery. He, too, is honest about "God". He does not join those who say that all is meaningless. He obviously stands open to the communication of meaning, precisely because he has a sense of mystery.

12-6-64   -4-

Men who know less still demand proof of meaning. "An evil and adulterous generation seeks for a sign but no sign shall be given to it." We may know too much to speak about "God" as we used to speak. We have to be honest about that. We do not know enough to speak about "God" in a new cosmological sense, but we can stand in the presence of mystery, "become again as children." We can still express that mystery in worship, poetry, music, and paradox. We can communicate in liturgy what we cannot otherwise say.

The mystery does not prove "God's existence", but it helps us to understand the use of theological language. Our language wrestles with the task of expressing the mystery of life. Whatever we may think about Advent, we ought to recognize the mystery and imagination in the Christmas story. That story ex presses poetically what cannot be otherwise expressed. It presents a poetic perception of "God" in human experience. The story of angels, stars, shepherds, wise men, a virgin confronts us with symbolism without which we should not want to live as Christians. We do not have "to take this literally" in order to see its meaning for us. The story tells us something true about the purpose of our lives. Just so, our language expresses our faith, our convictions about what life is all about. We point to the realm of mystery, and our language about Jesus Christ is an attempt to say what that mystery means to the living of our lives. Our language about Jesus Christ responds to and expresses the mystery which we have called "God". We do not use our language to say that our experience of the mystery is significant or important--but only to say that our experience convicted us. We commend it as an experience that has the power to convict man. To be honest about "God" leads us to the profound truth expressed by Advent--Jesus alone.

18. 12/13/64   Jesus in the Place of God

The Christian faith proclaims that through Jesus, God became human. Rev. Asbury uses this sermon's Biblical reference from John to express the authority of God through Jesus, a human being. The passage contains the familiar, "I am the way, and the truth, and the life…." This expression of authority helps solve the riddle of the relationship between God and humanity. In Asbury's words, it cleans up the language and provides a rationale for faith, that is, Christian conviction. It bridges the sacred to the secular and frees humans to act…to do the Right Thing in difficult and even overwhelming situations. Jesus is the model for doing the Right Thing, and this is what Advent and Christmas are about.

Westminster Presbyterian Church
Wooster, Ohio
Rev. Beverly Asbury, Minister
December 13, 1964

JESUS IN THE PLACE OF GOD
John 14: 1-11

Over a hundred people stayed last Sunday for over an hour to have a dialogue about the sermon. It may not be a compliment that we had to talk about the sermon twice as long as it took to deliver it. But it surely indicated that some interest and questions were sparked, to say nothing of the confusion generated. You will remember that we were calling for a recognition that we have reached a critical point in the evolution of our "God concepts." It was proposed that, if we could understand the purpose of theological language, we could recover some of the efficacy of the experience the "God concepts" have served to express. We admitted then that we were seeking a new language to express what we have used the word "God" to express. We admitted that we were after a "clean" theological language because the old version of that language isn't working very well.

In the dialogue, there were some "dirty" questions about this "clean" language. One young theologian asked, "Ok, so you get a "cleaned" language. So what?" Here's what! Let me quote Kyle Haselden in What's Ahead For the Churches? (Sheed and Ward, New York, 1964): "For many Christians today....the issues are: science versus religion, evolution versus an infallible Bible, social salvation versus personal salvation, theological liberalism versus fundamentalism. These battles were fought out and settled years ago, but Christians still bark at the empty logs. The new problems sweep over us and through us---problems of ethnic and racial relationships which tax all human ingenuity, problems of embarrassing abundance and humilating poverty side by side, of unprofitable leisure and unwanted idleness, of exploding populations, of ignorance, disease, urban decay, crime-ridden cities.......So run the real problems, passing the churches by; for the churches are otherwise engaged, preoccupied with hollow logs."

This preacher-theologian would hope that a "clean" language would help us understand what the chief business of the Christian faith really is. Perhaps a "clean" language can help us distinguished what is important from what is not. It could give us an opportunity to clear away some "problems" and get on with the works of our faith. This may be what some call "Christian revisionism", and you may then classify me as a "Christian revisionist". (This disturbs me a bit, because I recall a "revisionist" of another "faith." His name is Khrushchev, and look at the way he went!) But let us face it----Christianity is no stranger to change. In a recent article in Focus, John E. Haag pointed out: "At the beginning of (Christianity's) struggle, when it was an upstart challenger to Mithraism for the domination of Rome, it tried every trick in the book, adopting whatever rituals would draw the crowd." (And we might recall that Christmas was one of those.) Haag adds that Christianity may well be at just such a crucial stage today, and it certainly has to do something. Many of our religious expressions and devices no longer do what they were designed to do. They drive people away instead of drawing them. They do not set people free but generate guilt and anxiety. To face the difficulty with our "God-talk" does not mean "devitalizing" our faith; it means an attempt to revitalize it.

A lot of questions about this attempt have been raised, and we can't answer them all today---and maybe not at all. But this question has to be faced: If one has to speak without "God-talk", if one has to do without concepts of transcendent deity, if one knows too much to assume "God" as a transcendent deity as he was assumed in the past---then what can be said of other traditional theological items?

Well, as this preacher-theologian (who is a convicted Christian) sees it, this Christian revisionism looks increasingly to Jesus. It means focusing more exclusively on Jesus than the theological liberals did and becoming even more Christocentric than the neo=orthodox theologians are. But with a difference! To focus on Jesus in this way is not to condone the idolatry of Jesus we see among the literalists and fundamentalists. In fact, they begin with a notion of transcendent deity and begin their understanding of Jesus in the light of deity. In other words, Jesus does not disclose for them the nature of "God". Rather, when they say that "Jesus is God", they seem to say that their concept of deity determines the nature of Jesus. They "deify" Jesus. They simply exchange words--"Jesus" for "God"--but the meaning is always in the same "transcendent deity" framework. They don't deal with the "God-problem", with the difficulties of "God-talk". They simply compound the problem by denying his manhood, and making him into a transcendent deity. They do not touch the original problem.

What we are saying now, therefore, is not the same as what the literalist would say. Rather, we are saying that we look to Jesus as the paradigm(the pattern, model, example) of faith, as the one who suffers at the hands of a godless world out of love, for that world. When we see Jesus in this way, we escape the problem of "God-talk". We begin with Jesus as a man, void of any presupposed concepts of transcendent deity. In Bonhoeffer's terms we approach Jesus as men-come-of-age who have no need of a "God-hypothesis". We may end up saying something (who knows what?) about "God" after encountering Jesus, but we can't know that(or what) then. What we see here is a man who stood in the line of prophets who considered themselves as slaves of a living truth which compelled them to speak. We see Jesus as a man grasped and convicted by what he called his "Father". We see Jesus as one who embodies everything we have used the word "God" to represent. Jesus "fleshes out" everything we have used the concept "God" to express. He says in the Fourth Gospel, "I am the way, the truth, and the life; no one comes to the Father(God) but by me."

Perhaps here is where we need to see that we are not really saying something new, but giving new expression to our faith. We are using new terms to disclose the truth confused and hidden by the strange-sounding language of "God-talk". We can see this by shifting gears for a moment, in order to express this in orthodox terms. In the prologue to the Fourth Gospel, we read: In the beginning was the Word, and the Word was with God, and the Word was God. ....And the Word became flesh, and dwelt among us (and we beheld his glory, glory as of the only begotten from the Father.) (John 1: 1,14) The "Word" the logos if you will, passes the grasp of our understanding. We may feel that "it" is "there", but we have no relation to "it". So, how do we "know" "it". "It" has to become incarnate, to dwell in a man. So we are told in orthodox terms, that Jesus is the bringer of the Word of God, of the Word that is God. Jesus is identified with God. The Fourth Gospel says, "No one has ever seen God." And it says of Jesus,"He who has seen me has seen the Father." Jesus has made known, tocput it in orthodox Biblical terms, everything we mean by the word "God"; in fact, Jesus in place of God.

Remember the story where Jesus forgives the sins of the sick man.(Mark 2:1-12) Immediately, Jesus was questioned: "How can this fellow speak like this?" "He is insulting God." "This is blasphemy." "Who besides God can forgive sins?" Jesus had acted in freedom and with authority to take the place of God. Jesus did not leave it to "God" to forgive men; he forgave them. He acts for "God". And when he calls in his teachings for men to live without anxiety about the future, he shows them by his own conduct that he is free from anxiety. He shows himself as the paradigm of faith. He makes no claims for himself, outside the Fourth Gospel. He cites no authority. He seems free of every need for status, and he resists every attempt made to bestow it upon him. He discloses himself as the man for other men, the man who

grants a model, and yes, a power to become. "But to all who received him, who believed in his name, he gave power to become children of God." In other words, something about him grasped others, caught them up, and empowered them.

Men so grasped saw him then and see him now as One standing in place of God.
Jesus was free to love his neighbor, no matter whomt he neighbor may be. He was free
to live without regard to himself--free to put other first. He continually exposed
himself to those whom others av oided. He taught that freedom lies in service, and
he expressed his freedom in humble service to others. And those who see him as the
paradigm of faith find perfect freedom in his service. They have no further need of
old concepts of trancendence, of deity. Jesus takes the place of "God", and moves us
beyond the vague, the ambiguous, the confusing concepts.

Look again at the Fourth Gospel, which asserts that Jesus is the full and adequate disclosure of everything the word "God" expresses. In the Farewell Discourse,
we hear Phillip assuring Jesus that his and the disciples' difficulties would be ended if Jesus would grant them a vision, the sight of the Father of whom he speaks.
Philip wants to be shown the "Father", and he implies that there is something yet to
be shown, something lacking in what Jesus has disclosed up until then. Philip really
says, "Show us the 'God' of whom you speak."

Jesus clearly replies that the disciples should stop looking for the "Father".
Do we not see the clear implication that we should not find "God" and that the quest
to do so is futile? No man has seen "God". No man can find "God". Man has to live
without "God". Philip, the questioner, meets silence on the "God" problem; he is
pointed to Jesus. That seems to be the New Testament answer to the question about
"God", and if we take it seriously, it will serve well as an answer, thank you.

Whatever it is men seek and call "God" can be found by finding Jesus of Nazareth.
Whatever the word "God" means--as the truth about ourselves, our world, as the key
to human life and destiny--can be and is found in Jesus. For those who have been
grasped by him who see him as the paradigm of faith, he takes the place of "God". He
becomes the criterion for their understanding of themselves.

The New Testament required only one affirmation for early Christian: "Jesus is
Lord". Even men with a "God-problem" may be prepared to confess that. To say that
Jesus is Lord is to say that Jesus and the "Father" are one. Jesus becomes the key
to understanding and living our lives meaningfully. By looking to Jesus, as the
Fourth Gospel tells us, we find our only meaningful and useful answers to our "God"
questions. In orthodox terms, is this not what the Christian means when he says that
Jesus is the revelation of "God", the "incarnation of God"?

So, when the words of Jesus begin to give purpose, scope, and energy to our lives
when they grasp us and remake us, we acknowledge Jesus as Lord, our Lord. We stand
convinced that Jesus is "unique", because we certainly had not seen "God" until Jesus
makes "him" known to us. The Fourth Gospel seems to say, to use a "Clean"language,
that there is no "God" but Jesus. And what a "happy answer" this is. There may be
no way to express it other than poetry and music. Perhaps, and even undoubtedly, it
will be better expressed in the music of today's worship than it is in these words.
Why? Because this is an answer of joy. Jesus brings joy to those who have been
bound in the fallacies of ideal concepts by giving them a way out. Jesus brings joy
by granting us the courage to face our ignorance and live meaningfully despite it.
Jesus brings joy which can be expressed in poem and song by providing us a human experience that transcends the ordinary.

12-13-64

Jesus takes the place of "God". Our frame of reference shifts from heaven to earth, from "transcendent deity" to human being, from theological concepts to ethical action. Already today our choir called us to see this as it sang, <u>To Shepherds as They Watched by Night</u>: " Oh, then rejoice that through His Son,

> God is with sinners now at one;
> Made like yourselves of flesh and blood,
> Your brother is th' eternal God."

That is what Advent is all about. Blake said it in his poem:

> 'If Thou humblest Thyself, Thou humblest Me.
> Thou also dwell'st in Eternity.
> Thou art a Man: God is no more:
> Thy own Humanity learn to adore,
> For that is My spirit of life.'

Those who call themselves Christians are those who have seen in the remarkable man, Jesus, everything they mean by the word, "God". Those who call themselves Christians are those who have been so grasped by him that they have what they need to live their lives meaningfully. Those who call themselves Christians say that "Jesus is Lord"; he takes the place of "God".

"O Come let us adore him, Christ the Lord."

End of First Semester

19. 12/20/64   **Jesus Our Neighbor**   End of December

This sermon is the fourth of a series of four and summarizes the three sermons that preceded it. In this Cycle of Sermons, it marks the end of Rev. Asbury's sermons on Christian foundations and the beginning of his sermons on Christian conviction in practice.

The story in Luke (told also in Matthew 13:54-58 and Mark 6:1-6) used for this sermon shows Jesus taking responsibility for his actions, some of which were unpopular. Rev. Asbury points out that Jesus did not deflect blame or hide from criticism (even though, as Luke continued, "No prophet is acceptable in his own country"). Similarly, Asbury contends, when conditions are unpleasant or even overwhelming, we act with Christian conviction "when we move beyond indifference and understand love as more than a duty, goodness as more than an unpleasant task. ...[N]eighborliness does not mean mutual indulgence and false toleration." Doing the Right Thing means "to be more compassionate toward others; on setting free those who are oppressed by poverty, ignorance, and shame...."

[*Nota bene:* The concept of "who is my neighbor" is explored pointedly in Sermon #26.]

Jesus lifted the yoke of rules from a God-of-the-gap by his manifestation of God-in-humanity. He provided "...a renewal; a freedom from past guilt, a new start." Through love, humility, and serving others, we discover God. Jesus is the neighbor and the model for acting with conviction. Making the model visible for our neighbor is the greatest Christmas gift of all.

Advent IV

Westminster Presbyterian Church
Wooster, Ohio
Rev. Beverly Asbury, Minister
December 20, 1964

JESUS OUR NEIGHBOR
Luke 4: 16-30

Much of man's desire for a transcendent deity arises from his own failures and sufferings. Man has looked for a transcendent deity on whom he could blame his inadequacies and to whom he could shift his responsibilities. No small part of man's need for a belief in a transcendent deity, no matter how pagan in Christian terms, comes out of the desire to contract out of history, to transcend "upward" and escape.

What we have been saying during this Advent season is simply that that desire of man leads up a blind alley. We know too much to turn naively to a notion of transcendent deity as we once turned. We have learned in this vastly complicated and interdependent world that man is responsible for the human confusion of human history. We sense no meaning coming into it from "beyond". We know that our job is not to get out of life--"Now is my soul troubled. And what shall I say? 'Father, save me from this hour?' No, for this purpose I have come to this hour." Our job, in other words, is to find meaning in human existence, to discover the meaning in what has been "given Our task has been termed "transcendence downwards"--not to get out of life but to find within the human situation itself a redeeming center and a healing grace. And this is a task peculiarly conducive to the Christians, because Jesus came into the human situation. He did not run away from it. He suffered and died at its hands. He lived meaningfully and redemptively within it. He lived in such a way as to give men healing and freedom. His life granted grace and joy to those who encountered him. Jesus was their neighbor, the center of grace and meaning. And Jesus promises to be our neighbor, the way to genuine humanity, the truth of our human situation, and the life which is offered us.

In Nazareth, according to custom, he stood in the synagogue on the Sabbath and read from the prophet Isaiah. Then he pronounced, "Today this scripture has been fulfilled in your hearing." The promise of the Law and the Prophets, the hopes of the Israelites--the epitome of all great expectations--have been fulfilled in this man. Here, in this man, we see one without permanent address, a poor risk, without assets, with nothing to offer except himself, who now makes claims for himself. The reasons he makes these claims cannot be clear to his hearers. In the face of misunderstanding and mininterpretation, he has courage to claim that today, right now, in the hearing of those gathered, these words of hope have been fulfilled. Jesus, in effect, says, "I, your neighbor, a man of Nazareth, am your hope."

Surely, we can understand the reaction. Jesus' words clearly imply, do they not, that the meaning of human existence can be found in him, that we enter into life by way of a personal relationship with him. Jesus' words require a definite commitment to him as the center of human wholeness and selfhood. He makes a claim which can only be tested by accepting it. You can only "come and see" if it is so. In Mark 11: 28ff, Jesus is asked, "By what authority do you do these things?" He asked a question back. "Was baptism of John from heaven or from men?" His questioners were unwilling to answer, and so they said, "We do not know." And Jesus said to them, "Neither will I tell you by what authority I do these things." The essence of his answer is "What do you think?" You cannot prove his claims without entering into his life. In Matthew 11:25, Jesus says, "Come to me, all who labor and are heavy-laden and I will give you rest. Take my yoke upon you and learn from me; for I am gentle and lowly in heart, and you will find rest for your souls." Who can know the validity of the invitation's promise without testing it?

Advent IV

So did his hearer's react. They were aware of the graciousness of his words. They surely were touched by them. They would like to believe them. They spoke well of him. But they knew as well that these words might make fools of them. What if they were not true? "Is not this Joseph's son?" Is not this man one of us? What can you expect from one of us? How can he be the fulfillment of our longings? He is making fools of us.

Don't rob this story. It does not call for the introduction of pious or doctrinal considerations which will relieve its offensiveness, so clearly understood by its first hearers. "When they heard this, all in the synagogue were filled with wrath. And they rose up and put him out of the city, and led him to the brow of the hill on which the city was built, that they might throw him down headlong."

Jesus' claim to be the fulfillment of our hopes is transcendence downward. It replaces those notions of transcendent deity which we have used to soften our fears and anxieties. It puts our neighbor in the place of "God". We are told that "God" is here, not "up there". We are pointed to our neighbor, "Joseph's son; and our neighbor demands a complete reversal of our values and expectations. "New wines must be put into new wineskins." This neighbor disturbs us because he bursts the wineskins of old concepts. Love replaces law. Love renews us. Love places us in freedom, with all its dangers, and with all its opportunities.

Remember the woman who comes to Jesus and washes his feet with her tears. They were the tears of a sinner. She has lived on (or off) love. Now she loves. She has been "caught" by Jesus. Jesus does not speak directly to her. He speaks about her: "Her sins are forgiven." He doesn't pronounce absolution; he states a fact. He acknowledges that her sins are forgiven. He could do nothing about her sins in terms of past event. He acknowledges a new direction. Her life had found one who could redirect it. And that is what one needs --not an undoing, but a renewal; a freedom from past guilt, a new start. That is the woman's forgiveness! And it came from her neighbor, Joseph's son.

What a surprise! And that it is! So there is something more than offense to those who meet this neighbor. We can compare it to the experience we have with those whom we have known and have taken for granted. Then what we had least suspected hits us --"There is more to him than meets the eye." Such an experience comes suddenly, and it takes the form of joyful insight which we want to share. It breaks through the humdrum of our days and reminds us that we find our grea test fulfillment in and through the neighbor.

This points again to the fact that we should not and need not look for signs of God. Jesus tells us again and again that he will give no signs. He is the sign. Jesus our neighbor becomes our sign. He challenges us by his presence. He makes us realize our condition. His presence does something about it. You don't have to look elsewhere; he is the man at the gate (Luke 10: 16-19ff). He is the sign of the Lord's demand and the Lord's presence. Our neighbor is in the midst of us, Immanuel, God-with-us.

How beautifully this is expressed in poem and song at Christmas. One song,"The Gifts They Gave", has these words:
Jesus our brother kind and good
Was humbly born in a stable of wood
And the friendly beasts around him stood.
Jesus, our brother, kind and good.

And then the song tells of the gifts of the animals--the donkey, a ride to Mary; the sheep, a coat wooly and warm; the dove, cooed him to sleep that he should not cry. Then:

> Every beast by some good spell
>
> In stable dark was glad to tell
> Of the gifts he gave to Immanuel
> The gifts he gave Immanuel.

We could sing as well of the gifts that Jesus our neighbor gives to us. That gift, the truest Christmas gift of all, lies in the fact that Jesus' words explicate the promise we may expect from our neighbor. In a meeting with our neighbor, we find health, wholeness, completion. A letter from a student this week expressed it this way. "One thing that I am finding more and more about academic life, at least from the student point of view, is the lack of direct commitment to other people. There are certainly commitments that one has, but they are not as direct as I would like with others at present. Without commitment to others, I don't think that life is meaningful. By participating in (a civil rights project last summer) at the grass roots, I found a real sense of direction that was particularly meaningful to me; I would like to renew that sense if possible."

This very dedicated student knows Jesus as his neighbor and understands the meaning Jesus brings to human life. Our legs become useful and their use purposeful where there is someone they can take us to and someone to send us out. Our useless hand finds a new use when it meets another hand to shake. When we meet neighbor as neighbor, we have our eyes opened. The demonic obsession of loneliness, self-centeredness, possessiveness, can be driven out by the courage of my neighbor who is ready to face me in my egotism. This is the healing the neighbor can bring, and we recognize it because we have known Jesus as our neighbor.

We move beyond intellectual thoughts and beyond religious promise when such a relationship of neighborliness is what we most desire. The promise of Jesus lives only when we move beyond indifference and understand love as more than a duty, goodness as more than an unpleasant task. We learn from Jesus that neighborliness does not mean mutual indulgence and false toleration. Neighborliness is based on great expectations of releasing those who are captive to guilt and anxiety; on helping our fellows to see what they have not seen before and so to be more compassionate toward others; on setting free those who are oppressed by poverty, ignorance, and shame; on proclaiming the forgiveness of the Lord.

Christmas teaches us to be glad of the neighbor. The meaning of our life as the student so clearly saw depends on the neighbor. Our neighbor does not cramp our expectations; he gives them a shape, a human shape--as God gave us a human shape, the fulfillment of a neighbor.

The words of Jesus create for us a vision of what we can be, to a far-distant fulfillment. They hold promise and stretch our hopes beyond the confines of our present life. In our neighbor, our brother born in a manger, we learn to live against dying, to die for life, to enter into the pathos and glory of others--and there begin to love as we have already been loved.

Up to this point, we have dealt with the challenges confronting students upon moving into college, the secular environment in which adults find themselves, and the development of a foundation or stance upon which actions can occur. The next 10 sermons – until the beginning of Lent – describe those actions in detail and develop them atop the previously laid foundation.

20. 12/30/62 A New Year

This sermon heralds the New Year 1963. It is optimistic in tone, as New Year's sermons generally are. The year 1962 just past was mostly congenial. After all, it was Camelot. The year 1962 was highlighted by events such as the release by the Soviet Union of US spy pilot Francis Gary Powers (subject of the 2015 movie, *Bridge of Spies*), Jacqueline Kennedy's televised tour of the White House, opening of the Seattle World's Fair and its Space Needle, James Meredith's entry into the University of Mississippi as its first black student, the beginning of Johnny Carson's 30-year run as host of the *Tonight Show*, Richard Nixon's parting words after losing the California governor's election: "You won't have Dick Nixon to kick around anymore," and Cuba's release of the last 1000+ participants from the Bay of Pigs invasion. How heavy these events weigh on history's scale is for the reader to judge. Yes, in 1962 the Cold War continued, there were some airplane crashes, there were some space successes and some space failures, two of the Flying Wallendas died in an accident, the US Supreme Court ruled compulsory prayer unconstitutional, Marilyn Monroe died, Cesar Chavez sought improvement of conditions for migrant workers and founded the National Farm Workers Association (a prelude to the Delano Grape Strike of 1965) and, most significantly, the US and Soviet Union averted nuclear war during the Cuban Missile Crisis. What was unrealized at the time was that 1962 was the last year of the '50s. Thus, the context for this sermon at the end of 1962 more closely resembled the past than it resembled the unseen future hurtling toward us from the near horizon. What was to arrive in 1963 and thereafter was to be much different from what we had known before.

The reference for the sermon comes from the First Letter of John, which is a short epistle thought perhaps to have been written by the same author as the Gospel of John. The letter opposes proliferation of the notion that Jesus appeared to be human but really wasn't, a concept known as *docetism*.

The structure of this epistle is known as a *paraenesis*, which is a generally amiable philosophical exhortation to continue in a particular way of life or belief. This was probably appropriate for a letter addressed to a community of believers at the end of the First Century, that is, for them to continue to see Jesus as truly human. However, as a sermon reading for the New Year, 1963, its use was unintentionally ironic in that the context of life in the US was about to change.

In the way that I John argues for union of body and spirit in Jesus as *both/and* rather than *either/or*, this sermon is noteworthy – even prophetic – in its effort to reconcile *liberalism* and *conservatism*. Such a reconciliation is at least as important in 2015 and 2016 (and longer?) as it was in 1963. As a reconciliation, the sermon breaks the static concepts of political liberalism *vs.* political conservatism. It does so by asking if these two poles appear to be opposites simply because people view them from a perspective that is already polarized. Rev. Asbury's argument is that acting through Christian conviction is a both/and endeavor.

Westminster Presbyterian Church
Wooster, Ohio
Mr. Beverly Asbury, Minister

December 30, 1962

A NEW YEAR: THE FUTURE
I John 5: 1-12

In the last few days, I have been reading the
second revised edition of Clinton Rossiter's Conservatism
in America (Vintage, N.Y., 1962). This book has, in a
short seven years, become a classic in its field. It
deserves the honors which it has received because it does
a masterful job of defining and delineating two of the
stickiest words in our vocabulary: liberalism and conservatism. Among the other things that Rossiter says in
his preliminary definitions, he says this: "...when he
(the liberal) faces a showdown over some thoughtful plan
to improve the lot of men, he will choose change over
stability, experiment over continuity, the future over
the past...(the conservative's) natural preferences are
for stability over change, continuity over experiment,
the past over the future...."

As one looks at time, then, the liberal is optimistic
and prefers the future to the past, and the conservative
is pessimistic and prefers the past to the future. As
a Christian it is possible to be either liberal or conservative. The liberal Christian stresses that man who
is created in the image of God is essentially good, and,
given the opportunity and the will, can improve the world.
Thus, the liberal looks to the future, to progress, to
betterment, to change. On the other hand, the conservative
Chrisitan stresses that man is a sinner. The conservative
exphasis on man as irrational, lazy, selfish, cruel, and
depraved leads him to a pessimistic view of change, and
so there is a preference for what is known, for present
checks-and-balances.

However, beyond all this, must we not admit that,
for the Christian, this need not be just an either/or?
Can it not, must it not also be a both/and: Surely, the
Christian is sometimes the most liberal of conservatives
and at other times the most conservative of liberals (and
this is not meant to rule out other possible combinations
or positions). This is to say for a Christian what Rossiter
claims for these positions apart from the faith: "In all
genuine liberals there is a sober strain of conservatism,
in genuine conservatives a piquant strain of liberalism..."

This can be said of the Christian because he has a
past: He knows God's Creation, God's Presence among men,
God's act of redemption in a Man. A Christian has a hold
on the past which he cannot ignore or deny, and that makes

him a conservative. Yet, a Christian also knows that God's kingdom has not yet come on earth, and he has been called to hope for it. He looks to the future, and that makes him a liberal. The Christian is a man in history, a sinner, but he is also a man touched by eternity, a precious soul, a religious entity. He has urges toward evil, but these are matched by God's grace which gives him high aspirations for good. Men know every sort of inequality, but every man is a man--a physical and spiritual entity--and is thus entitled by God and nature to be treated as an end rather than as a means.

Man, Christian man, can be either conservative or liberal. Better yet, he can be both liberal and conservative. But that does not exhaust the matter. As we face the Year of our Lord, 1963, I cannot for the sake of me believe that it is enough for Christian man to let it go at this. It would seem to be a matter of not only being in the world but also of the world to think that the matter is ended with some balanced position on the conservative/liberal axis. Change and resistance to change may be the laws of life on earth, but must life be lived only in terms of welcoming or fearing change? As we face the future, we do face it as conservative liberals or liberal conservatives, but can we not also transcent it?

If man is the alloy of human and spiritual, if man has been given a particle of the eternal, then he can transcend and conquer that which is always changing. Through the eternal one can fathom the future. The eternal power is in man; it is faith: "This is the victory that overcomes the world, our faith." Faith expects victory. The New English Bible translates First John in this manner: "For to love God is to keep his commandments; and they are not burdensome, because every child of God is victor over the godless world. The victory that defeats the world is our faith, for who is victor over the world but he who believes that Jesus is the Son of God?" (5: 3-5) The Christian, therefore, transcends the usual alignments because, in Paul's words, he expects that all things will work together for good for those who love God and are called of God according to His purpose to do His will. Those who love God have an expectation of the future which anticipates victory, and such an expectation has already conquered the future. The Christian, consequently, is done with the future before he begins on the present. What one has conquered no longer has the power to disturb, and this gives us our transcendence. This transcendence does not mean that we are above it all, but rather that we can be more vigorous in the present.

To have faith, to believe, means a certainty about the future. Christian faith, from the New Testament onward,

affirms that historical life is never utterly bereft of
meaning, but that confused flashes of meaning, which
sometimes illumine and sometimes are blotted out by history,
find their only meaning in God who is not contained in our
notions of time. But do we have that sense of certainty
about the future? A group of students gathered around a
professor of New Testament during the Korean War asking,
"Would Communism be destroyed?" He replied that we seemed
to want solutions apart from God. Were we Christians
really certain about the future? Though we seemed to
believe, did we really? He had confronted us with the
question: "Do you really expect victory?" This question
makes the obscurity of conservatism and liberalism more
difficult. If we expected nothing, we really did not
believe. But if we merely waited upon some particular
event grounding our hope upon some particular thing--such
as victory over the Reds--then we did not believe either.
The New Testament pushes us beyond conservatism and
liberalism into something far more important, because it
teaches us that only one who is finished with the future
can be wholly and undividedly firm in the present.

Only when one knows that the future has been decided
can he act in the present with vigor. One can be finished
with the future when one has conquered it. And that is
exactly what faith does. It expects victory. It looks
for conquest. Every time I catch myself not expecting
victory, I know that I do not believe. Every time I
become just a liberal or just a conservative, I know that
I have not overcome the world by believing that Jesus is
the Son of God.

It is not easy to believe. But the first condition
for believing is to know in all honesty and truth whether
I really do believe or not. The easiest way to go astray
is to seek some assurance that our expectations will be
realized, instead of seeking for an assurance of faith that
we believe. The hardest but surest way is to test myself
and to confess my view of the future. Do I expect history
to be a solution to my problems as a man? Or do I expect
history to be part of the problem for which man has to
find a solution?

As we face the future, there shall be times of con-
servatism--of cherishing the past and what it means, of
protecting the good which has been given. There shall
also be times of liberalism--of welcoming change and
expecting improvements, of moving to greater effectiveness
and relevance. Through these times, and also above and
beyond them, we shall face the future in faith, expecting
victory, overcoming the world. Let me quote for you a
paragraph from Soren Kierkegaard:

"Today, on the first day of the year, when
the thought of the future obtrudes itself

-4-

upon men, I will not glut my soul with all
sorts of expectations, nor split it up by
imagining all sorts of things. I will collect
myself together, and hale and happy, please
God, I will go forth to meet the future. Let
it bring what it will or may. Many expectations
will be disappointed, many fulfilled. That
is bound to be, as experience has taught me.
But there is one expectation that will not
be disappointed--experience has not taught me
this, but neither has it the power to disavow
it--and that is the expectation of faith. And
this is VICTORY." (Edifying Discourses, Vol. 1,
p. 32f)

Prayer by Kierkegaard:

Father in heaven! How is a man nought without
thee! How is all he knows but a broken fragment
if he knows not thee! How is all he undertakes
only a half task, if thou art not the master
of the building! Do thou then move those who
live without God in the world that they might
seek thee. Form the hearts of those who seek
thee that they might wait for thee. For well
do we know that all seeking has its promise.
Why then not the seeking that seeks thee? But
we know also that all seeking has its pain, and
so too does the seeking that seeks thee. Well
do we know that to seek does not mean that a
man must go into the wide world; for the more
glorious the thing he seeks, the nearer to him
does it lie. And if he seek thee, O Lord, thou
art the nearest of all things to him. But for
that very reason he perhaps has not yet found
thee. So teach him to wait. Though the years
pass, grant that he may wait. Even though he
lose everything that is not worth gaining, if
he yet waited for thee, then he did not lose.
So be it, Amen.

21. **1/12/64** **The Gospel as "Blik"** – a return again to the series of sermons on "The Secular Meaning of the Christian Faith."

Christian action is grounded in *Blik*, a German word that implies *commitment* as well as *view* or *position*. A *Blik* provides the freedom of action that Jesus modeled. This sermon explores deeply the concept of *Blik* and establishes a theme that feeds other sermons in this Cycle.

The *Blik* that Rev. Asbury suggests is contained in the word *kenosis*, the Greek verb that appears in Paul's letter to the Philippians 2:7. It means "emptying oneself" or "pouring oneself out," and the concept is referred to on the sermon's second page, third paragraph from the bottom. A kenotic ethic is often referred to as an ethic of service and self-sacrifice (shown as an example in Sermon #35 and explored as a comprehensive disposition in Sermon #44). Kenosis engenders freedom because when one deeply empties oneself, one has nothing left to lose and is, thus, entirely free. Contemporary examples of kenosis are evident in the way many musicians, actors, and artists pour themselves into their practices, performances, and works…traits referred to by C.S. Lewis in his book, *Mere Christianity*. Paul pointed out to the Philippians that Jesus exhibited a kenotic ethic, and Paul advocated that Philippians should do likewise. Asbury observes that a kenotic *Blik* sets one free, just as it set Jesus free to enter into "the thick of social and political conflict." At the beginning of 1964, when this sermon was delivered, perhaps if more people throughout the country had practiced a kenotic ethic, collectively they might have mended the unraveling of events already underway.

VI in series

WESTMINSTER PRESBYTERIAN CHURCH
Wooster, Ohio
Rev. Beverly Asbury, Minister
January 12, 1964

THE GOSPEL AS "BLIK"
Philippians 2: 1-11
Text 5-11

It goes without saying that if the Christian faith had been confined to the "eye witnesses" of Easter, we should not be here today. From the very beginning, the Apostles proclaimed the Gospel to others, and some of the hearers responded positively to it. Those who heard and became Christians then understood themselves as sharing in that new freedom which was defined by the freedom of Jesus. They possessed a new perspective upon themselves, their life, and the world. The experience of this new freedom and perspective has traditionally been called "conversion".

Within this framework we understand Paul as a Christian. He was not an "eye witness". Yet, he was able to say (I Cor. 9: 1,2): "Am I not free? Am I not an Apostle? Have I not seen Jesus our Lord?" Paul appeals to his own freedom, his own experience, his perspective which has changed his life. Most contemporary Christians would not say "I have seen the Lord" but they would not be reluctant to say "I have seen the light". In saying this, he shares the experience of the Apostles. His experience is different, because he was not an historical witness to the Easter-event. Nevertheless, as one who has had an experience of discernment, his experience is at one with that of the Apostles. Indeed, it can be said that the experience of discernment depends logically and historically upon that of the Apostles, and it is for that reason that we today so often use their language to express our faith.

In other words, the language of the Apostles and the language of contemporary Christians alike claims a universal significance of a particular, historical person-Jesus of Nazareth. Christians of all ages have made the claim that encounter with this remarkably free man produces responses either of a feeling of judgment on us in our insecurity or else a new freedom in our lives. Christians claim that the Gospel is about a free man. Yes, but more--a free man who has set other men free. Yes, even more--a free man who sets other men free as no other man has done or can do. These claims have no empirical grounds; they express the firmness of the believer's convictions. These claims acknowledge that the believers' understanding of themselves and their lives and all things is determined by their understanding of Jesus.

This exclusiveness of the Christian's claim carries with it a universal note as well. The Gospel claims that, in the history of Jesus of Nazareth, something eternal, absolute, universal--something it calls "God", was manifested. These are precisely the claims that Paul makes in the second chapter of Philippians. The language is difficult, but the meaning can be clear.

We find in the eleventh verse the earliest and most basic form of the Christian confession--"Jesus is Lord." This is the perspective. This is the view of Jesus which is valid regardless of circumstances. It is this historical perspective which gives weight to the traditional assertion that there are practical consequences for the man who confesses the Lordship of Jesus. Paul obviously agrees that Christian faith involves a way of life. In other words, one could not make the confession that Jesus is Lord unless he was able to see some men sometimes act in freedom and love. If one never experiences a Christian living for others, one has no "empirical" grounding for a confession of faith. For Jesus to be Lord, he must have set others free and given them a new perspective.

Thus, in the first four verses Paul points out that this historical perspective should prevent disunity. Unity-in Christ must also mean unity-with-other Christians. Christian love keeps men as one. The existence of human pity and compassion comes from the discernment of the pity and compassion of Jesus, and one cannot possess it and still turn on the brethren. Paul insists the "encouragement in Christ" the "incentive of love" means that one cannot live for himself--the Lordship of Christ requires living for others, sets one free to live for others.

When Paul admonishes "reflect in your own minds the mind of Jesus Christ", he indicates anew that faith constitutes a certain understanding of self, man, history, and the whole world, and that this universal perspective has its norm in Jesus of Nazareth. Some of the linguistic philosophers have invented the word "blik" to express non-theologically what Paul says here. A "blik" is an orientation, a commitment to see the world in a certain way, and a way of life which follows inevitably upon this orientation. In other words, everything we do depends upon our basic outlook upon the world. A "blik" involves a perspective entailing a commitment. Paul here expresses a "blik".

Jesus of Nazareth has become the occasion and the definition of the way Christians look upon themselves and their world. This perspective is not a point of view selected by the believer. When Paul says,"Have this mind among you which you have in Christ Jesus", he does not mean that a person must now coerce himself into an outlook. Rather, he means that those who have been grasped by this perspective must live out the perspective of which Jesus is the norm. This is the Gospel as a "Blik"--it is a way of looking and a concomitant way of acting. The "mind of Christ" is given in the sense of perspective. But when you are grasped by it, you must respond to it. Thus, when Paul says that we should reflect the mind of Christ, he goes on to define it in terms of Jesus' action--that he freely lived for others.

The very reason that Paul can state that Jesus was "in the form of God" lies not in a preconception of his nature so much as it does in the fact that Jesus possessed the essential characteristics of what the word "God" means. Again, so far from living for himself, he gave up his freedom for others--he literally emptied himself, poured out his freedom that it might be shared by other men. He lived for others, in full service to mankind. Call it "love" or call it "freedom", we see th quality which enables and compells him to enter into the condition of man and to be treated in the cruelest way. Because of what we see in Jesus, we, who believe, confess his "divinity", that He is like, that He is what the word "God" means to us. He takes the place of God for us not because he grasps for our worship but because he gives himself for our freedom.

Those who have experienced this freedom know that we have a "Blik", a new way of looking at ourselves and our world and a new way of acting in it. We have a name, therefore, that is for us above all other names. It is not the name "Jesus", but the name OF Jesus. It is what this name means as historical perspective to which we respond. It is what we discern in and by this name that teaches who we are, why we are here, and what we must do.

The man who says "Jesus is Lord" is saying that the history of Jesus and of what happened on Easter has had the effect on him of setting him free. The man who says that "Jesus is Lord" means that he has been so grasped that he can and must recommend to others to see Jesus, himself, the world in the same way and to act accordingly. To say that "Jesus is Lord" means that every other claim on us is a relative claim. When Jesus becomes the point of orientation, the Christian is freed

VI in series-3

from final or ultimate loyalty to the nation, family, church, or any other person. The Christian has been liberated for service to these centers of relative value, but he can never again belong to them. Furthermore, he will never rest content so long as these relative centers of value serve only themselves instead of others.

When "Jesus is Lord" we stand the same risk as he stood. His freedom led him into the thick of social and political conflict. It is inconceivable that it would not be so for one who shares his freedom. To have this freedom carries with it a necessary way o f acting. Yet it is true that we Christians often seethose who do not call themselves "Christian" acting with greater freedom and love for others than "Christians" do. Since we know that Jesus is Lord, Lord of the world and not limited in his Lordship to the Church, we understand that all free men, no matter where they say they have found their freedom, have caught it from the same source as we. From our perspective as Christians we discern that freedom wherever and in whomever it is found comes from Christ. The free man may not have the same "blik" as we have---he may not recognize its relationship to the history of Jesus of Nazareth. But we recognize that relationship, and we know that his "blik" has been made possible by "Jesus Blik". Our freedom has a basic relationship to the story of Jesus, and the way we act is a response to and a reflection of the way of Jesus of Nazareth.

We do not have to speak here of absolute being, even Being itself. We do not have to refer to that which is "beyond" or "behind" it all. We do not have to speak of some final ground and end of creation. We can remain silent on these questions, because there is "the silence of God". What we have to tell is the history of Jesus and the strange story of how his freedom has become contagious. That history is the context in which the light dawns and in which freedom proves to be contagious to us again. That history of Jesus is our Good News. It is our "blik"-- our way of looking at things, our freedom to live for others, our way of acting. Let every tongue confess that "Jesus is Lord."

(As was the case with several preceding sermons and as will be the case with several following sermons, this one is indebted to Paul Van Buren's "The Secular Meaning of the Gospel, Macmillan, New York, 1963.)

22. 1/10/65 Ethics for Christians Today

The references in Mark (also found in Matthew 22:34-40 and Luke 10:25-28) and Romans present what is known as the Great Commandment. The sermon uses it as a backdrop for Christian action in a secular world.

Many themes of previous sermon converge here: maturity (Sermon #3), patience (Sermons #1,2,3), *I-Thou* & agape (Sermon #6), neighbor (#19, 22), conservatism/liberalism (Sermon #20; see Reinhold Niebur's statement that is cited at the top of this sermon's p. 3), service and kenosis (Sermon #21), and especially the enduring theme of Christian conviction in a secular world (Sermons #10,11,12,14,15,18,21) that runs throughout this Cycle of Sermons.

This sermon advises that, instead of retreating into practical atheism, as many students did 50 years ago (and still do now), one should adopt the principles of Christian commitment – *Blik*, if you wish – and act accordingly in order to attend to our neighbor. Acting ethically to correct injustices is neither a liberal nor a conservative stance. It is not a union or management stance and it is not a technological or primitive stance. Rather, it is a Gospel *Blik*. It is not either/or but, rather, both/and. Moreover, when one adopts the paradigm of Christian commitment, indifference is not an option. It is each person's responsibility to act – a responsibility that cannot be escaped or delegated to anyone else.

Rev. Asbury pondered the social and political events of 1963 and 1964 in light of the Great Commandment and preached this sermon. To what extent would the sermon remain the same today?

The concept of "who is my neighbor" is explored pointedly in Sermon #26.

Westminster Presbyterian Church
Wooster, Ohio
Rev. Beverly Asbury, Minister
January 10, 1965

ETHICS FOR CHRISTIANS TODAY
Mark 12: 28-34
Romans 13: 8-10

Despite periodic student revolts from time to time and despite significant student participation in demonstrations for civil rights, one does not get the impression that present-day students are boldly revolting against all traditional values and patterns of our society. The Christian Century recently(12/30/64) called to our attention a limited but suggestive study of current student attitudes. This study indicates that students, rather than attem pting to overthrow social structures which they find irrelevant, will be more inclined to retreat from them. It points out that students today have replaced the "lapsed ideologies of public action" with "an ideology of privacy". There is the current attitude of "privatism" which the individual expresses as "It's nobody else's business". This represents a kind of personal isolationism, a self-declared ex ile from concern with others and other's concern for them. Thus, broad social concerns are "not my business." Avoid personal engagement and entanglement.

The study concluded that many students find "traditional values are not so much oppressive as irrelevant. These students don't reject the "Thou shall nots"; they simply ignore them as irrelevant. The real atheism today is not one of rational logical attack. Today's atheism has no crusading zeal. It makes no determined systematic, public attempt to win converts. Rather than overt atheism, we see a "practical atheism", an operational atheism. Those who may go to church and even mumble through a creed go out and operate on the basis of a "practical atheism." In other words, they don't fight religion or "God", they just ignore both so far as the important decisions of life are concerned. They do not present us, for the most part, with irresponsible rebellion but with a private ideology that ignores or dismisses traditional values. The students outwardly appear docile, as though they accepted the values endorsed by the society. They seem outwardly not to be fighting the older generation. And they are not. Inwardly, they have dismissed that generation's values; they no longer even try to talk with it. They leave it alone and ask to be left alone. Paul Goodman, in Growing Up Absurd, has illustrated some of this operational difference. He points out that the new generation follows the logic of the older gen eration, for it has seen values espoused but never practiced. Thus, it ignores the tauted values and lives without considering them. It operates as though these values were unimportant, and it has, in fact, never seen their operational importance. They disaffiliate from the social, political, and religious concerns of other generations. They keep silent about the irrelevancies even if it means that evil dominates in society.

Many who have adopted this posture of a "world-come-of -age" are more-or-less within the life of the Church. Many who do not openly rebel nevertheless feel that traditional values and ethics say nothing to them. Many of those more-or-less within the Christian heritage are no longer swayed by the prohibitions of the "Thou shalt not" commandments. But they are not closed to an understanding of morality based on motivation rather than on authoritarianism. And the Church can be thankful for that and for the opportunity this gives the Church itself to recognize that the New Testament did not accept absolutist and legalistic ethics. Christ put ethics and morality on a new base--that of love, respect, and freedom--and it is to that that we can and must turn in this time when the absolutes are being rejected again.

Now, let me make this as clear as I know how to make it. This new situation does not present a threat to the Church so much as offering the Church an opportunity to recapture the true basis of its own ethic. The new indifference to the "Thou shalt nots" gives us an opportunity to aim at a higher code of ethics, rooted in Jesus Christ and his relationship to us. This gives us the chance to rethink our ethics and offer a valid and meaningful alternative to the "private ideology". The real sin of our day, the breaking the bonds of the covenant relationship, may not be so much a matter of "pride", as St. Augustine thought, as it is indifference. Man's real way of breaking human relationships now may not lie so much in his admiration of his "good works" as in the lack of any "good works" at all. In short, sin can be primarily our indifference, our lack of concern, our "retirement" from service to others. It is this situation that we must address ourselves.

The Church today has no other resource than that of the New Testament. Today as ever before she is bound only by the love made manifest in the Lord Jesus. Today as ever before the Church stands under the double commandment of love. The only basis for a Christian ethic lies in the New Testament challenge to act responsibly and in freedom for the welfare of the neighbor. As K. F. Logstrup has said: "A man has always something of his neighbor's life in his power. It may be a small thing, a passing emotion, a good mood that can be aroused or spoilt, a resentment that can be heightened or dispelled. But it can also be a terrifyingly great thing----it can depend on you whether your neighbor lives or died." Just so does the basis of Christian ethics fly in the face of the "private ideology". Yet, you cannot deduce from the love commandment what are the actual opportunities and actions open for the Christian. The New Testament comes from a history other than our own, and it's demands are not transferable to our new time.

For example, the New Testament treats the political and social realms as marginal to the true nature of man's life, but we must today give these very realms the decisive place in any Christian's responsible acting. Each of us in a democratic society shares responsibility with every other citizen for what happens in politics. We cannot escape into the anonymity of a "private ideology" or stay unaware of what is happening. Precisely because of this the New Testament seems irrelevant to this generation. The New Testament sayings and exhortations stay at the level of the individual or the family. The New Testament has an attitude of acceptance of the world. This generation knows that the really important decisions are not made by individuals and that the family is no longer the decision-making context. This generation looks less to accepting the world than to dominating and shaping it. The New Testament categories hardly apply in a society of scientific penetration and technological specialization because it now becomes difficult to distinguish between technical and ethical decisions. When management and unions today make decisions about working conditions, wages, and the like, they enter an ethical realm. What they decide technically affects human relationships and purposes. The decision to use computers has ethical implications, because men's lives as well as profits, are at stake. When researchers seek to test discoveries, such as a new drug, they have tremendous ethical decisions to make. When the Pentagon decides the size of weapons, it makes not only a technical decision involving money and armaments, but also an ethical decision involving employment, industry, and the lives (and deaths) of millions.

It would be asking too much of the New Testament to provide direct answers to the problems we face in this new time. Furthermore, if we had simple, direct, and absolute answers, then we would no longer have the Christian Faith. Discipleship has always had a cost, and it still does. The meaning of discipleship has to be worked out in every new period of history. History does not repeat itself. It places on us new, previously unknowable patterns of behavior. Discipleship means a further exploring of the old paths---and a pioneering of new paths. Pioneering had always been full of dangers; it still is. But we have to risk and then account for what we have done.

The behavior of the Christian in new times requires a running conversation between the New Testament and our contemporary situation. The ethics of discipleship must emerge from a dialogue between the historical New Testament examples and analogies for the fulfillment of the love commandment and our present history which requires action for which there is no blueprint and no escape from responsibility. Reinhold Niebuhr has said: "The Christian will not take any established order overseriously: he will not disturb any established order irresponsibly." The Christian will have profound respect for all ordering institutions and customs, and he is most ready to reform them when this can be done without undue hurt and violence. The Christian brings to society something which is always needed: a critical loyalty and a loyal criticism. And that stands in contrast to the indifference of a "private ideology".

It recognizes that personal responsibility can never be handed over to another man in the same situation. It also recognizes that you cannot hand personal responsibility over to the Ten Commandments or to the New Testament itself, because they are removed from us by so many deep and significant differences. Paul said "Owe no one anything, except to love one another; for he who loves his neighbor fulfills the law....Love does no wrong to a neighbor; therefore love is the fulfilling of the law. Let us face honestly that much we call "love" does great harm to the neighbor. We too often deceive ourselves about what is and is not love and fail to allow sufficient time to test it. So, we end up seeing our "love" do harm. The result is that many people reject the "love ethic" as inadequate, as only slightly better than no ethic at all! However, this basis for ethics for Christians today does not aim at a lower code of morality. It aims at a higher attitude toward the person, a personal relationship of responsibility and of love that will pervade all human relationships. This ethic aims for a relationship not based on laws but for concern of the person, rooted in Jesus' concern for the neighbor. The difference between love and lust must never be forgotten. Lust seeks only for one's appetite. It has no real concern for the other. It does not reason or care, and it destroys the genuine personality of the other. Love seeks first the other's fulfillment. It is filled with concern for the other. It cares less for one's appetite than for the well-being of the other's personhood. Such love does not destroy; it builds and completes. An ethic grounded in love always seeks the welfare of the other.

This position does not differ basically from that of any earlier generation. Certainly, it is not too different from that of the first disciples. They had nothing to go on beyond the free, even wayward, and obviously unsystematic speech and behavior of Jesus. They could not evade the challenge of responsible and genuine obedience to the Lord by relying on some preordained code. This fact did not free them any more than it frees us from all need of external controls and internal discipline. Paul cautioned time and again that freedom did not grant license to do as one pleased to have a "private ideology". The New Testament called for mature reason to discover the true situation and the action it called for.

So today in our new situation we must reason maturely about it and what action it requires. We must be in constant dialogue with the New Testament. Marty E. Marty in Varieties of Unbelief has said, "The modern world moves by images of what is seen and heard. Both secular unbelievers and religious unbelievers, from opposite motives can yawn and lose curiosity in the presence of the Christian witness if the believing community shows no regard for the world as it is and if it does not move in the world in a way congruent with its profession. It is the ethical concern that is leading to a restudy of self-serving institutionalism and religious narcissism among Christians today. Karl Jaspers is no doubt correct when he says, 'If the churches dared.....to put themselves in jeopardy, the Word would be credible everywhere

every day, on the lips of priests and theologians.' To make the Word credible is not
the same thing as saying that it will be believed. But a new situation for hearing
presents itself. For this task the churches need to seek the grace of patience,
perhaps having to be content with comparative formlessness for some generations.
While the churches revise their institutions and make their word credible, they dare
not wait for fulfillment in a kind of false perfectionism. In the spirit of Luther's
dictum that 'God carves the rotten wood and rides the lame horse,' they are free to
work with history as they find it, not as they wish it could be remade." The one
thing we are not allowed is indifference. Rebellion is healthier than disengagement.
Those who rebel can still care; they can still love; they can still act to redeem
society's evils and irrelevancies. To those still more-or-less within the life of
the Church--we can point to the insight that "love, utterly unconditional love,
admits of no accommodation. Jesus himself never resolves these choices for us: he
is content with the knowledge that if we have the heart of the matter in us, if our
eye is single, then love will find its way--its own way....."(J.A.T. Robinson).
Love is the fulfilling of the law--it does no wrong to the neighbor.

23. 1/31/65   Guilt and Responsibility

This sermon is about injustice, indifference, and hope. The context for
the sermon is the unrelenting procession of racial and political events
that wounded the nation. One of these events was the prolonged
stabbing murder of Kitty Genovese. At the time, it was [incorrectly]
reported to have occurred while 38 nearby apartment dwellers ignored
her screams and her cries for help. [Subsequent investigations of the
event revealed major inaccuracies in press reports, including arbitrary
use of the number "38." These inaccuracies do not eliminate the
damning inaction of bystanders, nor do they diminish Rev. Asbury's
message.] Rev. Asbury's theme is to emphasize the Christian moral
imperative to act in the face of injustice, and he does this by building
his sermon on a play, *Incident at Vichy*, written by Arthur Miller.
Repeating the concept from prior sermons that indifference is not an
option, Asbury shows how action to prevent or correct injustice is a
moral duty, even to the point of personal sacrifice. What is our moral
stance regarding the unjustly persecuted, the refugee, the immigrant?
This is the burden of the Cross. As the Genesis reference for this
sermon points out, we are our brothers' keeper and we are are also our
own keeper.

For other examples of the Christian imperative to reject moral
paralysis, see Sermons #16 and #45.

Westminster Presbyterian Church
Wooster, Ohio
Rev. Beverly Asbury, Minister
January 31, 1965

GUILT AND RESPONSIBILITY
Genesis 4: 8-16
John 15: 12-17

In a very real sense, the sermon today has been written by the noted playwright, Arthur Miller. Of course, he doesn't know that he has written it. He might even repudiate it. He would have good reasons: I have not been able to put my hands on a copy of his new play, "Incident at Vichy", which opened last month at Lincoln Center Repetory Theater. On the other hand, I have studied the reviews and responses to the play, and, more importantly, I draw today upon Miller's own words about the play, printed in the NY Times Magazine on January 3.

Miller obviously has written a play that is a moral inquest. That does not make it a good play, and I have no personal basis on which to give you a critical judgment on the dramatic production. Indeed, that is not my concern at all today. The concern here and now is with his message rather than with the play itself. The message attempts to pinpoint the "weaknesses and fears in all of us as the source of never-ending inhumanities visited by man upon man". (NY Times review 1/3/65).

This is how he relates it in the NY Times Magazine:

"About ten years a European friend of mine told me a story. In 1942, said he, a man he knew was picked up on the street in Vichy, France, during a sudden roundup of Jews, taken to a police station and simply told to wait. Refugees of all sorts had been living in Vichy since the invasion of France because the relatively milder regime of Marshal Petain had fended off some of the more brutal aspects of German occupation. With false papers, which were not hard to buy, a Jew or a politically suspect person could stay alive in the so-called Unoccupied Zone, which covered the southern half of the country. The racial laws, for one thing, had not been applied by Petain.

In the police station the arrested man found others waiting to be questioned, and he took his place in line. A door at the front of the line would open, a Vichy policeman would beckon, a suspect would go in. Some soon came out again and walked free into the street. Most did not reappear. The rumor moved down the line that this was a Gestapp operation, and that the circumcised would have to produce immaculate proof of their Gentileness, while the uncircumcised would, of course, go free.

The friend of my friend was a Jew. As he got closer and closer to the fatal door he became more and more certain that his death was near. Finally, there was only one man between him and that door. Presently, this last man was ordered into the office. Nothing stood between the Jew and meaningless abrupt slaughter.

The door opened. The man who had been the last to go came out. My friend's friend stood paralyzed, waiting for the policeman to appear and beckon him into the office. But instead of walking past him with his pass to freedom, the Gentile who had just come out stopped in front on my friend's friend, thrust his pass into his hand, and whispered for him to go. He went.

He had never before laid eyes on his saviour. He never saw him again. "

1-31-65

This story surely stands in contrast to the indifference and unconcern of our day. It stands in contradiction to the silence of the people who watched the woman murdered in Queens. It judges our own drifting lives and our withered wills which dare not even cry out in protest. Arthur Miller says that he has not written a play about Nazism, and that seems a justifiable claim. In writing about the crude horrors of the Nazi regime, he has raised the fundamental question about the nature of man. He points to symbolic and personal connection which all men have with violence of the world.

Miller says that if we find it incomprehensible how the Nazi horrors came to pass, we might understand it better when we contemplate our helplessness today toward the violence in our streets. He wonders if we are concerned enough to look within ourselves for a grain of its cause. Can it be that we are responsible for the evil? Do we care about the Negro ghetto? Do we think that our unwillingness to have Negro neighbors has no connection with the violence of the inner city? Do we not imagine that our protection of our "property rights" can lead to attacks on our property by those w ho can have no equal rights of property? As Miller points out, the news announcement of a prominent man's cancer of the lung is followed by the commercial: "Kent satisfies best!" Says Miller: We smile, even laugh; we must lest we scream. And in the laughter, we dissolve by that much. Is it possible to say convincingly that this destruction of an ethic also destroys my will to oppose violence in the streets? We do not have many wills, but only one; it cannot be continuously compromised without atrophy setting in altogether."

Again, the first question is not what we should do about it. Rather, we must first discover again our own relationship to evil, its reflection of ourselves. In fact, the story of Cain in Genesis has to do with this, with us. It asks not simply, "Am I my brother's keeper?" It also asks, "Am I my own keeper?" Here we see that human life is fraught with tension, pain, frustration, hostility. This is the universal human plight. The darkness of human life is not some exceptional condition. It is not some rare illness, alien to most men. It cannot be expurgated by polemic. Hostility and aggression lie hidden in every human being. This is not an accusation. This is not a reprehensible sin about which we can do something through an act of the will. This is a fact to be accepted, to be aware of, to guard against. When men are unaware of the hostilities that reside within them, wanton violence breaks out in the human community.

But oh how we deceive ourselves! We proclaim that we are innocent. Because we do not like being confronted with our complicity with evil, with the evil that lies in us, with the mixed motives behind our actions, with the revelation that we put "the best face" on the things we are and do. "Cain said to the Lord, 'My punishment is greater than I can bear...'" We have immense difficulties in facing ourselves. We fail to detect our own hostility in our own actions. Cain does not simply demonstrate the violence in us that leads to the disruption of human community; he also teaches us that the sight of our own evil is the highest agony a man can know. Cain stands as our Biblical reminder that the har_dest thing for us to relate to is our own crime against fellow human beings.

How painful it is to reflect upon our relationship with evil? How much of our fear of the Negro comes, as Miller says, from the subterranean knowledge that his lowliness has found our consent, and that he is demanding from us what we have taken from him and keep taking from him through our pride? If hundreds of men have been lynched, how many more thousands have been humiliated and brutalized by words and deed, gone unprotested by us?

Yet, surely it cannot be enough to stress man's guilt nor can it be enough to evaporate it. Guilt is not something that should be made everything or nothing. To insist on guilt though a blanket indictment can lead to neurosis and violence. To dismiss it as insignificant can lead to personal joy and relief and at the same time a personal unconcern and indifference about evil done to others. Arthur Miller says about his play: "I have no 'solution' to human guilt....., only a kind of remark, no more. I cannot conceive of guilt as having an existence without the existence of injustice...."

However, Miller really seems to see much more than this, and I believe that I do—and not simply because I am a "preacher". Miller could not bear to end his play pessimistically. He spares no one. The virus of indifference in all men is exposed. We are made to see Cain in ourselves. Even the most civilized of men harbors the germ of prejudice. Every man has his "Jew", the stranger, on whom to turn his back. In spite of the recesses of our nature, Miller holds out a shred of hope, the gesture of sacrifice by which an unknown man saves a condemned Jew.

Miller stops here. He says:"I do not know why any man actually sacrifices himself any more than I know why people commit suicide. The explanation will always be the otherside of the grave, and even that is doubtful." Now, I am not inclined to dismiss this in the way one knocks over a straw man, but as a Christian I believe that we do know something of why a man sacrifices himself. Indeed, we would not be Christians if we did not understand something of this. The act of Jesus to sacrifice himself discloses for us the nature and meaning of love. To love another enough to lay down your life reveals the purpose of human life. So look at the Christians who become mature and perfected as they love one another. We stand in a tradition of men who have willingly endured persecution and have readily laid down their lives for the brethren. (For example, The Deputy and Father Fontana; the German ministers, including Bonhoeffer.) This love, this charity for a fellow man alone marks the true life of the Church. The voluntary sacrifice for another is the supreme expression of love.

The deaths of the three young men in Mississippi last summer made a difference because they were volunteers. They were preceded in death by thousands who were lynched and beaten. But these three were not inevitable victims of Mississippi. They were volunteers, and the sacrifice of their lives opened the way to new responsibility. They died and others may live because of them. Greater love has no man than one who will take the place of another man in death. Such an act offers an alternative to human drift. It gives us another and better clue to the meaning of life. Such an act illumines the fact that the opposite of love is not hate but indifference. Hate may seek to take the life of another man, but our indifference allows it. The opposite of indifference lies in a love that will sacrifice itself and so in that act transform guilt into responsibility.

At the end of "Incident in Vichy", a Jew is suddenly given a pass to freedom. He accepts it in awe, wonder, astonishment. Along with the gift of his freedom he accepts the guilt of surviving one who laid down his life for him. Everything now depends on what he makes of his guilt, on how he uses his survival. Just so, the Christian understands the death of Jesus to hand us a pass—a pass from guilt to responsibility,from indifference to love. Those who live owe a debt to those who die—we owe a debt for living; the debt, as Miller says, to those who are wronged.

The Cross stands as our constant reminder that evil is overcome only by action. The "problem of Evil" has no solution other than action to conquer it. Guilt must be transformed into responsibility—the responsibility to be our own keeper and the keeper of our brother. "You did not choose me, but I chose you and appointed you that you should go and bear fruit..This I command you, to love one another." "Greater love has no man than this, that a man lay down his life for his friends."

This is the way from guilt and indifference to responsibility,to the very meaning of human life.

24. 2/9/64   **The Measure of All Men** – part of the series of sermons on "The Secular Meaning of the Christian Faith."   End of January

"Greater love has no man than this, that a man lay down his life for his friends." This is the familiar core of the Biblical passage from John that accompanies this sermon. Here, the passage is used as a foundation for action in a specific incident. In Sermon #41, the passage is used again to provide a more generalized ethic for living a moral life.

The burden of the Cross is theological. It is also intensely personal because Jesus was human. This sermon focuses on a then-current racial incident and accompanying police brutality in Hattiesburg, Mississippi, at the height of racial troubles. The incident is poignant and painful. The lesson: Being measured by the Cross requires courage.

IX in Series

Westminster Presbyterian Church
Wooster, Ohio
Rev. Beverly Asbury, Minister
February 9, 1964
Race Relations Sunday

THE MEASURE OF ALL MEN
John 15: 12-25

We have made it as plain as possible. The Christian's orientation is determined by the history of Jesus and Easter. When the Christian says that Jesus was a man, he uses historical language. He points to the history of Jesus, to his freedom in contrast to the bondage of other men, to his love for others, to his authority and immediacy among men. When the Christian then says that Jesus is "true man", he indicates that, for him, Jesus is the measure of all men. Here the Christian points to his unqualified belief that Jesus is the definition of a free human being. The Christian holds that he is what he is because of Jesus Christ. It proclaims that Jesus shapes a man's thinking and determines his particular way of looking at the world and his way of acting in the world. Thus, when a Christian asserts the "divinity" of Jesus, he means that Jesus has become the center of his picture of the universe. Jesus has become the measure of himself, the measure of all men, the measure of the world. Jesus has so become the measure of things that a man is freed for his neighbor.

Indeed, we have been saying without apology that we find it difficult to understand Jesus in term of metaphysical philosophy. We stumble and fall every time we use static categories to talk about Jesus. But we can understand Jesus as a man, a free man, who did not merely challenge other men to be free. He set them free. Those who know Jesus are not merely challenged to take up a cross. Rather, they are given a new measure of freedom which had been Jesus' during his life. They are free to live as he lived, free to bear a cross as he bore one, free to love others as he loved all men.

Whatever else Jesus may mean to the contemporary Christian, he means a point of reference. He is the measure of where we must stand, the measure of where we must be in conscience and in culture. Is not this what it means to say that we have been chosen? We do not have the right to choose where we, as Christians, shall stand. We have been caught up by the contagious freedom of Jesus, and he alone becomes the measurement of all that we must be and do. We have been chosen for love, and his love becomes the mea sure of our lives. We have to stand where love leads us to stand. It is a love that takes place in the middle of the real world, the ugly, banal, godless world of America today.

A very few days ago, an arrest was made in Hattiesburg, Mississippi. The man arrested was a young Yale law student. He was standing outside a voter registration station. He was there by invitation of the United Presbyterian Commission on Religion and Race, and his presence was known to the Justice Department of the United States. He stood there as an observer, as a witness to a line of Negroes seeking entrance, seeking to register, seeking to exercise their franchise. He stood on a corner, watching, so that some day he could serve as a witness in a trial before a court of justice in this land. The police came and put him under arrest. He inquired on what charge he was being arrested. He was put into a jail cell alone. Before the United Presbyterian representative could arrive to post a bond for him, a so-called drunk was put into the same cell. Then, with the jailer and a policeman standing outside, that "drunk" proceeded to beat up the student without mercy.

The drunk was then removed from the cell. And by the time a representative of the Commission on Religion and Race arrived, the student had to be carried from his cell, a bloody mess. (The only charge filed against him thereafter was one of resisting arrest.)

That young man, and last week nine of our ministers, including Wooster graduate "Cash" Register, stood where they felt they must. Dr. Eugene Carson Blake said in Columbus this week: "The Churchmen arrested in Mississippi were there and ran afoul of the state because they believe freedom to vote in our democracy is a moral issue for which the Church has some responsibility......" This is another way of saying that they have measured themselves in the light of Jesus. They too were chosen to lay down something of their lives for others.

These men stand as reminders that our rationalizations and ambivalence will not do. We Christians must admit that while demonstrations are deplorable, they are also deplorably necessary. There have been and will continue to be times when negotiations fail and demonstrations become necessary. Indeed, demonstrations should not be the first method used, but Christians should not hesitate to demonstrate when that remains the only method to challenge ambivalence toward injustice. We say "love your neighbor as yourself, but remember that self-preservation comes first." They say "love as you have been loved, bear fruit by standing for others." Jesus chose us to go out into the world, and the only way to be a Christian is to be Christian. Too many of us measure ourselves instead by the
"need to feel important
the need to show authority
the need for special privilege
the need to feel superior
the need to condescend
the need to dominate
the need to hate
the need to oppress
the need for a scapegoat."
We Christians know that these are unworthy measurements, and we know that we cannot tolerate them any longer without the total collapse of our integrity. Recently, the leaders of our denomination concerned with civil rights were invited into the office of a member of the Justice Department, who has direct responsibility for civil rights laws. That official expressed his conviction that without passage of the bill currently before Congress, America would undoubtedly experience the "blood bath" which William Stringfellow and others have been predicting. He felt that there was definite danger even if the law were passed. However, he felt confident that the fabric of our society would be irreparably rendered even though the law were passed. In the face of this appraisal, where must we Christians stand?
Christ is our measure, and we can only stand where he stood--alongside the neighbor, for the neighbor. We may know ever so little about what to believe, but we know where we must be. We are there to love, even though our love is not perfect or secure or confident. We are there because we have to be, to love one another.

Christ is the measure. And those Christians who stand in the cause for racial justice are not hoodlums, not "rebels without a cause". They are not beatniks on a binge. They are not eggheads enchanted with their own words. Rather, they are representatives of that numberless host who have caught the vision of a redeemed society. They are putting the Church where it ought to be. They have joined in the labors of one who laid down his life for men. They are men who, like Martin Luther King, dream of the rebirth of a people and the remaking of the nation. They join him in translating the bold venture of faith into the assurance of ultimate triumph. They share his words and feeling---"free at last, free at last; thank God Almighty, we're free at last." We must recognize that we Christians must also be free to set the victims of injustice free from hatred of those who have oppressed them. We cannot ignore that hatred was expressed and felt on both sides in the recent turmoil in Cleveland. Just because a Christian feels that he must come down on the side of integration does not set him free to hate them who disagree. No matter how unpopular it may be among his fellows, he must work to free them from their hatred, for he is called to reconcile all men unto God and to one another.

Furthermore, we must understand that if Jesus is the measure of what we must do, of where we must stand, we must also look to him as the measure of the world's reaction. A disciple is not above his master. A servant is not above his Lord. The world rejected Jesus. It hated his love and his freedom. We cannot expect something different. The "world" simply means any human society that organizes itself without God. There is bound to be conflict between those who measure themselves by the freedom and love of Jesus and those who measure themselves by the needs of the world. The world suspects those who are different; those who are willing to be "fools" for the sake of their convictions. Anyone who takes seriously this matter of measuring himself and the world by Jesus Christ is almost certain to be regarded as a madman, an eccentric, a danger. He cannot expect life to be comfortable for him. Christians must stop arguing with the consequences of their faith. Sixty Methodist ministers have lost their pulpits in the state of Mississippi in the last twelve months because they dared to mention race or brotherhood, even in the mildest terms. A school teacher in Georgia recently lost his job because he wrote a letter to the editor of the Atlanta Constitution in which he appealed for tolerance and brotherhood. Obviously, there are consequences involved in taking a stand.

The World acutely dislikes people whose lives are a condemnation of it. Ask any Christian who has stood in a line or occupied a seat in a restaurant in a racial demonstration. He will tell you of the pressure and dangers which come when you practice a standard different than the standard of the world. He will tell you that nonconformity is always suspect and that one hates to be rejected. Yet, If Jesus is the measurements of our lives, we know that we must have the courage to be different and that we must accept the risks and dangers that go with it..

We can do no other. We must love as we have been loved. The issues are joined, the struggle is on. There is no turning back---"anyone who sets his hand to the plow and then looks back is not fit for the kingdom of God." Christ is our measure, and we shall refuse to be duped, distracted, or dismayed. We shall keep insistent pressure on every crass, overt evil of segregation. We shall become known again, perhaps, as the "undaunted faithful". As a necessary and legitimate expression of identification with the freedom and love of Jesus, we turn with penitent hearts, enlightened minds, and free spirits to bring all men into the full heritage of the faith.

We have every weapon consonant with the love of Christ. We have every advantage bestowed by the freedom of Christ. And because of Easter and the freedom we have caught from the living Christ, we are confident that doors now closed will be opened, opportunities now denied will be extended, injustices now ignored or defended will be set right, shameless violations of human personality will be restrained by the recognition of the image of God in the fact of every man. These things will come to pass when we accept Christ as the measure of all men, accept the risks that go with being a Christian, and love as he commanded us to do.

25. 3/8/64   The Gospel in Hattiesburg

Rev. Asbury traveled to Hattiesburg to act according to the Christian imperative as he had preached it. He walked the talk. The walk was frightening and it required courage. The event recounted in the middle of the first page of this sermon is eerily similar to the event that brought about the death of James Brown on August 9, 2014 in Ferguson, Missouri. Other tragedies have followed elsewhere. The visible parallels compel one to notice the unevenness of change in race relations over the past 50 years.

The sermon closes with an intriguing thought: "The Bible for me this day is not a book about what happened <u>once</u> but a book about what is happening <u>today</u>" [*emphasis original*]. Similarly, the message in this sermon is not a lesson only about what happened in 1964 but a lesson about what is happening today.

This sermon is riveting. It is Rev. Asbury's summary, his affirmation, and his witness.

The sermon uses the same Biblical reference that is used for Sermon #19 – about taking action as a responsibility. That sermon, although placed earlier in this Cycle, was actually delivered nine months after this one.

Lent IV

Westminster Presbyterian Church
Wooster, Ohio
Rev. Beverly Asbury, Minister
March 8, 1964

THE GOSPEL IN HATTIESBURG
Luke 4: 16-30

Here we were--white ministers in Hattiesburg, Forrest County, Mississippi.
Two Presbyterians from Ohio; one Presbyterian from Wichita, Kansas; two Mennonites
and a Jewish Rabbi from the same state; a Presbyterian minister from The Commission
on Ecumenical Mission,(COMAR), Paul McClanahan, who is father of two Wooster students and a Wooster graduate himself; the Presbyterian University Pastor from the
State University of Iowa. Our guide and coordinator was John Cameron, a Negro Baptist minister, the only educated full-time Negro clergyman in the city which numbers
7,500 Negroes among its 35,000 citizens. Here we were--uneasy, unwelcome by a majority of the community, a little afraid of what was to come, but more than eager
to do what was right and to witness to our faith. It is not stretching a point to
claim that we were there because the Gospel of Jesus Christ had led us there.

We wanted to serve the purpose of the Church and were firm in our resolve to
be ministers and messengers of reconciliation. We were working in harmony with
the Student Nonviolent Coordinating Committee, and the philosophy of that truly
remarkable group of young men and women grows out of and supports the Christian
ministry to which we were committed. We felt it our job to preach good news to
the poor--in a county where the per capita income of whites is less than $1800
a year and that of Negros less than $1400 a year, and where 32% of the Negro fami-
lies live off less than $3000 a year. We felt it our duty to proclaim release to
captives in a county where men are often arrested without a charge and held incom-
municato. We felt we could only proclaim release to those who feel so enslaved
that their cry is literally "Freedom Now". Our mission could only be conceived
in terms of giving sight to the blind--and educationally there are many "blind"
in a State where there are no compulsory school attendance laws and where the per
capita expenditure for white education is $176 a year and for Negroes $9.60 a year.
In a situation of pressure and tension it was especially meaningful to see one's
work as setting at liberty those who are oppressed--yes, oppressed , in a State
where the lives of white men are worth more than the lives of Negroes. For example,
last Sunday night in Jackson, according to the report in the HATTIESBURG AMERICAN,
a deputy sheriff killed a Negro man. The name of the officer was not released.
Why? The story says that two deputies were checking reports of gunfire at a night-
club. They saw two men running from the scene and ordered them to stop. One of
the men stopped, turned toward the officer who then shot the Negro in the abdomen.
The deputy said he thought the Negro was going to attack.

This is the acceptable year of the Lord, and we knew that we could only define
our ministry in Hattiesburg in terms of the ministry of our Lord. Moreover, we
knew and know now that we had no monopoly on the gospel in Hattiesburg. There are
Churches there--many of them; well-staffed; prosperous. Three of them are Presbyterian Churches. But let me tell you something significant. The only white man
in Hattiesburg last week who was willing to talk with me and the others was willing
to do so only late at night. We had to sneak to his home--he wouldn't or couldn't
come to our office in the Negro quarter. We had to go in a furtive manner in order
even to escape our rather constant police surveillance. But under those conditions
we were entertained in a white home. Whose home? I'll tell you. The home of the
Jewish Rabbi. The home of a man, born in the North, sick of having his integrity
threatened by double-thinking; at a loss over the University of Southern Mississippi where professors are on notice to tolerate no mention of race in the classroom

Lent IV

and where one student was chastized for mentioning an "integrated personality".

The late night welcome into the Rabbi's home symbolizes and symptomizes the sickness of the Gospel in Hattiesburg Churches. The Gospel is being preached there, but obviously in a truncated form. The Presbyterian ministers have held that "The provinces of church and state are perfectly distinct, and one has no right to usurp the judgment of the other." What is missing in those Presbyterian Churches of Hat- iesburg is any recognition that racial injustice is a moral and a Christian problem rather than a civic or political one. So missing is this essential point that the ministers of Hattiesburg feel that the white ministers from the North are not ministers at all; are not concerned with the Gospel but only with social issues. Thus, they refused to meet with us and one even refused to talk with me over the phone. The phones are "bugged" and he was witnessing to his "loyalty" by refusing to talk. He later sent word that he'd talk if I called from a pay station, if he got home from jury duty. He didn't, and we never talked. Laymen are the same. The prosecuting attorney of the county in a fit of anger refused to shake hands with one of our ministers. The attorney called himself a Christian but denied that he was in any sense a "brother" to any of us. Obviously, we were considered by him to be enemies, and just as obviously his faith did not know or observe the teaching of Jesus to love the enemy and pray for those who spite you. The salvation of souls is preached in Hattiesburg but it seemingly has no relevance beyond the private confines of personal life. The Protestant ministers and Roman Catholic priests not only will not speak to the visiting white brothers, but they also do not know or speak to their Negro counterparts in that city.

But there is more to be said about the Gospel in Hattiesburg. Across the tracks and in the distinct areas of 9 Negro quarters, you get another view of the Church and its witness. It looks strange to those who expect to see the Church in conventional molds. But to those who know the marks of the Church; to those who look for the reading of the Word and prayer, for the breaking of bread and fellowship, it is not hard to find the Church. You find it among women who do maid work-- working 7 days a week with every other Saturday off, making an average of $16-18 a week. You find it among old men and women whose fear has gradually abated. You find it most especially among the very young who are not afraid, who are resolved never to fear as their parents do, who seek and demand freedom--now! You find the Church among those who have every right and reason to have given up on the Christian faith, because it is Christians they have to fight to gain their rights. You experience the Church vibrantly and brilliantly in mass meetings, those relevant and thrilling revivals of the spirit. When men and women hold hands around a church and close a meeting by singing "We Shall Overcome", you feel the Spirit of the Lord as you have not for a long time. You even feel the presence of the Church in those Negro taverns where the white ministers eat--for those are the only places open to them on an inter-racial basis. Until this past week only one of those taverns would serve the white ministers, because the owners were afraid of bombing. But now that it is evident that we are there to stay, at least for the forseeable future, others have opened their doors. The breaking of bread there under those conditions are reminiscent of Jesus eating with sinners, in places condemned by the religious folk. Yet, I tell you, never has communion of bread and cup been more real than with those Christians and Jews, Negroes and whites gathered around a table with a jukebox blaring.

In Hattiesburg, not all the ministers of the Gospel are ordained. You should know the SNCC(STUDENT NONVIOLENT COORDINATING COMMITTEE(commonly called "Snick")) workers. Henry Bailey, who was born there, served in the United States army, tried to register, went north, earned $150 a week, and returned to work at the "Snick" rate of $9.54 a week. You should see John Cameron, Henry Bailey, and Dickie Flowers, committed as few other people you know, go out to set their people free. You should witness their tremendously irenic spirit, full of peace, relaxed, seemingly free of hatred, free to laugh at those who persecute them, and unconcerned that they haven't been paid for five weeks. You should know those young boys out of school who man the picket line because they are prophets of a free future when they can eat in the Forrest Hotel or even in the Governor's Mansion. You should meet the 75 year-old man who lost his pension for walking in the picket line, but who doesn't complain because he doesn't want his grandchildren to be subject to police brutality.

The Gospel in Hattiesburg is found on those unpaved streets, lined by houses and shacks called home by thousands. You hear the Gospel at the so-called "tea parties" where Negro workers are trained to go out and canvass their blocks for folks to register. You hear a woman named Mary relate in a soft voice how "her" white folks fired her when her name appeared in the paper as a registrant. She tells how she, and others, have been so resourceful in finding other sources of income. She ends by praying for those who fired her, and she gives courage to others to go out and ask the impossible--to ask people to risk all for their right to vote. You hear parents tell you that they can't live with their children any longer if they don't get out and register, and you hear the children ask why they, 9,10, and up, can't cut school to man the picket line, that gives courage to their elders to enter the courthouse. You meet young people who have been kicked out of their churches because their pastors are so afraid of white wrath that they won't go along with this registra tion project. Believe it or not, the youth don't leave the Church; they merely go to another one where the Gospel of love and freedom is preached, where they are heard when they sing: "Let my people go."

Well, there we were in Hattiesburg. Anyone of us could talk to our people for hours about the experience. Some of the things that happened couldn't be repeated in polite company, certainly not from the pulpit. Perhaps you will give me the chance at a more informal time or in a chapel talk to tell other aspects of this story. But today, I had to tell about the Gospel in Hattiesburg. And I must tell you now about our part in that ministry.

Our being there helps immensely and immeasureably to dissipate fear. We are the only friendly white men known to Negroes who want their freedom. For example, there was the old man at the mass meeting who found out that I was born in Georgia and said that up until then, he would have been afraid to sleep in the house with a white man..He said that he realized that he too needed to be "converted" from fear and hatred to love, and he thanked me for coming. We were needed desperately, and God willing, there will be hundreds more like us. We have helped to give courage to over 600 Negroes who have now taken the registration test. We have stood for reconciliation in a community where alienation and estrangement hold sway. We have marched--yes around and around the courthouse lawn. Our path took us around the American flag and in front of the Confederate monument. The flag represented the hope of the Negro's future in this free land. The monument represents Hattiesburg's pillar of salt for those who look back only to a lost past and cannot discern the new day. But there was another symbol--the unbroken circle of the line, moving slowly, moving with dignity 8 hours a day. That was a circle of faith. To see it in my mind reminds me that we shall never hear the promise of the Gospel until we have first been challenged by its tumult and its demand that we make a creative response to our Lord. If some call us agitators, I remind them that God is a God not only of history but also a God of conflict-a God whose Son declared: "I came to cast fire upon the earth; and would that it were already kindled! Do you think that I have come to give peace on earth? No, I tell you, but rather division.....
You know how to interpret the appearance of earth and sky; but why do you not know

Lent IV

how to interpret the present time?"   (Luke 12: 49ff)

The Bible for me this day is a book not about what happened once but a book about what is happening today.   The Christian faith can no more be concerned only with the distant past or the distant future; it must be filled with the drama of here and now; and my name and yours must be in it.   The Gospel in Hattiesburg and Wooster must come as a ceaseless demand to participate in God's redeeming purpose:

> to preach good news to the poor
>
> tp proclaim release to the captive
>
> to recover the sight of the blind
>
> to set at liberty those who are oppressed
>
> to proclaim the acceptable year of the Lord.

26. 4/29/64   Christ's Deputies

This sermon follows up the Gospel in Hattiesburg sermon (Sermon #25) and the typical agitation such a sermon can cause in a congregation. The agitation centered on whether Christians should "be involved with social issues," specifically with the social issue of racism in Hattiesburg.

Rev. Asbury weaves together three passages from Luke to serve as his sermon's foundation. The first passage (found also in Matthew 12:46-50 and Mark 3:31-35) mentions "those who hear the word of God and *do* it" [emphasis added]. The second passage (found also in Matthew 16:24-28 and Mark 8:34 - 9: 1) contains several admonitions, including "For what does it profit a man if he gains the whole world and loses or forfeits himself?" And the third passage is the familiar story, found only in Luke, of the Good Samaritan who stops to help the beaten and bloody victim of a robbery. That story of unpretentious assistance concludes with Jesus's exhortation, "Go and do likewise."

Injustice in general – and racial injustice in particular – leaves people beaten in poverty and robbed of spirit. The sermon responds to the query about "being involved with social issues" by citing the play *The Deputy* by Rolf Hochhuth. The play poses a moral conundrum: Can a papal nuncio join the Nazi SS and passively watch persecution of the Jews even as Germany sides with the Vatican in its fight against communism? What is the proper response to this moral dilemma in terms of individual behavior? What is the proper response in terms of policy?

These questions are neither trivial nor merely academic. One perspective is made visible through what the code-breaking team at London's Bletchley Park faced during World War II, as told in the 2014 movie, *The Imitation Game*, based on Andrew Hodges' 1992 book, *Alan Turing: The Enigma*. Upon learning of German military movements – infantry, panzer divisions, and U-boats – through Enigma cipher messages, the Allies could not take defensive measures, even to alert their own naval convoys, unless confirming information was also obtained from other sources. If the Allies used information gathered only from Enigma to save convoys from U-boat attack, such use would have tipped off German intelligence that the Enigma code had been broken. Consequently, some intelligence from the broken Enigma cipher that could have saved lives was withheld, and some battles and convoys were sacrificed. However overall, fewer lives were lost and the war was won. This approach is what *Star Trek's* Mr. Spock summarized in his well-known ethic, "The needs of the many outweigh the needs of the few – or the one."

The other perspective is captured in Loren Eiseley's short story, *The Star Thrower*. A sojourner walking on an ocean beach observes thousands of starfish washed up after a storm. Ahead of him, he sees a solitary stranger, standing seemingly at the end of the storm's rainbow, repetitiously bending over, picking up something, and hurling it into the waves. Upon approaching the stranger, he sees that what the stranger is throwing back into the ocean are sea stars…but only the living ones. "Of what use is this?" the sojourner inquires. "No matter how many you throw back, you can't save more than a tiny fraction of them. In the long run, who cares of this?" The sojourner departs, ponders, and eventually returns to rejoin the star thrower in the overwhelming task. "I understand," says the sojourner: The starfish cares.

Deep ethical principles stand behind both perspectives. The decisions and consequences that arise from either perspective can be agonizing. *The Imitation Game* subtly raises the question of whether the secret weight of deaths carried by Alan Turing contributed to his own eventual suicide.

Rev. Asbury also cites a lesson that came out of the bombing of Birmingham. Alabama's, 16th Street Baptist Church, which killed four girls, ages 11-14, and wounded 22 other people. The day after the bombing, Charles Morgan, Jr., a rising Birmingham attorney, publicly blamed everyone who had failed to oppose racial hatred – this at a luncheon that involved Birmingham's white establishment. Addressing the silence of Birmingham's leaders, he said, "That is where you breed the atmosphere for atrocities." Not stated in the sermon is that Morgan and his family subsequently received death threats that caused him to close his Birmingham law office and move to another state.

The lesson here is that acting with Christian conviction is not for sissies. "Neighbors" and "brothers" (and sisters) are persons. To stand idly by when persons have serious needs is not a Christian option. Conversely, acting overtly and courageously in their behalf is often not all that attractive either. But isn't acting in behalf of neighbors, brothers, and sisters the meaning of the Great Commandment (Sermon #22)? And as agonizing as the choices might be, Rev. Asbury asks, what *is* the expected role for a deputy of Jesus?

Westminster Presbyterian Church
Wooster, Ohio

Rev. Beverly Asbury, Minister
April 29, 1964

CHRIST'S DEPUTIES
Luke 8: 19-21;
9: 23-27
10: 30-37

On the Sunday following my return from the Minister's Project in Hattiesburg, there was a man from my hometown in Georgia in this congregation. He was considerably agitated by the sermon that day and afterwards he minced no words in saying so. He even made a verbal presentation of his cred entials for chewing me out. He claimed that he had the right to do so because we were both from the same town and state, and because our families were on speaking terms. He felt that he had a claim on me because we were both Presbyterians. And on the basis of these claims, he argued that the sermon of that morning should never have been preached. He claimed that this is a time for "golden silence." He made no claims on me on the basis of Christian faith, and he seemed at a loss when I asked him if I were not my brother's keeper?

No other question is really so important and urgent. That question outweighs all considerations of birth, heritage, hometown, church traditions: Are we the representatives of Christ? Are we the deputies of Christ to the poor, the hungry, the naked, the dispossessed, the imprisoned? Those who are really our brothers and sisters are those who have heard the word of God and do it.

Last September 16 (1963), a young attorney by the name of Charles Morgan, Jr. addressed a luncheon club in Birmingham, Alabama. Charles Morgan was a man on the make--a rising star in political circles, a man with a future. He was speaking the day after the Sunday on which four children had been killed by a bomb in the 16th St. Baptist Church. He began with a simple question that Monday: Who did it? Who threw the bomb? And he gave a simple answer:
"
"We all did it. Every last one of us... The 'who' is every little individual who talks about the 'niggers'..The 'who' is every governor who ever shouted for lawlessness....It is all the Christians and all their ministers who spoke too late....It is the coward in each one of us... What's it like living in Birmingham? No one ever really has and no one will until this city becomes a part of the United States. Birmingham is not a dying city, It is dead."
(A Time To Speak, Harper and Row, 1964.)

Mr. Morgan now lives in Alexandria, Va., and he aptly indicts us all--all of us who are passive in the face of the enemies of society. He justly observes that atrocities do not take place in social vacuums. They take place where men will not be their brothers' keepers, where they hear the word of God and fail to do it, where they will not hear at all. That is where you breed the atmosphere for atrocities.

This is the same issue raised by the recently opened play, THE DEPUTY.*
In THE DEPUTY, Rolf Hochhuth faces the questions of how it could have been possible for more than 6 million Jews to have been murdered in Nazi Germany. He comes to the

*Grove Press, Inc., 1964

Apr÷26-2

conclusion that there must have been millions of indifferent people, cowards, too-careful tacticians who were not their brothers' keepers, who created the climate in which the Nazi agents could practice their cruelties. THE DEPUTY stands as a judgment on all who never bothered to lift a finger or say a word in protest when mass murders were getting under way.

The play begins by introducing Kurt Gerstein, an idealist who joins the SS in order to have an opportunity to observe the death camps with his own eyes. After visiting the Auschwitz gas chambers, Gerstein calls on the papal Nuncio to describe to him scenes "Whose horror makes Dante's 'Inferno' seem like a kindergarten." As a man the Nuncio condemns Hitler's cruelties, but as a diplomat and an opportunist he considers them a by=product that must be overlooked in the fight against communism.

Gerstein recognizes that there is no help to be had here. However, in the Nuncio's office he meets Riccardo Fontana, an Italian Jesuit, who is appalled at the story Gerstein tells him. Son of a nobleman on friendly terms with Pius XII, Father Fontana goes to Rome and calls on the cardinal who is secretary of state. Finally he reaches the Pope himself with his terrible tale. He urges Pius to protest publicly against the persecution of the Jews, to denounce the concordat with Germany--or at the very least to say something. He listens in abject despair to the answer: "Indeed, the terror against the Jews is atrocious. But we must not permit it to exasperate us to the point where we forget that we must in the future look to Germany as the protectors of Rome. Germany must remain viable not only to preserve the frontiers with the east but also to maintain equilibrium on the continent, an equilibrium that is more important than unification."

Riccardo Fontana realizes that the Vatican will remain silent and he harshly judges Pius XII for valuing neutrality more than is proper for the Deputy of Christ. Since the Pope will not act as "God's substitute on earth", Fontana decides to become the "real deputy". He joins a group of Roman Jews, is arrested with them and sent forth to Auschwitz and its gas chambers--since "in this era a Christian cannot survive if he is consistent." He must take up his Cross. His fate is not better than his Lord's. Jesus was a Jew! And so Riccardo Fontana, with the Star of David pinned on him, joins the fate of those who learn from Jesus that the way to find life is to lose it.

The principal characters of this play are based either partly or entirely on real persons. Out of the history of real persons, a play has been written. Out of the history of real persons, the questions come to us: Could not more have been done for the neighbor? Can you not expect Christians, the deputies of Christ, to cry out for those who cannot cry out for themselves? Are we our brother's keepers? Do we hear the word of God and do it, or must we forever be rewriting the Word by laying aside the Cross?

Too often we do not even cry out to warn our fellow Christians, much less to cry out for those who stand outside the Church. In the parable of the Good Samaritan we should always remember that those who passed the beaten, bleeding, helpless man by were a Priest and a Levite. They had an "acceptable" reason for passing by the wounded man--they were busy serving their church. Perhaps Pius XII thought he too had an acceptable reason. He had concern for his Church. He encouraged individual action. Monasteries and Convents took Jews in and fed them and smuggled them to other lands. But there was no official action. The crematories operated without ceasing. Trains arrived on tight schedules. The fires burned day and night. The average cremated at Auschwitz was over 5000 a day. As Riccardo put it: "Let us admit at last: these flames are also our trial by fire! Who will, in times to come, respect us still as moral arbiters if, in this time, we fail so miserably?"

Apr-26-3

The time for Christ's deputies to speak has long since arrived.. At least two Presbyterian ministers I know, who have endured a real urban racial crisis, will tell you that. They had had a "good relationship" with the church people. They played golf with them and they blessed their parties by their attendance. But when they finally spoke on a crucial issue, they found a "good relationship" turning sour. They found that nothing can be built on social amenities; that only the Gospel would suffice. They found, as we all do, that the only basis on which we can relate to people is Jesus Christ and that that basis gives us a cross to bear. When we face that cross, we find that we can no longer be silent or pass by on the other side. "Who will, in times to come, respect us still as moral arbiters if, in this time, we fail so miserably?"

Our time calls for inquiry and self-examination. It requires that we confess that we share in the guilt. We belong to a nation that did not open its doors wide enough or early enough to relieve the Jewish situation--a nation that is now divided about opening all its doors to its own citizens of color. We also share the human guilt of submitting passively to evil or trying to save ourselves or our business by collaborating or pussyfooting. We are also the guilty, law-abiding citizens who avert our eyes and ears and see and hear no evil.

Every man, no less than the Pope, must make choices. The avoidance of choosing is itself an act of choice. "Guilt is not only the bad we do but also the good we neglect." Riccardo puts its well: "Doing nothing is as bad as taking part. It is -- I don't know--perhaps still less forgiveable. We are priests! God can forgive a hangman for such work, but not a priest, not the Pope!" We are priests. We have been called to take up our Cross daily and follow Jesus Christ. Bystanders and fence-straddlers are never innocent. They are guilty by silence. It is, as Charles Morgan, Jr., so aptly states, the time to speak. We are all part of the same humanity. If a Jew suffers, we suffer. If a Negro suffers, we suffer.

YOU ARE PRIESTS! YOU ARE CHRIST'S DEPUTIES! YOU! YOU ARE! YOU ARE DEPUTIES OF CHRIST!

Christians cannot knowingly yield to the spirit of murder. That is the lesson of THE DEPUTY to all Christ's deputies. The question is not what good will it do to speak out. The question is whether Christ's deputies can do other than speaking out. Hear the words of Father Riccardo Fontana:

> "A deputy of Christ
> who sees these things and nonetheless
> permits reasons of state to seal his lips--
> who wastes even one day in thought,
> hestitates even for an hour
> to lift his anguished voice
> in one anathema to chill the blood
> of every last man on earth--
> that (Deputy) is ....a criminal."

Hear the words of Jesus Christ:

> "If any man would come after me, let him deny himself and take up his
> cross daily and follow me. For whoever would save his life will lose it;
> but whoever loses his life for my sake, he will save it. For what does
> it profit a man if he gains the whole world and loses or forfeits himself?"

27. 2/14/65   Race Relations Sunday: Made of One Blood

This is a Communion Sunday sermon. This sermon's Biblical passage in Acts contains the often-used statement about God: "In him we live and move and have our being." That phrase comes from a speech, summarized in Acts, that Paul gave to some learned colleagues in Athens, Greece. Paul proceeded to assert that "we are indeed his offspring." Rev. Asbury uses the passage as a Communion message to emphasize the unity of humanity. The invisible God of Paul's speech is God to *all* who live and move and have being, That, Asbury suggests, becomes a "Christian strategy in a world of racial crisis" and gives meaning to our lives. When we celebrate Communion, we celebrate the humanity of Jesus and the recognition that humans, regardless of race, are of one blood.

Communion
Race Relations Sunday

Westminster Presbyterian Church
Wooster, Ohio
Rev. Beverly Asbury, Minister
February 14, 1965

MADE OF ONE BLOOD
Acts 17: 22-31

Athens had no political importance at the time Paul spoke, and it did not rate as a great commercial center. How ever, it still carried great weight in intellectual circles and was famed for the number of religious cults which found hospitality there. Paul concedes that the Athenians are "uncommonly scrupulous" in religious matters— they are intellectually open, even if not personally receptive to new points of view.

On this occasion, the kernel of Paul's speech lies in his reference to the "Unknown God". This speech is addressed to intellectuals. Their problem is delineated by Paul: they worship an unknown God. In fact, their problem is the perennial problem of the intellect—it cannot know by rational pow er the nature of whatever reality we refer to by the name "God". It remains the problem today but it is magnified by dramatically new circumstances. Walter Lipmann and others have underlined for us that the impact of science upon religious certainty has produced "virtual despair". Those who are intellectually aware have become personally aware too of the uncertainty of religious categories, of the unknowability of "God". The philosopher, Huston Smith, says man is "lost in a universe where the meaning of life and of the social order are no longer given from on high and transmitted from the ancestors but have to be invented and discovered and experimented with."

Paul exposes that to us as well as to the Athenians. He demonstrates to us that we have to give content to our concepts of deity or else face that we worship what we do not know. If what we call "God" cannot be found in a shrine, then neither can "God" be found in a concept. Linguistic analysis may and does have its limitations, but its contribution lies in its exposure of the fa ct that most people do not know what they mean by the word "God". For example: "It doesn't make any difference what you believe as long as you believe." Can one conclude from this attitude that Christians should be content to have an empty "God-concept"; to worship what they do not know, just so long as they worship? Should not Paul's address to the intellectual community move us to abandon or revise these concepts? Surely, it should if we hope to be Christians. Yet, it is just as difficult for us as for the Athenians. And even more so, for we have nothing to fall back on, as Lippmann has made clear. Or do we?

Of course, Paul indicates that we do. It would seem that abandonment of certain concepts can lead to despair, but it could also lead to openness to the Christian message. Paul gives new content to the concept of "God", but we grasp that content only when we recognize that our problem is not "God" but man. The real problem of living is posed in the questions: Who are we? What is the meaning of life? What is our Destiny?

In other words, the analysis of language only goes so far. It goes far enough to expose the problem of the meaning of the words we use. It illustrates how we often know not of what we speak. But in the end it is a sterile approach. This is so, because our problem lies not merely in the meaning of our words but in the meaning of our meaning. One philosopher has said that "man is condemned to meaning". We forever ask, "What does it mean?" Some months ago I happened to get interested in Samuel Beckett's plays. After reading through "Waiting For Godot" and "Endgame" and all the others, I myself felt nothing but despair. Beckett not only seems convinced of total meaninglessness, but he also communicates it to others. The only thing that seemed to offer relief came from the recognition that he obviously found meaning even in meaninglessness. If he really took himself literally and believed completely in what he

2-14-65

was saying, he w ould stop writing in recognition of its meaninglessness. However, he, too, is condemned to meaning. He, too, must ask what does life mean? To talk about "God" apart from what our lives mean is a futile, irrelevant, meaningless exercise. Our problem is not with a "deity concept"; it is with a man concept. The only time the "deity question" really carries weight is when I am raising an existential question. Linguistic analysis may help me to see the futility of other questions; it may open me up to probe other areas. But ultimately what I want to know about is the meaning of my life, the meaning of the meaning I see in my life.

Paul proclaims what every intellectual Christian discovers—that the meaning we seek comes not through our concepts but through a disclosure of meaning. That meaning is disclosed in Jesus. It is Jesus who reveals that the meaning of man's life lies in a relationship of love to men. We discover in Jesus that life has no meaning apart from giving our lives in service to others. The event we call Easter makes known to us that new meaning is given to us; that new life comes into the old. Christians are those who confess that Jesus reveals what it means to be genuinely human. Christians confess Jesus to be Lord, to be God, to be Son of God and Son of Man, because he gives the power to become truly and fully human. The Jesus Christ-event gives meaning to man's life.

We do not need then biological or anthropological proof that all men have a common claim on life and its prerogatives. No, we have in Jesus Christ the theological truth that all men are made of one blood. We do not deny the scientific evidence, but we do not find it determinative. Even if genetic differences could be demonstrated, we should still maintain the theological truth. The meaning of life is what we are after, and that meaning lies in the affirmation of our common humanity, in the affirmation of the genuine humanity disclosed in Jesus Christ and made open to all men.

If this means that we affirm a "Christian Humanism", then, so be it; because it was a Man, a Man-for-others, whom Paul confessed to be the very disclosure of "God". That's how humanistic Christianity is and must be to be Christian. "What you worship but do not know—this is what I proclaim. The stupendous claim of the New Testament is that somehow a particular human being disclosed the very nature of God, and in that particular human being we may see and understand God's attitude toward man. Thus, we do proclaim the meaning of human life in Jesus Christ. And we had best face the question: if Jesus Christ is not a true figure of man, where do we look? If not Christian humanism, then what basis for genuine or authentic humanity? And this is what we seek—the meaning of our life, death, and destiny—not the meaning of empty concepts which cannot be known.

The time is at hand to make it clear to the Church itself that this is its mission — to increase the love of God among men. And unless we know what it is to be a man and to love men, we shall never know what it is to worship God. Our Christian strategy in a world of racial crisis must be based upon the meaning of love in Jesus Christ. To serve men in his name is an end in itself. To suffer is not the worst thing that can happen to us; the worst thing is not to believe in anything worth suffering for. And Jesus Christ embodies a meaning worth suffering for. He frees us for love, for acts to make men know their unity. And this very table to which we come points to his love for all men, and to the love which makes us one. And so it points to the meaning of being a man.

28. 9/15/63 A "Protestant" Picture of the Human Situation   End of February

This is the first to two sermons to refer to Golding's book, *Lord of the Flies,* and to other books with similar themes. *Lord of the Flies* was published in 1954 and subsequently made into movies, one of which starred Marlon Brando in 1963, thus making it a current topic in the '60s. Golding received the Nobel Prize 20 years later.

In this sermon, *Lord of the Flies* is set against a Psalm passage that marvels at traits, albeit hidden, that make human beings worthy of regard: "What is man that thou are mindful of him…?" Part of the reason for mindfulness comes from Paul's advice to the Ephesians (see Biblical reference for Sermon #8) not to fall into "hardness of heart," callousness, greed, licentiousness, corruption, deceit, and satisfaction without compassion. Thus, the present sermon asks, what happens when humans act selfishly as isolated individuals, estranged from each other, and disconnected? One way to re-establish connection is to act through Christian love. Through the love of Jesus, humanity binds itself together across ethnic, racial, and ideological barriers.

This particular sermon is placed out-of-date; it originally occurred at the beginning of the 1963-64 college year, the *Year that Everything Happened* (see notes for Sermon #11). Specifically during the summer of '63, Governor George Wallace symbolically blocked the door to the University of Alabama, civil rights worker Medgar Evers was assassinated in Jackson, Mississippi, President Kennedy gave his *Ich bin ein Berliner* speech, and Martin Luther King, Jr., gave his *I Have a Dream* speech. Coincidentally, the date of this particular sermon is the day of the bombing of Birmingham's 16th Street Baptist Church. Rev. Asbury argues in his sermon that if we stop at the lesson of arrogance, estrangement, insensitivity, and violence conveyed by the *Lord of the Flies*, there is no reason to begin the college year…or *any* year.

Rev. Asbury was not alone in his concern. The same premise – consequences of arrogance, estrangement, insensitivity, and violence – forms the core of Eugene Burdick's and William Lederer's 1958 novel, *The Ugly American.* The novel was read in colleges and discussed widely. During the spring prior to this sermon, *The Ugly American* came out as a movie.

This sermon is positioned here in the Cycle of Sermons because it directly reinforces the theme that we are Made of One Blood.

Westminster Presbyterian Church
Wooster, Ohio
Rev. Beverly Asbury, Minister
September 15, 1963

A 'PROTESTANT' PICTURE OF THE HUMAN SITUATION
Psalm 8:1-9; Ephesians 4:17-24

In speaking of one of Picasso's paintings, Paul Tillich expressed his view that a 'Protestant' picture means not covering up anything but looking at the human situation "in its depths of estrangement and despair". Part of the Protestant heritage lies in looking boldly and honestly at man and the world in which he lives. The very principle of Protestantism requires that every veil of deception be lifted and that the unvarnished truth be faced.

Perhaps for these reasons primarily, much of the fiction of recent decades has been welcomed by a growing number of alert and aware Protestant Christians. Many Protestants have refused to reject as lewd, vulgar, and pornographic all literature which has contained four letter words and dealt with sex. While some of the recent fiction has been all those and more--including poor writing and craftsmanship--the best of the writers have uncovered the "depths of estrangement and despair" in the human situation. Thus, Protestant Christians who know their theology have found relevant content for the concept of human sinfulness in such fiction.

Camus and Updike, William Faulkner, Tennessee Williams, and William Inge have all succeeded in exposing the sores and miseries of mankind. Indeed, sometimes Williams seems to be in love with morbidity, while others like Beckett not only expose the human condition but also come close to sheer nihilism about it.

A novel with great popularity among college students is William Golding's LORD OF THE FLIES. It has had some popularity for quite a few years with quite a few preachers as well. The novel tells the story of the crash of a plane of boys who were being removed from their country due to an atomic war. The crash was on an island, and the boys were the only apparent survivors of the war. The novel concerns itself with these young boys who have been quite civilized and well-trained. As time progresses, divisions take place. Trust evaporates. Hatred and cruelty emerges. They put on their own version of war, and man in this microcosm ends up the cannibal, the primitive barbarian. This altogether bleak and hopeless picture of human nature nevertheless has both Christian and Protestant implications. It speaks of the estrangements and alienations which we mean by sin. It devastatingly displays the emptiness of our cliches about man getting better and better, more and more moral as the years roll inexorably on. Golding succeeds in showing how thin the veneer of civilization really is, and the Protestant recognizes this as an authentic picture of despair.

Two plays by Edward Albee, THE ZOO STORY and THE AMERICAN DREAM, have a particularly American flavor, but the message of there being only futility and absurdity to human existence sounds not unlike Golding's. With forcefulness and irony, Albee attacks the notion of the perfectibility of man. In THE ZOO STORY, there are just two characters, Peter and Jerry. Peter is a middle-aged, middle-class man, sitting on a bench in Central Park, and Jerry, in his late thirties, and not so conventional, is coming from the zoo. He goes to Peter's bench and makes conversation. From that point, the audience (or the reader) knows that one man represents the bourgeois and moralistic American while the other represents the outsider. He stands for the ones who do not belong to society. The middle-class Peter is literate, cultured, and has a wife, two daughters, cats and parakeets. He belongs. Life is good. Jerry has on on and nothing. He does not belong and he cannot relate. One of his stories to Peter is how he has failed to establish genuine contact with a dog, and the play confronts us with the inability of the outsider to have a genuine relationship with any other human being. Of course, at the end of the play, it is clear that Peter is also an outsider-- all human beings are, and so all humans live in utter estrangement.

The author uses Jerry to demonstrate this. Jerry, while telling that he had been to the zoo to find out how people exist with animals, how animals exist with each other, and with people too, begins to nudge Peter off the bench on which he spends each Sunday afternoon. Jerry punches Peter and presses him over until Peter becomes hysterical about his bench and his right on it. At the end you have two animals fighting, estranged, out of contact-- a zoo story.

Edward Albee has produced an even more raw slice of life in his award-winning play, WHO'S AFRAID OF VIRGINIA WOOLF?, but the raw slice of the ZOO STORY fits Tillich's definition of 'Protestant'. How can we doubt man's essential alienation in this great year of racial revolution? Indeed, do we not often assume that men are animals? We debate a test ban treaty not so much in moral terms as we do in terms of security, ability to kill and over-kill, of enemies to be killed if we could get away free. Can we doubt that we would invade Cuba and impose our will were it not for fear of Russian retaliation? Did we not look upon the Washington Marchers more or less as non-rational creatures who would erupt into violence at the slightest provocation? Were we not surprised when the demonstration turned out to be peaceful? The ZOO STORY is unpleasant reading because it reveals something of the nature of our existence which we face all too seldom.

But, from that point of view, Albee's THE AMERICAN DREAM has an even greater Protestantism about it. It has about it a complete willingness to face the ultimate facts of the human condition in America. This play shows an American family-- Mommy, Daddy, and Grandma--in search of a replacement for the adopted child that went wrong and died. The missing member of the family arrives in the shape of a terrifically handsome young man, the embodiment of the American dream. He admits that he consists only of his muscles, his good looks. He is dead on the inside, devoid of genuine feeling. He has no capacity for the experience of love, and he has none of the depth required for a genuine relationship with anyone. He will do anything for money, even become a member of the family.

In THE AMERICAN DREAM, Albee pours scorn on the ideals of family life, togetherness and physical fitness. He squarely attacks all forms of sentimentality that keep Americans from facing the true condition of their life. The oily glibness of the characters succeeds in exposing again how we sink to the level of the least common denominator, how we who pride ourselves so much in our individualism resemble nothing so much as dead forms and empty shells. One cannot read Albee without being made to surrender some of the unctious, self-righteous, sentimental romanticism with which Americans look at human nature. Every last pretense is stripped away, and even "the American dream" ends up in the Zoo.

Again, if Tillich's definition is correct, the 'Protestant' means looking at the depths of human estrangement without deception, then we have been talking about a 'Protestant' picture of man in the books and plays produced by Golding and Albee. However, to be sure, this cannot be all that 'Protestant' means. To have a Christian and a Protestant view of man, man must also be considered in the context of his creaturely and sinful relationship to God. It is the business of Christian and Protestant theology to study also what God has revealed to be man's needs and the actions God has taken to meet these needs. Albee and Golding stop short of considering man in relationship to ultimate reality. While they specify needs, they need a larger and acknowledged context for doing so. To allege that man is an animal--whatever kind of animal--implies a context, for there is no such thing as a man looking at himself with total objectivity.

The Protestant Christian knows that and acknowledges his context. To look at man apart from his relationship with God is abstraction. In the same way, as Calvin made clear, to take a look at God apart from his relationship with man is also an abstraction. Man cannot exclude himself and know anything about God. What he does know is something about the God in the God-man relationship. Is this not to say then that the Christian cannot make a study of God without also studying man? And vice versa? Thus, a Protestant picture of man cannot stop with the depths of his alienation and despair, for the relationship that obtains between man and God does not stop there.

The eighth Psalm does not deny the insignificance of man, but man's insignificance is contemplated in terms of the glory of God. And as insignificant as man is, his very relationship to God gives him a true significance. Man is not Creator but a creature in creation--yet a creature with a high purpose. The Protestant Christian then does not end up nihilistic. Despite man's estrangement and because of his relationship to an ultimate reality, he is capable of good. Indeed, do Albee and Golding expose man's despair only to make him despair all the more, or do they in an unexamined way expose in the belief that seeing things without pretense man can begin again?

If they do not mean this, then the Protestant Christian does, and in that sense Paul was the first Protestant: "I say this and I solemnly lay it upon you-- you must no longer live the kind of life the Gentiles live." Paul attacks precisely what Albee attacks: life concerned with empty things that do not matter, minds darkened because of ignorance. Paul too pours scorn on the American dream-- glamour without feeling, petrified hearts that lust after satisfaction but have no genuine compassion. This Protestant preceded our theatre of the absurd in exposing life that has become so hardened that it has lost the capacity and power of feeling. Paul basically saw all that we see today, but he did not end where we too often end.

His Protestant picture of the human situation shares the perspective of the eighth Psalm, for he sees man in the context of his relationship to God. It is not a natural optimism that leads him to believe that man can do away with that kind of life. After all, it was Paul who confessed that the things he would do, he did not do, and the things he would not do, he did anyway. His 'optimism', if it be that, is based on and in God as made known in Jesus Christ. Beyond alienation and estrangement lay reconciliation. Beyond barbarism was the hope of peace. Beyond hedonism exists a higher way of life. Love, forgiveness, compassion, reason are all possibilities because these are properties of the God with whom we have to do.

If we stop with the LORD OF THE FLIES, or THE ZOO STORY, or THE AMERICAN DREAM, then there is little reason to begin this year--either in church or college. If, however, we begin with these Protestant pictures, we can move on in both Church and College to a more complete Protestant picture of the human situation-- one where the God-man relationship shall hold new life and one where we shall yet see the possibility of a new beginning for mankind.

29. 10/6/63   Law and Gospel

Like the previous sermon, this one also mentions Golding's book, *Lord of the Flies*, and adds into the discussion the lyrics of a Kingston Trio song of the time, *The Merry Minuet*, ("They're rioting in Africa, there's strife in Iran...."). It is alarming that Rev. Asbury's message of 50 years ago is still as relevant today as it was when he gave the sermon. Racial and political strife are disturbingly unchanged from what they were a half century ago. Given society's slowness to change, how should students, who can be especially idealistic, engage in civil disobedience as part of Christian activism? What is the Christian stance with respect to keeping – and breaking – the law? Are there higher laws, higher even than the Decalogue, that is, higher than the Ten Commandments?

Rev. Asbury occupied a sensitive position because his ministry included a college. On the one hand, the social and political environments of the time encouraged student activism, an activism that Asbury shared (see especially Sermons #24 and 25)! Moreover, college readings for first year Wooster students included Thoreau's *Walden* and the accompanying essay, *On Civil Disobedience*, hardly arguments for remaining naïve, unreflective, and uninvolved. On the other hand, the "ivory tower" environment of the college campus constrained involvement. Colleges and universities, while officially abhorring social injustice, responsibly feared the sort of tragic consequences of student involvement that could – and did – later befall Kent State University in 1970.

So, how does a minister preach moral indignation to energetic, idealistic students and yet temper the message against injustice with advice for moderation and awareness of the law? At the time of this sermon, people existed who were poor in spirit, who mourned, who hungered and thirsted for righteousness, and who were persecuted unjustly. Rev. Asbury acknowledges the conditions of turmoil in contemporary society by citing Matthew's passage on the Beatitudes (also found in Luke, 6:20-23), with its counsel of restraint. Yes, circumstances are unfair and laws are improper. Rebelling against society and defying laws has appeal. Yet, the subsequent passage from Matthew raises the question of what Jesus meant when he said that he came not to break the law but to fulfill it. In his response, Asbury appeals to a higher law, one of love. The Psalmist's message is that higher laws and ordinances of God are "more to be desired...than gold, even much fine gold." A person who lives by these higher laws issues a powerful command to self: "Let the words of my mouth and the meditation of my heart be acceptable in thy sight...."

This sermon meditates on these thoughts around the communion table.

"A Pattern for Life" II

Westminster Presbyterian Church
Wooster, Ohio
Rev. Beverly Asbury, Minister
October 6, 1963

LAW AND GOSPEL
Psalm 19
Matthew 5: 1-12, 17-20

Almost from the very beginning of the Church, Christians have been tempted to reject the law. One of the earliest divisions among Christians occurred over the issue of the place of the Old Testament in the Church of the new covenant. The stories about Jesus reported again and again how he broke what Jews called the Law. He did not observe the regulations. He healed on the Sabbath and He did not keep the laws on handwashing. He was crucified as a law breaker. He spoke of a new covenant, a law written, as Jeremiah had prophesied, on the heart. Love replaced Law as the basis for morality, and this led to the oversimplification that the Old Testament was one of Law and the New Testament was one of love and grace. Thus, many advocated that the Old Testament Law be dismissed entirely. So great a Church Father as Augustine said: "Love and do as you please."

Yet, we have read the Decalogue here today. We always read it at the Celebration of Holy Communion. Why at the eucharist, when more than any other time we are in fact celebrating--full of joy over the love and grace of God? Does it not seem out of place?

With questions like that, which are natural to any seeking Christian, we find it all the more astonishing that Jesus said that the entire jot and tittle of the law must be performed. In our text for today, Jesus comes very close to sounding like a Jewish legalist. For that reason, some Christians have suggested that we take note that this saying is found in the Gospel according to Matthew; that Matthew is the most Jewish of the Gospels; that Matthew was writing for the particular purpose of convincing the Jews. They would then have us conclude that Jesus did not say these things at all--that Matthew really put them in his mouth.

This, however, is not a very likely answer. Those of us who do now or have once proposed such a way to rationalize our way around this statement have not stopped to ask in what sense Jesus was speaking of Law. We have also revealed our own personal resentment of the hollow actions and dead forms imposed on us by legalism. Yet, we would not deny the need for law in our kind of world. Rejecting legalism as we do in a personal sense, we still call for obedience to the law in a social sense, and we are committed to rule. Our situation was well expressed for us a few years ago by the Kingston Trio in their song, "The Merry Minuet":

> They're rioting in Africa;
> They're starving in Spain;
> There's hurricanes in Florida;
> And Texas needs rain.
>
> The whole world's festering with unhappy souls,
> The French hate the Germans,
> The Germans hate the Poles,
> Italians hate Yugoslavs,
> South Africans hate the Dutch,
> And I don't like anybody very much!

> But we can be thankful and tranquil and proud,
> For man's been endowed with a mushroomed shaped cloud!
> And we know for certain That some lovely day,
> Someone will set the sparks off --
> and we will all be blown away!
>
> They're rioting in Africa;
> There's strife in Iran;
> What nature doesn't do to us
> Will be done by our fellow man!

No responsible person wants to be lawless or unlawful. We may often want to be free of laws, but history makes abundantly clear what we can expect when we live without them. In the absence of Law, on either the personal or social level, man's inhumanity comes to the fore just as surely as Golding depicts it in LORD OF THE FLIES.

Without law none of us can do "alright". We must then have reassurance that the love of God does not abolish the Law. Indeed, it could not abolish the Law in so far as the Law itself revealed the nature and will of God. To abolish His own Law would mean that God contradicts His own nature. To be sure the only Law that Jesus condemned was the Oral or Scribal Law--not the Commandments and not the Torah.

As we examine Jesus' relationship to the Law, we find that the Old Testament contains relatively few rules and regulations. We find more broad principles which must be taken and interpreted and applied. These are the great principles out of which a man must find his own rules of life. To the later Jews, the principles were not enough, and they set out explicitly what they thought to be implicit in the principles. They devised a rule and regulation for every possible situation of life. No better example of this reduction of Law to laws can be seen than in the multiplicity of injunctions about the Sabbath which arise out of the commandment.

However, these rules are not the essence of faith. It is one thing to reject the legalism of petty rules, regulations, and procedures. It is quite another thing to reject the Law. It is that Law which Jesus says he came to fulfill--to bring out its real meaning. Its real meaning lies in expressing our ultimate moral obligation. That is why the Decalogue begins with the four commandments that are theological or religious in nature. They express what we find to be true--that we are under an impossible demand. And Jesus recalled for us that the one great principle was that in all things a man must seek God's will, and that, when he knows it, he must dedicate his whole life to obeying it.

John Knox has expressed this very meaningfully: "Revelation does not so much give us new truth as make us aware of truth which, it seems, we once knew but had forgotten, just as redemption is not so much the creation of the new as it is the restoration of the old....The law of love, which is the law of Christ, is no superimposed command.... That law is the law of our own life. It is the voice of eternity in our hearts. It is part of the evidence, present in our being, that man essentially and ultimately belongs, not to this world and age, but to the Kingdom of God; and that he is subject to a demand higher and more exacting than any human tribunal can impose, any human wisdom can justify, or any human effort can fulfill."
(The Ethic of Jesus ....P 51f)

Here we recognize that Jesus could not deny the great principles behind the ten commandments without denying the nature of God and man. He reaffirms the need for reverence for God and respect for our fellowmen and ourselves. Law is based on that reverence and respect, and Law arises not out of petty rules but only out of love. The Law of Jesus, then, does not consist of sacrifices, but of mercy; not of prohibitions of what man may not do but of commandments of what men may do to base their lives on love. What Jesus speaks of is the permanent stuff of which the God-man relationship and the man-man relationship is made. The Christian faith, then, does not expect less than was expected of the Jews. The Christian's righteousness is to be greater. Jesus herein warns us in a definite manner that Christian faith is not easy. The grace of God does not abolish all the duties, responsibilities, and demands of the Law. The Christian has no basis on which to say "Now I can do as I like." While we are not called to be Scribes and Pharisees whose one motive is to fulfill the demands of the Law, we are called to the motive of love wherein our one desire comes to be fulfilling the Law to show our gratitude for the love in Christ which has claimed us.

The Jew aimed to satisfy the law of God, and to the demands of the law there is forever a limit. The Christian aims to show his gratitude for the love and grace of God, and love has no limits either in time or eternity. This is the radical nature of Christian faith—we must go beyond the Law. Love faces us with a task far greater than the law, with an obligation more binding than that of the law. This is our situation.

As we come to the Table on this World Communion Sunday we are not offered a release from the Law. We are offered the Gospel which places upon us the obligation to fulfill the Law. We are called to this not to be relieved of the task of building a better world but to attain the means by which we live more than ever in a right relationship with men. But as the Gospel places upon us the task of fulfilling the law, let us not assume it with despair but with joy, for it is not a burden, heavy and oppressive. The invitation to this Table is stated by Jesus: "Come unto me all ye who labor and are heavy-laden, and I will give you rest. Take my yoke upon you and learn of me; for I am gentle and lowly in heart, and you will find rest for your souls. For my yoke is easy, and my burden is light."

Law is relieved by Love. Love is informed by Law.

The following six sermons are Lenten and Easter sermons. They form a hesitation in the sequence of sermons on Christian activism and they permit reflection on the foundation of faith and love that underlies duties to others and self. By means of this hesitation, they set the stage for the sermons that follow thereafter.

30. 2/23/64   **Breaking Open the Circle** – part of the series of sermons on "The Secular Meaning of the Christian Faith."   ___LENT___

Being a Christian means, in a sense, accepting an election. When one accepts the election, one inherits duties and obligations. It has been said that what makes sense about Christianity is the humanity of Jesus. Another way this has been said is that Christmas makes sense only from the perspective of Easter. Because Jesus was human, capable of experiencing life, suffering, and even dying, some of the duties and obligations of Christianity are secular in nature. Rev. Asbury explains the verses in Ephesians that serve as the basis for this sermon. The duties and obligations conferred by election are inescapable. Above all, they are grounded in love.

Series XI
Lent II

Westminster Presbyterian Church
Wooster, Ohio
Rev. Beverly Asbury, Minister
February 23, 1964

BREAKING OPEN THE CIRCLE
Ephesians 1: 3-14
Text: 3-10

At other times and in other places, meeting strangers with whom one is supposed to converse and having only the identification of being a Presbyterian minister, this minister has experienced the topic of predestination as a recurring piece of conversation. It seems that when people have nothing else to say or find more comfort in idle talk than in silence, or know next to nothing about the Presbyterian Church, they give themselves away by turning to predestination. They have a popular notion of what it is all about, and it seems that no matter what you say, the popular notion remains and prevails. They retain the topic as a conversation piece to use on the next occasion on which they perchance are thrown again with a Presbyterian minister, and they will go over the same ground again--again accomplishing next to nothing.

If this appears to you to be cynical, then you must account that ministers also get weary of giving answers to questions which weren't seriously meant in the first place. You must also acknowledge that even your ministers get fatigued from battling with stereotypes. Perhaps more significantly, the cynicism about this subject among ministers arises simply because there _is_ something important to say here to Christians ---something that can't be heard or said so long as the questions are put as they are put and for the reasons they are put.

Today, let us move beyond idle curiosity and cynical attitudes and look seriously at this doctrine. Let us bring to bear the insights of the "secular meaning of the Christian faith" on the doctrine of the purpose of God, so often called predestination and more properly called the doctrine of election. As we do this, we need to recognize that there has been a renaissance of this doctrine in modern theology, and, therefore, we are not simply talking about past concerns. Furthermore, modern theology has drawn heavily on our text for today in its consideration of predestination or election, and we can turn to it as a sound basis of our consideration.

This section of Paul's letter to the Ephesians is long and complicated. In Greek, it constitutes one long, rambling sentence. It goes on and on, and it has no stages of logical development. It is difficult to read as a lesson in morning worship, and it is no less difficult to follow and understand. However, a study of the passage indicates that Paul's mind seems to run along three lines. First, he speaks of God's choice as a fact. Secondly, he deals with God's choice as a gift. Thirdly, he develops the purpose of God's choice. At the risk of being arbitrary, but with the purpose of clarifying this old and difficult doctrine of predestination or election, let us develop these three lines of thought. Let us look now to them and behold what is the meaning of this doctrine in the light of the meaning of our faith.

I THE FACT OF GOD'S CHOICE

In his own thought-forms, Paul says that even before time began, the very nature of God's love determined his purpose to adopt man as sons of God. That is, Paul contends that it belongs to the very nature of God to intend a relationship of love between himself and man. This means that a God of love must, out of his own necessity to love, will to reconcile us to himself. Thus, we have to do here with God's choice of man--the same thing expressed in John 15:16, where Jesus said: "You did not choose me, but I chose you......" This is entirely consistent with the Old Testament witness. While there is evident witness to the elected(chosen) people in the Old Testament, one always sees clearly that behind those elected (chosen) people stands the electing(choosing) God. It is always God who elects, because it is his nature to do so.

The fact of God's choice then has nothing whatever to do with naked sovereignty or irresistible power. It has to do with his nature of love as disclosed fully in Jesus. Thus we do not fully or completely know God's choice until we encounter Jesus. In Jesus, we discern that the electing God and the elected man have become one. That is, behind Jesus we discern God. In other words, man discerns in Jesus a man elected for other men, who stands for other men. The whole doctrine of election begins to make sense only when we see Jesus as elected for all other men. And at the very moment we separate this doctrine of election from Jesus Christ, we get right back to the silent, irrational, unknown God. If we remove the figure of Jesus from this doctrine, we return to the idea of orthodoxy that some men are elected for salvation and others pre-destined to damnation. The old form of this doctrine would have it that God chose some men only. When, however, we ground election in the history of Jesus and the Easter-event, we see that God, in choosing one man only for the sake of all men, has chosen all men.

In grounding this doctrine in Jesus, we discern a God as one who loves in freedom, as one who acts to relate himself to man and the world. Here, the fact of God's election lies in our discerning that in Jesus God has turned toward us and offered us a new humanity and fellowship with him.

This leads us to Paul's second line of thought:

II THE BOUNTY OF GOD'S CHOICE

Paul sees election as pure grace. The act of election gives the gift of freedom. We discern in Jesus a man of remarkable freedom who, after Easter, sets us free from our state of alienation and estrangement. To grant us that freedom cost Jesus his life. Those who have experienced that freedom and who have known forgiveness know the meaning of a gift. They know that they have received what they had no right or cause to expect. The choice of God discerned in Jesus is a bounty. It opens a way to a new life, a new being. Yet, not all have experienced this.

Then we are back to the sticky question. Is this gift offered to all? Or only to some? The old orthodox form said the gift was for some. Our position today, based on Ephesians, holds that this gift is offered to all men. What, then, is the difference between the two positions?

Well, the difference lies in the attitude toward men and what is thought to be significant about them. The old doctrine tends to distinguish between those who respond to the Gospel and those who do not. Calvin's doctrine of double predestination(based on his Roman Catholic heritage) was admittedly aimed at explaining how and why some responded and others did not. Later theology has hesitated to identify believers with the elect, but it has tended to do so nevertheless. As one reads orthodox theology, it is difficult to escape the notion that God loves those who respond to him. Consequently, it seems that the orthodox form holds that the most important thing to know about a man is whether he is a Christian. This may be qualified in a great many ways, but the clincher comes in the general attitude of the orthodox Christian. The clincher is that his attitude and conduct toward believers will differ from that toward unbelievers. He may use biblical texts to justify his position, but the real persuasion lies in the fact that he has become a believer and judges others on the basis of whether they believe as he does. He responds to God's love by loving those who have responded to God's love.

The newer form holds that God loves not only those who love him but also his enemies. The newer form contends that God loves those who reject his love. In the light of the Cross and Easter, God's gift of love is for man as man. In Jesus, one discerns that God loves all men, regardless of their response, and that Christian love is for all men, every man—including one's enemies. In this form, the most important thing about a man, therefore, is simply his manhood. The clincher here is that one's conduct is grounded in bounty of God's gift in Jesus to all men. A Christian must treat a man the same, regardless of his "race, creed, or color", as we Americans put it, because God's gift knows no bounds.

This now leads us to consider Paul's last line of reasoning:

III THE PURPOSE OF GOD'S ELECTION

That purpose is that all men hear God's promise and discern that it has been fulfilled in the life, death, and resurrection of Jesus. All men are potentially the elect--the gift, as we have said is for all. It is God's purpose that all men be reconciled. This reconciliation potentially is open to all. It is offered to all. The actually elect are distinguished from the potentially elect by the fact that they discern that they have been made free in Jesus Christ and respond in joyful service.

Must we not say, therefore, that the purpose of God's choice implies that Christians should be different from other men--not more filled with religiosity but freer than others to love and suffer and serve. God's purpose clearly means that Christians are IN this world, not out of it, but they are now in it for the purpose of reconciliation. One cannot really read and take seriously the teachings of Jesus without recognizing that Christians must love their enemies. A Christian must love his enemy because of his manhood whatever else may be true of an enemy, it is true that he is a man, a person who stands in need of love. The Christian's service is to break open the circle of election to all other men. The Christian's service is to live for others and break open the circle of election to them. The Christian seeks to offer his new humanity to others. It is not enough simply to be a new man. New manhood is a gift to be used. The main point is not one's private salvation; he cannot rest secure in that. The main point is that one's salvation is subordinate to sharing in Christ's ongoing work of reconciliation. The secular meaning of this doctrine is that there are no "outsiders"; there are no northerners; there are no southerners; there are no class or racial distinctions. Potentially all men are "in" rather than out, and it is the purpose of the actually elected to bring the potentially elected in. The secular meaning of this doctrine also lies in the fact that there are now no "outside" activities for the Christian. Politics, economics, business--what have you, are all in the sphere of the Christian's life where he works to realize the election of all men.

In Jesus we find that God's purpose all along has been to make men one with him and with one another. In Jesus we findthat God works to love us and set us free for this work. The intention of history expressed in Jesus is the unity of men, the salvation of all men. The Christian has faith that this purpose is being worked out, and he also has the task of so living in such a way as to open that purpose to others and them to it.

31. **3/1/64** **The World of Men and Things** – part of the series of sermons on "The Secular Meaning of the Christian Faith"

This sermon concludes the series on The Secular Meaning of the Christian Faith . It also is the fourth of six Lenten and Easter sermons in this Cycle. The sermon reprises the foundational principle, or *Blik,* and the examination of the Apostles' Creed that began with Sermons #11 and 12. As a Lenten offering, this sermon also expands the theme of election found in the preceding sermon. The expansion gives us a philosophy of history and a philosophy of life.

The *Blik* underlying the philosophy of history and life comes from the Biblical reference in Colossians. Paul founded several churches in Asia Minor. The one at Colossae is located about 100 miles from the one at Ephesus. Like the letter to the Ephesians, the letter to the Colossians was probably written by Paul sometime in the mid-late first century A.D. – although doubts about authorship exist.

Interestingly, this sermon uses the Colossians citation to take on creation (beginning in the sermon's fourth paragraph) as a component of Easter faith. Rev. Asbury speaks of the "meaning and intention of creation" from *Blik*. He does not try to finesse scientific hypotheses and mechanisms of where the universe came from. Through this reorientation, he uses Lent and Easter to sidestep the narrow creationist view of physical origins and evolutionary processes in the universe. The letter to the Colossians dealt with attitudes, and so does Asbury. Accordingly, this sermon expands the foundation for Christian faith and action.

Series XII   Westminster Presbyterian Church   Lent III
Wooster, Ohio
Rev. Beverly Asbury, Minister
March 1, 1964

THE WORLD OF MEN AND THINGS
Colossians 1: 15-23

"I believe in God the Father Almighty, Maker of Heaven and Earth." After 11 sermons in a series more or less related to the concerns of the Creed, we come back to its beginning affirmation--that God is the maker of heaven and earth. We turn now to the doctrine of creation, and, hopefully, we are mindful of the conclusions reached in other sermons.

At least, the first affirmation of the Apostles' Creed clearly rests in the faith of those who make it. That is, those who claim that God created the heavens and the earth are distinctly making a statement of faith--not a statement of "fact". The doctrine of creation, therefore, is not really the first thing that a Christian confesses. Rather, he is able to make this confession only because he already has a faith, a "blik", a point-of-view, a reference point. That is also why this series has dealt with so many other aspects of Christian faith before turning to this doctrine, and it is why we spoke last week of the doctrine of "election".

"Election" also is something one confesses from the side of faith. It affirms that one has discerned a new relationship with God in Jesus. And we need to make clear again and again that the doctrine of election must not be made a logical attempt to bind God. God condemned the friends of Job for legislating from human terms how God must act toward men, and we too must guard against such "logical explanations" which draw from human experience and bind God. The doctrine of "Election" really expresses our point of view and does not tell us how to act. It confesses that the Christian motivation is love and the purpose is reconciliation. It confesses that we have been set free from legalism in order to decide within each given situation how best to enter into the responsible love relationship. The doctrine of election, to use the words of Edwin Markham, is our confession that: "In love is all the law we need; in Christ is all the God to know." It is our affirmation that Jesus, the Christ, the man in whom we have discerned God, is the completion of the intention of creation in the life of man.

Thus, we are led by the doctrine of election to the consideration of what creation is all about. We have to do, obviously, not with an explanation of the physical origin of the world and universe. In the words of Bonhoeffer, we don't need God as a "working hypothesis" to explain the evolutionary process or even the newly discovered omega minus particles. Instead, we are really speaking of the meaning and intention of creation to be at one with him. And we speak in our faith, out of the perspective of God's election of man.

When, therefore, we say that Jesus is the "first-born of all creation", we do not speak of him having been "born" at the beginning of creation. This assertion has no time connection. Rather, this very wording arises out of the concept of election. Israel as a nation is the firstborn of God(Exodus 4:22). It means that Israel is chosen of God for a purpose. The title "firstborn" is a title of honor, and assigned to Jesus, it means that he plays a unique role in the meaning and purpose of creation. Just as Israel was given the purpose of making God known, Jesus now comes into the title as the task is given to him; because God and his intention have been discerned in Jesus. Jesus, the firstborn, is the man elected to elect all men.

Thus, Jesus is the one who gives meaning and cohesion to the world. Again, to confess that "in him all things were created" means that we find meaning, purpose, and significance in Jesus the Christ. Bonhoeffer in his book on ETHICS(P.262) said:

"It is vain to seek to know God's will for created things without reference to Christ
...To live as man before God can mean only to exist not for oneself but for God and
for other men." Our election leads us to see that the meaning of the world lies in
what we have discerned in Jesus and in the Easter-event of crucifixion and resurrection. Our life then is sought in terms of being obedient to what we have discerned
in him. To see all things created in Christ means that he is truly our "blik"--or,
more conventionally, it means that we now think Christologically about our lives
and our world.

Our confession that all things were created "through him" expresses anew our
faith that "all the God we know" is found in Jesus. Our confession that all things
were created "for him" ex presses anew what we hold to be the goal or intention of
creation--namely, our reconcilation to God, the unity and completion of all things
in God. The goal of creation lies in breaking open the circle until all men confess
their "election", their freedom from God to live for others and to love all others.
Obviously, the goal of creation has not been fulfilled--some men are still only potentially elect; chaos and strife seem to characterize our world; all around us we
see brokenness, fragmentation, wars, enmities, hatred, dividedness. Even so, we who
discern God in Jesus and who have been "elected" to the ministry of reconciliation
confess that in Jesus "all things hold together". He gives cohesion to a world that
otherwise has little or none. He provides the basis for a unity where none other
might exist. He holds together the conflicting parts of the "world" in which each
self lives and the "world" in which we seek community.

The doctrine of creation is our affirmation of God's purpose to have fellowship
with men. The world becomes God's creation for us only as we discern by faith that
we have been elected for fellowship and reconciliation. The Christian looks then
upon the world of men and things with a positive attitude. Indeed, we can say that
when Christians have been world-denying, when they have pronounced the world as inherently evil, they have been less than true to the doctrine of creation. They have
misunderstood their election, for they have failed to recognize that they have been
called to face the world's sin with confidence and hope--indeed, with a peace which
passeth understanding. Christians cannot allow anything in the world, except the
Biblical history centering in the history of Jesus of Nazareth, to determine his
orientation. If he did allow anything else to determine it, his orientation would
be "idolatry"--it would be untrue to his faith that all things hold together in Jesus.

Here we see plainly that a confession of election and creation also expresses
our conviction that God has an appointed goal for history. Our philosophy of history
lies in the belief that nothing can separate us from the love of God which we have
found in Jesus. Thus, we find ourselves free to act--free to act confidently--be-
cause we know that the redemption of the world is assured. D. T. Niles, the great
Ceylonese Christian, has written in UPON THE EARTH: "The Acts of the Apostles is the
story of men who felt that the pressure of a victory that was certain as well as of
a combat that was crucial. They seem never to have been plagued by the question,
'How can the combat be critical if the victory is certain?' May it be that we, for
whom the question is so important, find it so because we are neither certain of the
victory nor are involved to the death in the combat? (II Peter 3:4; Heb. 12:4) May
it not also be that we have got ourselves into a position in which we feel the need
to convince ourselves that the task to which we are called is indeed urgent, when
our real need should be to be so committed to the task that we cannot escape its
compulsion?"

To believe in God as "maker of heaven and earth" means for us that the world
of men and things is the realm, the locale of our election where we work in confidence for reconciliation. It is our confession that we have to do with God our
Father in the spontaneous events of life. It is our confession that in unity with
God, the world of men and things is a good world. It is our conviction that we
must witness to that unity.

32. 3/21/65   Communion

This Lenten Communion sermon emphasizes that accepting election requires us to serve others in our social and political actions, even as we would serve others a meal.

There is no Biblical reference associated with this sermon, but if there were, a suitable choice could come from I Corinthians mentioned by Rev. Asbury in the first paragraph of his sermon. Commonly, I Corinthians 11:23-29 is used at Communions, but the Biblical verses that surround this particular passage provide the background that Asbury actually uses for this sermon.

Communion   Westminster Presbyterian Church
Lent III   Wooster, Ohio
                        Rev. Beverly Asbury, Minister
                        March 21, 1965

The Church at Corinth had more than its share of problems. It had many divisions but it had particularly difficult problems in the area of worship. The observance of the Lord's supper, the central act of the Church's worship, was a cause of division, and the practices in Corinth greatly distressed Paul. Thus, when he writes the Corinthians about the Lord's Supper, he says that he cannot commend them, for they come together not for the better but for the worse. He points to their divisions and factions. He does not equivocate in his judgment: "When you gather together, it is not the Lord's Supper that you eat." And he gives the reason: "each one goes ahead with his meal" (with no consideration of the others) and "one is hungry and one is drunk" (because not even common manners prevail.)

Such a situation could only result from the fact that the Eucharist was at this time a common meal. Later in this chapter Paul tells us that the service began with the breaking of bread, and only after supper was there participation in the cup. In between there was a full meal, a "pot luck" if you will, provided by the more affluent members. Those same members began to eat before the others arrived, gorging themselves consuming most of the provisions, and letting the others go hungry. The ones who came late because of their work received the least. And so there was a scandal: drunkenness at the Table of the Lord; and worse yet, drunk with a false sense of superiority and an indifference to the needs of the brethren.

Such could not be the Supper of the Lord. Such actions destroys the character of the meal. A meal with religious trappings and ritualistic blessings cannot make up for a lack of love. Where love is lacking, there is no church; let alone no Supper of the Lord. Paul brings his irony to bear on this, for he sees no need for the factionalism which distorts and perverts the gospel. Where the "good news" really exists, true Christians will be identified partly by the absence of petty strife. Paul declared that he could not commend the Corinthians, because they were petty. And he took their pettiness seriously. He did not simply dismiss it as "human nature.

He could not, because he viewed this as more than an ordinary meal. It involved a common meal, but its meaning transcended the common. This Supper has a special nature. But if the fellowship has been destroyed, that eliminates the possibility that a common meal might become the Lord's Supper; becuase Paul believes that the presence of Jesus is not primarily in the elements of bread and wine but in the dramatic act of the Supper. Christ is present in the breaking of bread, the emptying of the cup. These events re-enact the passion. These symbolic acts accomplish the very thing they portray--the redemptive action of the love of God made known in Jesus' death.

This action should be repeated in remembrance of Jesus Christ; not as a simple memory of past event but as an act of remembering the past event of his death present and real for the man of faith in our day. To repeat the action dramatizes God's saving action of the past by making it present. More than that, it proclaims what God has done in Jesus so that men may respond with faith. It proclaims that the Supper is supremely action, fundamentally an action of God which the church is called to share. Here every man of faith proclaims in a clear and unmistakeable fashion the gospel to which he is committed and how he intends to act on it.

Since Paul sees this Supper as the continual re-enactment of God's saving action, it is no small wonder than he concerns himself with those who take it the wrong way. He warns the Corinthians not to take the Supper in an unworthy manner. One who uses the meal for reveling and drunkenness has failed to recognize the action of the meal that makes Christ present. This way of partaking centers in the self. It fails to seek the welfare of the "other", for it begins and ends with the needs of ego and physical appetite. Such conduct misses the action--which is for others. One's conduct that fails to remember Jesus, fails to proclaim him, fails to commit himself in hope and action--that conduct makes one a guilty participant. A failure to discern what the meal means and calls forth profanes God's name, the name of Jesus.

Well, so much for the Corinthians and their profanity. What of ours? We don't revel and get drunk at the Lord's Supper. Thus, if we pay any attention at all to the admonition not take the meal in an unworthy manner, we concentrate inwardly on personal and/or pietistic considerations. We make unworthiness such an individual and puritanical matter that we miss the heart of what Paul has to say to us about the action.

In fact, Howard Moody in a recent article in Christianity and Crisis (1/25/65) gives us an excellent indication of what it means to profane God's name today: "I remember my father telling me as a youth that uttering the profanity "Goddamn" was the unforgiveable sin of blasphemy as well as the breaking of the Third Commandment. It is the Christian's devious manner of avoiding the hard truth that 'taking God's name in vain' is a far more profound sin than profanity. It is not the vulgar utterance from our lips but our deeds that truly profane human life. Christ always warned that you can't judge a man by his speech. Not everyone who says words like 'Lord, Lord' even spoken with great reverence and peity, 'does the truth' of those words; conversely many people who speak roughly in the raw language of vulgarity live in awe of and respect for the mystery of humanity.

"The true profanity against God is to refuse to take him seriously; the truly 'dirty' word is the one used to deny and denigrate the humanness of another person. ....the word 'NIGGER' from the sneering lips of a Bull Connor. Obscenity ought to be much closer to the biblical definition of blasphemy against God and man."

That definition is the modern counterpart of Paul's. The Corinthians refused to take the action of the Supper seriously and they profaned God's name. And when we turn our back on the love of the brethren, we take the Supper unworthily and profane God's name. We profane God's name whenever we "play it so safe" as never to risk "breaking our bodies" to meet the needs of others; as never to "empty ourselves" in service of those around us who need the attention and love we can give. We profane God's name when everything we do must be so planned and calculated as to rule out the inspiration and direction of the Holy Spirit. To take this meal worthily means recognizing God's redemptive action in the Supper--the action of remembering a past event; an action that makes that event present. To take this meal worthily means a proclamation of our hope in Jesus Christ to reconcile all men; of our commitment to act in love for all our brethren; of our intention to share, as symbolized in One Great Hour of Sharing, in the common life of mankind as a redemptive sign of God's love.

33. 4/4/65   **Identity Through Suffering**   <u>End of March</u>

Leadership frequently has associated with it necessary duties and responsibilities that are unpleasant and maybe even dangerous. Anwar Sadat, Mohandas Gandhi, Nelson Mandela, and Martin Luther King, Jr. took on causes that ruffled tradition and disturbed the authority of others. The circumstances they faced have been documented as filled with discomfort, argument, animosity, and hate. Also documented were their premonitions of imprisonment and death. Yet, they continued in their tasks. Much more recently, young Malala Yousafzai has persevered despite her injury and her own awareness of continued danger.

This sermon is a prelude to Good Friday and to Easter. Given Jesus's challenge to authority in his own time and his own life trajectory, it is hard to imagine him not having premonitions of peril. The story in Mark that supports this sermon (also found in Matthew 20:20-28 and in abbreviated form in Luke 22:24-27) confirms this. His disciples yearned for glory and greatness, and Jesus reminded them that these are not goals but, rather, occasional corollaries: "Whoever would be first among you must be slave to all."

Doing the right thing – and leading others to do it, too – might not be convenient. Nevertheless, correcting injustices – those of race, gender, origin, physical difference, religious difference, ideology, politics – and mustering the courage to do it is the way of Christian leadership.

This sermon was delivered a week after Martin Luther King, Jr.'s civil rights march from Selma to Montgomery, a month after Bloody Sunday in Selma, and bit more than a year after Rev. Asbury's sermon about his own sojourn to Hattiesburg (see notes for Sermon #4; see again Sermon #25).

Westminster Presbyterian Church
Wooster, Ohio
Rev. Beverly Asbury, Minister
4 April 1965

IDENTITY THROUGH SUFFERING
Mark 10: 35-45

They were on the road, going to Jerusalem. This creates the framework for the third announcement of the Passion. We get the undeniable impression that Jesus knew very well what was in store for him. In the first Passion announcement (8:31-33) Jesus has already indicated that he knew what was to come and had already accepted the fact of his suffering. Yet, the disciples were not in the least impressed by his three predictions. Peter rebuked Jesus for predicting a course so contradictory to the prospects for the Messiah. Jesus rejected Peter's rebuke, and, in so doing, rejected the "cheerful and sensible" kind of religion that delivers from suffering. He pointed to the ways of God; to the cost of discipleship.

Even so, his twelve did not understand. Later(9: 30-32), in the second announcement, they still did not grasp his meaning that the Son of man will suffer at the hand of men. And the narrative reports "they were afraid to ask him."

The followers were afraid to know and accept the truth, but Jesus knew and accepted it as they went along this road. He knew that he was leaving comparative safety for a place of danger. He was going from a place of little cost to where the costs could be quite high, indeed. He recognized that the journey crossed a frontier, and this is one frontier that many fear to cross. Jesus could not stay in quiet Galilee. He went to the extreme even though his disciples seem to have urged that he stop somewhat short of Jerusalem. But even if this road led from comfort to pain, he had to go the distance. This action represents the test of his profession as the Son of Man, the Man-for-Others.

As he traveled this road, two of the disciples, James and John, the sons of Zebedee, came up to him. These two are part of the inner group, and they requested a promise from Jesus. This may be quite naive, and it is characteristic of popular stories of the time. However, it clearly illustrates that they have missed the point of this journey. They were sincere. They were earnest. They asked him to grant what they asked of him. And Jesus wanted to know what it was they asked. And so they told him, a special and favored place in his glory.

Don't we find this to be a natural human desire? For example, in the March on Montgomery, the followers of Martin Luther King felt the same way. Let us be close. We love you. We follow you. We want to be with you, whatever happens. This is their search for identity. They are sincerely and earnestly wrong in their search. If they had understood his predictions of suffering, perhaps they would have made no request at all. But since they had failed to understand, their concern was less with his purpose than with their place. They needed an identity, an image, a relationship and so they bluntly asked for it.

Jesus told them that they didn't know what they were asking. And he posed some questions to them. Basically, he said, Are you ready to share my fate? Are you prepared to accept the purpose, the hazards, the cup of suffering, and the baptism of overwhelming disaster? His question to them is simple: Are you ready to offer your lives?

James and John simply did not grasp the fact that Jesus' way was to be one of service and not of pride, ambition, and conquest. And, frankly, we don't either, most of the time. How many of us stand ready to expose our nerve ends to the hurt of others, to be sensitive enough to let our hearts hurt with the anguish of others.

Sensitivity, a mark of holy worldliness, surely is a part of the cup of suffering, and James and John do not have it in this story. And neither do we have it when our pose is one of clamlike indifference and easy comfort in the face of need. We do not have it when our concern, like theirs, lies in seeking a place of glory, because we then shy away from conflict with the evil and dangerous powers of our day. Jesus' answer to James and John, and to us, points the way to the suffering which he goes now to face.

They indicate that they are willing and able to take his cup and baptism. This may be the optimism born of false hope and misunderstanding. This may be their under-estimation of what lies ahead. They may not yet have counted the cost. Later, they forsook him and fled. They were not able when the first severe test came. It's always easier to commit oneself in general than it is in specifics. People don't know where we stand unless we stand. The details test the claims we make, for they may violently rearrange our cosy mental world, our luxury and comfort. James and John and the rest of us, had better understand that the request to share and the indication of our readiness exposes us to unexpected dangers.

It is no great wonder that the other disciples were indignant when they heard about the request. They did not understand either, and they would naturally get "worked up" by the realization that someone was pushing ahead of them. They would be just as concerned about their place, their image, their identity as James and John. Personal frustration results when we find that someone has outwitted us in achieving what we ourselves wanted. When we are outmaneuvered, we too get angry.

But Jesus turns this world of ours upside down. The usual rules of leadership and authority are suspended. They shall not be so with disciples. Whoever would be great must be the servant, and whoever would be first must be the slave of all. For example: the San Anselmo students,(Presbyterian Seminarians),did the dirty work on the Montgomery March. This answer of Jesus has been addressed to all the disciples, to the common problem of men. Men shall be measured precisely by this standard of service, "For the Son of Man also came not to be served but to serve, and to give his life as a ransom for many."

Disciples must accept the role of "mere servants." Mark gives us here a theo-logical statement. It constitutes his clue to Christology. It is in this light that Mark understands the person, the mission and message of Jesus. Identity comes through suffering. This verse states the ultimate object of the Son of Man's life on earth: service and death as a way of "buying" men into a right relationship with God. Ex: Jesus here seen as the representative of God before men; Jesus substituting for God; Jesus embodying God. This is not Paul's idea of atonement: Jesus representing man before an angry God. It is Jesus serving and suffering to disclose the true nature of live and grace of God. This is what it means to "minister"----to serve.

Last week, a question, a good one, was put in our Dialogue following morning wor-ship. The questioner wondered how long "demonstrations" would have to continue. This week I have read a quotation from Harvey Seifert's new book which seems to give the answer:

"Persuasion, negotiation, political action, and economic pressure are still the basic nonviolent methods to be relied upon for social change. Only in-frequently will these be pushed to such length of unconventionality as to result in dramatic suffering. Yet at all times, these four general methods will be more adequate if they are inspired by a love willing to suffer. The pain actually imposed upon us may involve only the minor inconveniences of absorbing time and energy, or the surrender of some forms of social advance-ment, or the personal tensions of social controversy. Even so, our willing-ness to accept these may make the difference between creative contribution and futile gesture, and between obedience and rebellion toward God.

Although these supportive attitudes are necessary to keep our methods most effective, they are nevertheless very much in short supply. The cultural ideal of our time seems to embody more of agressive, egoistic, domination of others than it includes persistent, altruistic spending of self. A moderate measure of suffering for the sake of others is accepted as part of our image of parenthood. The quality is quite obscured, however, in commonly accepted economic and political roles. Even while we are working toward generally good ends, we want to protect our comfort in the process.

Both Biblical and sociological insight suggest that we ought to be more ready to embody sacrificial elements in all of our daily social interaction. In an unjust world we cannot escape the displeasure of the protectors of wickedness. Affluence cannot shield us from it. Since evil always resists eradication, progress is impossible without pain. Whenever in social reform it seems possible to sidestep suffering, we had better be suspicious of that alternative, lest it be a rationalization of selfish desire. In an imperfect world the burden of proof is on the side of the placid life. When one of the colonial Quakers, Mary Dyer, was already standing on the gallows and was then reprieved at the last moment, she felt "disturbed". She hesitated to obey the command to step down, for she wanted to wait on the Lord "to know his pleasure in so sudden a change." Were we more deeply dedicated, we would more often hesitate to escape from perilous testimony." (Harry Seifert, in Conquest by Suffering: The Process and Prospects of Nonviolent Resistance. Westminster Press)

Surely, such a stance for the Church would put if "off limits" for many contemporary men, but it would put the Church squarely where it belongs. And it may open the way into the Church and its mission for those for whom it is currently "off limits --reflective, critical spirits, persons who see no connection of religion to their lives, urban man. James Reston recently pointed out in the Times that many young people today look to the Civil Rights Movement as the contemporary counterpart of the religion of their ancestors. To put the Church back into the central, gnawing social problems of our age may open it up to the sizeable and growing minority which grows weary and ill of being identified with the one institution which above all others professes to believe in the value of each person without implementing its belief in service and urgent action.

But whether it opens or closes the Church to men is beside the point. What is to the point is faithfulness to the Son of Man. The Church must seek its identity in obedience to him, no matter what. It must be the servant of all; the slave of all, for its Lord came to serve, not to be served. Thus, the Church's one concern must no be passive but the active expression of faith in Jesus through entering into his suffering in and for the world.

In this day when men wonder who they are, even more than James and John wondered how tremendous it would be for the Church to know who it is and what it must do! To have this identity, we must undergo much basic revision and renewal. But this critical times demands no less of us. Just as the meaning of Jesus comes clear in his service and suffering, let the Church find her identity in suffering, in following the Lord, in giving her life as a ransom for many.

34. 4/11/65   Conflicts in the Souls of Men   Palm Sunday

The sweetness of Palm Sunday is here mirrored in its conflict with the impending agony of Good Friday. The specific Luke events used by Rev. Asbury are also told by Matthew 26:30-41 and Mark 14:26-38. The background story that Asbury uses for his sermon begins in Matthew 26, Mark 14, and Luke 22. Asbury's referral to Jesus's anointment at Bethany, that Luke omits in his Passion narrative, appears in Matthew 26:6-13 and Mark 14:3-9. Luke actually positioned the anointment in a different time and place – see Luke 7:36-50. Finally, the Luke Gesthemane narrative ends without the often used quotation that, according to both Matthew and Mark, Jesus uttered to Peter about the disciples falling asleep: "The spirit indeed is willing, but the flesh is weak."

There is conflict evident in the events between Palm Sunday and Good Friday. There is also conflict in contemporary racial injustice, political strife, war, economic inequity, and gender discrimination. These are conflicts where the spirit may plead for right action, yet the flesh finds pretexts, excuses, and weakness to justify inaction. Many of our personal choices pale in comparison with the choice Jesus faced. The message: Through the model of Jesus's leadership, surely we can find ways to take actions that resolve conflicts in our own time.

Palm Sunday

Westminster Presbyterian Church
Wooster, Ohio
Rev. Beverly Asbury, Minister
April 11, 1965

CONFLICTS IN THE SOULS OF MEN
Luke 22: 39-46

In the Gospel according to Luke, the transition from the Temple to the Passion is marked by Jesus' going into the city. Luke abandons Mark's day-by-day arrangement, and the last events begin to transpire with the last meal. The symbolism of the amointing at Bethany is missing from Luke's account. Instead, the situation is characterized by the reappearance of Satan: "Now the feast of Unleavened Bread drew near, which is called the Passover. And the chief priests and the scribes were seeking how to put him to death; for they feared the people. Then Satan entered into Judas Iscariot, who was of the number of the twelve; he went away and conferred with the chief priests and captains how he might betray him to them..."Thus, a new period of temptation begins (vss 28, 40, 46), which will continue after Jesus is gone. This fact of temptation, of inner conflict, of a struggle, forms the background for the Passion narrative. There has been a transition to a new epoch. Different conditions now prevail. Peace under the protection of Jesus is now a thing of the past. The disciples are now exposed to temptation, yet they are given assurance that they are not deserted

In the light of this setting, we can consider the dark premonitions in Jesus' mind in the hour on the Mount of Olives. According to Luke, Jesus went out according to his usual practice, and the disciples simply followed along. In contrast to the distress and agony depicted by Mark, Luke gives us the impression that Jesus' attitude is more collected and that he has accepted his fate. Yet, he still conveys to his disciples the conflict that goes on within him: "Pray that you don't enter into temptation." Perhaps, this is to say, don't desert me now. In any case, he does not withdraw very far--"just a stone's throw".

Then we witness the drama, the conflict in the soul of this man of Nazareth. He feels caught between the commitment to fulfill his role, his mission; to live out his teachings; to be obedient, on one hand, and the desire to avoid rejection, betrayal, the curse of being classed a criminal, on the other. We do get here a sense of great agony. This conflict had to be resolved. It's a real conflict, with great intensity. His sweat dropped to the ground like great clots of blood. And if this were not enough, he was troubled as well that his disciples might leave him during this critical period. This distressing anxiety leads Jesus to hope that he will not have to drink the cup of rejection.

The real nature of this conflict receives its underscoring from the fact that Jesus had earlier predicted his death. He had known what was to come. He had deliberately set out for Jerusalem, with the full knowledge that the journey led to death. He had faced hostility before, and he had told of a sharp trial and suffering ahead. Why, then, does this conflict appear now? Because Jesus is a man, a human being. Just because he foretold something did not make it easier to accept when it came. We human beings are that way. To know that death is coming does not make it easier to accept. We do not know in advance that we can endure what we know is coming. We can only hope and pray. And, surely, our anxiety increases as we doubt that those closest to us "are asleep" to our need and conflict.

Jesus resolves his conflict. He submits himself. Then relief comes, as it does when a decision is made, even if the decision has unpleasant consequences. But then to turn, as Jesus did, and find the disciples sleeping must come as something more than a disappointment. And it underlines again that temptation is not over for man; that conflict will continue in the souls of men; that men are confronted ever with agonizing decisions about their lives and the lives of others. This story reminds us that the Christian never makes a decision once-and-for-all.

Last year, a novel entitled The Martyred, by Richard E. Kim, told a story about the conflicts in the souls of contemporary men. This story is poignant and reflective, and it is a kind of mystery, in the religious sense. The tale is narrated by a young Korean intelligence officer by the name of Captain Lee. Captain Lee has charge of an investigation of the murder of Korean ministers by the North Korean Communists just prior to the outbreak of hostilities in June, 1950. Fourteen ministers had been taken, but two had survived. The South Korean forces, then occupying part of North Korea, found it important for reasons of political and military propaganda to investigate this matter. The inquiry centers on the questions as to why and how two ministers had escaped death. Had they betrayed the others? Were the twelve true martyrs? How exactly had they died? How had they behaved?

The conflicts in the souls of men who are servants of the Church slowly come out. We never learn exactly how and why the two ministers escape. We never get a clear answer as to the behavior of the martyred men. Rather, we get many answers from which to choose. The narrator searches for a solution, and we end up sharing the search. In the best sense of the word, we are left wondering, for what can you do but wonder at the conflicts that go on in the inner-self of a man?

One of the two surviving ministers has lost hold of reality as a result of the experience of his survival and his witnessing the murder of the others. The other, a Mr. Shin, stands as a complex human being. As we meet him, we are faced by many questions. How great was his guilt? How can he carry on as a minister? Was he truly a Judas? Is a Judas ever to be forgiven? Can there be a Golgotha without him? We catch a sense of deep pain within Mr. Shin. We see him as a participant in a tragedy that has both depraved and exalted him. We learn from him that one of the martyrs, a man of fanatical faith, had died an agnostic, a man in conflict, a man unsure. Yet we also see in this survivor, this Reverend Mr. Shin, a man who will not tell the Christians of Korea about the last moments of doubt; he would rather accept the guilt of betrayal and seek forgiveness.

You might wonder how he could avoid telling the truth. But what is the "truth"? That is far from clear. As you look at men from different angles, from different levels of understanding, with varying degrees of involvement, you see different things. What is true? Can you represent the truth as "objective"? Can you only say, then, that Christians face temptation, that they are full of conflicts in the soul? Mr. Shin has a great conflict; if he tells the "truth" about the "martyrs", that means personal relief for him but the destruction of the hope for those who revere their memory; or he may withhold the "truth" and so personally suffer as one accused of treason but **upholding** the memory of those to whom the Korean Christians look in hope. The author, Richard Kim, was raised a Christian. His grandfather was a Presbyterian minister, and he was shot by the Communists the day after the war broke out. It would seem that Kim writes out of his own sense of commitment and conflict.

Perhaps because of this, Kim catches the basic characteristic of the human condition. In a moving, convincing way, he does not give us all the answers. He ennobles us as men by leaving us with our problems illuminated but still ours to bear and solve. We learn much about the conflicts in our souls. This novel reminds us that men cannot endure suffering without the hope and the promise of justice. If men are in despair, if men are hopeless, if you will, they have the "sickness unto death". Men must hope. Mr. Shin lets them hope. And if many are to live unenslaved by hopelessness, a few must bear cruel and even holy burdens. (Kim dedicates his novel to the memory of Albert Camus "whose insight into a 'strange form of love' overcame for me the nihilism of the trenches and bunkers of Korea."

Palm Sunday
4-11-65

-3-

This strange form of love, for Christians, is also that expressed in Jesus as he resolved his conflict: "Not my will, but thine, be done." Our understanding of him comes from his acceptance of his death, from his willingness to bear a cruel burden out of love for others. And in so doing he gives us hope about the conflicts in our own souls. His strange form of love somehow grasps us and gives us the faith, courage, and strength to live our lives meaningfully, without despair. We discover something of who we are through this act of love to do the will of the Father.

But the conflict remains. It is forever t here to be dealt with. And it is generally, for us, on a lesser level than The Martyred. Recently, some of us talked with a man who said that he would do what was right if it "didn't cost him money." This man goes to church every Sunday, but he revealed the conflict in his soul. This man is a good man, but he illustrates the level of conflict that most of us know abou If we do not have his particular conflict, we suffer from the conflict of wishing on one hand to forgive him, and, on the other selfrighteously to condemn him. Any way, none of us really wants to do what is right when it costs us something dear. Remove this cup from me--because I do not want to be removed from my profits, my popularity, my luxury, my status. John Ciardi in the Saturday Review of April 10, 1965, writes about a banker who asked him, "Do poets steal?" Says Ciardi: "I dodged by asking him another question. 'What have you got...that's worth the time it would take me to steal it?' If I wasn't prepared to declare myself irremediably honest, I could at least make the point that nothing I could imagine him to have in his vaults, and nothing immediat ely visible to me, offered any real temptation.....Certainly(poets) are (not) indifferent to money and possessions. But most poets, and all the good ones have the shaping of their own attention as their central passion. Material possessions, aside from those that furnish a life more or less congenially, just aren't worth the time they take. I am myself w illing enough to get rich negligently, but it's no deal if it has to take more than passing attention."

Well, Jesus had a central passion too: To do God's will; to fulfill his role as Son of Man. And so must we, if we would be Christian; if we would decide the conflicts in our souls; if we would do more than merely endure them; if we would be spared the disabling dichotomies of many gods. Jesus told his disciples to rise and pray that they enter not into temptation. Surely, he says to us that we should not deceive ourselves about our conflicts. There may be no simple answers. We may have to live with certain ambiguities. But we must also decide. We must decide which path we shall take out of the conflicts of our souls.

The road of Palm Sunday led to Good Friday. The road of overcoming the insanity of hatred and the folly of indifference may lead us from our luxury into suffering. The road to better human relations leads us into great risks and may move from an affluent society to a Kingdom of the poor in heart. We must decide what road we shall take out of the conflicts of our souls. Dag Hammarskjold said this: "He who has surrendered himself to it knows the Way ends on the Cross--even when it is leading him through the jubilation of Gennesaret or the the triumphal entry into Jerusalem. Do not seek death. Death will find you. But seek the road that makes death a fulfillment."

35. 4/18/65   **To Be A New Man**   Easter

The Biblical story of the empty tomb and subsequent events, as told in the Luke narrative, also appears in Matthew 28:1-15 and Mark 16:1-13.

Sermon #33, the Palm Sunday sermon (#34) and this Easter sermon (#35) share the same context. Rev. Asbury delivered them in sequence, one week apart each. Some context has already been mentioned in the notes to Sermon #33. In this sermon, Rev. Asbury refers to the funeral of James Reeb. A background explanation was not necessary at the time the sermon was originally delivered, but now, 50 years later, it is:

Selma, Alabama, is situated on the west bank of a river known as Majors Creek. Montgomery, the state capital, lies about 50 miles to the east. Racial segregation in the South at the time was by law (*de jure*) rather than by circumstance (*de facto*). By law, voting by African-Americans was restricted, so civil rights workers were attempting to bring about changes in voting rights laws. Some of the attempts involved demonstrations and marches to state capitals, including to Montgomery, Alabama. On Sunday, March 7, 1965, about 550 people set off on a march from Selma to Montgomery. They got to the county line across the Pettus Bridge, which spans Majors Creek – hardly out of town – and were met by state troopers and a posse. The result came to be known as Bloody Sunday. A second march of about 2500 people set out two days later on Tuesday, March 9. However, in the interim, a federal restraining order was raised that temporarily prohibited the march. Obeying the law, the marchers stopped at the bridge. That night, three white Unitarian-Universalist ministers received brutal beatings and one of the ministers, James Reeb, died two days later. On March 17, the federal restraining order was lifted, but any walk along the highway to Montgomery was to be limited to 300 people. Therefore, on March 21, 300 people set out walking, but thousands more traveled along by car. Thus, on March 24, some 25,000 people showed up at the Alabama state capitol. On the capitol steps, Martin Luther King, Jr., gave his *How Long, Not Long* speech.

The March to Montgomery was not the end. More beatings and killings ensued that night and beyond. The immediacy of blood-spattered television coverage, which was new at the time, horrified a nation. During the events described above, President Johnson sent to Congress the outline of the Voting Rights Act of 1965. The bill passed Congress and was signed into law during the summer.

Rev. Asbury amplifies his message of spiritual renewal out of the depths of despair by citing Saul Bellow's 1964 novel, *Herzog*. The epiphany available in the novel and from Jesus is that there is tremendous freedom available when one yields one's life – if not literally, then at least spiritually. When one has nothing left to lose, one is free to become a new person (see comments on *kenosis* found in the notes for Sermons #21 and #44). The civil rights workers and marchers in Alabama felt that they had nothing to lose. Thus, they risked everything. Easter epitomizes the surprise gift of freedom when everything is risked. When one yields to the imperative of humble service, one suddenly becomes rich and free. Through a resurrection of spirit, a person, a state, and a nation can change. When one has nothing left to lose – even one's life – one suddenly and unexpectedly gains everything.

Westminster Presbyterian Church
Wooster, Ohio
Rev. Beverly Asbury, Minister
April 18, 1965

TO BE A NEW MAN
Luke 24: 1-16, 27-35

The preaching of the Early Church presents Jesus to us as the model of true and full manhood, the man in whom men discerned the whole presence of God.   In his manhood, Jesus made such a unique response to God that he was obviously seen to be a remarkably free man--a man free from self-concern; a man free to love others, no matter who the "other" may be; a man free to be himself, a genuine human being. His relationship with God was understood to be the source of his freedom. He lives as though he were related to God. That is, one who says he trusts God, who says he has chosen to live as though there were hope and meaning in human existence, but is fearful, despairing, and unloving is displaying a profound contradiction. Jesus lives as one who has faith, who hopes for what is not seen, who has chosen for meaning, and he lives consistently. So the New Testament presents Jesus to us as an exceptionally free man.

Then the New Testament calls upon those who follow Jesus to do so by living and acting as he did. Yet, the New Testament faithfully records the fact that even those closest followers, who had been attracted by Jesus' remarkable freedom, did not share in it.   There were no Christians prior to Easter. All the disciples were disloyal after his arrest. The historical Jesus did not receive the response of faith. The followers had tasted his freedom only momentarily and fleetingly, and they produced no freedom in others. Prior to Easter, nothing pointed to Easter. Nothing!

We have no evidence that the disciples expected anything after his murder on a Cross. Yet, on the other side of Easter, they w ere changed men. Apparently, they were caught up in something like the freedom of Jesus himself. They became men who put aside self-concern. They became men-for-others. They became new men, who despite their past fail ures now could and did face death without fear. They became men, as Jesus had been a man. And let us not underestimate what that means!

At the memorial service held in the First Presbyterian Church of Casper, Wyoming, for James Reeb, Robert A. Reed, his longtime friend, had this to say:

"Conventional Christians has missed Bonhoeffer's insight that to be a Christian is first of all to be a man! Jim's lifelong struggle was to be a full, free, and compassionate human being. He died as he lived, seeking to take some meaningful action on behalf of brotherhood and justice. To become a man is the first business of life. These words of Morris West, the Catholic novelist, describe for me the kind of man Jim had become: 'It cost so much to be a full human being that there are very few who have the enlightenment, or the courage, to pay the price. One has to abandon altogether the search for security, and reach out to the risk of living with both arms. One has to embrace the world like a lover, and yet demand no easy return of love. One has to accept pain as a condition of existence. One has to court doubt and darkness as the cost of existence. One needs a will stubborn in conflict, but apt always to the total acceptance of every consequence of living and dying.'"

So if becoming Christians means first becoming men, then the disciples, after Easter, became men. They paid the price and accepted the consequences. But why? What gives Christians the power to choose to become fully human? What happened to the disciples at Easter to give them this participation in the freedom of Jesus?

4-18-65   -2-

Surely, we can say no more than the New Testament says. That must be our guide as we seek an interpretation of the meaning and significance of Easter. In the New Testament, the earliest tradition was recorded by Paul in I Corinthians 15. He wrote some twenty years after the Easter-event and he recounted what he had received as oral tradition----that Jesus had appeared to Peter, than to the 12, then to a number of other disciples. That later and more developed tradition, from which we read this morning, tells of Jesus' tomb and it gives details of various appearances of Jesus. However, neither tradition speaks of the actual "resurrection". The New Testament devotes not a single word to an account of the actual rising. Rather, with the one word "resurrection", the New Testament points to the whole event of Easter; the accounts begin with his appearances, or with the empty tomb. At least, if we are to say no more than the New Testament said, we must face the fact that whatever "resurrection" means, it does not mean resuscitation. A case of resuscitation does not require a response of faith. It may evoke admiration at the skill involved. It might even be acknowledged as "miraculous", just as we so acknowledge delicate heart surgery. Even given our bent for the worldly, we should probably call it "incredible". But a case of resuscitation does not make us believers. The old saying has it that "Seeing is believing", but when it comes to the Christian faith, that saying breaks down. Seeing is not believing. Perhaps, we are closer to the faith in its Biblical understanding when we put it "Believing is not seeing". "Faith is the assurance of things hoped for; the evidence of things not seen."

The other night a man in Ohio saw smoke emerging from a house. On a hunch he broke in and saved a three year old child who had been left alone. Someone could ask "Was that a case of duty?" Well, the evidence won't settle the question. It's not irrelevant, for he acted. But why he acted cannot be discerned from the action alone Just so with the resurrection, to ask if it "happened" cannot be answered empirically The evidence is insufficient. What happened to cause such a change in the disciples after Easter is no longer open to historical investigation. We can only say that something happened, and that the intention of the New Testament obviously never included a description of physical resuscitation. And even if it had, it would not have settled for us the question of why men responded with belief.

The New Testament indicates that the disciples had not expected anything and reacted with disbelief at the first reports that Jesus had been seen. They dismissed an account of the "empty tomb" as an "idle tale". Paul tells us that the "risen Christ" did not have a body of "flesh and blood". From Luke we learn that there was great difficulty in recognizing Jesus, even though he bore the marks of the crucifixion. According to the text, he ate with them, appeared and disappeared at will in a most unbodily fashion. There is no doubt that the Gospel gives an account of a most unusual experience. Easter was for Peter and the others a situation in which they discerned Jesus in a new way. Against the background of Jesus of Nazareth, they now experience him in a way they did not expect. A life that had seemed to end in failure, now took on new and important meaning. This experience of new meaning gave them a power to become new men.

Somehow such an experience has come to seem foreign to us. As a result of our technological revolution, we have been technicized, rendered efficient, and diminished as human beings. In the face of the quantitative transformation of our age by electronic computers, we have a prevailing mood of feeling the irrelevance of the human. But it still happens that some men become new men; that some men struggle sensitively, intelligently, and imaginatively to keep sane and make sense out of the world; that some men like James Reeb "reach out to the risk of living with both arms."

Saul Bellow's novel Herzog also gives us a contemporary account of the kind of discernment situation in which men are set free to be men. Herzog is about Moses Herzog, a man in his late forties, an intelligent man, a man who is reasonably familiar with the best that has been thought and said. He is also a man who has made a

Easter
4-18-65   -3-

mess of his life and is trying valiantly to discover what his life or any human life
can mean. He is, in many ways, a sick man and knows it. He is, in many ways,,a
foolish man, and he knows that too. But both sickness and foolishness form the
world's setting in which we have to make difficult value judgments, and this novel
tells its story in terms of such judgments.

Parts of the story are unpleasant to read, and the novel itself is not easily
read. The entire story is not important for the sermon this morning. It is enough
that you understand that Herzog is an historical man living in posthistory; a Jew
with a history stretching back over many generations who has to live in a world with
little sense of that history. Understandably enough, Herzog is a little out of his
mind. He spends a good deal of his time writing brilliant, outlandish letters to all
kinds of people. He never mails any of them. As someone has said, "They are gestures
that replace action in his hopelessness."

He goes to Chicago to see his daughter who lives with his divorced wife. He
spends an afternoon with her at the park and all goes well until he has a minor auto
accident. Because he is carrying a revolver, which is carefully explained, he is held
by police. On the way to the police station, he meditates:"But what is the problem of
this generation? Not God is dead, that point was passed long ago. Perhaps it should
be stated, Death is God. This generation thinks--and this is its thought of thoughts
--that nothing faithful, vulernable, fragile can be durable or have any true power.."
This is the turning point; his discernment situation; something unexpected happens.

Something in the pathos of this experience changes Herzog. He returns home and
writes letters more furiously than ever and begins to achieve stability. He writes to
God: "How my mind has struggled to make coherent sense. I have not been too good at
it. But I have desired to do your unknowable will, taking it, you, without symbols.
Everything of intense significance. Especially if divested of me." Herzog knows that
the "bitter cup will come around again" by and by but now in the present he has found
joy. He has hold of a new life. He learns enough of what it is to be a new man that
he knows that he is not out of his mind. He has learned to hope. Whether he stays
out of a mental institution depends now largely on if he can keep this hold on hope;
if he can live the hope out in a meaningful life.

H erzog's experience gave him a new hold on life. And the Easter faith gave a
new perspective on life. The disciples had an experience in which they discerned a
"risen Jesus", who was different from but inseparably related to the Jesus of Nazaret
They saw Jesus in a new way, and they shared in the freedom which he alone had previously possess. On Easter, the disciples found that Jesus had a new power, a power
which he now exercised--a power to set them free, and power given to them to set
others free. Easter, w hatever else it was, was the experience of sharing in the free
dom to love and live for others.

Ah, but is this not subjective? It's just like what happened to Herzog. How can
you speak about this experience? Let us admit it: of course, it's subjective. All
experiences are. Objects don't experience anything. Only persons have experiences.
So, it could be no other way. On Easter, the disciples experienced Jesus in a thoroughly new way, and it made a difference in their lives. And that is what counts!

It just doesn't matter what we believe to be "true" unless that "truth" is able
to make a difference; unless it generates "meanings" which make a difference in both
life and language. What happened to Herzog gave him a new meaning; he had a change
and it opened up a better life. What happened on Easter gave the disciples something
that made a fundamental change in their l ife and thought. The proof of Easter lies
in the fact that their lives change; they become new men. They can point to them- -
selves and say"see, here it is, here's the difference."

Easter marks that point where they confess Jesus as Lord. Easter marks the point
for us at which we find the power to be new men. Easter marks the points in our live
in which we see Jesus in a new way; at the times in our l ives when we experience
his presence in such a way that we are set free. Easter is what we proclaim: a setting free from the dominion of death and a setting free for the life of the world.
This we proclaim as the Good News for mankind.

At the time of this writing, the collegiate academic year generally runs from late August to early May. Fifty years ago, the spring semester ended in early June. In both arrangements, summer semester is scheduled as a separate entity. Nevertheless, the next sequence of sermons continues the calendar year from early May through the summer, and does so by calling on sermons that were delivered during the regular school year when students were present to hear them (and for May, they actually were). The theme is Christian action in a secular world: How should we approach difficult social issues that we might prefer to avoid? The first four sermons (#36-39) deal with the search for inner guidelines...including the turmoil that often accompanies the search. The core of what follows (sermons #40-48) probes how the Christian stance interacts with the secular world, including poverty, wealth, discrimination, violence, pride, and religiosity. The last four sermons (#49-52) return to reprise the opening theme of the Christian stance.

To be a pastor is to accept an election. The poignancy of such an election is described vividly in sermons #30-35. Therefore, it is important to realize that Rev. Asbury's ideas were evolving even as he was maturing as the elected pastor to a College. Some of that evolution appears as battles that he shared with us in his sermons; others remain appropriately opaque, although they are hinted at by Prof. Tait in his manuscript described in Wooster Magazine. *They are also documented more fully in the archives of Andrews Library. Dissatisfaction and impatience appear in these sermons, and some of both overflow into righteous anger. The moral imperative that is revealed is **not** to sit idly by while worldly injustices accumulate. Thus, the power of the sermons derives, in part, from the observation that some of Rev. Asbury's battles against injustice were **our** battles. The reasons, the passions, the struggles with faith and secular obligations were – and are – our struggles to this day. Students wanted to fix the entire world back then, and we were wounded that we couldn't do so. We still want to fix it today, if only we had the strength (faith?) to do it. Stated in Biblical language, "I believe; help my unbelief." The journey through the following sermons may help medicate the wound and cure the unbelief --- in order to promote our own acts of faith in a secular world.*

[Ed. note: Color Day at Wooster usually occurred around the second weekend in May. Because calendar days change from year to year, two Color Day sermons are included here, #38 and #39. Their inclusion is much less due to a calendar reason and much more due to the reason that both sermons reinforce an important theme.]

36. 9/20/64   Christian Stance: Inner Guidelines

Faith or good works? Are we judged by our character or by our deeds? This sermon, the first of a pair on the subject, recommends that adopting the perspective or attitude of Jesus, that is, a Christian *Blik*, is a way to achieve the right balance of attitude and action.

Rev. Asbury has used the Beatitudes previously as a reference in this Cycle (Sermons #6 and 29). For this particular sermon on Christian *Blik* he calls upon Matthew for two additional elements: First, "You have heard that it was said, 'You shall love your neighbor and hate your enemy.' But I say to you, love your enemies…" (Matthew 4:43-44 (also found in Luke 6:27)), and second, "You, therefore, must be perfect, as your heavenly Father is perfect" (Matthew 5:48 (also found in Luke 6:36)). Asbury presents these pronouncements from the Sermon on the Mount as guidelines for Christian attitude and action.

There has been scholarly argument about what it means to be "perfect" in either attitude or action – and whether achieving perfection in the eyes of God is even possible. The Greek word in Matthew is written in English as *telios*, and it is usually translated as *perfect*, less commonly as *complete*. Because the immediate context is one of loving one's enemies, a suggested alternative translation has been *mature*. That is, "Be mature [in love], even as your heavenly Father is mature." A perfect, complete, or mature love is reserved, respectful, fully formed, and forgiving. Godly love that is perfect, complete, and mature "sends rain on the just and on the unjust" (Matthew 5:45). This thought leads to Luke's treatment of the same message: "Be merciful, even as your Father is merciful." Luke uses an altogether different Greek word, written in English as *oiktirmon*, and translated consistently as *merciful*. Again, the context is to "love your enemies…[and be] kind to the ungrateful and the selfish" (Luke 6:35).

Rev. Asbury takes the position that a Christian *Blik* is a balanced attitude that is perfect/complete/mature/merciful. It melds together the two questions, "What must I do?" and "What must I be?" The balance offers, first, humility to accept self and others and, second, conviction to act for the recovery of goodness in society. The Christian stance is not a set of rules but, rather, a construction of inner guidelines.

Westminster Presbyterian Church
Wooster, Ohio
Rev. Beverly Asbury, Minister
September 20, 1964

THE CHRISTIAN STANCE: INNER GUIDELINES
Matthew 5: 1-11; 43-48

A Christian has every right to be suspicious of words that lead nowhere. After reading books and hearing sermons most of our lives about "Christian principles" we begin to wonder where, if anywhere they do lead. "If I speak in the tongues of men and of angels and have not love, I am a noisy gong and a clanging cymbal." Words have been so important to Protestant Christians that those same Christians have often been blinded to the pressing concerns of human life. Many Christians seem to hold that the set of words you use about God and the Christian faith are more important than anything else. But, quite frankly, it seems to me that, important as the tone and quality of theological words are in our time, our style of life is more important than the style of our words. Some Christians may vary widely in doctrine---some may be unquestioning, undoubting, secure in and satisfied with the training and doctrine which they have received; but there will be others looking for the radical reformulation of doctrine, which we discussed last Sunday. Regardless of doctrinal differences or present uncertainties in theology, Christians of all doctrinal shades should have a profound concern for the Christian style of life.

The Christian faith should lead us to a certain posture, a stance in the world. Our words should tell what we believe, and why we believe it, and where it has led us. If we have a Christian vision, then that vision ought to spill over into our lives. And the world rightly tests our faith not by our words but by how the words work themselves out in our lives. Let me use again the word "blik" to express what we are saying. "Blik" is a way of saying things, a world in view, that carries with it, of necessity, a way of acting. Simply, the proof of our words lies in our action. They work themselves out fragmentarily and incompletely, but unless they are seen in our way of moving and acting, they are nothing. Principles must lead somewhere or else they are useless. They must lead to a Christian stance.

Now, since we have said that a "blik" is a way of looking that leads to a way of acting, let us examine this week the way of looking and next week the action to which it leads. (This separation cannot be complete.) This approach recognizes that the authentic place for our living lies in our personal interior. Our outward actions are re-presentations of what we inwardly hold to be true (unless, of course, we are trying to be deceptive.) Thus, our first question is not,"What must we do?" To treat that as the question of first importance would be to continue to give exhortation and instruction that takes no account of the interior life and thus leads nowhere. Christians preaching that tells people what their outward actions should be has all the marks of irrelevance to personal life and ineffectiveness in changing society. The contents of a Christian's stance in the world cannot be stated or even revised without first envisioning or re-envisioning the interior life of man. This may be the new starting place for contemporary Christianity rather than doctrinal reformulation. Out of this revisioning of guidelines may come doctrines relevant to our living.

Again, then, the most difficult question faced by the Christian today is not "What must I do?" Rather, the question pressing us is "What must I be?" And there is a very correct and proper way of answering the question. We are to be perfect, "even as our heavenly Father is perfect." What should we be? Everything the Sermon on the Mount says we should be. In short, the Christian can correctly hold that the pattern for our life is the man Jesus. Yet, many of us have discovered that the correct way of answering the question, "What must I be?", is not a very helpful way. In the first place, we do not know enough about Jesus as a man among men. His Lordship over our lives does not easily and automatically become in us a style of life appropriate for the demands of our time and place. There are no direct lines from the Sermon on the Mount to my interior life. Rather, I must use the resources of my mind and heart to re-envision my interior life and my stance in the world in the light of those teachings and the Lordship of Christ. In order to have a Christian stance in the world, in order that my actions may square with my interior life and my words, I need to have some guidelines. They must in some way be determined by the Lordship of Christ. Even if they fall short of the admonition to be perfect, a Christian must be able to follow them in good conscience and with integrity.

What then are some inner guidelines of a "blik" that lead us to proper ethical action?

First, as Bonhoeffer and William Hamilton have helped us to see, we need a sense of reserve in our dealings with others.

Bonhoeffer points out in his Letters and Papers from Prison (pp 22-3) that we have to fight for a wholesome reserve between man and man or else all human values will be drowned in anarchy. He felt strongly that chaos was at the door where men lost the feeling for the human quality and the power of reserve. In a day of false sociality, of make-believe togetherness, reserve is considered anti-social. Those who have the dignity of reserve find their sincerity questioned, because reserve means the end of popularity seeking. Reserve requires depth and quality of friendship rather than flippant acquaintance and easy acceptance. As Bonhoeffer put it: "Culturally it means a return from the newspaper and the radio to the book, from feverish activity to unhurried leisure, from dissipation to recollection, from sensationalism to reflection, from virtuosity to art, from snobbery to modesty, and from extravagance to moderation."

In contrast to the "Hi there" heartiness of our present life, reserve suggests that you reach another person truly in a slow and even difficult manner. Mere talk and mere being together mean little. One sign of the lack of reserve in our day is the first-name mania. Everybody rushes to be on a first-name basis within moments of an introduction and this ought to make us uncomfortable. How well I remember my commencement at Yale Divinity School! After conferring of degrees, the professor with whom I had worked and studied for three years said, "Now you can call me Julian." Frankly, I would have felt just as comfortable walking to the pearly gates and shouting,"Hi, St. Pete". Surely respect and reserve go together.

Reserve also means a willingness to leave the other person alone--to let him be himself, apart from us. Every man needs a genuine space between himself and others. This does not mean that we should be guided by cultivated hostility and arrogance, but it does mean recognizing that love and acceptance can also suffocate. This means that the Christian dares to defend the privacy of interior life--his and the other's. Every man has a right to be solitary--apart from us. This is not anti-social; it is the power to grant respect to the other man. It means loving another as you love yourself. It means that love suggests both a closeness and a distance between one another. Authentic human=love cannot tolerate a clinging vine or an invading parasite. Love allows the other the space in which to be a private self. And thus, an important inner guideline for a Christian stance in the world must be reserve, the respect for the inner life of the other.

9-20-64

Secondly, as Alec Vidler has taught us, a Christian has to be an inner combination of tolerance and anger. Tolerance becomes the inner life of a Christian because he knows in Jesus Christ that God is teaching and chastening all men. To me, tolerance means the inner ability to stand in the presence of what disturbs us, threatens us, displeases us. It arises out of the inner conviction that we do not have all the answers, that God has much yet to teach us, and because we have been and are tolerated by both God and other men. Any man who has ever stood in the need of forgiveness and received it knows the meaning of toleration, and he finds himself thereafter less and less intolerant of others.

But at the other extreme lies anger. Let us never doubt that in the Christian life this is equally right and necessary. The interior life of a Christian should be marked by an anger, a constant fighting against the claims of proud and secure men who claim all the answers and have no tolerance for others. This is what William Hamilton calls generous anger—anger that is not malicious; anger that fights out in the open and without fears. Anger ought openly to be displayed in the face of injustice, indignity and inhumanity.

Tolerance and anger! These are poles, to be sure, but they do not contradict each other. The life of Jesus exemplifies both poles. Jesus showed tolerance to the broken, rejected, and lost by expressing his openness and love. He showed his anger and scorn to the self-righteous and knowledgeably secure by the sharpness of his words and actions. Nevertheless, we do have a problem in balancing these poles in our life. To be too tolerant leads us to empty-headed indifference. To be too angry leads us to absolutism and tyranny. We have both weapons in our inner life. Perhaps our best rule of thumb is to be tolerant to the victims of intolerance and reserve our anger for those who are so secure and protected that they care not for the weak and undefended.

A third guideline for inner lives can be simply expressed: our stance must make room, in a world of noise and movement, for times of silence, waiting, and contemplation. Some would call this prayer and others would not. No matter the name, the interior life needs a time in which to set its bearings. Unless this is done, we find that we do not determine our schedules but that our schedules run our lives. Without a period to examine our work, what we are doing and why, we have no clear idea of our motivations. A time of silence, apartness, and examination can relieve us from spending our time taking bearings from town or campus or country club in order to test what we do. The Christian's direction should not be set by the world's estimate of him. A man discovers quickly what poor guidance is received there. Thus, this guideline means a fight for a time of precious freedom from the world--a time in which to take one's own bearings, set one's own course.

Lastly, we need to be guided by and toward a recovery of goodness. Recent theology has zeroed in on sin, self-righteousness, and the moralistic goodness which leads to pride. We have cast out the Pharisee and stressed that all men are sinners. Preachers, including this one, have held long and sometimes eloquently that men must face their evil nature before they can receive forgiveness. All this contains part of the truth. We have reached the point, it seems to me, when we are afraid that being good means being unChristian or falsely pious. Let's remind ourselves that an essential point of Biblical theology affirms that we are created in the image of God. How fractured that image maybe by our sin, how distorted it may be by our pride and idolatry, it still resides within us. Man is not so totally depraved that he lacks all capacity for goodness.

Let it be said that a Christian stance in the world will surely fall short of

9-20-64

-4-

being Christian if it lacks goodness. The inner life must seek to recover goodness
so that goodness will be manifest in our dealings with men. The Church can today
give an unashamed defense of goodness even if it cannot say precisely what goodness
means. At least, we know that goodness involves a willingness to stand with the
underdog in society; an openness to the claims and rights of others; opposition to
pompousness, injustice, and coercion. Not least of all, goodness means a refusal
to call attention to one's own goodness.

The search for goodness does not mean blindness to the theological and psychological truths, why lists of virtues cannot lead to goodness. Christians must
know that one cannot become good simply by willing to be good. Paul and Freud would
agree on this. We cannot be unaware of Paul's confession in Romans that he does
not do the things that he would do, and ends up doing the things that he would not
do. The Christian knows this about his own life. But the Christian also knows
that moral character is not totally independent of inner discipline and will. We
grant that the human personality has a very low receptivity to injunctions from
its own will, but we still can defend the good man--the man ever open not only to
radical and heroic acts of faith but also to the humbler goodness required in the
less pressing hours of our days. The Christian can acknowledge the Lord's admonition to "Be perfect even as your heavenly Father is perfect." No matter how far
short we fall, His words remain our guideline.

These, then, are the inner guidelines which can lead us next Sunday to a
consideration of a stance in the world, a style of life meaningful to Christians
in our day.

End of Second Semester

37. 9/27/64   **Christian Stance: Rebellion and Resignation**   <u>End of April</u> `

This sermon is the second of a pair, both of which were given near the beginning of a school year. Both occurred after a summer of civil unrest, racial strife, poverty, and political discord....see the notes for Sermon #1. The end of the summer of '64, when this sermon was written, was the end of the racially tragic *Mississippi Summer*, less than a year after the assassination of JFK, less than two years after the Cuban missile crisis, a bit more than three years after the U2 incident, and at the height of the Cold War. It was the time of the Johnson-Goldwater presidential campaign..."a choice, not an echo." It was 1963-64, the years when "everything happened." By the way, Sermon #1 in this book immediately preceded in time this pair of sermons.

Unrest was growing on US campuses. The motto, "Don't trust anyone over 30" carried influence; students on campus, who were separated from parental restrictions, behaved accordingly. Drinking, sex, relationships, beliefs, the draft – for many students, these elements took on new guises. Some students took active roles in sit-ins, protests, and marches. Regardless of their perspectives, students wondered, "Is this really the world that awaits us?"

This sermon explores uncertainty – and even dissatisfaction – in the world. The story of Jesus revolves around his own dissatisfaction with oppression, arrogance, insensitivity, and poverty and his efforts to do something about them. Rev. Asbury uses Mark's Gethsemane story (also found Matthew 26:36-46 and Luke 22:40-46) to probe Jesus's dissatisfaction, his conflict, and even his uncertainty. Asbury's analogy is Jesus's stance for his cause vis-à-vis students' stances for their causes. Jesus showed that the Christian stance is not passive and withdrawn. It is also not easy. It is involved and humane. College students are especially good at being involved. Thus, the sermon argues not for rebellion but, rather, for involvement tempered with maturity, reserve and, when appropriate, acceptance. In Asbury's words, "All things do not come quickly or easily."

Rev. Asbury mentions a Charles Shulz *Peanuts* cartoon to illustrate a point about working for change in a world of imperfections. Asbury was not the only one to notice deeper messages in *Peanuts*. In 1965, less than a year after this sermon, Robert L. Short published his book, *The Gospel According to Peanuts*.

Westminster Presbyterian Church
Wooster, Ohio
Rev. Beverly Asbury, Minister
September 27, 1964

THE CHRISTIAN STANCE: REBELLION AND RESIGNATION
Mark 14: 32-42

Last spring just before commencement a student visiting my home caught me up short with her words. This was a student whom I had known quite well, I thought, from the beginning of my ministry here. Since she was about to be graduated, she felt that the time had come for her to give an evaluation of my work in this church. Her words, which really got me, went something like this: "You care too much and we're suspicious of anyone who's committed and involved." Certainly, this was meant as criticism, meant to say that there would be less suspicions of a minister if he played it "cool". However it was meant, I finally decided that it was as fine a compliment as one has a right to hope for. After all, I'm a Calvinist, and Calvinism has been marked by an active and aggressive relationship to the world. A man who stands in the tradition of John Calvin wishes to shape the world into a more suitable instrument for God's glory. He works to create a commonwealth, not just for the "elect" but for all men. He seeks to use government to bring about justice and peace. The Church to the Calvinist is a disciplined community that has been called "To comfort the afflicted and to afflict the comfortable." No Calvinist can really "play it cool"; rather he is marked by earnestness and seriousness since all things relate to God's purpose.

Yet, there is no denying that the Calvinist spirit has been challenged today. I cannot change my spirit to be what the student wanted me to be, but I know as well that she is not open to the "causes" espoused by Calvinism. Two quite different forces oppose the Calvinist spirit, and they quite unwittingly embrace one another in this. For lack of better names, we can call those in one force "conformists" and those in the other "beatniks." How different and yet how alike in opposition to the Calvinist spirit. Both reject the idea of reshaping the world. The Conformist manipulates himself to fit into the world. The "beat" leaves it for his own form of social monasticism. Neither aims at transforming the world. The Calvinist continues to say, without being heard, that we should be out in the world, transforming it as God's redeeming agents. We should face it that activism belongs to the minority, only a few are going to participate in such ventures as the Mississippi summer project, and most people do not hear us when we call for active involvement.

But when you are not heard, what shall you do? How do you say it? Do you shout? Shall we weep for the majority? Or scold them, or create neat and imaginative programs by which to restore zest? Or do we face the death of the Calvinist activism and find a new stance, related to the inner guidelines. Let this Calvinist suggest the latter. Having tried and failed at the others, the time has come to find a new style of life that leads to appropriate action. In the light of our "blik", we seek a pattern of action for our day as relevant as the Calvinist pattern has been for other days.

Our clue to this new pattern of action can be found in the Gethesmane story. "Abba, Father, all things are possible to Thee; remove this cup from me; yet not what I will, but what Thou wilt." This passage has expressed for many contemporary Christians more clearly than any other movement of the Christian life. Here in the agony of Jesus where He fell on the ground, prayed, and sweated like great drops of blood, we find in acute form the tension between rebellion and resignation. Jesus submits Himself to God's purpose only after openly expressing His own desire, His rebellion against a will contradicting His own. Here Jesus shares our humanity in

9-27-64

its fulness, and here we sense that we share in the fulness of Jesus' life. Our stance as Christians will have to include both these actions. They will have to exist in tension in our lives just as they existed in the life of Jesus.

Rebellion belongs to our stance. Even good Calvinists understand that. The tolerance/anger polarity occasionally resolves itself into anger against an unjust world. Even the traditional Christian rebels against an unsatisfactory world. Nevertheless, we ought to recognize that rebellion becomes more and more difficult. As the current political campaign shows us, it is harder and harder to locate what it is we should be rebelling against. Politics in our country has largely moved away from rebellion and has been replaced with adjustment, compromise, and manipulation. Indeed, the very success of the process has so frustrated potential rebels that they react against the world--- and think that reaction and rebellion are one and the same.

Nevertheless, rebellion can still be a part of our Christian lives, and it is especially so for the student generation. The rebellion of the young against the old goes on--rebellion against the father and the family. We should pity the one who fails to rebel against capricious demands of love. We should not be afraid of those who rebel against the past, the authority which has "sinned" against them. But those who rebell must l earn, after rebellion, to forgive and love, for the past has given us our lives. The Gethsemane story would seem to endorse a break with the past that allows us to become conscious of our present life; even to rebel against God, to accuse him of injustice, impotence, irrelevance in order to learn who God is. It seems to me that it is difficult to be honest with oneself in our day unless we have so rebelled. If religious faith comes at all to many, this will be the way of its coming. Rebellion can be a means to self-knowledge and of the knowledge of God.

Nevertheless, rebellion has its dangers and risks. Rebellion involves loneliness, and too many take it only as an invitation to irresponsibility and mundane bohemian life. Rebellion is not that easy. Let us rescue it from its false friends----those who conform to valueless living in the name of rebellion. Let us reinterpret it as a way, a means to knowledge, rather than an end in itself. Let us defend it as legitimate and necessary. But then let us declare in no uncertain terms that rebellion is inadequate. Jesus' last words in Gethsemane were: "Yet not what I will, but what thou wilt." Rebellion can never be the last word of the Christian life, though it may seem so to American Christians who have been nourished on activism.

Much can be said for rebellion's opposite number: resignation. Such a passive notion is generally condemned as a part of that dread disease conformity. Resignation, not withstanding our suspicions, can be a means to knowledge. It grows out of our reserve, our tolerance, our meditation, and even out of our search for goodness. Let's put it this way. Rebellion acts in freedom, and to win more freedom. The freedom won rebellion is a freedom to do and to act----a freedom from what impairs freedom. The Civil Rights struggle, with its sit-ins and demonstrations and picketing; symbolizes the way in which freedom is attained by rebellion. This is an important way to freedom when others deny human rights. The truth is that there is another kind of freedom too---just as desirable. This is the freedom within a world, a freedom that cannot be won by rebellion. This was never so clearly illustrated for me as it was when the Jewish Rabbi from Kansas returned from a long night's visit in the white community of Hattiesburg. Confronting the southern Negroes who were with us, the Rabbi declared: "You are the ones who are really free." And he was right. The Negroes were free from fear and hatred and free within themselves to love and to forgive. This kind of freedom is not won by action. It comes through acceptance and resignation. Furthermore, this kind of freedom is not mere undisciplined submission. It requires discipline to accept the structures within which one's life is given, which are unalterable. Such resignation, or acceptance, or submission is the way in which one comes to live with imperfections. Just this morning, I found a theological message for today in the comic strip, Peanuts by Schulz. The strip shows Linus with a yoke on his neck, and Charley Brown says, "What in the world is that?" Linus replies, "This is a "yoke" ...I'm going to use it for a special school report. " Linus continues,"I'm going to tell how the yoke is a symbol of subjection of one individual to another, as Esau to Jacob(Genesis 27:40)." He goes on, "Then I'll tell how the yoke was sometimes placed literally on the neck of a person reduced to submission...my reference will be Jeremiah 28:10." Linus goes on and on, "Then I'll tell of the yoke placed on Israel by Solomon and Rehoboam (I Kings 12:9) and wind up by talking about the yoke of sin suggested in Lamentations 1:14 and the "easy" yoke of Matthew 11:29." He finally concludes, "I think that will cover the subject pretty well...." Charley Brown stands in a daze. Then he turns and shouts at Linus, who has walked away, " What about the "yoke of inferiority" you've given me?!" This is precisely the point. We must accept some things about ourselves which cannot be changed, and this is the way one checks his own vocational ambitions.

To be sure, there are dangers here too. We may and do make mistakes about what we can and cannot alter. Still, the strange thing is that acceptance of something as unalterable often alters it. In Reinhold Niebuhr's words, to have "The serenity to accept thethings I cannot change" often ends up as the condition of change. How often in the last 12 years I have seen persons rage at terminal illness. One lady who will always live in my memory fought her death for months. She finally came to a mood of resignation and acceptance, and she helped her family and friends watching her die. She never accepted her death piously, but accept it she did, with grace and blessing to others. There are other times than death when resignation brings us to self-know-ledge. The act of waiting has much to teach if we understand that the Christian life is more than rebellion. The Christian learns by waiting, by acceptance, by resignation, to use rebellion as a means to restructuring society.

The choice before the Christian does not lie between conformity on one hand and beatnikism on the other. Either choice would resolve the tension. The Christian stance lives with the tension expressed in the Gethsemane story. One sentence by Bonhoeffer deserves our continuing consideration. Its significance to us is almost inexhaustible. He said: "Man is challenged to participate in the sufferings of God at the hand of a godless world." The man who loves God and loves the world enough to do this must know how to rebel, how to fight the world, how not to lose his soul to the world's allure. He will also need to learn the discipline of resignation and waiting, for all things do not come quickly or easily.

William Hamilton has said that the Christian today can choose between an open and a concealed break with the culture in which he lives. The open break, the act of rebellion, has great attractions. It is dramatic, visible, easily praised. It can be symbolized. For example, the "inner city ministry" seems to be the only one of interest to many seminarians today. Here is the break, open and dramatic.

But there can be a concealed break as well, and it is more difficult in a good many ways. There is the danger in it that we go on as before, thinking that our bad thoughts about culture are enough. Must we not say, then, immediately that since a concealed break is not so dramatic and visible, it must take on some visible form? Words are not enough for those who conclude that the open break is not the only way to break from the trap. They too must participate in the sufferings of God--- in this case not by escaping from the broken world by rebellion but by returning to it, making an inner break with it, suffering patiently its sorrows and joys.

9-27-64

-4-

Neither way is better. Both are necessary. Both are true ways of salvation. We shall always need the open, radical, dramatic break with the broken world. But that is not the only way. The way of resignation--the less obvious, less dramatic, less noticeable way-----may be the more difficlut way, and it can involve genuine courage. It can be the suffering in the world that searches and waits for a break, a way out, a way to life abundant. If we seem to commend it more than rebellion, let us hope that it is due to the fact that rebellion has spokesmen enough in our day----and because we can undertake the discipline of resignation in the conviction that it is one way in which we can think, live, and obey God. Not our will, but His be done.

38. 5/14/63   **You Was Never My Age**   Color Day

During the month before this sermon, Birmingham, Alabama, developed into the focus of civil rights sit-ins. Martin Luther King, Jr., was put behind bars, from where he issued his *Letters from a Birmingham Jail*. Television screens became filled with appalling scenes of Birmingham Alabama's Commissioner of Public Safety Bull Connor's fire hoses turned violently on demonstrating men, women, and children. Often it appeared that there was a world of "them" and a world of "us."

Part of the usual estrangement of students is that they (we?) believe that parents and professors and college administrators don't know what it's like to be "us." They were never "us" even as this Color Day weekend was not the same as Color Day weekends a generation ago. This sermon agrees with that perspective in the sense that the world was different for "us" as students then, even as it is different for "them" as students now. Both worlds can be uncomfortable.

After Rev. Asbury makes use of the quotation from *West Side Story* (see introduction to Sermon #16) as his title, he invokes Paul, who enjoined his church in Corinth: "We are afflicted in every way, but not crushed; perplexed, but not driven to despair; persecuted, but not forsaken; struck down, but not destroyed…" (II Corinthians 4:8-9). Resolution for the discomfort of estrangement comes, in part, from *transference*. That is, the Christian stance includes the responsibility to transfer the teachings of Jesus "beyond [church] walls into a world that is not its age…to live in and know the age that is new and revolutionary." Even in a world of revolution and ferment, the Christian stance includes "the responsibility to support all attempts to make this desperate world more just and righteous." Transference includes, but is not limited to, reframing lessons across space and time. Transference in a Christian setting also means accepting the model of Jesus and applying it to contemporary, secular problems – which also means not giving up or giving in.

Westminster Presbyterian Church
Wooster, Ohio

Rev. Beverly Asbury, Minister
May 14, 1963

"YOU WAS NEVER MY AGE"
II Corinthians 4: 1-12

The world we live in never stands still. It is never the same. The changes of the present time are almost unprecedented in history, and our very social foundations seem to be cracking under the explosive forces of the 20th Century. Whatever one's convictions, he can hardly doubt that the events of Birmingham have momentous significance for our future as a nation, and he may well suspect that recent events are only a prelude to a more revolutionary period in race relations in our land. What ought to be equally clear to us is that the direction taken by Christians during this time will also have far-reaching effects not only for the future of the Church but also for the future of mankind. All around us voices tell of change and call us to change.

Perhaps most of you have seen that most exciting musical by the name of West Side Story. The music by Leonard Bernstein is magnificent, but not the type we usually whistle. The scene is harsh and crude. The story is an old one, an adaptation of Romeo and Juliet. And yet it is a new story-- the story of ferment and revolt, a story as close to us as the events of recent weeks.

Neither the language nor the characters of West Side Story can be regarded as typical of most American towns or neighborhoods, except for one scene; in fact, one line of dialogue. The scene is a small drug store on the West Side of New York City. The Jets, a gang of native New Yorkers, and the Sharks, a gang of Puerto Ricans, have decided to fight it out--to have a rumble. The Jets use the drug store as their headquarters. In this particular scene, three Jets are present, Baby John, A-rab, and Action, along with Doc, who runs the store. The time is midnight and Doc speaks: "Curfew, gentlemen. You should be home in bed." A-rab replies: "We're gonna have a war council here, Doc. We're gonna decide on weapons for a big time rumble." The startled Doc answers: "Weapons. Rumble. Couldn't you play basketball... Why, when I was your age....." At this point, Action breaks in: "When you was my age, when my old man was my age, when my brother was my age; old man, you was never my age. The sooner you creeps get hip to that, the sooner you'll dig us."
Every parent or teacher has heard himself say at some time: "When I was your age...". And every non-parent and non-teacher here will some day hear himself say the same thing. This is a line of dialogue that belongs to the human drama. But the really important words of the dialogue are those delivered by Action:"You was never my age." These are important words, because they are true. They are true of our whole world. That sentence is true of you and me. It is true for the marchers in Birmingham. It is true for the students of colleges and universities. It will even be true when the students here this morning sometime say to some younger person, "when I was your age", and they will be wrong. No one will ever be your age again. It may very well not be a better world each day, each generation, but it is a new world, a changing world, a world that is not our age.

One idea of our world has been expressed by Lawrence Ferlinghetti, a "beatnik" poet, in "The World is a Beautiful Place."(adapted)

"The world is a beautiful place
to be born into
if you don't mind happiness

```
          not always being
          so very much fun
if you don't mind a touch of hell
          now and then
just when everything is fine
          because even in heaven
they don't sing
          all the time.

The world is a beautiful place
          to be born into
if you don't mind some people dying
          all the time
or maybe only starving
          some of the time
which isn't half so bad
          if it isn't you.

Oh, the world is a beautiful place
          to be born into
if you don't much mind
          a few dead minds
in the higher places
          or a bomb or two
now and then
          in your upturned faces
or such other improprieties
          as our Name Brand society
is prey to
          with its men of distinction
and its men of extinction
          and its priests
And other patrolmen
          and its varied segregations
and congressional investigations
          that our fool flesh
          is heir to

Yes, the world is the best place of all
          for a lot of such things as
making the fun scene
          and making the love scene
and making the sad scene
          and singing low songs and having inspirations
and walking around
          looking at everything
and smelling flowers
          and even thinking
and kissing people and
          waving hats and dancing
 and going swimming in rivers
          or picnics
          in the middle of summer
and just generally
          'living it up'
Yes
     but right in the middle of it
Comes the smiling  mortician".
```

Such a harsh and pessimistic description of the world we live in may not
be to our liking. But our world is not a very funny place. It is different than
it has ever been. The world of the present students on this Color Day Weekend is
not the same "age" of the world of the Color Day of former students. Some of us
belong to a generation of students--not so old--that didn't know television and
can even remember when families talked to each other. Now there is a generation
which has a history that includes only a cold war, a 'police action' in Korea,
more cold war, Cuba, Laos, Berlin, the threat of Communism, the threat of extreme
right-wing groups that, in mis-guided 'patriotism', find a 'red' in every pulpit
and under every rock and behind every demonstration for equal rights. When Action
says "You was never my age", he was quite correct. We, some of us, can remember
another world--a non-pushbutton world, a world free from the threat of atomic, hydrogen, and neutron bombs. Some here can remember another, far less complicated
world, when the Amish were not the only ones who used horses and buggies.

But we have never been the age of the students of the present generation.
A recent article, "College Morals Mirror Our Society", by Grace and Fred Hechinger,
appeared in the April 14 issue of The NEW YORK TIMES MAGAZINE, and it pointed out
some of the basic changes in the American social scene. No words were minced over
the fact that student attitudes are today pitted against the traditional restrictions and exhortations of college life. Those who read the article could not miss
the point that students were saying: "You was never my age." Indeed, many of them
had greater social freedom in high school than they have in college, and it profits nothing to point out that the college rules of today would have seemed like
'libertine idealism' 20 years ago. The youth of today are not 'my age'. To quote
the TIMES' article: "Young men and women today have been reared under pressures,
exerted from an increasingly early age, to render them socially 'mature' long before their time, with the accent on physical rather than intellectual and moral
growing up."

Those of this age know a world of early dating and going steady, teen-age joy
rides, unchaperoned parties, and loud music. This age asks for the privilege of
entertaining visitors of the opposite sex in dormitory rooms, and one is far less
than honest if he does not recognize that sex is the predominant interest and
motive in seeking a change. Those who differ, who were never this age, are generally dismissed as "Victorian", "puritanical", and "prudish".

But what of the Church? Where does it stand in this world that is so new?
What does the Christian faith have to say to those who are not of its age? What
stand does it take in a revolutionary period?

First, the Church needs to reassert the truth and reality of the Christian
faith--both so desperately needed by those living in a new age. With Paul we can
say that we never lose heart in the great task that has been given to us, even
in the face of attacks that confront us with our own irrelevance and hypocrisy.
When our motives are misinterpreted, when our actions are misconstrued, and when
our words are twisted out of their real meaning, we dare to remember that we have
a treasure--in earthen vessels. For us, the treasure is more important than the
vessel. What is said about us is far less important than the power and mercy of
God at work in and through us. The truth of the faith lies in saying and living:
We are sore pressed at every point, but not hemmed in. We are at our wit's end,
but never at our hope's end. We are persecuted by men, but never abandoned by God.
We are knocked down, but never knocked out. In our bodies we have to run the same
risk of death as Jesus Christ did, so that in our body the same life as Jesus
lived may be clear for all to see.

-4-

Nevertheless, the world that is not our age still pleads with those who call themselves Christian. In effect, the world says to us: Quit hiding behind legalistic defenses--rules that reflect another age. Come out from behind the crass gold of your institutionalized cross. Leave it behind on the scrap heap of worn-out art objects. Come out and come down boldly singing your Golgotha where it can be heard, where it counts. Quit evading the world by speaking as if another day had lingered on; speak to this day where people are no more confined by the four walls of the church.

The world says, then, about what Paul says: that if a man would share the life of Christ, he must share the risks of Christ, that if a man wishes to live with Christ, he must be ready to die with Christ. In a world that is not our age, we are called to be men and women who respond to the Gospel--secular men and women constituted by the Holy Spirit to be servants to the world, earthen vessels bodying forth a great power of life. We are like pots and pans; not pretty but useful not admired except for what they hold. God has called us to be men and women who will live in a new age in order to announce to this age what the LIVING GOD is doing in this new age and what God requires of us in it. We are God's instruments for his work. Our work is done in the world but it is God's work. A year ago, Vassar's president Sarah Blanding told students that, if they wished to indulge in premarital sex relations or excessive drinking, they must withdraw from school. She created a furor, and, though a majority of students supported her, it was a small majority. The minority attitude was: "You was never my age." It was expressed: "students (are) mature enough to regulate their own personal lives." This view grows out of a moral relativism, a nihilism, and it rejects any absolute standards. Correct: I am not that age and hope never to be. But, the Christian must be careful not to equate his moral standards with certain legalistic expressions of the mores. Yet he stands ever ready to remind the world constantly through his thinking and acting of the costly grace by which Christ has freed the world from false gods. The Christian confesses the need for moral standards, regardless of whether others violate them in private. He refuses to accept as right "What a majority does or what the 'elite' practices."

To put it another way, the Church of 1963 has the responsibility to go beyond its walls into a world that is not its age. The Christian has the responsibility to live in and know the age that is new and revolutionary. He has no excuse to stand apart from it. He even has the responsibility to support it in all its attempts to make this desperate world more just and righteous. He may even have to get his hands "dirty" in the process. But, the Christian must also strongly oppose immoral behavior--as much so in personal relations as in race relations. There are times when Christians are ready to accept that "You was never my age." He must stand in the world without being of it--because he knows that one reason why he can never be totally of this age is that he belongs first to the age of Christ. If we have the complete conviction that what happens to us is happening literally for Christ's sake, then we can face and bear the rejection of that very world we should like so much to help.

We live in a desperate world, a world of revolution and ferment. It is so uncertain that our very existence is uncertain. But we can be sure that if we are hard-pressed on every side, we are never hemmed in, bewildered but never at hope's end; hunted but never abandoned to fate, struck down but not left to die. Whatever our world is, it is still the world of Jesus Christ.

39. 5/8/66   Do We Count?   Color Day

Estrangement is a common theme in Biblical literature (*see also Sermon #45 below*). It permeates Adam and Eve's separation from God in the story of the Garden of Eden. It emanates from the lips of Jesus on the cross when he asks why God has abandoned him. Estrangement is emotionally powerful. Estranged people – the dispossessed, the minorities, the poor, the immigrants, the refugees, the needy, the orphaned, and the sick – become marginalized. Students and teenagers can feel themselves estranged…suddenly alone, powerless, and among the forsaken and abandoned. Marginalized people often distrust the "system" and when they act, they frequently rebel against it.

Rev. Asbury picked Biblical references usually used around Palm Sunday and Easter (see Sermons #34 and 35). Here he uses them to show the path toward finding meaning in a world that presses in with large problems. The path can be hard and the price high, but one "counts" when one selects a cause, estimates the cost, pays it, and moves toward achievement.

This sermon is the fourth of four on the cultivation of inner guidelines.

Westminster Presbyterian Church
Wooster, Ohio
Rev. Beverly Asbury, Minister
May 8, 1966

DO WE COUNT?
Luke 7: 36-8: 3; Mark 16: 9-11

Yesterday, as most of you participated in or witnessed the Color Day spectacle,
I was hearing a report on poverty in Ohio. We were informed that the Ohio Legisla-
ture set minimum standards for "welfare" in the State in 1959. Since that time the
State of Ohio has never met more than 75% of those minimum standards for decent living. Today, due to inflation and the rising cost of living, it meets about 60% of
the minimum. Those who receive "welfare" feel imprisoned by this failure, by unjust
laws, and especially by our myths that they are lazy, slovenly, slothful. They have
to live with our distrust and on pennies a day for food. And they rightfully want
to know----do their lives count? Do we care what happens to them? Will we discard
them on the trash pile of our myths and reject the value of their lives? Do they
count?

Now, this is not a sermon about poverty; it is about the value of human life.
The subject of man's identity and meaning presses upon great numbers of thoughtful
people, and the concern is more than a fad. No one is proposing facile answers.
In fact, answers of any kind seem to be in short supply. Everyone has an analysis,
but one has much rougher sledding in finding constructive proposals. Indeed, it
seemed to me that our Second Centennial Scholar, Lewis Mumford, had difficulties
proposing even the way to answers. When it came down to the meaning of man's life,
he could tell us at length that something was wrong and what he thought had brought
it about. He protested that he hoped, but his tone showed little of it. The machine has taken over, he said, and in this mad culture man doesn't count.

Well, that really is the question--does man count? Do we count? Do you count?
Do I count? In other words, does our life have any meaning at all?

Dr. Erick Fromm, the psychoanalyst, spoke to this question a few weeks ago
(The NY Times, April 14, 1966). He was speaking to fellow professionals when he
observed: "We are too exclusively concerned with what is produced by the family or
by the vicissitudes of the instincts and not concerned enough with the pathology of
normalcy--the drive to conform--that prevents a man from knowing his own fears, his
angers, his hopelessness." Fromm pointed out that sex and love are less repressed
now and have become a part of the consumer culture. "Sex is something to 'get',
something cheap and relatively accessible, and love is something that, if you don't
'get'it, you're deprived, like a baby without milk". He then said that what was
truly repressed today was "the underlying anxiety, depression, loneliness, boredom
and pain about the meaninglessness of life.........A man sits in front of a bad television program and does not know that he is bored; he reads of the Vietcong casualties and does not recall the teachings of religion; he learns of the dangers of nuclear holocaust and does not feel fear; he joins the rat race of commerce, where
personal worth is measured in terms of market values, and is not aware of his anxiety. Ulcers speak louder than the mind.".......Theologians and philosophers have
been saying for a century that God is dead, but what we confront now is the possibility that man is dead, transformed into a thing, a producer, a consumer, an idol-
ator of things."

Our boredom finds expression in so many different ways. Recently, I read a
novel entitled THE STERILE CUCKOO. It was one of the funniest novels that I've
read in a long time. The novel portrays two college kids who give themselves to
each other, but they are giving before either has come to understand who he is and
what his life is all about. They engage in a number of hilarious events but one is

more struck by the sadness of two great kids who lust for life, who live it zestful-ly, but who cannot reach across their individual and mutual emptiness. It is when they attempt to be "serious", when they recognize the emptiness of their drinking and sex life that things fall apart. Life has no meaning for them beyond that level --not yet anyway. What was marvelous was their play--as joyful play always is. It was an attempt to break through to meaning. However, they were "playing for keeps" before either had a right to do so. Therefore, as is generally the case, it was not for keeps at all. The novel ends a year after these kids have parted. A note from the girl tells the boy that by the time he reads it she will have taken her life. His first instinct is to write for her hometown paper to see if she did it. But he doesn't. And the novel ends with his feeling that maybe she'll turn up later in his life.

One is tempted to make too much out of the ending. For me, I'll let it stand as an enigma--as to whether he cared at all. What seems more certain is that this young man, like so many others like him, will settle himself down into the "pathol-ogy of normalcy". There's no indication that he's come any closer to meaning than before. Not even the spontaneous joy of this affair has permeated his life, and one suspects that his life will not count for much. At least, I would have felt bet-ter if the novelist had grasped what Fromm meant when he said: "If enough people be-come aware of their shared misery, they will probably affect changes. Anger may often be less sick than adjustment."

Another novel that approaches the same question: "Do we count?", was the winner of last year's Harper award--P. S. WILKINSON. It's about a young Yale graduate who spends his immediate post-college years in the Army, as many of you may also have to do. After his discharge he goes through the throes of deciding how to spend his life. Obviously, this places him not among the Big Men On Campus, the "take-charge guys" who have never doubted their destiny, or, more likely, have been afraid to expose their doubts even to themselves. Nor does he belong to the "poor boy" group which works its way through college with the goal of worldly success in mind. No, P. S. Wilkinson belongs to a small but growing number of students who come from mid-dle class homes and are "faced with the outward life-pattern of their parents" and can't stand the prospect, as Professor Kenneth Kenniston as expressed it in the re-cent issue of the Yale Alumni Magazine.

P. S. Wilkinson is not awkward; he doesn't lack ambition; he has been and could be popular. He simply does not know how to count in this life, and he knows that the way of his parents and most of his successful friends does not count! P. S. Wilkinson's great sin in the eyes of his father and peers is "underachievement". He is capable of simple personal expressions of moral indignation. He resents conven-tional adulthood. He finds it difficult to "weld any connection" (as Professor Ken-niston states it) between his own personal search for meaning and the continual .....pressures he faces. And he sees no sense in "achievement". Here again, the novel closes on something less than a clear note. Whatever answer P. S. Wilkinson has found appears more likely to be personal and existential rather than universally. applicable to others of his generation. One would wish that personal answers, which are so necessary, would also be personal in more than an individual sense.

Yet, over and over again, we learn that men today want to count. Peter Drucker discusses that in the May issue of HARPER'S. He and others like him, such as Rich-ard L. Cutler, vice president for student affairs at the University of Michigan, agree that today's students are antagonistic to the 'system', to the bureaucratic organization. They distrust or reject the tedious process of solving problems "ac-cording to the rule", because they suspect that they count less than the "rules". They don't trust the system, especially when it seems that those running it place the system above personal interests. They discount pleas for order as manipulatory, and they call for immediate solutions without really knowing what solutions they are willing to accept as right and just.

What really is at stake is the desire to count for something. In a world of ugliness, fearing the threats of Vietnam and China as well as the explosiveness of the racial and urban and technological revolutions, facing man's beastiality; seeing men starve when it is not necessary; one wonders what one's life means and how one can count! As one man has put it (The NY Times Magazine 4/24/66,P.69), "the load on single men will grow. For the size of the circle each man stands in as a single self is not only diminishing, but the space enclosed is filling up." Reinhold Niebuhr, who has proved to be right about so many things, put it well when he warned thirty years ago that we could not preoccupy ourselves with social problems to the exclusion of the personal dimension of man's life.

In this light Drucker and others see a new personalism on the rise. It carries with it both great threat--if it forgets the social problems of our day in its preoccupation with the personal--and great promise--if it can help men to come to a new personal identity in this mass world in which we live. In the search for a new personal meaning, for a way out of boredom and loneliness into real human identity and commitment, we can expect false starts and wrong-headed moves. Those who are today using LSD may often be irresponsible thrill seekers, misguided cultists, and persons with psychological problems, but others are sincerely seeking greater meaning than they currently have. They refuse to accept the absurdities of life around them, and so they take chances on side-tracking the mind and inducing psychosis. This cannot be condoned, but it can be understood that some people who don't count are looking for a way into meaning and out of life as it now stands.

One could go on and on analyzing and detailing. We could describe the student who "is too smart to fight" and who opts out of the draft as a CO on purely "personal" reasons. He's looking for meaning too, because he does not find it in "Vietnam". He wants his life to count for more. And that is true too for the activists. He commits himself only on specific issues. His action as often as not is a simple personal expression, ethically or religious motivated, by which he seeks meaning. The activist has an answer, "Go to the ghetto, the core of the city." Yesterday, it was "Go to Mississippi". Tomorrow, it may be "Go to Washington". Then it will be elsewhere that he calls us to march. He may not have faced his inner dilemmas emotionally, but he surely expresses his conviction that one must begin with action, not introspection.

God help the church and all its members if it does not identify today with all these men and women who search for meaning, who seek to have their lives count. God help us all if we cannot spot this struggle for what it is: an attempt to develop what we have traditionally called the "spiritual life" of man. It's in a new guise; the words and expressions are different, but the struggle is the same--to be what God intended us to be, to have a sense of worth, the feeling that we count. The hope here is to be able to feel, think, and express what is real in oneself and in society. I submit that it is the business of the Church to awaken persons, to arouse their consciences before catastrophe comes crashing down upon their heads.... in order that men may yet turn from unworthy pursuits and find value and wholeness.

It is well for us to remember, as we consider our contemporary problems of personal meaning, that Jesus first appeared on Easter to a woman from whom he had cast seven devils. His original encounter with her should be enough to indicate that he was concerned to help Mary Magdalene face reality. In this perspective, Christian religion should never be an attempt to help people escape reality. The ability to count in life does not lie in a false assessment of one's abilities and competency. One may count more when he accepts the true situation, sees what he has to offer, and knows that these are many gifts. Religious concern, as Anton Boisen has said, appears where men are facing the facts and making an attempt at constructing something from them. He says that the religious man is one who no matter how morally unworthy he may have been is moving to become better. The religious man has to struggle, as it were.

"This woman to whom Jesus appeared first on Easter may be taken as the representative of struggling humanity. Not of the perfect, not of the correct, not of the wise was she, but of those who in the face of odds are moving to become better." To count. "The divine (the meaning of life) comes first, not to the perfect, not to the strong, but, to those in whom the need is greatest and the struggle hardest." (Boisen in the C.T.S. Register, Feb. 1966) And in that struggle, the Mary Magdalenes the P.S. Wilkinsons, the seeking students may get some glimpses of truth which are hidden from the wise and the prudent. They may learn what it means to count while those who already count their possessions as life itself will find that they have lost their own souls.

Jesus appeared to Mary Magdalene from whom he had cast out seven devils, because perhaps her mind was sensitized through inner conflict. She was able to perceive a presence that others could not. She had suffered and struggled. And she had learned through it all to love. And perhaps Jesus appeared to her because she loved much, not necessarily a personal love for him, but because she was one of those who love righteousness and put up a determined struggle against odds for the attainment of the good life. Again, I submit that the Church has the message which goes to the heart of the problem with which persons are faced----the insight that God is love and that love is the fulfilling of the law.

"To be cut off from those who for us are most worthy of life.....means death just as truly as for a cell to be cut off from the organism to which it belongs. Such estrangement is the root evil in most cases of mental illness, and salvation is to be found through the re-establishment of right relationship with the undying love manifested in Jesus. This takes place whenever we are able with Paul to make the discovery that in the eyes of the love that rules the universe any man is good and worthy of honor in so far as he is moving to become better." The people "on welfare" in Ohio are planning a march in June, a march to Columbus to ask the State to meet its own minimum standards. But the most important thing is that these people want to become better, to give their children a chance to grow, to count for something of value in this life. We in the Church can either condemn this march as irresponsible or listen to the marchers, learn from them, and respond as fellow human beings. We may learn to forgive and to be forgiven. "This is the good news set forth in the New Testament, that for all who are willing to come to the light, there is forgiveness and life. Such a discovery sets men free from the tyranny of the standardized and makes them one with the fellowship which is striving for the attainment of that which is not yet, but ought to be, both in personal character and social order." (Quotes are from Anton Boisen in the Chicago Theological Seminary Register)

Perhaps this is what it means to learn again from Jesus what it means to count in life and how we can count. While it surely means increasing your capacity to think critically, because man is empty when he ceases to think, because an empty man can hardly expect to meet the living God--while we shall have to learn to question and seek, that in itself is not enough. What more we need...can be called spiritual struggle, a heightened sensitivity to the reality and presence of love. We shall both be relearning a great lesson about our lives and learning it in significantly new forms. The role of powerless and suffering love will be recognized again in shaping our values.

We look to this with hope, for it came to Mary Magdalene, a lost soul possessed with seven devils, who learned to love righteousness and to struggle for a good life. We look with hope as men possessed by demons of our day in technological and totalitarian guise, ready also to learn what is right and worthy of human life, ready also to make sensible judgments about the kind of world God intends for us to live in, ready to count in making those judgments stick--no matter the sacrifice. For greater love has no man than this, that he learn to count by laying down his life for his neighbor. And he who would lose his life for Christ's sake will find life and meaning as he never knew it before.

40. 10/13/63 The Foundation of Christian Ethics – A Pattern for Life

This sermon begins a group of nine that describes how a Christian stance copes with specific problems in the secular world.

As originally delivered by Rev. Asbury, this sermon was part of a series with its own particular premise. That series is not reproduced in full here. Chronologically, this sermon followed Sermon #29 in this Cycle, and that one fit better where it is in the Cycle for thematic reasons. This sermon and the one that follows immediately (Sermon #41) take on the issue of secular engagement. The premise is that Jesus did not face away from the world, and neither should we. Christians do not have to approve of the world 100% in order to live productively in it. There is humility in dealing with things that are less than perfect (see notes for Sermon #36 on the Biblical reference in Matthew about being perfect). Consequently, Christian action is not mechanical re-enactment of what Jesus or anyone else has done before us. It is not slavish obedience to rules. Rather, it is the use of inner guidelines to do right things.

Rev. Asbury uses as a partial foundation for this sermon Jesus's approach to ethics from the Sermon on the Mount that ends with Matthew 5:48. He also uses Psalm 51, which is often called the *Miserere*, after its first words, "Have mercy on me...."

A psalm is a poem, typically structured for one verse to express an idea and for the paired verse that follows to restate the same idea in different words. Psalm 51 follows this parallel structure. Psalm 51 in particular has been set to music many times, including in the 1630s by Italian composer Gregorio Allegri. Some 140 years later, in April, 1770, Wolfgang Amadeus Mozart heard Allegri's *Miserere*. The often retold account is that immediately afterwards, 14-year-old Mozart wrote out the entire *Miserere* score from memory. A day or so later, Mozart heard *Miserere* again and returned to his draft score in order to correct a few mistakes.

"A Pattern For Life" III

Westminster Presbyterian Church
Wooster, Ohio
Rev. Beverly Asbury, Minister
October 13, 1963

THE FOUNDATION OF CHRISTIAN ETHICS
Psalm 51
Matthew 5: 21-48

Last week we celebrated the sacrament of Holy Communion. This sacrament is the service of the church which regularly dramatizes for us the story of Jesus Christ --crucified and risen. The truth in Christ is expressed in the service, and it relates us to the truth as we participate in the drama of the liturgy--the "work of the people". For that reason, a conscious attempt was made to provide participation, to make the service a truly "Protestant" one in which we take part and take hold of the truth of God's action.

Of course, the only important thing to some worshippers was that the service took 10 minutes more of their time than they usually give. Certainly that gives others of us the right to wonder out loud if perhaps the symbol of "time" has become more important to us than the symbols of the sacrament. The day may be upon us when the symbols of space capsules, and mushroom clouds, the structures of DNA and ANA molecules, the presence of tail fins and TV screens deserve more of our time than the symbols dramatized in the sacraments. I have no intention of drawing pious moralisms about how much time we give to other things while we set aside a strict 60 minutes a week for the worship of God. However, it does seem clear that the usual symbols of our culture occupy our attention. Yet, are they the symbols by which we desire to live? Are these the symbols which draw us into a relationship of being in the truth?

Do not misunderstand what I am saying! I would not and do not defend symbols for the sake of the symbolism. I have no desire to draw people away from the world. Indeed, I agree with George MacLeod in the point he makes in his story about St. Nicholas Church, high above the Mersey River in Liverpool. The city's commerce moves on the river, and the marketplace is at the river's edge. Up high, the church used to turn its back upon these centers of human toil and finance. The Church seemed to beckon those who entered to direct their gaze to a distant altar shrouded in gloom. But the church was shattered by bombs. Today, in the framework of its ruins, a hut of modern design has appeared--FACING THE OTHER WAY. The former porch is now the chancel, and the backdrop now is a clear view of the river and market place. MacLeod calls this a parable for the modern church. It must turn around and face the common life of men. Instead of drawing men into a quiet sanctuary, it must carry Christ's broken body into the market place. MacLeod simply argues that the cross must not simply be on the steeple but at the center of life--on the town's garbage heap; at the crossroad. He concludes that Christ died "at the kind of place where cynics talk smut, and thieves curse, and soldiers gamble. Besides that is what he died about.....and that is where churchmen should be and what churchmen should be about."

I agree. Evangelism has to do with relating the Gospel to the world. And I do not mean "relating "by using a sneaky strategy to plug religion such as we see in the current United Presbyterian -Stan Freberg commercials--"doesn't it get a litle lonely sometimes, out on that limb without him? Why try and go it alone? The blessings you lose may be your own." Rather, the Gospel has to be related to the world by living in the world as secular men and women who are attempting to respond to God. Christians in the modern world have to "dereligionize" Christianity. To

-2-

do this in our kind of world with our interest in "time" may well require new symbols. To do this in our world of "busyness" may rightly mean new designs, a "facing the other way."

However, to carry MacLeod's story further, we have to recall that what was turned around was still the church. What faced the common life of men had a new orientation, a new bearing, a rediscovered mission. But the center was still the Cross. It was placed in a new position in order that it might still carry the implication of the redemptive power of suffering and love.

The Church must not only turn to the world. It must have something to say to the world; some content, some message to relate to the world.

Now, I find among my non-church friends, even my non-Christian friends, a friendly welcome for a new stance in the Church. They express delight that the Church will face and recognize their world. However, they do not always stand ready to welcome the message which it brings, even when it's "dereligionized." They do not open themselves to the tall order of the New Testament: "Ye, therefore, must be perfect even as your heavenly Father is perfect," no matter how it's stated. Their response is one of "here we go again...a new posture but the same old stuff... We can't be perfect. What are you asking? On one hand, you face our world and take it as it is; on the other, you reject it and call for perfection? Make up your minds; are you Christians going to accept the world or reject it, and separate yourselves from it?"

Well, we Christians want to live in the world, but we cannot approve it when it is less than fully human. We believe this to be God's world and we have no intention of ignoring or escaping it. But we know that we are not of it, and, while, we do not reject the world, we know ourselves to stand under the admonition to transform it. In so far as we are Christians we intend to follow Christ in the world. We live in the world for H is sake, that man may be restored to his true manhood.

For the Christian, this is not an abstraction. Christ was the perfect man. Abstractions will not do, for the Christian is not called to pursue an ideal but to share the achievement, man reconciled to God. We are to love as we have been loved. He asks that we go where He has gone and do as He did. He asks nothing less than self-giving. This is not an ideal: it is an act, a deed. Example: There was something of a family crisis in Wooster recently about which few people knew. Almost by accident, I was involved as a minister, although the people concerned were not members of this church. The crisis concerned neighborhood hostility which was directed at the family because of an action which they had taken. The action, in my eyes, was a Christian one which deserved support. However, the family wished to withdraw in the face of resentment. I asked them not to. They inquired if I expected more of them than I expected of others. Without religiosity, I replied,"Yes", because Jesus promised that we should all have to bear a cross."It was truly meaningful to say the words of Jesus, "In as much as ye have done it unto one of the least of these, ye did it unto Me." To ask them to act in that manner was not abstract. It was "evangelism" --relating the Gospel to the world. That's why we face the world. Yet even that is not enough. Jesus requires not only outward acts of righteousness but also the right inward springs of action. When Jesus asks that we love as we have been loved, it is not enough merely to treat our neighbors rightly. We must also think of them rightly. He forces upon us the insight that hateful and lustful desire are not just unhealthy psychological conditions for the persons who have them: they are wrongs done to the persons toward whom they are directed.

3

Yet there is more to be said to time-bound, time-conscious Christians. And to the worldly-wise, non-Christians. That is, even if we had never heard of Jesus' teaching about love, about inner motives and outward acts, indeed, about perfection, we should still find ourselves under an obligation. We do find ourselves under an impossible demand. It is part of our humanity. Whenever we set any limits to our ultimate moral obligations, we know that we are deceiving ourselves. We know that when we say: "We have done all that we ought to do. We are all that we ought to be", we are deluding ourselves. If Jesus had not taught us that God's will for us is perfection, we could say with some reverence, "Well, He should have." If Christian symbols do not communicate the truth, the symbols may be inadequate, but the truth remains unchanged. The demands for perfection is true; it is strenuous, it is exacting, and it is impossible for finite, sinful men in a finite, sinful world. But it is what God created man to be, even though we find it an impossible demand.

Alright, let us face it as that. The standard of Jesus means that every one of us is in default. None of us can stand this judgment. Even those who have lived an outward life of moral perfection can hardly deny the inner desire for the wrong things. In terms of the teaching of Jesus, who can stand? Who is not guilty of murder? Which of us has not killed something of the spirit of another person through our ego, our rejection, our meanness? Who has never looked lustfully and committed adultery in his heart? Who has not known spiritual and personal divorce from those to whom he was supposedly most committed? Who has never sworn falsely? Can anyone anywhere deny the urge for revenge? How many love their enemies? How many avoid, evade, ignore them!

At this point, we get the ethical teachings of Jesus into perspective if we now understand that He has not offered us detailed guidance for conduct in this or that situation. The Sermon on the Mount is not an iron-clad law, which has the intention of producing a new Pharisaism, more intolerant and intolerable than the old. Again, these dramatic pictures appeal to our conscience by the way of our imagination. They show us true human manhood. They are seemingly harsh and uncompromising demands, but there is the prospect of fulfillment, not because of who we are, but because God is what He is. They lead us, then, not to despair but to repentance, to the gospel of forgiveness. The teachings of Jesus show us forgiveness as the creative power of God, releasing men for action. When perfection is seen in context of love and forgiveness, it represents not the dread of an impossibility so much as it does excitement of unlimited possibilities. Because of this, the Christian does not always have to look for success. He dares to enlist in what men deem to be "lost causes", because he knows that faithfulness and forgiveness weigh far more heavily than failure.

Let us put it this way. God does not ask us to engage in the mechanical imitation of Christ. For example, once the Twelve had lived with Jesus and learned his ways, they were sent out to do things on their own. Each situation in which we live calls for us to act. Each of our situations is unique and demands a unique response. We are not tied hand and foot to a written code, but we are not left alone. The ethical teachings of Jesus do not provide exact rules of behavior in particular situations, but they set before us the ethical task which is obligatory upon us as Christians in the world.

The Christian is called to follow Jesus. That is the Foundation of Christian ethics. But we must then bring a creative initiative to the task of living. God gives us the freedom to deal constructively and imaginatively with the problems of

-4-

our times. That's what it means to be "secular" --to live in the world where Christ was crucified. That's what it means to be "Christian"--responding to the Gospel in the world. That is our "liturgy"--our work--to live in the world. Not "to serve time" but to carry reconciliation into the market place. That is what time is for-- not to "get it over with", but to "get with it." The goal of perfection, then, is not abstract, remote, removed. It is to be like Christ, fully human as He was human, reconciled to God. It is the impossible possibility. Impossible because of who we are. Possible because of who God is, and what He has done. Our ethic derives its content, its form its authority from Him who died for the world. Those who feel its force most keenly are the ones who belong to the community of faith, which belongs to H im, but which faces the world. The Church is not then a "saved remnant"; it is a "saving remnant."

The Christian ethic is a living, growing thing. "Be perfect" refers to the present. "Love as I have loved you" extends from the past into the present and until the end of time. The achievement of the Christian ethic is always something original, unique, new, for it consists not of slavish obedience to rules and laws but of a living relationship to Christ. Christian ethics is active living. It is going to the heart, to the motives, to the core of every person and situation. Christian ethics has the power to respond in terms of feeling, word, and act. It carries with it courage, boldness, creativity. In short, to seek to be perfect, to seek to follow Christ requires a work of art. There is still "time" for that.

41. 10/20/63 The Love of Christ and the Moral Life –A Pattern for Life

<u>End of May</u>

Rev. Asbury refers on the first page of this sermon to a previous sermon, entitled *Law and the Gospel*, one that he says was difficult for him to write. That sermon is found in this Cycle as Sermon #29.

After a spring and summer of racial violence and fire hoses in Mississippi and Alabama, King's *I Have A Dream* speech, the 16th Street Baptist Church bombing, and escalating hostility in Vietnam, Rev. Asbury sought a unifying principle to guide proper action amidst the chaos. On one side was anger and a motivation for action against horrifying inhumanity. On the other side was hope for restraint and a yearning for resolution and peace.

This sermon summarizes the moral principle of a Christian stance: Action through love (*agape*; see Sermon #6). It continues to develop the premise from Sermon #40 that Christian ethics face toward, not away from, the secular world. Christian ethics do not involve a fixed line of behavior or a set of mechanical rules. Being human is a messy business. Did Jesus give us a fixed line of answers to guide us? Rev. Asbury's answer: "…A fixed line is too easy. [With a fixed line] you don't have to face the ambiguities of existence. You just rest on the attributes that we call Christian, and that's that." Instead of a fixed line, Jesus gave us the principle of love to guide action. Asbury contrasts the "religious person" with the "Christian person." This thesis statement appears on the first page, 2nd paragraph of his sermon. The entry to the rest of the sermon becomes visible in his core question that ends the 3rd paragraph.

From the sermon: "[Jesus] lived and died to restore our fallen and lost humanity – to make us fully human by restoring us, by reconciling us to serve our being…." Jesus was human and a friend to sinners. It is from these apparent ambiguities – preparing to risk all in order to rescue, willing to befriend the downtrodden in order to ennoble – that Christian responsibility and moral action flow.

This sermon's supporting passage from John ("Greater love has no man than this, that a man lay down his life for his friends…") is also used in Sermon #24. The connection there was to a specific racial incident. Here, the ethic is generalized for living a moral life. Interestingly, four months after he gave this sermon, Rev. Asbury put his words into action and went to Hattiesburg. See again Sermon #24.

"A Pattern for Life" IV

Westminster Presbyterian Church
Wooster, Ohio
Rev. Beverly Asbury, Minister
October 20, 1963

THE LOVE OF CHRIST AND THE MORAL LIFE
John 14:12-17; 15:12-17

It may not have shown. Perhaps it is better if it did not. But this series of four sermons on the theme, "A Pattern for Life", has come only with the greatest of difficulty. Each one has gone through several rewritings before being preached to you, and the one that seemed to be the least satisfactory, the one on "Law and Gospel", required the most in the way of Biblical and theological concentration. However, the difficulty has arisen in no small way from the fact that I am who I am--one who has come to the Christian faith via the road of great doubt and skepticism. All too often, I find that as soon as my skin has been scratched, the doubt rises to the surface.

Thus, even as a Christian, I have not and I cannot put aside the fact of my being a modern man, and I do not apologize for that. For I am convinced that Christians shall not really be able to get alongside modern man in our world until we stop being "religious" men and start being human men. That is, I am sure that I could have never become a minister if it had not been for those who "dereligionized" Christian- ity and gave me a new understanding of it. I am a Christian because God became a man in Jesus Christ and died for the sake of the world. What God became was man--a human being. What God did was for the world--the secular, the material, the non-religious.

My fear has been that these sermons on morality would appear to be an attempt to make Christians religious. No one has any business making Christianity into reli- gion, for that would mean correcting the work of Christ. Christ did not live and die that we men might be human-plus-something, called religion. Christ lived and died to restore our fallen and lost humanity--to make us fully human by restoring us, by re- conciling us to the source of our being, God himself. Thus, I have been confronted with the question: "Is it legitimate to look for a pattern of Christian living in the closing decades of the twentieth century?" Can we even talk about a pattern for life without being "religious"?

I ask this simply because most people equate the Christian pattern with a fix- ed line. Recently, a student group pushed me hard for a "moral line". They wanted to know what was "right" and what "wrong" without having to make any decision. They wanted to be told. In the face of my unwillingness to give a "line", one responded that she was tempted to be a Roman Catholic, where she would be "told". I am not even sure this is fair to Roman Catholics today. Yet this point is that a fixed line is too easy. You don't have to face the ambiguities of existence. You just rest on the attributes which we call Christian, and that's that. The trouble comes in that these attributes are usually negative: don't drink, don't smoke, don't gamble, don't mow the lawn on Sunday. I suspect, out of experience, doubt, and skepticism, that the desire for a line to follow is also the desire for a mask, a Christian "front" behind which to hide our personality, about which we are not too happy or too sure. Behind the desire to be told may lie the desire to keep a good face on ourselves and show only what is good. How many think that's what it means to be Christian! No wonder we get so depressed in private about the way we carry on in public! Dare we forget that Jesus was the "friend of sinners"!

The guilt under which we labor all too often comes from the belief that there is
a certain way of life which all Christians ought to adopt. Our society usually reinforces this idea through its spokesmen who say that the problems of the world would
be eased if only we would follow the absolutes of the Sermon on the Mount exactly
and point-by-point. We feel guilty even though we know this to be a fruitless admonition. Nevertheless, the religious corner of our otherwise fully secular life keeps
telling us that we need a line, a system, a law. I will not even ask you to excuse
my saying so, but I believe that to be the mere paying of lip-service to God. Those
who talk most about a certain way of life being the only way have turned grace into
law; they have oversimplified complex questions; and they have resolved questions
without having made a personal decision or commitment. They think that in so doing
they have appeased God, and have found a safe haven from the storms of everyday life.
It is amazing, for example, how those who don't drink, who have chosen the way of
voluntary abstenance, feel that alcoholism is not their problem. Those who don't
drink often show no concern for the alcoholic. Yet, it's just as amazing that those
who do drink, who have chosen in good conscience not to abstain, so often ignore the
social consequences of drinking. They too dismiss alcoholism as not being their problem. They can "handle it". Drinkers and non-drinkers make a religious justification of their positions, concerned only about themselves. They forget that they have
social responsibilities no matter their personal habits.

Those of us who have been purged of religiosity know that responsibility can
never be escaped. We know that the easy answers of religion are false. That is why
I have had to struggle so to preach about a pattern for life. I have wanted to avoid
pitfalls. But you certainly have the right to ask that I now draw out for you the
implications of the last three sermons. You have the right to ask me to explicate
what kind of life emerges for the Christian in the last years of the Century, even
if there are no easy answers.

Here, we must repeat what was said in the first sermon. Ethics is not an independent and separate discipline. It grows out of a relationship with God. Ethics
has to do with discipleship--living out the relationship in daily life. Since God
first loves us, we then love Him; the love of God requires that we love others as He
loves them; and as He loves us. Discipleship is the acting out of the relationship,
and we can say then that ethics is the outward manifestation of the inward relationship with God. The Christian faith is God-centered. Christian action arises out of
what God has done. You cannot really talk about the Christian pattern for life, then,
without an acceptance of the way of life which Jesus teaches and exemplifies.

Having accepted Christ means that we now understand morality has to do with a
new relationship towards men, created by a new relationship with God. However, we
must also understand that Jesus has not made our moral decisions for us. His example
and precepts must be translated by us into action in our secular lives--in our lives
in the world. Jesus could not have decided every questions for us without robbing
us of our humanity. To be human inevitably involves decision-making. There is always the question: "What should you do?" Again, one of the ways that religion is a
disservice to man lies in its robbing man of the necessity of making decisions.
"Religious man" plays it safe; he has the answers; he never makes a mistake. The
"man in Christ" can never play it safe; he lives with the ambiguities of existence;
he knows that he may be wrong and that his motives may be mixed; he lives by grace
in a relationship with God. John Hospers in a new book puts a theoretical question:
To relieve all hunger in India for a day, would you be willing to walk down the
street naked in broad daylight for two hours (or until police caught you) without
explanation to anyone then or in the future? The point is not so much the action.
The point is simply that the Christian cannot count on his own righteousness or rightness; he counts on God's forgiveness. The "religious man" attempts by rules and

regulations to mend the manners of mankind and ends up only treating the symptoms of man's predicament. The "Christian man" must forever be translating the Law of Christ the love of God, into concrete practical decisions by moving beyond self-love into a relationship of love in depth in his own situation. How can anyone tell you how to love? You love as you have been loved. The "religious man" concentrates on himself-- on his goodness and his salvation. The "Christian man" lives for others, for the moral ideal lies not in a code or social order--it lies in a life where love to God and man is the spring of every thought and word and action.

Dietrich Bonhoeffer wrote in his LETTERS AND PAPERS FROM PRISON(April 30, 1944): "I often ask myself why a Christian instinct frequently draws me more to the religion-less than to the religious, by which I mean not with any intention of evangelizing them but rather, I might almost say, 'in brotherhood'. While I often shrink with religious people from speaking of God by name--because that Name somehow seems to me here not to ring true, and I strike myself as rather dishonest (it is especially bad when others start talking in religious jargon: then I dry up almost completely and feel somehow oppressed and ill at ease)--with people who have no religion I am able on occasion to speak of God quite openly and as it were naturally."

So often I feel the same way. This is what I call the secularization of our-selves. It is the recognition that there can be no line, no formula for relating to people. There is Love; there are the Laws of God. But we must translate them by loving and relating; by taking each persons as he is. When we do that we find a kind of liberation, a new freedom--perhaps a conversion. Morality cannot be thought a burden when it is so great a joy. We discover that we Christians are not different from other men. Indeed, we share with non-Christians a common humanity. The point at which we are different is that we know the Gospel and that we stand ready to relate in love to others.

We can share with each other the insights we have gained through experience of relating. But we must always remember that Christ's Pattern for Life is love and that the patterns we draw forth must be our own--ever new and fresh as each situation is itself unique. In each situation we must weigh up, without sentimentality or ro-manticism, the pattern of living we must exhibit there. There can be no generaliza-tions. We must play it,if not by ear, then by openness to the grace of God. Each Christian provides his own content from his own rapport with the world around him. Jesus said: "Greater works than these will he do..." In keeping his commandments, we go beyond where he went. His Spirit is present with us in each new situation, but the decisions are ours-- new, unique, particular, imaginative--for this is the world in which we live.

In this sermon so far, I have stressed the radical openness which a Christian must have toward the world. Christians must be open to the future; to the world, to their neighbors. Now, I must stress again that the only real openness comes from a committment to Jesus Christ. He is the fulfillment of the Law. He is the way, the truth, and the life. He embodies love. He is our peace and our reconciliation.

No Christian can do what this sermon ha' advocated doing in the world in a non-religious way unless he rests on the ultimate love of God in Christ. We cannot ope--rate this way without the knowledge of love and forgiveness. We have not chosen this way; we have been chosen by Christ for it. He has chosen us to bear fruit--by loving one another. Bonhoeffer said that the Christian must have a "secret discipline". He never elaborated what he meant. I think that he meant an inner commitment to Christ. to bring the fundamental principles of the Gospel to bear on human situations. For

-4-

it to be secret means so linking oneself to Christ that it does not automatically cut you off from men as the old patterns did. We do what we do then, as Hospers' question makes clear: we do what we have to do without explanation. Acting in love, we do not have to remind others of why we act. We act because we must--without explanation--because God loves us. It means being totally in the world--but never left alone, always armed with Christ's insight into the nature of man and his common life.

This commitment to Christ enables us and binds us to pronounce moral judgments on human conduct--even beyond the Church's membership. When we cease to be "religious", then we can cease making "religious" pronouncements for "religious" people. When we re-enter secular humanity--as God did in Christ--then we can speak relevantly to the world of men and affairs. This we can do when, as secular Christians, we understand that Christ did not give us a specialized code of regulations for a society of optional membership, but instead lived and died for the world. So, when we pronounce judgments, we do so to bear witness to what the Gospel declares about the eternal nature of God as disclosed in Christ, out of which all our moral obligations come.

You may not be satisfied with all this, for you may have expected to see clearly the meaning of a pattern of living in these years. I used to despair when I did not see the results of my work. Now, under God's guidance, I have learned better. We are called only to be faithful, only to love. The results are in God's hands. They are the fruits for His sake. We cannot expect to see the meaning of the political situations in which we are involved, of what our neighbor is up to, of what will come of our efforts. We can only do what we should be content to do: love as Christ loved; serve as Christ served; let our lives be hidden in Christ as His is hidden in God's.

42. 4/24/66   The Coming Agony

Chronologically this sermon existed in the middle of the turmoil of the 1960s. Although probably not specifically intended to do so, it stands as a forecast of the world that the about-to-graduate Class of '66 would face. Some of the turmoil depicted in the sermon is specific to the Presbyterian church, but the message has a broader impact. It asks the question, amidst conditions of societal difficulty and distress, should individuals and the church, at one extreme, turn inward to find solace in a "churchy church" (see particularly Sermon #7) or, at the other extreme, "take the teachings of Jesus beyond [church] walls into a world that is not its age" (see especially Sermon #38)? Whereas this sermon predicts that the coming social changes will be difficult – even agonizing – it is unlikely that the predicted time scale for the agony was seen to extend into the next century, which is now 50 years later. Nevertheless, the social issues pictured in this sermon are the same today: race, injustice, poverty, ideology, territory, immigration, and war. Regardless of the passage of 50 years, the insights in the sermon are prescient. Solutions may appear to be ambiguous, and they definitely are not easy. Nevertheless, there is a moral imperative here, and to *not* act – that is, to remain a slave to past errors – is to bring about even more, prolonged agony.

Two Biblical passages are used in this sermon. The Matthew reference raises the question of authority for undertaking proper actions. Does moral backing come from a set of authoritative rules, the observance of which provides justification? Or does moral backing come from an inner perspective of responsibility, specifically the model provided by Jesus? Rev. Asbury contends that the second option prevails.

The second Biblical passage comes from I Peter. This is a letter written in the late-middle first century to be delivered to several churches in Asia Minor that were being harassed by Rome. The authorship of the letter has been debated…maybe Peter, more likely an aide or emissary. Whoever wrote it, the message in I Peter is to persevere in the midst of difficuly…"to keep the faith, baby." *

*(The phrase was actually uttered by Adam Clayton Powell in January, 1967.)

WESTMINSTER PRESBYTERIAN CHURCH
Wooster, Ohio
Rev. Beverly Asbury, Minister
April 24, 1966

THE COMING AGONY
Matthew 21: 23-32;42-46
I Peter 4: 12-19

Signs abound that there is increasing agony today in the life of the Church.
The evidence comes not only from this country but word from Thailand, Korea, and India indicates that the agony has a deep relation to the rapidly changing social orders in which men today are living. The conflict between the ways of the past and
the uncharted ways of the emerging world would be real with or without the Church,
but we cannot doubt that the Church has been caught up in it. We see it in the
Church's anguish about her role, her pain of mind and spirit in questioning what,
if any, future she has among men. And men of faith differ, and they agonize over
the fact that they differ.

There are many today in the life of the Church who wish that it were possible
to avoid this agony. At least, how much nicer it would be if all Christians could
agree among themselves! That is the point of view of those who want peace where,
in fact, there is no peace---where we have piously thought harmony to be the absence
of controversy; where we have failed to recognize controversy and conflict as creative. And if this is what we of the Church of Jesus Christ think and desire, we
had better face the fact that we seek to improve upon our Master; we expect a better
fate than his.

We can scarcely afford to forget that the lifetime of Jesus was marked by conflict between him and the current understandings of Scripture, tradition, and au--
thority. While it would be false on the face of it to claim that he sought controversy and conflict for the sake of it, it is to the point to recall that he did not
avoid them in order to avoid them. Conflict has to be seen as one of the characteristics of Jesus' ministry, and I would propose to you that these conflicts must be
understood as the paradigm(the model) of the later ones that have marked and will
continue to mark the life of the Church which follows him.

In our lesson for the morning we read how the leading Jewish authorities challenge Jesus' right to cleanse the temple, heal the sick, accept messianic tributes,
and now to teach with authority in the temple. Who gave it to him? Their implied
answer is that he has no real authority; certainly God gave him none; he is self-
appointed and to be condemned.

Instead of giving a direct answer, Jesus asks a counter question--'the baptism
of John: was it from God, or from men?' Jesus knows that his work and John's is
connected, and that the Jewish leaders, in failing to see that God had sent John,
had forfeited their right to judge John's successor. They argued among themselves..
Now just imagine, Jesus set people to arguing! If they answer,'from God', they condemn themselves for not responding to God's prophet, and Jesus can condemn them.
But if they answer 'from men', as they would like to do, the people who consider
John a prophet will repudiate them.

These leaders profess inability to answer, but this is no escape from their
dilemma. They really confess by this that they are incompetent to judge one who
except for Jesus has been the most prominent preacher of their day. If they cannot
tell about John, how can they judge Jesus? Jesus really has answered their ques-
tion--his authority has the same source as John's.

4=24=66

Jesus follows this incident with the first of three parables which drives home this point. This parable about two sons has a clear intention. The son who refuses his father's command to his face, then has second thoughts and fulfills it, is closer to the heart of the matter than the dutifully polite son who does no work. Jesus himself points the moral. The early behavior of tax collectors and prostitutes rejects God's claims on them but they have ultimately obeyed the call. The religious leaders promise but do not obey; they keep the traditional forms of worship but do not fulfill God's will! Jesus may not finally exclude the leaders from the kingdom; they could still respond. But as things now stand, the outcasts are entering the kingdom, and there is no evidence that the respectable leaders, the prominent members of the church, will respond. Even the sight of the outcasts entering the kingdom has not changed their attitude.

At the end of the third parable with the same moral, Jesus refers to the Psalm: "The stone which the builders rejected has become the main corner-stone." And then the point is repeated for all to know: the kingdom will be taken from the disobedient and prominent religious leaders. And you can hardly be more authoritative, controversial, jarring, and abrasive than that. The conflict is on for sure. And his crucifixion and resurrection did not end the conflict, not for his people.

The conflict of Jesus became the paradigm of that in the early Church. The early Christians refused to bow to the authority of Rome. The controversy and conflict were intense, and the persecution by the government was seen by the faithful as a sign of the agony of God's breaking in upon history to bring his kingdom. Some of this is reflected in the later epistles included in the New Testament canon, as in the passage we read this morning from I. Peter.

This letter from a period of persecution announces that the time has come. God's new order has moved into history. Judgment comes upon the old order, and ordeal and agony result. The suffering of the Church is part of the process of God's bringing his purpose to pass. We are clearly told here that the Church is first--it must first face God's judgment. The Church itself must turn from the past to the future. The household of God is the community of penitence and faith which has endured the agony and the joy of passing "from death to life". Whatever the agony of conflict, such judgment on the Church should assure us of God's activity in history, his presence in our lives. This epistle seems to say: He will not let us alone and he will __not leave__ us __alone__. Thank God!

The time has come! It always does. It cannot be avoided. As the New Testament scholar, Rudolph Bultmann has said: "Man can never jump out of time but has only to choose whether his present is determined by the past or the future." Ever since Jesus walked the earth, that has been the issue. And, good friends, that is the issue today. That is the issue at heart in the conflict between Jesus and the religious leaders. That is the issue in the present and coming agony of Church of Jesus Christ, including this church. Are we to be determined by the past or open to the future? Christian faith is the choice of openness to the future--the expectation of the Kingdom of God!! Do we look to what has been or to what will be? Of course, some will feel that it is better to be tentative and willing to change whenever firmness invites hurt. Turning away is always easier, and that is often the American way, the way of silence, excluding life to preserve existence. But turning away is not the way of Jesus Christ. The time has come! Judgment begins with the Church and it must face the agony of giving answer.

The agony is upon us today as expressed now by a national group called the "Presbyterian Lay Committee,Inc." and by local groups (such as one in Mansfield) following dissident Southern Presbyterians calling themselves "Concerned Presbyterians". They are dedicated to an understanding of the Bible that comes out of the past and that seeks to ignore the scholarship of the last 100+ years. It seeks to keep the

Church "religious", out of political and social issues. Of course, the root of the opposition lies in Civil Rights. As one member expressed to me recently, he would not go downtown to a movie because he does not want to come into any contact with Negro people. His group wants the Church to tend its ecclesiastical affairs, distinguishing as it does between the affairs of men and the affairs of God. It sees the Church as a "spiritual" body with no temporal concern save where those concerns somehow make contact with "spiritual life".

k   This group of men represent tremendous corporate and personal financial resources, and they feel that there is a conspiracy against them. They see Eugene Carson Blake, Bishop Pike, and the NCC as enemies who are part of a world-wide conspiracy to take power away from them and their kind. Somehow Presbyterian Laymen, Inc. feel that these less-affluent servants of the Church have an overriding power to have their way, but these "Concerned Presbyterians" are determined to repossess power and prevent the final subversion of the Church. Theirs is a social paranoia which believes that demonic forces have captured the Church and led it into the secular realm. And so they ask, "by what authority do you do these things; engage in the racial, social, industrial, urban revolution of our time?"

And we might as well face it, the Church is divided today on this issue. Many ministers feel that their laymen only want the Church to reflect the prevailing values of the "American way", while many laymen feel alienated from their minister and accuse them of conspiracy, subversion, and worse. Disconfirmation bothers not these laymen. Psuedo-scholarship in such tracts as "None Dare Call it Treason" boosts morale and is accepted as the proof-positive of theses already held. And in all this is the fear that the call to a new Church mission in race, poverty, and the cities is a threat to entrepreneurial competition and that a decline in that will erode our national character. So their song emerges: "Gimme that old time religion!" But others of us answer, which "old time" do you wish---the first century or the 19th? They are not the same. You want it the way it _was_? Which way? A future opened by Jesus or one closed by Adam Smith and Karl Marx? There's the coming agony!

John Fry's sermon last week also symbolized the coming agony of the Church. To be sure, he was not heard well by all. However, assuming that he was understood, the comments on what he said indicate our agony. (Some felt that his sermon was no sermon; that they were insulted by it; that such a thing--whatever that means--such should never be heard from this pulpit again. And from the other side came a letter this week from a visitor last Sunday which said that the sermon was just "what some of the fat souls....need to hear to drag them out of the past.")* And this conflict may also indicate the agony between the ages, between the generations. It is natural, I guess, for men to want things to remain as they have known them, for them not to change--at least not too much. But it is also natural for a new generation in a rapidly changing time to want a radical openness to the future. The agony of two generations which cannot talk to each other even in the life of the Church may be coming upon us. That conflict can split the Church wide-open and will be more destructive than creative. It will certainly come upon us if we close our future by worshipping the forms of the 16th and 17th Century Reformation or the Neo-Puritan forms of the 19th.

You see, we are even in agony over the language we use. Some would much prefer never straying beyond the King James Version. Others insist that meaning and understanding today must be more important than "beauty" of language. Some would call the Church to good taste and others would refer to it as the middle-class tyranny of "good taste". How important are words! Important enough to fight about? Well, the agony is built into the Christian who would be open to the future but still have a sense of the past. This can be creative agony. The agony is a part of the Protes-

*The parenthesis indicates that these words were not spoken in the sermon. It was my fear that they would not conducive to reconciliation. Hoever, they are included here only to clarify the issue for those who are not familiar with it.

4-24-66   -4-

tant Principle that God alone is absolute; that words and concepts and dogmas change.
God is both "Thou", the Wholly Other, the transcendent One who stands over against
man, and "You", the constant Friend, the One close at hand to sustain and give peace,
the Abiding Presence of the immanent God. God ever produces change among us to keep
us alive and open to the future, to his Kingdom coming. And we agonize at every
point he challenges our false absolutes and casts down our idols. God, in fact,will
not let us alone and he will not leave us alone. He will not let us build a church
house and then set it apart from human concern and activities. He will not let us
alone to make property more important than people. He will not let us capture him in
words or hold him in the cages of our minds. When He becomes only a "Thou" to us,He
jars us by becoming a "You" as close and present as life itself; but when He becomes
only a "You" to us, He frees himself from our familiarity and becomes a "Thou". He
refuses to fit our forms.

Anne L. Morrow has put it well in a poem entitled "For Sale__A New Jesus":

FOR SALE--A NEW JESUS

FIND the doll of your own choice--
Buy him here, buy, buy,
him here. Three to choose from --
Buy the one made just for you.

Here's the intellectual's dream
(sold a hundred yesterday);
in English, Russian, French and
German, he chants the proof of his
incarnation. (A book of magic is
            enclosed.)

This is Jesus of action
(45 gyrations in all);
he bends, runs, walks on water;
swings his whip when faced with silver;
waves his arms to calm the sea; and
speaks, speaks --
speaks one word -- come.
Literalists, come buy this one
(the halo is of solid gold);
he writes the Scriptures one by
one in Paul's native English tongue.
Word for word, he's worth a fortune --
guaranteed for life.

Every doll has 27 different
costumes, faces, colors --
are you Eskimo, white, Negro, Martian?
Here is a body, face and pattern for
your discriminating taste.(and
if not, we will make one; what is
history to us?)

Find the doll of your own choice --
Buy him here, buy, buy,
him here. Three to choose from --
Buy the one made just for you.

(You there, come closer, friend --
beneath the counter is a
fourth doll: a terrific buy; but no real
pattern, no real system--no market for
these, you know? Here, take it, for
free. Wait! For free, I said. Wait!

                    The Christian Century
                    4-20-66

Jesus remains then the paradigm of our agony. We are not better than our Master,
We have a choice as Christians. Christian faith is a choice for openness--for freedom to the coming Kingdom rather than slavery to the kingdoms at hand. Only Jesus
and precious few of his followers have had the intellectual stamina, plus a sufficient reservoir of outrage at the past and the present to propose that men live with
openness to the future, by and with the grace of insecurity. Jesus points us ahead
to the coming, the certain coming of a Kingdom beyond madness and agony. Those who
propose that we look now to that Kingdom can expect to be called "sectarians","left-
wing revolutionaries", "visionaries", and "crackposts:. Well, let us richly deserve
such epithets. Others before us richly deserved them and paid that price to endure
the agony of becoming open to his Kingdom.

-5-

Let us endure the agony of identifying with tax collectors and prostitutes for
to them the Kingdom is open. Perhaps Georgia Harkness says it best in her poem--

THE AGONY OF God

I listen to the agony of God --
    I who am fed,
    Who never yet went hungry for a day.
    I see the dead --
    The children starved for lack of bread--
    I see, and try to pray.

I listen to the agony of God --
    I who am warm,
    Who never yet have lacked a sheltering home.
    In dull alarm
    The dispossessed of hut and farm
    Aimless and "transient" roam.

I listen to the agony of God--
    I who am strong,
With health, and love, and laughter in my soul.
    I see a throng
    Of stunted children reared in wrong,
    And wish to make them whole.

I listen to the agony of God--
    But know full well
    That not until I share their bitter cry--
    Earth's pain and hell--
    Can God within my spirit dwell
    To bring His kingdom nigh.

--Georgia Harkness

43. 2/10/63   To Reconcile Man and the World

Fifty years after this sermon was spoken, people continue to make – and argue about – public displays of religiosity. Who attends which crystal cathedral, which mosques and churches should be allowed to stand (or to be built), which buildings and what events should allow public prayer? There is division and even hate between people who think one way and those who think another. This sermon opens with the Biblical story of two people praying, one extolling the self and the other humbly coming to terms with shortcomings. It is a sermon about people who pridefully represent themselves as privileged, and thereby favored by God, and those who humbly acknowledge their own limitations. It is a sermon about hate. Rev. Asbury pointedly makes it also a sermon about reconciliation through love.

The word *reconcile* in the sermon's title also appears in the II Corinthians reference that supports this sermon. Paul wrote, "God was in Christ reconciling the world to himself, not counting their trespasses against them, and entrusting to us the message of reconciliation" (II Corinthians 5:19). To *reconcile* means to *bring into alignment* or to *find a common view*. The Apostle Paul and Rev. Asbury both make the argument that in a reconciled world, Jesus, in his humanity, becomes the model for how to interact with other humans. And when humankind and God are reconciled, "...we are ambassadors for Christ, God making his appeal through us. We beseech you on behalf of Christ, be reconciled to God" (II Corinthians 5:20). In a reconciled world, comparisons of privileges in society, achievements through careers, richness of possessions, and goodness in behaviors do not matter. In a reconciled world, it is not necessary to count the trespasses of others. In a reconciled world, people seek more than justice; they practice love (*agape*; see again Sermon #6) for each other.

Westminster Presbyterian Church
Wooster, Ohio
Mr. Beverly Asbury, Minister

February 10, 1963

TO RECONCILE MAN AND THE WORLD
II Corinthians 5: 16-21

Two men went up to the Temple to pray--one a Pharisee,
the other a tax-collector. One stood and prayed with himself:
"God, I thank thee that I am not as other men; greedy, dishonest, adulterous; or, for that matter, like this tax-collector. I fast twice a week; I pay tithes on all that I get."
But the other man kept his distance and would not even raise
his eyes to heaven, but beat upon his breast, saying, "O God,
have mercy upon me, sinner that I am."

Two persons went up to the Memorial Chapel at the College
of Wooster to pray, one a middle class Presbyterian, and the
other an uneducated negro bricklayer. One stood and prayed
thus with himself: "God, I thank thee that I have not been
raised as other men; that I am clean, serious, dignified, and
even sophisticated. Especially, O God, I thank thee that I
am not like this bricklayer. But the negro man with head
bowed, and with the feeling of pain and guilt said: "God, be
merciful to me, for I am a sinner."

It may appear to you in the context of the mission of
this church that we are really talking of two different people.
That is not so. We are really talking about two sides of each
one of us. They cut right down the middle of my heart and
yours. They divide my mind and yours, and they have no respect for our color or creed. These two voices are the two
voices of our conscience. One says to me: "Thank God, I am
not like other men." It says: "Nigger, damn Jew, dago, mac-
keral snapper, and spick. It points a finger and says, "kinky
hair, long nose, colored, beatnik, prostitute, apostate."
The other voice says to me: "O God, O God, be merciful to me,
sinful man that I am." The first closes a door and holds it.
It closes us in with ourselves--with our false religion of
pride and racism. The voice is one of hatred, and it justi-
fies itself by saying that the object it hates is itself
hateful. It is the voice of self-deification which tells us
again and again that the power of being is man's own possession.

The other voice opens a door. It opens it with bruised
knuckles and presses against it. It opens us up to God and
seeks to free us from the false religion of self-worship.
This voice tells us that our hatefulness is the product of
our hate and that we cannot hate as we do unless hate has
filled our own hearts. It sounds the note that we are that
in which we abide and participate. This is the voice of the
Incarnation of God in Christ, reminding us that man is made
in the image of God. It tells us that the image in us is a

2

gift of God's grace--not an acquisition; not a quality which man possesses. This voice repents of self-centeredness, for it knows full well that man is truly man and truly free only when he loves as God loves.

Two voices speak. The first voice produces one of the greatest, if not the greatest, problems in our history: The relation between races. In some areas of the world it may mean black men hating white men. In other, Blacks hating Browns and Browns hating Blacks; Blacks hating Blacks, Browns hating Browns, and Whites hating Whites. But in our land, it is predominately a matter of White and Negro, even though other minorities cannot be ignored. The first voice calls forth a great evil in every life. The other voice seeks a way out of the evil, a way to eradicate it, a way to salvation. It recognizes the mandates of God and man, and it understands the promises of the faith.

To which voice shall we listen? Obviously, we should not be where we are in human affairs if we had not listened to the first voice. Yet, we should not be here where we are, if we had not listened to the second voice. And the Christian knows that he would like to heed that voice--even when it goes against his in-grained prejudices. We want to listen to and live by that voice. But how?

The most popular answer these days is "obey the Law of the Land". Even those who do not respect the Law of the Land now admonish their followers to respect the "Fact" of the land. This view seems to hold that Law can hold our hatred in check, that Law can at least block the discrimination which grows out of our prejudice. Indeed, Law can and does produce a better society in which men live at peace with one another. Yet Law produces condemnation for it does not produce moral- ity in the heart of man. It does not overcome the voice of the heart that says the minority group is dirty, lazy, shift- less, uncouth, and immoral. The Christian respects the Law and upholds it for the good which it produces, but the Chris- tian also acknowledges its limitations, whether national or religious.

Those who stand in the Christian faith have been called to live responsibly in a nation of laws, but they have also been called into the body of Christ, into the fellowship of those who are even now being redeemed by the love of God. God has called us to be his people not because of, or in spite of, our ambition, morality, state of cleanliness, or level of intelligence. Rather, we know that all are unde- serving and yet loved and accepted of God the Father. The Christian message then is not first one of law and order, of man's rights, of constitutions. The message of the second voice in the life of the Christian is not: "Obey the Law and Respect the Supreme Court." Rather, it is the Good News of grace and redemption. It is the voice that tells us God was in Christ reconciling the world unto himself. God was in

Christ reconciling his children to one another and thus to himself. God was in Christ breaking down the walls of hostility that divide men from God and so from one another. God was in Christ loving the other voice in man--the voice of hatred and segregation--loving and accepting, forgiving even those who cannot yet love and forgive other men.

The Christian message on race is no less than the Christian message. It has to do with grace, not law, not order. It has to do with a grace that must be spelled out and applied over and over again in daily life. Our message is not the latest word. It may not be the most intellectually respectable word. It is the same scandal, the same stumbling block, the same offense to men. It does not reject either method or success, but it knows that its validity does not depend upon either success or method. Its validity depends upon the God who gave the message. The task of the Christian is to be faithful to the message of reconciliation--whether or not he is successful.

I know from almost ten years in the ministry that the ministry of reconciliation is not easy. When you see people shut out, beat up, threatened, and hurt, your reaction can well be one of hating those who hate. When you see a 12 year old boy refused service in bus stations across an entire state because he is a Negro, when you sense his bewilderment and fright, you may feel more like damning the insensitive and the prejudiced rather than reconciling them. That first voice is so real even in the heart and mind of the professing Christian that he stands in constant danger of being prejudiced against the prejudiced--in constant temptation to be self-righteous and not love those who are so unloving. It is difficult to remember then that the suffering of the minority group does not separate it from God, but that the sin of the majority group does separate it from God. But, remember we must.

"...If anyone is in Christ, he is a new creation....All this is from God, who through Christ reconciled us to himself and gave us the ministry of reconciliation....So We are ambassadors for Christ, God making his appeal through Us." The Christian is interested in something more than good race race relations. He is interested in man's relation with God. The Christian seeks justice, but he seeks more than that; he seeks love. The Christian seeks more than either desegration or integration; he seeks the unity of God's people. The Christian knows that the society in which he lives in not sinful because in segregates; rather, it segrates because it is sinful. But what is the sin?

Do not confuse the symptom with the sin. The real sin is not what we do to one another. The real sin lies in our attempt to deny the sovereignty of God. When a man knows that the first voice in him is truly an effort to negate the absolute supremacy of God, he can no longer be a racist.

4

From this point on, he can no longer be the Pharisee who desires self-justification. He cannot be the defensive, self-pitying man who looks for those who agree with him in order to make him feel secure. When the absolute sovereignty of God is accepted, he hears his voice which says,"God be merciful to me, sinful man that I am." Thereafter he can never forget God's authority, nor can he claim it for himself.

Will Campbell, in his book, Race and the Renewal of the Church, has this to say: "The Christian can now see that all his stereotypes about groups, even when true, have no real significance, for,...with Isaiah, he perceives that the inhabitants of the earth are as grasshoppers....The fate of having a Negro neighbor...fades in importance when God becomes the center of thought and life, and one acknowledges his absolute rule, authority, and government. There is no exception to this theological principle." Thus, the sovereignty of God is expressed in Deuteronomy 32:39: "See now that I, even I, am he, and there is no God beside me; I kill and I make alive; I wound and I heal; and there is none that can deliver out of my hand."

This is the beginning and end of Christian race relations, for it begins and ends in reconciliation to God. Calvin insisted on the priority of God's sovereignty and explained that when we begin with ourselves rather than God we see ourselves as more impressive, powerful, and glamorous than we actually are. To see ourselves as we are, we begin with God. To look in God's face is to get a painful exposure to our frailty and finiteness. It reminds us that God alone can dispose the lives of men. We cannot look at God, as Will Campbell reminds us, without "the shock of cemeteries," and that means the humility of seeing anew that all flesh is grass, that we are all here dying together. What man can really face his mortality and continue to divide men into colors, classes, and races? What man can face the finitude of his own life and still say; "O God, I thank thee that I am not as other men"?

We can only say: "God, be merciful to us, sinful men that we are." "Thou art the God, thou alone, of all the kingdoms of the earth; thou hast made heaven and earth." (II Kings 19:1 5) The sovereign God, our Lord Jesus Christ, is our sole referent in human relations. Nothing can be said of us except that we and all our fortunes and destinies belong to him. And it is enough for me and for you to know that God was in Christ reconciling the world unto himself--not counting our trespasses against us--and entrusting to us both the message and the ministry of reconciliation.

5

Prayer by Jacob Trapp

(O God) May this be our prayer:
to be oppressed rather than to oppress,
to suffer injuries rather than to inflict them.
As we look back over the road we have come
we see that the Present often persecutes
those who are sent to it from the Future.

Give us not to seek persecution,
nor court opposition,
but humbly measure our own
thoughts and deeds,
whether they are indeed of the Future.

Give us some portion of the Love that becomes
saviour to the one who crucifies.
And may we know that the Father of all beings
only listens when we speak
as brother of all beings. (Through Jesus Christ
                                    our Redeemer).

44. 11/14/65   A Messianic Pattern

William Sloan Coffin, Jr., a Yale colleague and personal friend of Rev. Asbury, visited Wooster during the Centennial Year to share his unique insights. One of his memorable warnings was, "If you stand for nothing, you are likely to fall for anything." Coffin poured himself into his Christian activism This sermon follows up on what Coffin said during his visit.

Here, Rev. Asbury approaches the reconciliation principle of Sermon #43 from another perspective, one of pouring oneself into a cause…the kenotic ethic of Sermon #21. In a reconciled world, people act from a disposition of servanthood and humility, even if actions are accompanied by self-denial. This behavior follows the messianic pattern. Appropriately, the Biblical reference from Philippians that was used for Sermon #21 is invoked again here.

The kenotic mental mindset or disposition is a necessary, but not sufficient, attribute. Rev. Asbury's theme that is captured in this Cycle of Sermons is that Christianity – to refine a phrase from the notes of Sermon #9 – is not a spectator sport. It is not an institutional mission, an aloof monument, or a mirage where people piously quote from a rule book. Rather, it is a real gathering of Pilgrim People who then pour themselves into lives "out there" in the secular world in order to repair it of hunger, poverty, racism, and war.

Student voices are impatient, concerned, skeptical, and frequently confused…no more and no less so at the College of Wooster in the 1960s. This sermon recognizes moral ambiguity in the secular world and suggests a messianic pattern – a disposition, a humility of service – as the prescription for making sense of, and healing, a tattered earth.

Westminster Presbyterian Church
Wooster, Ohio
Rev. Beverly Asbury, Minister
November 14, 1965

A MESSIANIC PATTERN
Philippians 2: 5-11

As Yale Chaplain William Sloan Coffin, Jr., reminded us this past week, student voices throughout the world today seem unanimous in calling for Christians to live according to what they profess to believe. These are voices of impatience, of concern, of confusion, voices of skepticism and protest, voices challenging traditional Christian concepts, beliefs, and actions. This generation calls for Christians to get outside the Church and live in the world. But as James Gustafson, also of Yale, recently put it: "....what informs, directs, governs, impels, and motivates that life in the world? One generation, living on its childhood religion, can afford to be antichurch and antireligion, but the compelling faith that drives this generation into identification with the world needs to be nurtured in others, and I know of no conceivable way of coming to faith in Jesus Christ apart from the religious tradition and institutions that have provided occasions for it in the past. Only the prejudiced could construe what I have said to imply that the Church is above criticism and reformation. It needs both, as does the world."

Haven't we, in other words, come at long last to recognize that it is more important to judge what institutions do rather than simply condemning the institution? God ministers through ambiguous structures. We readily admit that God works today in the morally ambiguous secular realms. Do we deny that he may also work through the equally ambiguous churches and religion? Isn't our real problem with the Church today one of reshaping what it does and can do rather than abolishing it entirely? One theologian (Hoekendijk) has called for "institutional self-emptying." He called this the "kenotic form" of the Church--the Church that empties itself so that it can take the form or shape that will best represent and identify with the human world around it.

This indicates that the Church today should be a fellowship of persons bound in a "messianic pattern", and we get some idea of that pattern in Philippians 2. Here in a letter the Philippian Church, we of the Church today are told to let this be the pattern or disposition that governs our common life. This letter to the Church which says "have this mind", "follow this pattern","let this be your disposition" does not refer to personal inner life. It refers to your life in your community of faith and hope. This disposition alone is fitting. This is the atmosphere and attitude of life which must befit those in Jesus Christ.

In the strophe hymn which follows, the "messianic pattern" is laid out for us: self-denial, servanthood, humiliation. Jesus was in the form of God. That is, his form of existence in some sense exhibited his true nature so that men of faith could confess that He was the Son of God. His form of life, the conditions of his existence, disclose the reality which he represents. Therefore, men of faith confess him to be the presence of God among them, the Son of God. Yet he did not grasp for equality with God. He stripped himself of that form. Literally, he emptied himself of that form of his existence, and took upon himself the form of a servant or slave. He took upon himself the fundamental condition of the life of man. What man is defines the self-emptying of Jesus. The letter generalizes and broadens our understanding of this by saying that Jesus took the shape of man, participating in the life of humanity. He was obedient. He stripped himself. This was his voluntary decision. He humbled himself.

The "messianic pattern" we see here consists of acts. This speaks not of the "divine nature" of Jesus. It speaks of his redeeming acts. Because he acts voluntarily to strip himself, to be obedient, to humble himself, to identify with man by

11-14-65

dying (and that, death on a cross) ...yes, because he acts, Christians can say "that at the name of Jesus every knee should bow...and that every tongue should acclaim him 'Jesus Christ is Lord'--to the glory of God the Father."

These acts--self-denial, servanthood, and humiliation--constitute the messianic pattern. And it is this pattern, this disposition that should govern our common life ---our life of faith and love as the Church. When Paul says "have this mind", he does not indicate an intellectual sense. He means that this should be the entire orientation of our emotions and will so that we act in this way. Be of this disposition, act in this pattern of self-emptying.

Obviously, we need to know this and what it means for our own faith and for the Church. If the church is to be a fellowship of persons following a "messianic pattern", our theological pretensions and false absolutes will have to be humanized. It is perfectly clear that "institutional self-emptying" does mean the death of some churches which conceive their lives purely in institutional terms. This will threaten religious authority, especially where preachers or ecclesiastical leaders presume status or where theological interpretations claim infallibility.

A "messianic pattern" means that even if the "world come of age" is not as mature as some think it is, it is one sight more mature than the paternalistic and pedagogical posture of the Church has assumed it to be. As a people bound to this pattern, we must accept a wiser world and learn to help it be itself. Hoekendijk points out to us that the Church's real center of interest is outside the Church --living and looking for those situations in the world that call for loving responsibility. We are to find out there what shape or form God's mission will take. The Church's role is not to carve a segment of holy space out of the world, to guard some piece of sacred ground. Rather it is to help the space of the world to be what God intended it to be -- a good and human creation.

The implications of this may shock the Church. They should! Look again at kenosis: the self-emptying of Jesus, and the "messianic pattern". Jesus stripped himself; he divested himself of all religious authority, of the form of God in favor of the form of man. Here we get a glimpse of what may be in store for those who follow the pattern--a giving up in preaching, teaching, and relating all claim to "mystery, miracle, and authority", to use Doestoevsky's phrase, all claim to a special kind of religious knowledge. This entails a stance which deliberately, voluntarily, and meticulously surrenders any claim to authority. For example, we must not expect men to listen just because we are speaking. If men are to listen, it will be because of the quality of our thought and not the sound of our words.

Even though this may shock, it may also enable us to be human to our fellowbeings. When we have no further need to convert, to cajole, to change, then we can love our fellows. Our witness is no longer burdened by having to teach or convince everyone we meet, or report to the FBI those with whom we disagree. We do not have to read a religious commercial every time we talk. We are freed from seeking to find a religious message in every play, movie, and novel. We can swing with jazz and appreciate it without asking its origins and whether it would be good in Church. We can accept art forms and know that it is enough that through them shine the mystery and creativity that brought them into being.

Theology in a kenotic church becomes not a weapon to use to convert agnostics and atheists, not a means to gain church members. Theology in this pattern becomes a means by which we clarify our own experience. It grows out of the pattern of Christian life; it reflects on who we are as a people bound together and how we are to act. Such a theological stance does not mourn the passing of "system building" or the demise of "proofs of God". It sees them as having been meaningful at a particular point, but we move ahead now doing theology in a more experiential sense.

To understand theology in any such dynamic way means that we must leave room for new forms or parables of church structure. For example, twenty years ago "serendipity" was a novel subject for a technical talk. Now, serendipity is a common subject. In science, it means the achievement of some high value through an unexpected stroke of good fortune. Putting it another way, you experience serendipity when you make a significant discovery accidentally. And, though it may seem peculiar to you, many of the most important and useful developments are serendipitous---pure accidents.

Well, the Church in the world is serendipitous. It accidentally happens where we do not expect it or where we are sure that it cannot. It happens as good fortune, and it happens whether men believe it or not. Like grace, the Church is one of the unexpected surprises of God, and we can seldom predict it. The Church never happens in the same way twice, and it is shaped tremendously by the people who perform and the space where it takes place. But it is always marked by the "messianic pattern", whenever it happens.

It is significant that the Church happens in a space or place. There has been an anti-building "kick" in the life of the Church, and churches with new buildings have operated with "hang-dog" guilt complexes. You begin to think that we should sell the building and go on the road. Yet, we see mission happen serendipitously in a building and realize that it must happen in some place or space. To deny this would be to deny the need for the Incarnation. Jesus takes the real form of a real man. The Church becomes a reality when it is incarnate, visible, concrete, occupying a certain space at a certain time. For example, let us not forget that in the South church buildings are bombed. We need not apologize for the building, whether it be irrelevant Gothic, like this Chapel, or stark modern, like the Church House, but for what happens there. If the building is only a religious ghetto, it won't matter and nobody will dislike, discuss it, "cuss" it, or scrawl obscenities on its doors.

Now, we meet here today in a Chapel used for every purpose. Political meetings take place here. So does every sort of musical event. Red China, sex, Peace Corps, education are discussed here. There are speeches, horseplay, prayers, hymns, and sermons. You name it, and almost everything you are willing to name out loud on Sunday morning has taken place here. So you hear the complaint that one would rather worship in a less familiar place--a specially holy place. Surely, we can be more perceptive in this matter.

The very familiarity of the space forms a proper setting for worship. As we come to offer worship, we come to a place we know--where life has been lived, issues faced, and where joy and laughter have been heard. This old building has a "holiness" all its own, not dependent on its being set aside but on its being a setting for the common concerns and cares of this life. This building constantly reminds us that faith and obedience are responses to particular times and places. It is where the Church is everywhere that it is nowhere; it is when the Church is exclusively eternal that it is never timely; it is when the Church is spiritual that it is never material to anyone. A building can be the space where the Church serendipitously happens--the shelter where the thoroughly secularized world can be itself and where men can care for one another with deep concern.

This obviously implies that the Church which empties itself, denies itself, and takes the form of a servant exists among those and for those who do not believe. One group in the life of the Protestant Church which fears this wants to limit it to those who know what the Christian faith is. They would make the Church a core group of committed and devoted persons. But a kenotic pattern moves us in another direction --- that of inclusiveness. The Church today should make little distinction between believer and unbeliever; between "true believers", inquirers, and nonbelievers. We should have such an openness that we are a community that includes persons of faith and unfaith. The touchstone of such a community is still the gospel, but the mood is one of waiting and seeking.

A poem from East Africa recently raised this question of the non-believer in our midst:

"If there is a God
He must be a God of our time
He must be a God of love
      Of living, limitless love
      To take away from our life the curse of pain
      That we may not die
            But live
      That we may be free again
      That we may be good again
      That we may love
NEVER HAVE I MET THAT GOD.

You who believe
      And shun our company
            Because we do not believe
You who live with God
      And cast us away
            Because we live without God
I will tell you why we cannot accept your God
Meeting you
      We do not meet
      Persons who love.
If your God were the God of love
      That could not be so.   (The Intercollegian, November, 1965)

We can show that love only by following the messianic pattern--including among us all who will associate or relate. What is important now is that a community of persons comes together with concern for the world, bound together in self-denial, servanthood, and humiliation--bound to each other and willing to lay organizational life on the line in loving service for the world. This secularized Christian community deprived of its religious authority, spiritual games and sacred places is freed to discover the new shape of mission in terms of human need and the social structures given us by the world. Our future is fraught with dangers, but the possibility of risk and denial are always with God's people. But what is also possible is that we may learn in a messianic pattern what it means for every knee to bow and every tongue confess that Jesus Christ is Lord.

(This sermon stands in debt to Howard Moody, pastor of Judson Memorial Church in New York City. Some of the ideas developed here either originated with him or expressed by him in full. Yet, it is a fair claim that many of them were developed here "simultaneously" or, at least, along parallel lines.)

45. 5/5/63   The Conscience of Man   End of June

An individual who follows the messianic pattern, who battles hate, and who faces agony in order to live the moral life, can become lonely, dispirited, and pained. Are we left so alone to do these things because God is dead? This sermon takes the position that humankind has lost its humanity – has lost its soul, so to speak – and it is *that* loss that makes it appear that God is dead (*see Item D in the* Epilog). Involvement in the secular world will restore our humanity and permit us to find God.

Loss of humanity and the imperative for moral action appeared in an influential fiction-based-on-fact movie of the early '60s, *Judgment at Nuremburg*. The time and setting are the 1947-48 Nuremburg trials, this particular one involving four German judges and prosecutors accused of Nazi atrocities. The chief judge of the tribunal, Dan Haywood (played by Spencer Tracy) is especially interested in one defendant, the German judge Ernst Janning (played by Burt Lancaster), who seems to resemble him in education and disposition. Perplexed, Haywood wonders how Janning could have strayed to use his courtroom to condemn so many people to death. Several deep ethical issues arise in the film, arguably the biggest when Hayward converses with Janning in his prison cell after the trial. Janning agrees that the tribunal convicted him justly but argues that although he feared the Nazis, he never expected things to get so bad. Haywood says, "Herr Janning, it came to that the first time you sentenced a man to death you knew to be innocent." [The Christian imperative to reject moral paralysis, even when it is difficult to do so, is also central to Sermons #16 and #23.]

This sermon explores Robert Bolt's play about Thomas More, *A Man For All Seasons*, (stage play in England , 1960; Oscar-winning film, 1966) as an example of how a person, acting alone, can find one's soul and, simultaneously, find one's God. Rev. Asbury uses the Biblical reference in Romans to reinforce his abiding theme that the Christian stance is faith *plus works* and that "there can be no works except that a [person] believes that there is something worth living and acting for." When the conscience awakens, a person acts with integrity, humility, and courage. Lonely? Sometimes. Risky? Perhaps. But what would happen to race relations, territorial conflicts, economic disputes, ideological differences, labor disagreements, and personal arguments if *everyone* acted with integrity, humility, and courage?

The God Is Dead viewpoint became the cover story of Time Magazine, April 8, 1966.

Westminster Presbyterian Church
Wooster, Ohio
Rev. Beverly Asbury, Minister
May 5, 1963

THE CONSCIENCE OF MAN
Romans 2: 1-16

If "faith is the assurance of things hoped for, the conviction of things not seen", then how does one get faith? Where does one begin? How does one commence his journey toward the certainty of realities unseen?

We live in an age that accepts the Nietzchean view that "God is dead". How do we accept a living God in the days we are living? One man has said that we are in the mess we are in because we are living the Christian tradition but not living it as though we believe it. To use post-Nietzchean jargon, we need the resurrection of "God" from the dead, or, to put it in more orthodox terms, we need to rediscover God. This we need in order to rediscover what it means to be man, to be a person in a depersonalized society, to be a self in a culture that robs us of distinctive selfhood. What we need is God if we are to have a framework, a perspective in and by which to understand who we are and why we are here, and a "dead God" will not do for that purpose.

The rediscovery of God and the rediscovery of man will not take place separately and independently. We confess our belief that we are in "the image of God". But this doctrine of the imago Dei is far from simple. Our image of God has changed, as I think Brooks Atkinson meant to say, and that means that we have changed our image of ourselves. From the human perspective the fate of our image of God and the fate of our image of ourselves is one and the same, —and vice versa. What we think of God correlates with what we think of ourselves. What we think of ourselves correlates with what we think of God. And if "God is dead", it may be and probably is because we have become less than man. Some have said that "God died" of an overdose of man, but I am more inclined to agree with those who believe that "God died" of an underdose of man. To put it the other way around, man died "of the same disease, whatever it was, that slew his Maker." In any case, the point is that the rediscovery of God and the rediscovery of man will take place together.

It was in this context that I recently viewed Robert Bolt's play, A MAN FOR ALL SEASONS. This play about Sir Thomas More is one in which the moral issues are clear, the hero purposeful and noble, and his action "evocative of unstinted approbation". The simplicity of the play is so direct that it becomes awesome. Sir Thomas More, lord chancellor to King Henry VIII, was a man of principle--a man of whom Robert Whittinton said: "And as time requireth a man of marvellous mirth and pastimes; and sometimes of as sad gravity: a man for all seasons."

It was More's conviction as a Citizen and as a Roman Catholic that Parliament has no right to sever "the connection with Rome" and to establish the King as Head of the Church. When it did so in order to void the marriage between Henry and Katherine of Aragon, it went beyond its authority. So More withheld his support. As this congregation well knows, this struggle between Rome and Henry was not ambiguous. A great deal was at stake, much more than the obvious issues of Henry's self-will and desire for a male heir. However, Bolt's play is less concerned with the judgment of history than with the central question: the right and duty of conscience to resist the encroachments of the state upon its prerogatives. This play then is predicated upon the thesis that More could not in good conscience sanction the actions of the king of parliament and that as a man of principle he would not do so.

More was a prudent man by nature and by training was a scholar of the law of England. He decided that his best course of action lay in silence. He was not looking for trouble. He was not tempted by martyrdom. He liked and enjoyed life, and he considered it a boon to be preserved by any means short of perjury. The king, however, could not settle for that. The silence of the lord chancellor on the question that had become the test of an Englishman's loyalty was more eloquent than words. The king, first in person and then through his aide, Thomas Cromwell, tried to wring from Thomas the simple words of approval. Every means was used without success. More was forced to resign. He was reduced to poverty. He was imprisoned. He was finally brought to trial, convicted of treason on false testimony, and beheaded. The state had asked him to forswear his conscience, and he could not say Yes.

This is a play about Man, the conscience of Man. Robert Bolt tells us: "The action of the play ends in 1535, but the play was written in 1960, and if in production one date must obscure the other, it is 1960 which I would wish clearly to occupy the stage." When one watches this play, or even reads it, he knows that it is no period piece. It has to do with the rediscovery of Man, and what we watch is ourselves in a 16th Century mode. To make this clear, Bolt used a character called the Common Man. This fellow is servant, boatman, pubkeeper, executioner, or what-have-you. He is used also as a commentator on the action of the play. "The 16th Century," he remarks, "was, like all centuries, the century of the common man." But as Tom Driver has said in the Christian Century: "The play's irony is that it takes the uncommon man to balance the common man's penchant for time-serving."

The author of this play is not a Christian, as he says "in the meaningful sense of the term." Bolt has, therefore, made no attempt to "convert" people to the Christian faith. However, he has done much to rediscover the nature and meaning of man, and he, consequently, clarified things for those who are Christians. Yes, even for others he has "resurrected God from the dead." In his preface to the play, Bolt wrote: "We feel--we know--the self to be an equivocal commodity. There are fewer and fewer things which, as they say, we 'cannot bring ourselves' to do...... But though few of us have anything in ourselves like an immortal soul which we regard as absolutely inviolable, yet most of us feel something which we should, on the whole, prefer not to violate. Most men feel when they swear an oath (the marriage vow for example) that they have invested something." Thus, for More, an oath was a definite contract, and any oath involved a sense of selfhood. More is presented as he must in fact have been -- a man so large in spirit, so intelligent in mind that his own limitations are known to him, so sure of his moral poise that he need not depend upon the courage of others, so in love with life that he has no desire to die for the cause if he can keep his convictions and live. At one point, where the "connection with Rome" is under attack, he is asked: "does this make sense? You'll forfeit all you've got--which includes the respect of your country-- for a theory?" More replies: "The Apostolic Succession of the Pope is--..Why, it's a theory, yes; you can't see it; can't touch it; it's a theory. But what matters to me is not whether it's true or not but that I believe it to be true, or rather, not that I _believe_ it, but _I_ believe it...." Again, upon being asked to concede and live, More replies: ".....I will not give in because I oppose it--I do--not my pride, not my spleen, nor any other of my appetites but _I_ do--_I_! ....."

There is the rediscovery of man. And of God, if you will. You cannot say that kind of thing as long as you believe that all is nothingness. Man is man when he can act as if there is _something_. Even when man does not see it very well, he has to act as if it is there. Indeed, unless he has the courage to act, to live as man, he may not see it at all. I am sure that we shall not see God unless we have the courage to act as Men. As Robert Bolt said: "Courage is the action of the

self even when all the 'reasons' one can find say not to act." More had the courage of himself, and he paid for it. He got beyond all the right 'reasons' into
courage, and he taught us what it means to be a Man, to have a conscience.

Robert Bolt may be officially silent about God. He is not agnostic or silent
about Man. And as we said at the beginning of this sermon, it may be that before
we can see God as God, we must first see man as man. We can rejoice that Bolt has
helped us to do that.

Something of the same lesson has recently come from an unexpected source. I
refer to the recent Easter encyclical letter of Pope John XXIII, which he addressed
to "all men of good will." The foundation of the Pope's long but closely reasoned
document is the conviction that "the Creator of the world has imprinted in man's
heart an order which his conscience reveals to him and enjoins him to obey." This
is the first conviction of Natural Law philosophy, which Protestants do not accept
but which is held by men of widely differing theological positions. In other words,
as Walter Lippmann recently pointed out, the Pope has not based his argument on
revelation or inspired teaching, but on a philosophical principle. Says Lipmann,
"It is that there is in all men at least the rudiments of a conscience, at least
some capacity to reason, and some inclination to follow it."

You may or may not agree with this. But it is clear that the Pope was speaking of Man as Man. His concern is peace on earth among men. He calls for men to
be men, saying "every human being is a person endowed with intelligence and free
will." He also states,(one is tempted to say'concedes'), that "every human being
has the right to honor God according to the dictates of an upright conscience...."
The Pope surely has said all this in full belief that when man rediscovers man,
he will rediscover God. Indeed, the Pope defends Man against every encroachment:
"...it follows that if civil authorities legislate for or allow anything that is
contrary to that order and therefore contrary to the law of God, neither the laws
made nor the authorizations granted can be binding on the conscience of the citizens.'

What does all this say then to the Christian Man, to those who even now profess faith that God lives and reigns? Surely, it says what Paul says to the Jews
in Romans ": that we shall not save ourselves from judgment as men simply because
we are Christians. We, of all men, can claim no favored position, no special privileges with God. We shall be judged, not be the words of our mouths in worship,
but by the kind of lives we lead to give meaning and content to those words. We
cannot trade on the mercy of God. The mercy of God is not for the Christian Man
"an invitation to sin (but) an incentive to repentance." It is the call to courage
to live as those who have the image of God in them. We too often fail to understand that Paul, the great apostle of justification by faith, also taught that God
will settle with each man according to his deeds. To Paul a faith which did not
issue in deeds would be a travesty and a parody of faith---indeed, no faith at all.
There can be no faith that does not issue in works and there can be no works which
are not the product of faith. The two are inextricably bound together. Thomas
More made that forever clear. Man is not man without works, but there are and can
be no works except that a man believes that there is something worth living and
acting for.

Thus, we have to believe with Paul that a man will be judged by his fidelity
to the highest it has been possible for him to know. If man has been true to the
highest he has known, God has not asked and cannot ask for more. And Paul surely
agrees that man has a conscience, a God-given conscience, and that man will be
judged according to his faithfulness to that conscience he possesses as a Man.

-4-

A MAN FOR ALL SEASONS ends with the Common Man, taking off his mask (having served as More's executioner), and commenting: "I'm breathing... Are you breathing too?...It's nice, isn't it? It isn't difficult to keep alive friends-- just don't make trouble --- of if you must make trouble, make the sort of trouble that's expected. Well, I don't need to tell you that. Good night, friends. If we should bump into one another recognize me."

If we do recognize him, we may never see God. But there is an uncommon Man, the most uncommon of all Men, who said: "If any man would come after me, let him deny himself and follow me. For whoever would save his life, will lose it; and whoever loses his life for my sake and the gospel's will save it." (Mark 8:34,35)

46. 2/13/66 Behind the Mask of Success

Too many people see prosperity as a sign of divine blessing and, alternatively, poverty as the opposite. The distinctive common-man prophet known as Amos spoke against those who trampled the poor. He revealed the hypocrisy behind the mask of success of those that did so. Amos mixed religion and politics.

Amos, who is classified today as one of the "12 minor prophets," preached in the middle of the 8th Century BC during the time of King Jeroboam II in the northern kingdom of Israel. He, Amos, came from an agricultural background. Hosea and Isaiah both lived at about the same time, but they were younger than Amos. Relative stability in Israel and trade with neighbors brought prosperity along with corruption and greed. Amos noticed disproportionate distribution of wealth between upper and lower classes and became the champion of the poor. One of Amos's themes was that pious ceremonies don't compensate for corrupt actions. He warned of regime overthrow if fraud, immorality, inequities, and social improprieties were not addressed – admonitions that were not well received by those in power and that quite likely got him banished.

Micah, another of the so-called minor prophets, was a younger contemporary of Amos who did his work in the southern kingdom of Judah. He told his audiences in Jerusalem that if they did not mend their ways, the city would be overthrown…which it was by the Babylonians a century and a half later.

Jesus echoes Micah's concerns in the Biblical reference from Matthew that supports this sermon (see also Luke 12:52-53, 14:26-27, and 17:33). The warning in Matthew contains the familiar words, "I have not come to bring peace, but a sword" (Matthew 10:34), and "…he who loses his life for my sake will find it" (Matthew 10:39).

Easing the burden of the poor, the discriminated, the dispossessed, the uneducated, and the homeless was not popular work in Amos's and Micah's time and it is neither popular nor profitable today. Nevertheless, this sermon makes the point that the person who follows the messianic pattern does not treat neighbors or other segments of society as *I - It* or *I - Thing*. Instead, the person of conscience treats other people, regardless of race, economic resources, or background, as *I-Thou* (ref. Sermons #6 and #22 and Item A in the Epilog). To use words from other sermons, the Christian *Blik* recognizes the real, secular world and *reconciles* it (Sermons #43 and #44) as *Thou*.

Note: Rev. Asbury's mention of "Coffin" in the sermon's first paragraph refers to the Wooster visit of William Sloan Coffin, Jr. approximately 4 months previously (see Sermon # 44).

Westminster Presbyterian Church
Wooster, Ohio
Rev. Beverly Asbury, Minister
February 13, 1966

BEHIND THE MASK OF SUCCESS
Amos 3:1-8; 8:1-12; 9:13-15
Micah 4: 1-7
Matthew 10: 34-39

It is no news that most men find it disconcerting when their ministers 'mix religion and politics'. After all, religion should be comforting, and that old saying about 'comforting the afflicted and afflicting the comfortable' does not really impress those who are providing the livelihood of such a 'prophet'. The natural expectation is that he should conform and reflect the prevailing views and by all means keep religion 'religious'. This expectation produces "kept men"; what Coffin called 'rat fink' prophets.

Furthermore, it is no news that through the centuries men of a prophetic calling or nature have felt that they had no alternative to 'mixing religion and politics'. The great 8th Century prophets knew that there was no alternative. Amos recalls that God has a special relationship to Israel, and "The Lord has spoken; who can but prophesy?" And that he did, in terms which some call 'gloom and doom'; but perhaps there was no alternative. This was an extremely prosperous time. Prosperity was taken as the sign of God's blessing. Who can argue with success? Still, Amos looked behind the mask of success. He saw those who trampled upon the poor and needy, who enjoyed the bounty of the land without regard for those who starved. And he related the political situation to the acts of God. Amos dared to prophesy that there would be a famine in the land as a result of what lay behind the mask of success--- a famine of hearing the words of the Lord. Only thereafter, only after the mask of success has been ripped off, the truth exposed and evil corrected, will the day come when the fortunes of Israel are restored. Only then will men really know what life is all about again. Only then will the reconciliation and peace prophesied by Micah be realized.

The prophets did not please the people nor would they have won a popularity contest. They mixed 'religion and politics'. In so doing they taught us that theology has to have a 'congruity with experience'. All good theology must be empirical. That is, there must be some way in which we can observe its principles at work in life as we live it or observe it in other men.

Theology in the Biblical tradition has to evince a tremendous ethical and social concern. Theology leads the Church to its social task--to create conditions in which men can be set free to love and serve the Lord. And the Church today cannot ignore the fact that politics provides the means by which to create these conditions. The voices of Amos, Micah, and Jesus must sound again in our day, mixing religion and politics.

This means, of course, that Christians have to be conscious of this world in relation to some other world or age. To look behind the mask of success requires a point of view. Call it what you will--a 'blik', a stance, a commitment, an ability to stand outside oneself, an eschatological itch. Eric Fromm, a psychoanalyst-philosopher, has recognized this in THE SANE SOCIETY in talking about man today. He says: "If man is created in the likeness of God, he is created as the bearer of infinite qualities. In idolatory man bows down and submits to the projection of one partial quality in himself. He does not experience himself as the center from which living acts of love and reason radiate. He becomes a thing, his neighbor becomes a thing, just as his gods are things." Man lives behind a mask when he loses a 'transcendental dimension'. Whenever man thinks that the world's relationships exhaust his possibilities, then he has lost all ability to stand outside himself in order to pierce behind the masks that he and other men wear.

Fromm reminds us, then, that when man confuses the world of man-made things with reality, he is involved in an idolatry which produces alienation. It would seem that Rheinhold Niebuhr was well aware of this, and this may be one of his more lasting contributions. His interest in every social question and his penetrating analysis of them grew out of his deep conviction in the reality of the Kingdom of God. We should learn from him that there must be a stance, a point of view by which one can keep things in perspective. The famous Dr. Spock tells us from his work with children that it is in the process of learning to differentiate ourselves from others who confront us that we achieve genuine self-consciousness. It is not wrong, therefore, to assume that we can have a searching self-consciousness of our age only in contradistinction to another age, or world, or dimension. That is, we can hardly mix religion and politics or look behind the mask of success in our day if we don't realize that there is a mask; that there is something hidden to be looked for.

For the Christian, it is a matter of knowing that he is IN but NOT OF the world. The Christian holds that authentic humanity means a consciousness of being in but not of the world, that we have a stance in the world because of conviction of an experienced reality which the world alone cannot contain. For example, to seek to redeem men, to buy them back, presupposes a view of redemption--of what it is into which men should be brought back. Jesus claims a higher loyalty: lose life to gain it. To talk about the reconciliation of men requires some understanding of to whom or to what men are to be reconciled. In short, men function on the basis of their view of the way things are. And Jesus is certainly not calling men to be other-worldly. Actually, he is calling men to live fearlessly in this world, to look behind the mask of success and be willing to sacrifice physical safety in order to find true life.

So it would seem that we really have no alternative to mixing religion and politics. If you don't think so, look behind the mask of success and then re-examine your own theology. Hear this prayer by Malcolm Boyd in ARE YOU RUNNING WITH ME, JESUS? It's called "The kids are smiling, Jesus, on the tenement stoop."

The little girl is the oldest, and she's apparently in charge of the younger two, her brothers.
But suddenly she's crying and her two brothers are trying to comfort her.
Now everything seems to be peaceful, and she's smiling again.
But what's ahead for them, lord? Home is this broken-down dump on a heartless, tough street. What kind of school will they go to? Will it be hopelessly overcrowded? Will it be a place that breeds despair? Will it change these kinds' happy smiles into angry, sullen masks they'll have to wear for the rest of their lives?
I look at their faces and realize how they are our victims, especially when we like to say they are beautiful children, but we don't change conditions which make their faces hard and their hearts cynical.
Have these kids got a chance, Jesus? Will they know anything about dignity, or love, or health? Jesus, looking at these kids, I'm afraid for them and for all of us.

That's behind the mask of success. "Have they got a chance, Jesus?" His theology makes him ask. And we must ask too in this time of prosperity.

Gunnar Myrdal has recently written about America that while 1/5 of the nation is very poor, that 1/5 contains $\frac{1}{4}$ of the nation's children. 25% of the children, and most of them will be functional illiterates because of bad schooling. They will live in slums that have a higher percentage of the old, sick, and disabled than the rest of society. They will have a higher fertility rate, and the crowding will be worse, not better. Beginning today, The Cleveland Plain Dealer is devoting a series of articles to the Negro in the city. The first article points out that the Negroes constitute 34% of Cleveland's population, but in that 34% can be found 45% of the city's children. Behind the mask of success lie gross inequalities that would make Amos a prophet of even greater gloom and doom.

In his light we can see that it is an old American tradition to do 'double think': professing loudly (and honestly, I think) elated principles which we then bluntly and constantly sin against in the way we organize our life and society. One of the things witnessed over and over again in a college community is the concern expressed by parents when they believe that their children are taking the principles they taught them too seriously. They have always wanted their children to believe in the rightness of certain things, but grow greatly disturbed when these young people predicate their lives on these principles. Seymour Melman in OUR DEPLETED SOCIETY has related this to growth rate of juvenile delinquency cases in the courts. He sees juvenile delinquency as one indicator of a wholesale rebellion against communities which cynically demand that the young comply with moral codes that place a high value on human life, although the adult community itself fails to behave according to these standards. Young men and women who grow up physically incompetent and functionally illiterate become our social castoffs, and from them we reap a bitter harvest of self-destructive and socially damaging behavior. They come at us from behind the mask of success which kept us from seeing them until too late. Now, Christians ought to be the first to insist that a double standard will not do. If principles are worth having, they are worth taking seriously. We must mix our principles and our practices and expect to practice our principles.

Those who stand in the Christian faith and look behind the mask of success with open eyes and challenged consciences will surely work to eradicate poverty. They will mix religion and politics, because what we have come to call the 'war on poverty' is an attempt to eradicate the causes of the existence and growing isolation of the American underclasses. Of course, as we look behind that mask, many find themselves asking: What will it cost? But if we have the spirit of Amos, Micah, and Jesus, we shall ask further: what kind of cost, human cost or financial cost? What shall be our criterion?

We are already seeing the human cost. Millions of young men and women are filled with resentment at being treated badly--a condition that they know could be changed in this wealthy land just as it could have been changed in ancient Israel. And when it is not changed, we see a rise in alcoholism among the young, narcotics addiction, and juvenile delinquency on an epidemic scale. The human cost is without measure, and as Gunnar Myrdal has shown, the war on poverty, in the long view, costs nothing, for it will assure higher earnings and profits for a majority of prosperous Americans. Furthermore, studies have shown that the improvement of neglected people and blighted neighborhoods do really reduce many classes of local government costs-- such as police, fire, public health.

Yet, even this does not do justice to the matter. As Walter Lippman has written in connection with the war in Vietnam, we are not now in this society faced with the 'same old question' of 'butter or guns'. We are not yet so involved in Asian land war that we must make that choice. Furthermore, it is not a question of 'butter'. It is a question of the crucial issues of an urban society, of cities fit for human life, of private lives being destroyed by suffocating purposelessness. It is a question of what Christians work for in society. In fact, even the Vietnamese situation and the need for a larger draft call each month has reminded us of the issue of functional illiteracy, where the rejection rate exceeds 50%. What have we to commend ourselves when we so freely accept the high cost of discarding people as unfit for the demands and responsibilities of this age. The Christian Church must press this on government--to spend for human ends rather than for ends of destruction.

We are in this world, but we are not of it. We should look more often behind the mask of success--not only to see what is there but also to see what is required of us. What does it mean that we have created in this land a superabundance of killing power without precedence? According to Government estimates we have six times the number of aircraft and missiles that the USSR has. Yet, our generals and indus-

tries call for more. We are able to deliver explosive power equivalent to 6 tons
(12,000 pounds) of TNT per person on this planet. Yet each year we seek more over-
kill. We spend over half our national budget on space and defense. Are we more
secure now than we were when we had only 3 tons of TNT per capita. Will we be more
secure next year when we have an even greater overkill? Why do we not complain about
what _that_ costs? How much of our prosperity can be accounted for in our spending
not for peace but for war? Since I arose a little earlier this morning, I had a
chance to look at the morning paper, including the financial page. I learned there
that the stock market, that barometer of American life, dropped on two successive
days last week. The Wall Street financial analysts attributed the drop to "the peace
scare." There was the obvious implication that some investors and industries consider peace a threat to prosperity. Why is it that our churches which profess faith
in a Prince of Peace speak so little about the high cost of peace? Are we afraid to
mix religion and politics?

When we look behind the mask of success, we see clearly that we are confronted
with a choice. The cost of sustained parasitic growth in our country is not even
measured by the large budgets for overkill. We suffer the penalty of depleted bodies
and minds. Look behind your mask and ask what kind of nation we will become if we
continue to neglect our children, our youth, our cities, our large Negro minority,
the quality of our lives. How shall we beat our swords into plowshares and our spears
into pruning hooks? That is the immediate and future agenda for Christians who would
mix their religion and politics behind the mask of success. That is the agenda of
those who spend over 7 billion a year on space journeys, 2 billion on more nuclear
weapons for overkill, and so on. That is the agenda for those who would rescue 9
million American families from dwellings that an underdeveloped country would mark
for replacement.

Behind the mask of our success, what shall be the quality of our lives? If you
seek only your own life, you will lose it. If you are willing to lose your life, you
will find it. The dimension of life given in Jesus Christ, the eschatological itch,
makes us responsible for what lies behind the mask of success. We must mix our religion with our politics--to redeem our religion and bring it into harmony with God's
purpose of a mankind free to love and serve; and to redeem our politics as the means
of fulfilling life and its promises rather than destroying it. Let this be our agenda
behind the mask of success.

47. 10/11/64   An Issue for Christians: Our Wealth and the World's Poverty

The appeal to the wisdom of Amos appears again. The sermon expresses anger about political persiflage and irresponsibility and takes issue with members of government who talk in public about how religious and righteous they are and yet act selfishly when they could do something significant to help those who suffer. The story is a familiar one across decades, centuries, and millennia.

From the sermon: "Amos spoke in a day not unlike our own. He lived in a period marked by affluence, stability, and economic growth. His people were not divided from one another by the effects of disaster but by the very results of luxury and abundance."

This sermon about the politics of poverty was delivered in the autumn of 1964, about five months after President Johnson's Great Society speech in May, and two and a half years after President Kennedy said, "If a free society cannot help the many who are poor, it cannot save the few who are rich" (see Sermons #5 and #6, which are also about poverty).

The "day not unlike our own" mentioned in this sermon was more than 50 years ago at the time of this writing. To what extent are the reproaches of Amos, Kennedy, Johnson, and Asbury appropriate now?

Issues I   Westminster Pr esbyterian Church
                                         Wooster, Ohio
                                  Rev. Beverly Asbury, Minister
                                       October 11, 1964

                AN ISSUE FOR CHRISTIANS: OUR WEALTH AND THE WORLD'S POVERTY
                         Amos 4: 1-5; 8: 4-6; 11-12; 5: 18-24

Men in developing countries looking for an ideology rarely turn to the Christian faith--they equate it with colonialism, the "white Man's religion", the past, the dead. The critics of Christianity within the Church refer to this as a post-Christian era--an age governed by assumptions no longer directly related to the Christian Church. Men who are seeking a way to preserve human values in a world of immense revolution often regard Christianity as so conservative as to be of little help. Reality seems to confirm their impression and opinion. Even those of us who stand convinced of the dynamic and revolutionary force of the good news about God's love in the world in Jesus Christ are puzzled by and wonder how to treat Paul's eschatological admonitions to be patient and conform.

However, we never forget that Jesus did change human life, and in His light Christians may today be more struck with the Biblical passages which radically question the status quo. This does not mean that a Christian can or should select particular passages to support his own political outlook. Quite fortunately, the Bible is not a sourcebook for ideologies. Very fortunately the Bible is not a textbook of general principles. The Bible is a story of a particular people in a particular time who confessed that God was present in their history--that their history was God's history with them.

And Christians are quick even now to say that God acts in the historical events of our time. But we should surely be sorely pressed to discern this in any clear and uncontradictory way. Any one event or circumstance which we pick out proves to be ambiguous. In this election year, some have called one candidate the "antichrist", but others have called him a "messiah". Some theologians have termed him a sign of God's blessing and others discern in him a sign of God's judgment on our land and culture. Let's face it, we like to think of our involvement in politics as our joining with God in his work in this world's history. But honesty and truth compel us to admit our puzzlement about where a Christian ought to stand on the issues of our times. We cannot easily write off those who stand on the other side of an issue. We find that many sincere, reasoning and reasonable, prayerful Christians differ with us in many particulars. (That confuses those who want simple divisions, and it perplexes those who want clarity.)

How often it is, when I read the Old Testament prophets, that I long for such men today. Don't we all want prophets who would discern the signs of the times and call the nations' rulers to repent and reorient the people toward God's purpose for the world? I confess that I have long yearned for a contemporary Amos, a man who would have the same passionate concern as the prophet who lived 2,700 years ago in the time of King Jeroboam II. I have secretly wished for God's man today who would show us the unjust practices between peo ple and nations, the responsibility for which lies to a large extent with those who call themselves "Christians". I have hoped for a man of courage and insight who would expose anew how we worship God in private life and see nothing wrong with seeking profit at the expense of the poor and needy.

We have no new Amos-- at least not one with authority for us. We do, however, have the old Amos and he is still worth listening to. He has authority for Christians who say that God reveals himself through the Scriptures. Listen to him:

> Hear, this, you who trample upon the needy, and bring the poor
> of the land to an end, saying, "When will the new moon be over,
> that we may sell grain?..And the sabbath, that we may offer
> wheat for sale....Woe to those who are at ease in Zion, and to
> those who feel secure on the mountain of Samaria, the notable
> men of the first of the nations.....

Amos spoke in a day not unlike our own. He lived in a period marked by affluence, stability, and economic growth. His people were not divided from one another by the effects of disaster but by the very results of luxury and abundance. This created what we today term a "social problem". Amos looked upon that problem, the breaking of the people of God into rich and poor, oppressor and oppressed, honored and dishonored, as an act of disobedience to God. You see, Israel had an even stronger notion of a classless society than the church has today. It knew the meaning of solidarity, for God had given the promised land and its wealth to all. Thus, when men were set against men on the basis of rich and poor, Amos. could not be silent.

Yet, we remember that Amos was not a professional prophet. He was a simple shepherd. He was not employed to speak about God. He was not well versed in theological terminology. This simple man was denounced by the priest Amaziah, who was employed by the king for service in the sanctuary. Amaziah found Amos' prophecy to be dangerous and destructive. Thus, he denounced him to the king. Amos had no authority. He spoke on his own--because he had to speak. "The lion has roared; who will not fear? The Lord God has spoken; who can but prophesy?"

Who feels compelled to speak today about modern forms of injustice, hypocrisy, inequality, bribery, exploitation? Whom is God using today as his instrument? Perhaps it will be someone such as Amos, a man with a secular vocation. Perhaps it will be a man with a non-religious language who doesn't seem qualified. But it does not have to be so. Christians do not have to wait for the words to come from elsewhere. One would think that it should not be too difficult for Christians to follow the example of Jesus and to identify themselves with the poor, the hungry, the oppressed, the unjustly treated. One would think that Christians would recognize that rich and developed countries have a responsibility to the world. One would think that men who have lived for so long under the influence of the Christian ethic would be the first to understand "charity" to mean more than a collection of clothes or money for bread.

In this election year, Christians have an important contribution to make to an understanding of the issue of our wealth in a world of poverty. If we seek Christian perspective, if we seek to be Christians first and Democrats and Republicans second, we have a word to speak to those who advocate the "Great Society." Christians must warn against utopian schemes, for men cannot themselves build the kingdom of God. Unless we are careful, unless we respect the meaning of selfhood, we shall end up building a Tower of Babel. More particularly, every Christian should be more than slightly disturbed by a "Great Society" that neglects the world outside America. Appeals to our covetousness, even if it is an election year, only increases the impression that we have done enough for others. To be sure, talk about aid to the world is not popular, but Christians can caution against the popular notion that our nation is generous and charitable because it has been giving one or two per cent of national income to developing countries as foreign aid. No society is great in Christian terms if it feels no responsibility for the poor of the world.

Yet, if the Christian has questions about the idolatry of a "Great Society",
he must, because he is a Christian, have even greater reservations about rampant
nationalism. Never have we heard greater appeals to our own selfishness than we
hear today. It does not matter that it is called "enlightened self-interest."
It is the same thing. It is utter and complete selfishness to offer help to those
alone who will bend utterly to our will. One must have a sense of total justification in order to offer aid simply to gain total devotion and reverence from the
other nations. Christians should shudder at the selfishness of men seeking election by advocating help to other nations only in the light of what will further
our own purpose.

Have we Christians so unwittingly become nationalists that we no longer care
for people because they are people? Back in 1951, at the height of the Korean
War, a number of us were students in seminary. During those days, there were
frequent Red Cross blood drives, for the demand was greater as a result of the
war. It was assumed that the blood we donated would end up in Korea. At one of
the donor stations, a fellow seminarian insistently inquired of the Red Cross---
"Who will get _my_ blood?" We couldn't figure out why he was so insistent. Finally,
he replied that he wanted the assurance that _his_ blood would not be given to a
Chinese--the enemy. That, as you might imagine, brought about quite a discussion
among ministerial students. Who is our enemy? Whom are we to love? Does the
saving of a human life matter, regardless of the conflict? Should Christians
ask first to whom the blood goes? Just so, today should we wonder first whose
life our wheat will save? Do we lead our country into continuing an ideological
struggle or do we form a consensus for resolving the struggle and building a better and more just world? Does Christianity, like partisan politics, stop at the
shore line? Do we care what happens to people in India, Africa, South America?
Did we mean what we used to call "foreign missions"? Do we not know that the
Churches alone cannot bring about the development of new nations in our kind of
economic world? Who calls today for more than charity?

In an article prepared for the World Student Christian Federation, it was
said: "Watch out! The suppression of foreign aid will be the cost of our own
well-being." The author then went on to prove it by figures--for those who call
foreign aid waste cannot be persuaded by moral or humanitarian arguments. The
author claimed that if the developed nations---U.S.A., Great Britain, France,
West Germany, and the like--suppress foreign aid, we shall in 1990 have a gap in
per capita income that will lead to a third world war. (The percapita income
would be $80 in undeveloped countries and $3900 in developed ones). He showed
that if we merely continue the present amount of foreign aid, the gap will be
$3800 to $150--still a great risk of war. But if we increased aid to a degree
where the relation in 1990 would be $3700 to $500, peaceful coexistence might be
possible between the developed and undeveloped nations. However, for that to be
done, it inevitably means a reduction in military expenditures-- a step no one yet
advocates with real seriousness.

On this issue, we have a choice that has vast consequences, and many of us
may live to see the consequences of that choice of how we use our wealth in a
world of poverty. Amos said:

> Therefore, because you trample upon the poor and take from him
> exactions of wheat, you have built houses of hewn stone, but you
> shall not dwell in them; you have planted pleasant vineyards,
> but you shall not drink her wine... Therefore he who is prudent
> will keep silent in such a time; for it is an evil time.(5:11-13)

10-11-64   -4-
Issues I

 That time has not yet come. There is still time to speak and to act. There
is still the opportunity to hear the representatives of developing countries
who speak, like Amos, with an astounding certainty of the basic right of all
nations to share the products of earth. Unlike Amos, they do not base this
right on the fact that God has given the land to all. But we know, as they do,
that men do not choose their places of birth and the land of living. We do not
need an explicit reference to God to recognize God's challenge in their voices.
We do not need to hear them use our religious language to know that they speak
a profoundly religious truth--that the welfare of mankind and not a nation is
the Christian's ultimate concern. This is an issue for Christians--how to use
our luxury in a world of poverty. And we have reason to hope! Because God is
at work in this world!

          "Behold the days are coming", says the Lord, "When the plowman
          shall overtake the reaper and the treader of grapes him who sows
          the seed; the mountains shall drip sweet wine, and the hills shall
          flow with it. I will restore the fortunes of my people Israel,
          and they shall rebuild the ruined cities and inhabit them...."
                                        (9: 13-14)

(This sermon acknowledges its debt to Student World, No. 2, 1964, on "Economic
   Power and Political Responsibility").

48. 10/25/64   An Issue for Christians: Morality and Legislation

This sermon is a generalization of the Christian stance on the law
introduced in Sermon #29. It probes the question, "Is it possible to
legislate morality?" Rev. Asbury's response is, probably not, but laws
can provide an environment where morality can flourish. He argues,
"Laws create the social conditions that either encourage or hamper the
growth of persons." Thus, the Christian stance encourages a special
kind of growth, namely: "…In Jesus, we have been called to produce
a just society, to legislate for a just and merciful order…where the law
of love operates."

This is the last of nine sermons describing specific interactions of the
Christian stance with the secular world.

Westminster Presbyterian Church
Wooster, Ohio
Rev. Beverly Asbury, Minister
October 25, 1964

AN ISSUE FOR CHRISTIANS: MORALITY AND LEGISLATION
Deuteronomy 10: 12--11:1; Matthew 5: 17-20

"You can't legislate morality." That truism has been repeated from one end of
the land to the other. Those who say it generally stand opposed to any legislation
in the field of human rights or to some specific piece of legislation which affects
them. The platitude has gained acceptance among a great many people. It is always
difficult to argue with a platitude or altruism. For one thing, those who utter one
don't want to examine critically what lies behind the statement and what it really
means. For another, most of us accept truisms in company where we wish not to be
offensive by protesting. Perhaps most significantly, we are often too intellectually
lazy to search for a deeper truth. So we let it pass -- "You can't legislate morality."

However, we should not let it pass. This truism represents an issue for Christians. It holds vast consequences for our understanding of law and order. It has
tremendous implications for our view of morality and ethical action in a revolutionary world. It influences the consensus under which we approach government at all
levels. Christians stand in a long tradition of law and morality, and we must examine the issue behind this truism with great seriousness.

Since we have termed this saying a "truism," we have at least admitted that it
contains a truth (not the whole truth, but a part of the truth). The truth expressed
recognizes that the law might not reflect the interior life, the private life of a
person. The law might not represent what one's inner life holds to be true, and so
that private life can consider the law antiquated, or too bold, unfair, and, strictly
speaking, unjust. In short, when you encounter law in your interior life, you often
see it either wearing the clothes of a policeman, a worn-out legislator, an unneces-
sarily imperceptive judge or as a preacher, weaving clothes of Avantgarde, far out
idealism. This is when one truly feels that morality cannot be legislated. The
images and convictions that lead one to action lie in the inner life, and they may
well differ with the law. So that is the truth to the truism. There is an inner
freedom--from the law, to one's own motivations. But there the truism stops.

The community, the society, the state or nation could not care less about the
entire region of right ideas within our private lifes. Law concerns our life in common. The law determined by a community seeks to provide checks, regularities of
procedures, and channels for settling open disputes. The community is interested in
making refined adjustments in its delicate balances of power, in protecting the
majorities and minorities. Law is related to social morality, and it arises from
deep roots within our own tradition. Morality itself is not confined simply to the
private life. It has to do with community, with the way we live in relation to one
another.

The Old Testament law grew out of a deep moral concern. The laws as they now
appear in the Old Testament show a developed and consistent prophetic note, at least
in the Deuteronomic Code. Justice is tempered in behalf of the offender; mercy is
pronounced toward the weak; a deep religious concern is manifested. The Law was seen
as the articulation of divine will for community under the Covenant. It was theological law, to be sure, but it did legislate morality. The law defended against the
perversion of justice. All the codes butress the rights of dependent classes and
aliens. Not all the codes express equally the principles of compassion and justice,
but the primary motivation is clear. They create the human conditions of community.

Yet, these Old Testament laws reach their heights in their attempts to express and prescribe what one shall inwardly be. Leviticus 19:17 says, "You shall not hate your brother in your heart, but you shall reason with your neighbor, lest you bear sin against him. You shall not take vengeance or bear any grudge against the sons of your own people, but you shall love the neighbor as yourself: I am the Lord." Again, one would have to admit that the fire of the free prophetic word is lost in every attempt to legislate the intrinsically unlegislatable, but those legislative attempts can express the prophetic motivation. The law of community affects our personal life. That is, law at its best, as expressed in Deuteronomy 10, is conceived out of the experienced reality of the merciful God. Law expresses the conviction that God created us all; that God is impartial toward men; that God still acts among us; that God has placed on us the responsibility for one another.

The keeping of the law is man's obligation, and Jesus expresses that strongly in the Sermon on the Mount. While he often manifests great freedom from petty legalisms that enslave; while he often acts with great freedom beyond the realm of law, while he broke laws that denied human need, he says that he came not to destroy the law but to fulfill it. He never denies that law expresses the purpose of life. He subordinates ritual law to moral duties. We learn from Jesus that law, from the human side, represents the covenant requirements for community. From the law we learn the essence of human being ---the I≠Thou relationship; the standing for another. The law, far from denying humanity, expresses the essential quality of human life, our responsibility under God for one another. In the light of Jesus, we understand that law cannot be partial to position and power. Those are non-essential and irrelevant distinctions. No one is seen as exempt from the law, from community--not even the rich and wealthy. Man will find fulfillment of his life only when his worship of God leads him to hold in inviolable respect the totality of his neighbor's life. Jesus expressed the law in its full significance.

Our internal and private motivations may or may not produce this responsibility. Community cannot wait until every private life agrees. You can't legislate morality even less love; but you can legislate conditions conducive to morality as love. As James Baldwin pointed out, some social structures make love impossible. You can't legislate brotherhood, but you can legislate conditions favorable to it. You don't wait for the day when all men desire brotherhood. We cannot wait for the day when every man can do what is right. The absence of external restraint is not the same thing as freedom. Law can permit the greatest possible liberty that doesn't in--fringe on the freedom of others. It may be true that there are no laws in heaven--but just look at how carefully heaven's residents are chosen! Law is one of our great teachers. No small part of our morality has been learned from the law. We take the law and make it internal--thus producing our morality. Each private life has a procedure by which it takes legislation and makes it internal and moral. No society could exist without this procedure, and the truism should never blind us to the importance of legislation even to our private notions of morality. For example, law on Civil Rights led to obedience to the law, and it is not inconceivable that acts of obedience can lead to changes of attitude and a new moral consensus. In city after city, public accommodations obeyed the new law, despite a century-old custom. It is conceivable that in time, that obedience will produce a changed attitude.

Christians know full well that legislation does not directly and immediately change a people's moral standards. In fact, as we have said, the law often lags behind our deepest moral insights and concerns. Our moral imaginations, following Jesus, often leap far beyond the legalisms of the day. Our compassion cannot be contained by the limits of legal justice. Yet, we must assert and reassert that laws do more than control overt expressions of anti-social behavior. They also

10-25-64   -3-

influence the inner attitudes of citizens. We accept the law that reflects what we hold to be true about man's life and reject other laws (i.e. murder of Jews, etc.).

Much of the public adopts as its own standards those which are expressed in public law. No on-going society can dispense with this process of internalization. Had not the South internally accepted the law on Civil Rights, we should have ended up with military occupation. As John Fry has pointed out, a few thousand policemen care for cities of millions, because we morally internalize the law. Most people will behave in a legally and orderly fashion éven if they never see a policeman or think of one. Democratic laws, then, declare and define what is commonly accepted. We Christians might wish to think that social practice follows inner assent, but we must acknowledge that it works the other way---inner assent follows social practices. Law indirectly improves social practice. We should not want that otherwise. Legislation does improve social morality. The level of social morality does then produce inner changes. There are many cases where law nurtures moral growth.

Legislation has great moral consequences. Who can doubt it? If there were no laws governing the sale of drugs or alcohol, what would result? If we had no laws regulating gambling, what would become of our conception of morality? If there were no laws governing prostitution or abortions, would we still hold that you can't legislate morality? In fact, the moral level acceptable to a society is expressed in the laws of that society. Laws create the social conditions which either encourage or hamper the growth of the person. Those who constantly warn us against obnoxious legislation have not been so quick to commend to us the positive possibilities of law. Law can be a protection of freedom and order when it reflects the statutes of God to stand for one's neighbor.

The Gospel does not do away with the law. It calls upon us to give it its full significance; to fulfill its spirit of community responsibility. The Gospel of Jesus Christ calls upon us to produce the inner morality expressed in the outward legislation--to go beyond the righteousness of the Pharisees by being the moral embodiment of God's law. In Jesus, we have been called to produce a just society, to legislate for a just and merciful order among all men, where the law of love operates.

49. 2/20/66 Christian Presence   End of July

These last four sermons of the Cycle look to the future. They emphasize Rev. Asbury's themes and aim them forward, which was an altogether appropriate thing to do for a class of college students nearing graduation in 1966. Consequently, Asbury's themes are relevant for citizens today. The sermons outline how to be a Christian *presence* in the secular world.

This is a communion sermon, and Rev. Asbury uses the occasion to point out that Christian presence is more than a position at the table. *Presence*, in Asbury's characterization, includes conversation, interaction, and influence. More than *being*, Christian presence is *doing*, an active engagement with secular issues and structures in the mode of the Biblical Amos and Micah (see Sermon #46).

College students, subconsciously, unintentionally, and for the most part unavoidably, endure a transition from being older teenagers to becoming young adults. College students have a more or less cosseted existence in an ivory tower of safety, an environment that ideally encourages reflection, a circumstance of mostly discrete responsibilities, and expectations that often terminate in grades. Grades validate students' behaviors and tell them where they are on the curve. Upon graduating, students leave the relative safety of a campus, receive little further encouragement to reflect, acquire responsibilities that expand greatly, and confront consequences weightier than grades. After college, grades disappear, leaving students unaware of where they are on the curve. *Presence* in the world means something beyond just showing up. It means making a difference without the guidance, boundaries, or cares about grades. The Biblical references from John and I Thessalonians that support this sermon indicate how Jesus was a presence in his world – not merely *being* there but *doing* things in order to make a difference. Rev. Asbury's sermon gives counsel on how to take an active Christian presence from college into a complex secular world and make a difference.

Note: This sermon refers to "The Name of God." For further explanation, see Items C, D, E, and F in the Epilog.

Westminster presbyterian church
Wooster, Ohio
Rev. Beverly A. Asbury, Minister
February 20, 1966

CHRISTIAN PRESENCE
John 5: 2-18; 20: 19-22
I Thessalonians 3: 11-13

The Church in the world today faces what appears to be an enigma. It is that we are more concerned on one hand with living out the Gospel in the world than we have been in several generations. However, on the other hand we have less confidence than ever in old terms such as 'evangelism', 'witness', and 'mission'! A new generation of Christians over the world has made it clear that the message entrusted to the Church must be involved in the affairs of men, and we saw that last week in a remarkable statement of the Central Committee of the World Council of Churches in which both United States policies and those of the Communists' nations were criticized. Yet, that same new generation does not expect the world will be made "Christian in this Century". The Christian Century and the goals, strategies, and methodologies of our denominations' missions boards were wrong. Some would say that such an approach was preoccupied with the soul at the expense of the whole of life, and that it is the latter with which we must be concerned today.

Be that as it may, our situation looks less enigmatic when we recognize that what a new generation seeks today arises out of the same commitment as the 'missionary' response of yesterday. It knows that the old response has been challenged, and that fact is recognized in the very way that our Church deals now with churches in other lands. We cannot save the remnants of a time now irrevocably past. We shall not witness a restoration of the ecclesiastical influence known in previous generations. To think so is not only to indulge in romanticism but also to be guilty of an impossible outlook on the world.

This does not mean that the Christian mission has been a failure. It does mean that it can no longer be understood as proselytism and membership enrollment; that men of other faiths and convictions can no longer be addressed as heathens by Christians who use piously moralistic tones or condescending dogmatic arguments; that we can never again face the world as if we were superior to men of other races and nations because of religion and morality. We cannot go on as before. In order to fulfill our mission in this new world, we must rid ourselves of all secret ideologies and ecclesiastical hopes. We must take seriously Walter Freytag's dictum: "Yesterday, missions had their problem; today, they are a problem."

The failure of the old way naturally leaves many persons feeling threatened and with nervous insecurity. We have been found almost completely unprepared for this time when we can no longer communicate to others but must now have conversations with others; when we have more to learn than to teach. The campus itself illuminates our problem. It must be admitted that many Churches which founded church-related colleges expected that students would be rescued from the influences of secular life and be brought into a Christian enclave which becomes the sphere of the presence of Christ. How else do you explain the location of most church-related colleges out in the rural areas? But we have learned, have we not, that even in those locations students and faculty will not consent to being a religious ghetto? A church committed to making the campus a community of religiosity is doomed as much to utter ridicule as to complete failure.

The commitment of Christians is still there, but we must seek a fresh understanding of what it means, of how Christians are to live out their lives in the world. The World Student Christian Federation has said that our mission today must take the form of a "faithful Christian presence" in the university and in society. And this may be exactly right: that our posture, our stance today should be one of presence. Some of you may feel that this term, Christian Presence, begs many questions, but can we not first consider that it may also express vividly and meaningfully what we should be about in the world today.

Listen to these words taken from a more lengthy World Student Christian Federation statement: "(Jesus') presence has shown God to us. And even after his death, he is present....(The word 'presence') tries to describe the adventure of being there in the name of Christ, often anonymously, listening before we speak, hoping that men will recognize Jesus for what he is and stay where they are, involved in the fierce fight against all that dehumanizes, ready to act against demonic powers, to identify with the outcast, merciless in ridiculing modern idols and new myths...." (Student World, Vol. LVIII, No. 4, 1964.)

Naturally, this position will have to be spelled out in each situation. It rejects rash answers and rigid structures. It is a perspective by which we see that Christians must be "engaged", involved in the concrete structures of society. It indicates a "priority"--namely, that you have to be present before the task of the Christian there can be clearly seen. It means that presence precedes witness, and yet acknowledges that the very act of being present is itself a witness.

It is like Moses wanting to know who it is that sends him to Pharoah. The reply, "I AM", means as we have said before that "I will be what I will be" or "I will do what I will do." It can and does also mean "I am He who shall be present". That's what YHWH means--the one who is present. YHWH cannot be typed or taped beforehand. He will be seen and known for what he is in the situation as men become aware of his presence and as they respond, as they act accordingly.

That in itself should make us suspicious of religious propaganda where we hear a stereotyped recital, unrelated to the world. We ought to be suspicious of our own words and answers learned by rote, regurgitated at the sound of a stock question, and offered as the last word. On some such occasion, the question may not be a stock one and our answer may be only a stone when men have asked for bread. Must we not instead be one with Moses and Isaiah not only in recognizing our poverty of understanding what we believe but also in trusting that while present we shall be given new words or an authentic silence.

Men of faith have never been given answers in advance. They ask, to be sure. They seek. However, they are given no answers; only assurances that The Name of God will be present. In fact, so overwhelming is the Hebrew sense of presence and of the call of the authenticly present that God is called the Shekinah, the Presence, the dwelling among men. And the Fourth Gospel proclaims the Shekinah becomes flesh in Jesus. Jesus is the Present One. Man finds the Presence of God in him; he locates God in Jesus; he remembers and names. In the way in which Jesus relates to men, they recognize presence. In the acts of making men whole, men discern a presence in him. And when questioned about what he is doing and by what authority, Jesus interprets himself as one who is sent. He who is present is also sent--to do the Father's work---and he then sends others to be present with their fellow men, to live with them, to respond to them.

Jesus drew his two Great Commandments from the Hebrew Scriptures. His second commandment comes from Leviticus 19: "You shall love the neighbor as yourself; I am the Lord." This means very truly, Love the neighbor, because I am the One who is beside the neighbor. If you do it to my neighbor, you do it to me. I am present. If you don't do it to my neighbor, you fail to do it to me. I am present there.

And the New Testament makes abundantly clear to us that the One who is present will be present—that this is not a fleeting momentary expression but the truth, the way things are. The One who has been present with Amos and Micah requiring justice, kindness, and involvement in the community of men is still present and will continue to be. The Ever-Present One whose spirit seeks man out even to the "uttermost part of the sea" and into the depths of hell will be present. Matthew presents him at the opening of his account as "God with us", present among men. And he ends it with a call to "Go" and a Promise that "I am present with you to the close of the age."

Christians have also confessed that Jesus was present for them in the reading and preaching of the Word, in the water of Baptism, in the bread and wine of the Lord's Supper. We have affirmed that we have known him in the acts of love toward us and other men; in the judgments we have felt in our lives; in the Peace we have known and the reconciliation we have experienced and witnessed. In Communion today we declare that He is present among us and will be present when his Kingdom comes.

In between his presence now and his presence then, we declare that we shall be present, that we shall work out for our time the meaning of his presence and the meaning of our presence among men. We do not declare what we shall do, what forms our witness shall take. We make no pretensions that we shall create a new Christian enclave. Rather, before the Present One we agree to live in faith, without final answers—to be present. We expose our willingness to be there, serving without ulterior motives and for the time being without too many words. And to be present in this way is already to express the Good News that we love because we have first been loved.

50. 3/6/66   Present Like Abraham I

This sermon begins a two-part valedictory message for Pilgrim People. Rev. Asbury uses the Genesis story of Abraham's journey into Canaan as a metaphor for a modern day college commencement. As with Abraham's journey, the modern journey for Pilgrim People can be hard.

Four abiding themes that permeate Asbury's sermons throughout this Cycle unite together here at the end:

- Christian *presence* is *doing* – even emptying oneself in the act – not merely being.
- *Doing* occurs throughout a never-finished journey by Pilgrim People.
- The beneficiaries of doing are *neighbors*, and they are to be treated as *I-Thou*.
- Pilgrim People do not inflict their will during a sojourn but humbly *reconcile* the secular world.

In the Genesis story that supports this sermon, Abraham leaves home to enter Canaan, where he builds altars and then moves onward to establish a *presence* elsewhere. In the metaphor, students leave home to enter college and acquire an education. Then they move onward to….

Note: Like the previous one, this sermon refers to "The Name of God." For further explanation, see Items C,D,E, and F in the Epilog.

Genesis 12

Westminster Presbyterian Church
Wooster, Ohio
Rev. Beverly A. Asbury, Minister
March 6, 1966

PRESENT LIKE ABRAHAM I

Two weeks ago, we began an examination of "Christian Presence." The term itself is vague and abstract. As a term, it could develop into nothing more than a new slogan to replace old slogans about evangelism. At least, unless we define it, it will mean something different to every person. And how will we go about defining it. Like so many other catch-words of church life, this one is quite unknown to the Bible, because the Bible does not deal in philosophical abstractions and systematic theories.

In the Bible a story is told--the story of God in the world, a story of his people. That's true of Jesus too. One man asked Jesus for a definition of 'neighbor', and Jesus told a story of a good Samaritan. It was a story not only of one who was present but also of one who did something. And he became the neighbor by what he did to the man left stripped and half-dead. So it is through the Bible, stories without abstractions and theories.

As we approach the meaning of Christian Presence, we should expect the same thing. The only way that we can expect to know what it means to be called by God to live in the middle of the world is to follow out the story. If we follow out the story as it is reported to us in the Bible, we may be able to understand our "Christian Presence". At least, the theme of being present as God's people is dealt with in the story of Abraham. Indeed, this early story expounds the theme more fully than anywhere else, and we do well to listen to it.

When telling their history, most people begin with their forefathers. We begin that way in the history of the United States. But Israel's history begins differently--"Now the whole earth had one language and few words." The nation is told, in effect,"You can only understand your own history if you know that you are a member of a great family of nations who were once supposed to belong together." Now, only the most literal minded and unimaginative will ask the pointless question: "When did all the nations ever speak the same language?" The point is that all nations should live together in harmony and peace. That is God's intention. However, when the nations do not understand each other, they destroy peace. When they think too much of themselves and go after a "Name" for themselves, then their claims to "sovereignty" lead to disruption of the human community. One contemporary example occurred in the state of Mississippi where the claims to sovereignty were taken so seriously that the state behaved as though it were located basically in the midst of a foreign power. It upheld its sovereignty to determine all matters concerning race regardless of the position of the people in the United States. The conflict of Mississippi's "sovereignty" with that of the National Government led to riots and the use of military force. Even today, there are many people in a number of states who are convinced that they are sovereign and right and all others wrong; they worship their own image of themselves. When you confuse your "name" with the "Name" that is idolatry. The prestige, influence, and security of a city and tower here indicate absolute claims to total "sovereignty". Man forgets the roots of sovereignty and misuses the powers given to him. He uses his technology, if you will, to live without reference to You-Know-Who, without reference to the way-things-are. From this arises the disruptive rivalry of men and nations with which we cannot successfully deal even the 20th Century.

Now, I, for one, do not take these early Biblical stories to be reliable historical sources. But I do take them to be reasonable depictions of the world in which the people of God lived, and still lives. They depict it as reasonably, realistically, vividly as anywhere else. This is still the world where men for

the sake of their reputations accept a challenge to race for the moon, and yet
are incapable of living on the same street with their brothers of a different
color. This is still the same world where national self-interest allows the
fighting of dirty wars in which non-combatants suffer the most. We say it is
for the sake of our prestige, our credibility. We must not have the name of a
"paper tiger"; we must use our power to make a name for ourselves among the peoples of Asia. This is the world that spends millions to advertise luxury goods
for the "name" they bestow, while hunger encompasses two-thirds of mankind and
drives those men to hatred. Yes, this is still the world in which God's people
live--the world in which Christians must be present.

It is the same world and God's people have been present in it before. So,
how did this people get started in the first place? A single man is called out
of this world, just as Jesus later creates a new people by calling "12 Jews to
save all of America." Here God calls one primitive Semite away from country,
kindred, family. He had to burn all the bridges which normally link a person to
the world. And right here we must learn that Christian Presence must never become a motto that allows us to forget that every new beginning requires a parting.
And any human being who has ever parted from anything dear knows well the pain
involved. We know this at many levels. When we really leave home for the first
time in such a way that the leaving will only be interrupted by vacations, we
sense that we are parting from something familiar and dear. Perhaps we only
realize later the meaning of taking leave from parents or home. And although
you may not believe it in this dreary season of the year, you will feel something
of the same pathos when you leave this college-----your friends, your teachers,
your co-workers, a part of your life. More particularly, when we are knowingly
parting permanently from something dear, the pathos is even more deeply felt. And
so, when the parting is a matter of finality, as it is in death, we have our own
profound sense of the irrevocable loss that comes in parting. If this is true
personally, it is also true institutionally. That is, every new beginning of and
in the Church requires a parting that cannot come without some agonizing and
trauma. But this parting is made more bearable when we realize with Abraham that
what lies ahead is decisive help and blessing to others.

Amid quarrelling nations and parties, races and classes, faculties and students and administrations, confessions and religions, the only one who can make
available the help, healing, and peace of God is the one whom God's call has released from allegiance to one party, one group or viewpoint, one people, one race,
one class, only one confession and religion. The one so released is perhaps more
suspect. Security may lie in identification with one party, if it's the right one,
the strong one. But real service or blessing ultimately can come only through one
who can transcend these lines of division. This doesn't mean that some of these
are not important; they are. Put it this way: Abraham never forgot his family;
he continues to think of them in his old age(Gen.24). But God's commission is
more important. For the sake of that he leaves country, family, kindred behind--
and each of us concerned with Christian Presence will learn that the first step
leads into a strange land where you quite naturally feel a stranger among your
own people. When the things that determine life for us are no longer prestige,
name, nation, and class, rank, salary, then we shall feel strange. But we shall
also know and have something more important going for us, going on in our lives,
and perhaps it's all important.

That's the way it was with Abraham. A man with 'no name' is to be given a
name; though alone in the world, he is to be a blessing to the whole world; though
nothing distinguishes him from others around him, he is to be the instrument of
reconciliation and peace. God only demands trust. And Abraham is so struck with
the notion that God not only wants to use him but actually can do so that he allows everything else to fall away. Here again, we Christians can learn that al-

though we are <u>no</u> <u>better</u>—that's right, no better than others, God entrusts to us the job of making his reconciliation known and available in this world. He gives our often so nameless, senseless, and useless lives a name, a meaning, and a purpose.

What does this look like? What's the shape of it? Well, next Sunday, I want to speak specifically about what we learn from Abraham about Christian Presence and the dangers in that presence. But, before we can really look at the shape of our meaning and purpose, we must recognize the first thing Abraham learns in the new, strange country.

What he learns first is that God can also talk with him there. Wherever he goes, God is there before him. And this is what precedes all presence of ours in the world. You-Know who is there before us. "There's the Name again." He has been at work and wants to show and explain to us something of what he is doing. Even when we go out to speak of God among non-Christian people, our faith quickly gives us the insight that God has already been there ahead of us. Those whom we assume to be heathen or pagan already know something about the One of whom we speak. Their knowledge may not be as full or complete as that revealed in Jesus Christ, but God has been at work out ahead of us. In a like manner, we discover that he goes before us down every unexplored path we take. As we feel led to take paths leading-we-know-not-where, even those paths that know nothing or care less about God, we find our journey down those paths one of exploring what God has been doing and saying ahead of us. We find our journey full of locating, pointing, naming. "See, You-Know-Who, the Unexpected One."

Therefore, the first thing that Abraham does is to put up a sign in this strange land—a sign of God's presence. He builds an altar and calls on the Name of the Lord. Now, you can be sure that we would today be more comfortable if we read that Abraham set out at once in that new country to bring about peace and justice. My, what a religious man! He built an altar. What an institutionalist! Today he would start by building a chapel or church! How terrible!

Well, don't miss the real point. Our presence and action in the world can at best reflect the presence and action of God in the world. The church exists as a community which proclaims that God is present; as a community that demonstrates in the quality of its life that God is present; as a community which understands its function to be present among men to serve them in the Name of the present God. This is what is at stake in the world which is bothered about making a name for itself; where once the powers of nature and now the powers of technology for social and economic development are what determine life and are its gods. In this world, there must be one man—or a group—who calls on the Name of the Lord and makes his word and power felt.

Let us remember that even the French worker-priests who tried to find a new approach to evangelize France did not do away with worship. Although they engaged in the life of the people as workers and miners, they still gathered to call on the Name of the Lord. Without a constant response to God's presence in the world, any presence of Christians is bound to be misunderstood, wrongly understood. The Christian who would be present has to take account of One who is present before him.

Even Abraham had to reckon with God's ubiquitous presence. When his journeys bring him to Egypt, he clearly fails to take account of the presence and protection of God. He takes to cunning and deceit. He exposes his wife to the danger of being shut away in Pharaoh's harem, all to save his own life. He plays with his own future, since it is through Sarah that he is to become the forefather of

Israel. And in risking himself, his wife, his future, he also risks the people
of Israel whose blessing he is supposed to become.

And it is this which happens to us when we lose sight of God's presence in
the world. We risk the very welfare and reconciliation of the world for the
sake of which we are there at all. And so we must first learn that we who would
be present must recognize first the presence of God; that we must first build an
altar without being tied to it; worshipping and _journeying on_ as did Abraham---
but being able to journey on and be present precisely because our worship has
acknowledged the presence of Another with us now.

This sermon, and others in the series, have been stimulated by the World Student
Christian Federation's statement on Christian Presence and by treatments of the
theme over the past two years in _Student World,_ especially No. 3, 1965--Geneva.

51. 3/13/66 Present Like Abraham II

This sermon is the second half of a valedictory metaphor, one that involves the Genesis story of Abraham.

Two of Rev. Asbury's major points:

- Abraham is not tied to a physical structure, that is, to his altars. He establishes a *presence* beyond them.
- As God takes aim to obliterate the city of Sodom, Abraham urges merciful treatment for good people there, even if there are only 10 of them to be found in the entire metropolis. Imagine the *chutzpah*: Abraham negotiates with God Almighty! He regards good people as neighbors who deserve divine treatment as *I-Thou*.

Abraham's presence of *doing* recalls the story of the star thrower found in the notes to Sermon #26: Who cares if I throw one starfish back into the ocean when so many are dying? That starfish cares.

Westminster Presbyterian Church
Wooster, Ohio
Rev. Beverly Asbury, Minister
March 13, 1966

PRESENT LIKE ABRAHAM II
Genesis 18:17-33; 22: 1-14

The people of God began with a single man, not a special one, but a primitive
Semite, who had to part with his past and undertake a journey. The journey is
filled with dangers, but this man Abraham discovers that God has gone ahead of him.
In our own lives we take paths too that are filled with the unexpected. Our journeys into vocations, marriage, and the like involve tremendous dangers. One friend
who made a deep impression on me reminded me on the day I left to begin my first
parish work that it was conceivable for me to fail; such a danger and possibility,
not to say probability, had not occurred to me. It is often that we begin our journeys into life oblivious of the dangers ahead of us. Yet, we too find that You-Know-
Who has been out there ahead of us, just as other human beings have walked these
paths earlier and found him there.

When Abraham realized this, he erected an altar; a signpost that recognizes the
presence of God; a marker of how far he has come and how far he has to go; but also
a marker of the Presence of One along the way. This altar is a symbol that Abraham's
presence in this strange new land reflects the presence of One who was already there.
Moreover, this altar reminds us that an act of worship is not a conclusion, because
Abraham does not pitch camp there and settle. From this altar, he journeys on in
trust. He is not tied down to the marker or signpost. It indicates why he is to
travel on. Abraham has no fixed home: he is already to move off again.

And this is what anyone who has a sense of purpose about his life knows----that
they must decamp again and again, never completely settling down, but always at the
disposal of that purpose. Only in this way can Abraham become a real blessing in
the next story. A dispute over the land breaks out between his men and those of his
nephew, Lot. Abraham now knows that to have the certainty of the presence of God
everywhere is more important than having the good land. Thus, he easily renounces
the rights and gives Lot his request, who takes the land to the Jordan. And here
again, Abraham demonstrates what the people of God are to be in the world; peace-
makers, people who don't insist on their own rights and interests, for the sake of
peace among them. Reconcilers, if you will, who are able to reconcile because they
are ready to look first to what is good for the other.

Lot chooses the good land around Sodom and Gomorrah without being aware of the
dangers involved. When he gets caught up in the war of the kings of Sodom against
their enemies, Abraham again proves to be available. He does not ask to know the
reasons. He does not spitefully say,"just what you deserve". WE do this, don't we,
when we see people around us not coming to terms with their problems and questions?
We feel the urge to say "the chickens are coming home to roost". We know the feeling inside us, "if you had listened to me". But not so Abraham: he comes and saves
Lot without questions or conditions. And we too experience that. When a crisis
occurs in our personal lives brought on by our own moral failure, someone comes and
stands by us without questions and judgment. When we are in real need, someone we
have spited or ignored or neglected comes into our self-imposed alienation and gives
what we never allowed ourselves to expect.

Wherever men follow Jesus Christ, this is their commission: to be on that spot
where men are in need and to step in on their behalf, that they may live free and
unhindered, that they may grow and act without disabling prejudices and idolatries.
Of course, we must recognize that the manner of stepping in has changed. It was natural for Abraham to step in with arms, but weapons today are the least appropriate

3-13-66

way of coming to the aid of our world. Yet, the commission remains--to be a service corps--a peace corps. And those who join this corps may find that this other thing happens---that people may realize that You-Know-Who is behind his service cadres. This is what happened to Melchizedek, the priest-king of the Canaanite town of Salem.

Abraham sees that it is all important not to let this insight of the surrounding peoples be challenged. Therefore, he refuses what we would so gladly accept: a reward! Yes, we would look for the reward for our service. A medal, a round of applause, a promotion, an honorary degree, a higher salary, an appointment to high office. And we lose our authenticity, our authority, our self-respect. Most of all, we lose our independence, our reliability to do what is right, whether it is popular or not. "Not a thread of a sandal thong or anything that is yours, lest you should say,'I have made Abram rich'".

Because Abraham is that independent, he has kept the freedom to intercede before God. Everything else Abraham has done previously now fades in comparison to what he does now. He now fights with God himself on behalf of the cities that want to live without him, for the cities which have become so disorderly that God wants to destroy them.

There are two outstanding things about this scene. First, the Lord cannot keep his intentions away from Abraham, because Abraham has been chosen to be a blessing to the world. So Abraham is imminently aware of what God intends to do. And that may well mean that we too who are his people living in the world for the welfare of it, that we too shall often realize more sharply than the world itself how near the danger-point it stands, how enmeshed and precarious it has become. The question then is how we will react. Will we succumb, as Christians have so generally done, to that temptation to turn our back so majestically to the world? You know, we too can feel that since we belong to God, we can leave the others to destruction.

And here is the second fascinating thing about this scene: Abraham sides with Sodom and Gomorrah. Man, what bargaining between him and God---a real good haggle. Oh, it's qualified a bit--"Oh let not the Lord be angry...", BUT... Abraham obviously is willing to become obnoxious before God rather than abandon them to destruction. His solidarity with Sodom and Gomorrah does not mean that he approved them; but it means that he will plead for everything that speaks well for them that they might be given one more chance.

And then the most astounding thing--God accepts to bargain; he never rebukes the impertinence; just the contrary, he lets himself be beaten down to the minimum price. The result even so is meagre; not even 10 men could be found. But that does not have to be the case always, and that is not the decisive point. It is instead that God is ready to take his people seriously when they take up the world's cause with him; he will give another chance to all for the sake of a precariously small number. And we also learn another thing here: we never withdraw and leave the world to itself; rather, we stand up in its midst for God and his causes, and we stand before God for the world and its safety.

Now, as I see it, that is the path which we must take to Christian Presence. The shape of this presence is peace and reconciliation. It is the shape of our speaking to the world of value, of reality, of the way things are--of God, if you will. It is also the shape of our presence before God on the world's behalf. Christian presence, then, means insisting among men on God's presence, insisting among men on the humanity of their fellow men, and not least of all insisting with God on the value of men and their world.

Again, as I see, this shape of Christian Presence carries with it a good many dangers, and most of the dangers arise less from external threat than from our own internal lack of faith.

First, we have before us that act of unfaith and lack of trust in which Abraham allows his wife to be taken by Pharoah rather than take the risk of harm himself. He did not trust the protection of God. The danger for us is that we shall try to preserve the Church and our existence as Christians by improper means. There is always the temptation to let the church be "an American institution", a "bulwark against communism". The church can protect its own life by reflecting the prevailing views of American society. It can underline the accepted morality and never challenge the status quo or the authority or power of those who rule. Yes, we can assimilate ourselves and attract as little attention as possible, having little power or promise, but acting as Chaplain to the prevailing ethos, punching society's TS card.

A second danger crops up when Abraham begins to worry that God's promise will not be fulfilled. So, he goes and plays a trick in order to have a son in whom God's promise could be fulfilled. He listens to Sarah's advice, and begets a son of her slave, Hagar.

And this is the danger to all of us who know that it is vital for the Church to make its message known. We realize that things are not going well. The Church is often 'out of it'. We see it ineffectual and powerless, and we conclude that this institution can never be a blessing to the whole world. Abraham in that setting went about helping God out by means which were normal in that day, and we may be tempted to do the same. We try, for example, to make the Church influential and important. Too often our attempt to mobilize and influence public opinion and governmental action arises out of this motive rather than the motive to see the right thing done. We may end up dazzled with our own power and yet fail to understand why many would consider us just one pressure group over against others. While it is important to get things done, we should never simply seek power or attention. And unless we are both honest and careful, our jazz and folk liturgies, coffee houses, and "peaceful protests" can degenerate to the level of gimmicks. What starts out as genuine, we find ending up as 'showboating' in a world in which the Church stands so often on the fringes. Such cheap ways of convincing others that we are powerful, or different from what they thought about us, can mislead us entirely from what we should be about. They can hide, in other words, the key thing about the life of God's people in the world: that they reflect the presence and action of God. They don't have to, but they can unless the church learns to wait and listen. The very things we have mentioned can be instruments of waiting and listening if we give up the concern for power, attention, status, and preservation of present forms.

Now, there is a third danger which faced Abraham, and it is qualitatively different in that God himself brings it on. God demands that Abraham sacrifice Isaac, the guarantee of the promise. This is an inhuman requirement. And yet even this can be asked of us as we live in the world as God's people. We can be asked to give up familiar and cherished forms of church life, of mission, of worship, of youth work ---things which we have previously believed to be God's ordained way of working. We can feel torn apart from the need to give up something which has worked and which we trust, and such a parting often seems to endanger our faith itself. However, when we overcome the danger and are ready for the sake of mission and authenticity to let go of former guarantees of God's presence, then we learn, like Abraham, that we receive them back renewed. Success in this last test brought renewed promise to Abraham and opened the future up.

3-13-66

-4-

And the future is what we too must think about. The Abraham story was retold in order to remind Israel over the centuries that it had received God's blessing only for the purpose of being a blessing to the nations of the world. Israel overlooked this calling and was increasingly condemned to a marginal existence, until it was violently scattered about through the nations. Yet, the hope remained that this people would be a blessing to all.

The Church of the New Testament knew this expectation fulfilled in its presence. "You are a city set upon a hill." Jesus used this to point the church to its function; the same function Isaiah had hoped for from Jerusalem--peace and justice shall go out from Zion. Jesus puts this together with the saying that the light of the Church shall so shine among men that they may see our good works and give glory to God, and in doing so reminds us that our presence in the world today can do no more ---but should in fact--reflect the presence of God.

Jesus has taken up the old promise and passed it on to us, his people. Therefore, we can read this story of Abraham as our own story, and we can take the words of promise as spoken to us, as our future--"I will bless you and you will be a blessing."   So BE it!

This sermon, and others in the series, have been stimulated by the World Student Christian Federation's statement on Christian Presence and by treatments of the theme over the past two years in Student World, especially No. 3, 1965--Geneva.

52. 5/22/66   Authentic Human Speech   Third week of August

The Matthew reference for this sermon (also found in Mark 4:10-12 and Luke 8:9-10) poses the disciples' question to Jesus about why he spoke in parables. The answer is captured in this declaration: Seek first to understand, then to be understood. To understand someone else – that is, listening deeply in order to see their issues and their perspectives – requires patience. Once understanding is achieved, THEN it is appropriate to make oneself understood – and that part requires courage. Understanding a parable requires deep listening and empathy, even having an *I-Thou* relationship with the speaker. Jesus did not speak in code; he spoke in a way that *neighbors* would understand. Interestingly, nearly 2100 years after Jesus made this point and 23 years after Asbury gave this sermon, the concept became the fifth habit in Stephen Covey's 1989 book, The *Seven Habits of Highly Effective People*.

Originally delivered on May 22, 1966, just before the graduation of Wooster's Centennial Class of '66, this was perhaps the last sermon we heard in person from Rev. Asbury. For altogether independent reasons, it is a particularly good one to conclude this Cycle of 52 sermons. The sermon is highly personal. It reflects Rev. Asbury's independence and his Christian stance of pouring oneself into humble, persistent service. Such a model of behavior forms a worthy benediction.

Westminster Presbyterian Church
Wooster, Ohio
Rev. Beverly Asbury, Minister
May 22, 1966

AUTHENTIC HUMAN SPEECH
Matthew 13: 10-17

The Christian Church in the United States is not accustomed to a serious and open challenge. The content of its message, the language of its proclamations, the structure of its organization, and the style of its leadership were developed in the context of society in which Christian beliefs were taken for granted. This is still the way it is in some of the more rural and isolated hamlets, or so we imagine, and this is the way that many people would like for it to be again. That fact makes it difficult for the churches to gain their bearing in the new situation of urban America.

Now, the Church can despair of it all and struggle to survive, or the Church can accept the need for a radical reformation. I am in the ministry today, at least partly, out of a conviction that came during my college years that the Church is being called to new patterns of obedience which must be reflected in new structures of institutional life.

This does not mean that churchmen today should expect the Church to light upon immediate solutions to all the problems that it has taken generations to face and accept. We are groping for answers today—sometimes desperately—and ad hoc answers should not be taken as final policies. However, the Church must in the future take the society more seriously than in the past. The Church has not really appreciated how much the individual person is influenced by social pressures over which he has little, if any, control. We can expect no widespread response to the Gospel by modern men until and unless we take account of those areas of social life which have such a profound affect upon human attitudes and behavior.

It is in this light that I find myself questioning the American Christian's ready and easy acceptance of Billy Graham and his style. Mind you, I do not doubt Dr. Graham's good intentions or his overwhelming sincerity. Rather, it is the content and style and language and technique that I find harmful in the long run.

The Graham Crusades have a startling similarity to 'soap-box' evangelism where the emphasis is on quick returns in the form of a personal response from individuals whose feelings of guilt have been successfully aroused. This whole technique seems preoccupied with only one thing—filling the empty pews of the churches today. Studies have shown that these massive efforts influence those who are already more-or-less committed to the Church. However, the serious part is that their very numbers lead a good many ministers and even more laymen to postpone the hard thinking about how to reach the modern man who is uncommitted.

The Graham Crusades confirm too many Christians in their antipathy to constructive social thinking and to the consideration of the new forms of life a radical reformation of the Church will take. Graham uses the King James Version of the Bible, an acceptable language, to be sure. Yet, when you combine its familiarity to those who hear it with his near-literalistic interpretations, you simply confirm to the man-outside-the-church that the Church is "out of it". The "ancient Gospel" sounds "ancient", archaic, petrified—concerned, it seems, solely with the saving of individual men and women from the perils of life in a world which is degenerating rapidly and will soon be consumed in the fires of hell.

My father was here part of this past week, and on Monday night as we sat a-
round the dinner table, we talked about the "gospel sings" which are held every
year at our county courthouse. These Sunday afternoon events, which I heard as a
child, had a gospel theme but were nevertheless quite commercial. Of course, Nash-
ville recognizes that and now records all this "music" to the accompanying jingle
of many profits. As we talked about all this, we sang some of the ones we remem-
bered. The words of one go like this: "Here I wander like a beggar through the
heat and the cold, for my burdens are so heavy and my sorrows untold. But to Jesus
I am clinging: let me hide, dear Lord, in Thee, for this old world with its sorrow
is an unfriendly world to me." Those who accept this view point, including our
dear Dr. Crane, oppose all those who attempt to proclaim the Gospel in twentieth
century terms; they oppose all who are concerned with a contemporary interpretation
of Christian ethics. They take every opportunity to denounce scholars and pastors
who are trying to communicate Christian truth in ways which make sense to those
who are outside the orbit of traditional belief.

The Church of which they are a part may survive, but, I repeat, I long ago
accepted the need not to survive but to reform the church to serve a new age. Our
world is largely secular, and we must hammer out some connection between the "eternal verities" and the world of modern men. This hammering will be done in a thunderstorm of criticism——(I am here to tell you that! At least if I haven't known a
thunderstorm, I have been exposed to a few showers, and one never knows but what
the thunder and lightening will follow.)——and the work will require great tenacity
and high courage. But this is not only worth doing; it is also imperative if we
would speak the authentic Gospel to modern man. That is, we must find an authentic
human speech with which to communicate the Gospel in every new age.

Jesus himself faced the problem of authentic speech. He spoke in parables to
the crowds, and his disciples inquired of him why he did so. Jesus quotes from
Isaiah to indicate that the people hear but do not grasp the truth, because their
heart, which in Hebraic manner includes intellectual capacity, has become dull.
Literally, their heart has become thick and calloused; they are not sensitive and
attentive; they hear with difficulty and do not keep alert. Then comes the ironi-
cal note; Jesus states that the result of their callousness and indifference——which
he tried to overcome with his parable illustrations———is unresponsiveness. With
sad irony Jesus says that they _fear_ they may see and hear and understand and turn
back, that is, repent, and receive from God healing, salvation, and blessing.
Their guilty callousness may turn them away from the very thing they need. Because
of the immense difficulty of arousing such people to their needs, Jesus uses parables. He searches for an authentic human speech, a way for presenting truth which
may penetrate the dullness and incomprehension which is leading people to their
doom. He seeks by parables to illustrate, clarify, and enforce truth and lead men
to the right decision as they faced his Kingdom teaching.

This kind of speech, which I have called "authentic", recognizes, as Tom F.
Driver of Union Seminary puts it (Christianity and Crisis, May 16, 1966), "no obligation to conform to accepted canons of style, beauty and rhetoric. At the same
time it feels free to employ any styles and techniques that are useful in the course
course of its swift flight to the target. This quality in the speech of the early
Church, as reflected in the New Testament, has been discussed by Amos Wilder in
The Language of the Gospel. The earliest Christian speech is "naive, it is not
studied; it is extempore and directed to the occasion, it is not calculated to
serve some future hour. This utterance is dynamic, actual, immediate, reckless of
posterity; not coded for catechists or repeaters."

Perhaps it was out of such a conviction that C. S. Lewis, no mean master of
the English language himself, wrote the "Introduction" in 1947 to J.B. Phillips'
translation of the New Testament Epistles, Letters to Young Churches. C.S. Lewis

speaks directly to those who find a modern translation both unnecessary and even offensive. He reminds such objectors that there was once great opposition to any English translation at all. He says, "Dozens of pious people in the sixteenth century shuddered at the idea of turning the time-honoured Latin of the Vulgate into our common and (as they thought) barbarous English." When the Bible was put into the "language men use", into the forms of authentic human speech, they felt it lost something. Lewis says that the only "sanctity" it could lose by being "modernized" was the "accidental kind which it never had for its writers or earliest readers." Lewis makes clear what Wilder says--that the New Testament was written in "vulgar, prosaic and unliterary language. The New Testament in original Greek is not a work of art. It really should not shock us to learn that the New Testament was written in crude language unless we are also shocked that God's son was a baby at his mother's breast, preached in unliterary language, and died on a very crude cross. As C. S. Lewis says, if we can stomach one we ought to be able to stomach the other. "The Incarnation is, in that sense, an irreverent doctrine: Christianity, in that sense, an incurably irreverent religion." The real beauty and sublimity of the New Testament, and of Jesus' life are of a different sort than the beauty we have come to expect from the King James Version.

I will not belabor Lewis's point that the King James Version has ceased to be a good, a clear translation. "It is no longer modern English; the meanings of words have changed. The same antique glamour which has made it (in the superficial sense) so 'beautiful', so 'sacred', so 'comforting', and so 'inspiring', has also made it in many places unintelligible."

Finally, Lewis reminds us that we must get away from the King James Version, "if for no other reason, simply because it is so beautiful and so solemn. Beauty exalts, but beauty also lulls. Early associations endear but they also confuse. Through that beautiful solemnity the transporting or horrifying realities of which the Books tells may come to us blunted and disarmed and we may only sigh with tranquil veneration when we ought to be burning with shame or struck dumb with terror or carried out of ourselves by ravishing hopes and adorations."

An authentic human speech, like the parables of Jesus, must be concerned with making people see and hear and understand and turn back and receive God's reconciliation and wholeness. And let us not forget that Jesus was not addressing these parables to the disciples. The disciples, according to Matthew, stand in strong contrast to the callousness of the people. The disciples see and hear. They can be grateful for they know that they live in dramatic days of powerful fulfillment. God is establishing his reign, and they know it. Jesus, then, can and must address his parables to those who don't know it and don't want to know it.

And, you see, this is very different from what Billy Graham is doing. (Since this sermon was written the Christian Century of May 25, 1966 has published a critique of Billy Graham by Cecil Northcott, pages 673-675. It is commended to you as a sound development of this theme.) And it is very different from the concern of those who want to keep the King James Version in use in the Church. Their concern often enough is with themselves and others who are already committed. And while there is a certain legitimacy to that, we cannot forget that Jesus taught that he came not for the saved but for the unsaved, not for the reconciled but for the unreconciled, not for those already loved but for the unlovely and unloved. It could not be clearer that the Church does not exist for its own sake. It does not even exist for the sake of those within it. It has been called into being as the faithful people of God for the sake of the world. God sent his son for the world, that it might not be condemned but redeemed. The Church, as the Body of Christ, has a mission not to itself but to the world which stands in need of reconciliation.

-4-

All this has been made abundantly clear in Pier Pasolini's movie <u>The Gospel According to St. Matthew</u>, which is now showing in Cleveland, and probably is the "first Biblical film that embodies true faith." Tom Driver has said that this "film presents us with nothing other than that genuine Word of which theologians so frequently write but of which they seldom find examples toward which to point. The origin of this Word is quite outside human invention and control, but it could never be present in culture if there did not also occur authentic human speech....."

Pasolini uses diverse styles and techniques in this movie, but he never employs them for their effect. Pasolini seems to understand that authentic speech does not care about effect; that it drives single-mindedly, as Driver puts it, toward the statement of its intent. This film detects this quality in Jesus. After the temptations, for example, Jesus walks on a lonely path toward Galilee. He meets a group of farmers carrying scythes and winnowing tools toward their fields. As he passes them, he says, "Repent, for the Kingdom of Heaven is at hand", and he keeps on going. They stop and stare, wondering whether he said what they thought he had said. And when Jesus gathers his disciples, he does not sit them down and lay out his mission for them to see. Instead he walks and talks to them as he goes along, striding out ahead of the group, tossing his words to the wind. Those in the rear have to run to catch up and try to hear what he is saying, all the while trying to keep their footing on the path.

In this context all the statements of Jesus about people not hearing, about ears that remain closed, become immensely important. "I speak in parables...because hearing they do not understand...." This is no riddle, for Jesus points straight to the fact that hearing the Word can be as much a matter of intent as speaking it. The disciples hear because they want to hear. "He that has ears to hear, let him hear."

It would be great irony if it appeared that the 'authentic speech' of Jesus Christ and his Church could not be heard by the 'disciples' within but only those without who have not come to faith. But it would also be a great triumph, because Jesus addressed his parables to such people. Yet, one can hope that the forms of authentic speech of which we have spoken can be heard by <u>all</u>: "....blessed are your eyes, for they see, and your ears, for they hear. Truly, I say to you, many prophets and righteous men longed to see what you see, and did not see it, and to hear what you hear, and did not hear it."

EPILOG

An epilog is a place to tie up loose ends, to reveal consequences, to add insights and explanations. Among the Wooster talks of Rev. Asbury are some that, even though they don't seem to fit into the Cycle, are integral to the collection and should not be left out. Among these are some sermons that amplify those that were included, a couple of chapel talks, and the last sermon he gave at Wooster. The final sermon was delivered on Dec. 4, 1966, six months after the Class of '66 had graduated. We in the Class of '66 did not hear it in person. Nevertheless, that important sermon is included here.

A. 11/24/64   Chapel Talk: The Love Life of a College Student

The first half of the 1960s was the time of the Second Wave of US Feminism, the first wave identified as accompanying women's suffrage in the early 1900s, led by Elizabeth Cady Stanton, Susan B. Anthony, and Harriet Tubman, among others. The Second Wave contributed to what became the sexual revolution. In 1956, social mores were such that the Ed Sullivan Show televised Elvis Presley only from the waist up in order shield viewers from his well-known pelvic gyrations. By 1960-66, the following events and publications occurred: President Kennedy's Commission on the Status of Women, chaired by Eleanor Roosevelt; Gloria Steinem's essays, first on the women's dilemma of career vs. marriage and, second, on women's treatment in men's clubs following her employment as a Playboy bunny; the book, *Sex and the Single Girl* by Helen Gurley Brown, followed by the movie starring Natalie Wood; the book *The Feminine Mystique* by Betty Friedan; formation of the National Organization for Women (NOW), with Betty Friedan as its first president, and the US Supreme Court decision favoring Planned Parenthood in *Griswold vs. Connecticut*, which struck down Connecticut's Comstock Law, made birth control publicly available, and established a reproductive right to privacy.

In this atmosphere, campus physician Dr. Viola Startzman worked with Rev. Asbury to present seminars on the role that love and sex – including pre-marital sex – played among 1960s college students. The 50+ years since those seminars and this chapel talk have seen the arrival of the US Supreme Court decision *Roe v. Wade*, attempts by some states to offset that decision, the continuing rise of female rights, the appearance of HIV/AIDS, refinements in The Pill, the appearance of surrogacy and *in vitro* fertilization, genetic manipulation, growing public acceptance of LGBT lifestyles, and the evolution of numerous related social and sexual mores. With all this on the unseen far horizon, Rev. Asbury develops enduring principles from Martin Buber's *I-Thou* concept, discusses Hugh Hefner's *Playboy* concept, outlines the marriage ceremony, birth control, and pregnancy, and closes by drawing on Paul's poetic words from I Corinthians 13 (also used in Sermon #6) – all in the same chapel talk.

[*Note:* The startling phrase, "kleptomaniacs, perverts, lesbians, and other kindred spirits" in this chapel talk refers to a student perspective printed elsewhere. The phrase is cited ironically, as is apparent from the context of the rest of the talk.]

THE LOVE LIFE OF A COLLEGE STUDENT
An Expanded Version of a Chapel Talk
Delivered on November 24, 1964
By Beverly Asbury, Pastor of
Westminster Presbyterian Church

The genesis of this talk lies in the Student Government Association's Seminars on Sex and Responsible Selfhood conducted by Dr. Startzman, the college physician, and myself. Much of the material which is covered in this talk is covered in those seminars but with both greater breadth and depth. This talk is not to replace the value of the seminars for any of you who have not attended them, but perhaps it is to acquaint you with the point of view and interest some of you in giving your time to them in the next semester. Much of the material which I present this morning grows out of my counseling experience as a pastor and as a college chaplain. Other parts of the material are directly drawn from and are both consciously and unconsciously indebted to Dean Ferm, the Chaplain at Mt. Holyoke College, and to a sermon he gave there over a year ago, using the title I have "borrowed" from him. I'm also indebted to Harry Smith, Presbyterian University Pastor to the University of North Carolina, and four talks which he gave at the Religion-in-Life Week a year ago at Florida State University. In other words, I do not claim that material which I use this morning is original with me. In fact, most of it is borrowed. What I claim to be my own is the point of view which I present here. The material simply expresses it. In this sense, this has become "my material" too. I simply wanted to acknowledge my debt to others and to the experience in this field which has been provided by counseling with many of you.

What I am about to say to you this morning is subject to greater misunderstanding, misquotation, and misinterpretation than anything else that I have ever said in this Chapel. For example, Dr. Startzman and I were invited to a recent meeting of the Ohio Deans' Association on this campus. The Association wanted Dr. Startzman and me to explain to them what we were doing in our Seminars on Sex and Responsible Selfhood. Dr. Startzman was accorded the privilege of making the first presentation. Her opening remarks were, and I quote,"Mr. Asbury and I do this sex thing together." Obviously, that remark brought a great deal of laughter, and it may well produce an act of expulsion of Wooster from the Association.(and maybe our expulsion from Wooster!) I use this simply to illustrate the dangers which are involved in talking on this subject. Some of you will feel that it is an improper subject for public presentation and mixed company. Many college and church officials across the land continue a kind of conspiracy of silence regarding this subject. Many people I know feel that if we ignore the problem it may disappear. I, obviously, do not feel that it will disappear, and I propose to approach it to you this morning in as open and mature fashion as I possibly can.

Now, there will be others of you who will say that I can hardly be objective concerning this problem. After all, I am a clergyman. And have you ever heard of a clergyman who advocated free love? Someone told me of one who did, and I understand that he is no longer a clergyman. Thus, some of you will say that there is a bias which is built into my occupation. Still others will say that the subject---the love life of a college student --cannot be dealt with by talking about it. You will think that it is so private and so special that it cannot be subject to public scrutiny without objectifying it and degrading it.

Yet this subject is of such intense importance that I would consider it cowardly to ignore it. I have chosen rather to face this subject with all the risk of misinterpretation and misquotation involved rather than to be irrelevant to what I consider a crucial issue facing this generation of college students. I know full well that my position, like every human position, is limited and fallible. I only

Ch. Tlk.

ask you not simply to look for loopholes in what I say, but to look for the position for you which has the fewest loopholes.

We live in a day when a great many people seem to assume that nothing in regard to sexuality is inviolably sacred. Even a cursory glance at certain aspects of social life on many college campuses indicates not only that sexual promiscuity is on the rise, but also that many students feel that what they do in this aspect of their lives is their own business--and no one else's! When the Dean of Harvard deplored the fact that a growing number of students were using their rooms for wild sex parties, the Harvard _Crimson_ seemed to suggest that sexual freedom is an analagous to freedom of religion and speech. When the president of Vassar College declared almost two years ago that sexual purity was a norm expected of Vassar students, a large segment of the student body protested that its behavior was none of her business. One student newspaper editorialized that the moral character of students should not be a criterion for admission. Apparently kleptomaniacs, perverts, lesbians, and other kindred spirits should not be discriminated against. Other colleges have experienced similar student declarations of independence, and one college not very far away from here has had great problems of its own in this area.

I'm not prepared this morning in my limited time to discuss all the causes for this revolution in moral standards. Others have done that, and many causes have been suggested: the insecurity of our times, the greater independence of college students, the more permissive attitude toward behavior, etc. The fact is that a change has occurred and is occurring. Our problem is what, if anything, should be done about it. And I do not mean for one minute to suggest that the revolution is entirely bad. I find it good in the sense that the revolution in morals rids us of the Victorian notion that sex is dirty. However, I conclude that it is bad in the sense that it has made sex cheap. It has cheapened something that is beautiful and holy, and it is leading to the destruction of certain basic values which most of us would prefer to maintain.

Having said this, I should now like to focus our attention on the problems of premarital behavior, although I recognize this to be one aspect of a larger problem. Certain ones of you already have your minds made up on this matter, but I hope that you will listen anyway. Primarily, however, I am speaking directly to those of you for whom the old "Thou shalt nots," have lost their sanction, but who want to develop a sensible rationale for premarital behavior, not only for yourselves but also in the hope that you can provide some positive support to the moral tone of our campus and our society. I shall point to a number of problems which must be thoroughly explored before one can wipe away the virtue of premarital purity. All the problems I mention are important, but I have attempted to mention them in order of increasing seriousness.

The first problem which is of concern to many people today is the rising incidence of venereal disease. This has been adequately documented both in the popular press and in studies which have been conducted in serious sociological fashion. It is a distressing report, and I take it that a college has the responsibility to point out the real dangers involved in the rise of venereal diseases in the youngor generation. Yet, even accepting the seriousness of this, it occurs to me that this is not the most serious problem to couples who claim to be in love and have refrained from relationship with others. Apparently, there is no danger of contracting a venereal disease for two persons who have remained pure outside their own relationship.

I want then to turn to the second problem which concerns one of the most tragic experiences that can happen, namely the unwanted pregnancy. This is one of the most tragic things for everyone involved--the unborn child, the parents, their parents, their friends, their future. Sometimes I think that the most effective way to present the dangers of premarital pregnancies is to have an unmarried mother and/or the unmarried father to tell at firsthand of their heartaches and headaches. Sometimes the saddest words I ever hear are those of the girl who is introducing a difficult subject by saying, "Mr. Asbury, I think that I am a 'little bit' pregnant." This is the quiet and simple introduction to one of the most perplexing and difficult problems with which a pastor or counselor ever deals. It is never easy to know what is the right thing to do. Marriage may or may not be the answer, and when it's not the answer, there are so many heartaches involved in bearing a child and placing that child for adoption. Now, to be sure, methods of artificial birth control are constantly being improved and being made available. The "pill" is the most effective deterent and may well become the most readily available. But let's face it: most unwanted pregnancies are the results of moments of passion when reason is thrown to the winds. In a moment of passion one does not think clearly; if he is thinking clearly, friends, he's not being passionate! But passion does not encompass it all. I have counseled with a great number of people who are not only passionate, but who are terribly irresponsible. I had a student to come to me at Westminster College where I was Chaplain. When he came for the first time, he said that his girl, who lived in a city a few hundred miles away, was pregnant. I counseled with him, and he certainly was not mature or ready to be married. I counseled with the girl, with both sets of parents. Finally, it was decided by all the parties involved that marriage was not the perfect answer but was the only one feasible in this instance. As it turned out, the girl was not pregnant. I thought surely that this young man had learned something from the experience and the counseling, but evidently he did not. The next time that I saw him was a few months later when he came in to tell me that he was in the same situation, but now with another girl. Again, I sought to deal with him in a non-judgmental fashion. However, I made it as clear as I absolutely could that I did not agree with his sexual standards or find them easy to understand. However, as a pastor, I went through with him, the girl, and with both sets of parents the same procedure as before. Before any decision had been reached, it was discovered that the girl was not pregnant. Now twice is pretty lucky! I thought surely this lustful, irresponsible student not only had learned a lesson but would produce a change in his standards and habits. This did not take place, and the next fall the same boy came in and told me that the girl who had been involved the year before was now indeed pregnant. I was at the end of my counseling rope. My non-directive and non-judgmental approach could only go so far. I really blew up. I wondered why, if he could not change his moral convictions and habits, he could not at least have enough respect for the girl and the parents and society-at-large to use a contraceptive. He replied that they had used a contraceptive "part of the time." This instance of total irresponsibility reminded me of nothing so much as the moral in one of James Thurber's favorites. The moral goes like this: "Love is blind but lust just doesn't give a good goddamn." In the most meaningful sense of that moral, this man was guilty of lust.

He illustrates that the unwanted pregnancy can well be a terrible situation for everyone involved. The best safety devices in the world and the best intentions will not stop conception in every case. I am my brother's keeper. The young man whom I have mentioned had no understanding of what that means. I have a responsibility to others that goes beyond myself, and even beyond the other person whom I love deeply. The young man whom I have mentioned, and everything that he symbolizes, doesn't begin to understand the word "responsibility".

Chap Tlk

-4-

However, let's assume that there is no possibility of venereal disease. Let us assume that man and woman are going to be 100% rational at all times and will take whatever precaution necessary to prevent pregnancy. What then? One must still face an even more serious problem and ask himself this: What is my motive in this relationship? Why am I so involved?

There are two things to be kept in mind here: First, the ideal relationship between two people who are deeply in love; and second, the sacred intimacy of the sexual act itself. Why do two people want to get married, ideally speaking? They want to get married because there is a compulsion which draws them into a new relationship which makes them want to share their lives together. This compulsion does not come automatically; nor does it usually come suddenly. Normally, it comes only after a period of time in which two people have learned to know each other as persons with growing intensity and intimacy. There are a number of conditions which people have to meet before they understand marriage to be something which comes, not out of need or necessity, but out of an act of will to give themselves one to another, to live their lives together in independence and interdependence.

The first condition which must be met is obviously that both parties must be willing to participate. Mutual involvement is essential. Love is primarily a verb not a noun. It means genuine mutual participation. So, is the desire to have sexual relationship a genuine mutual decision that is made freely and lovingly.

Then, there must be a sense of mutual trust between two individuals. Suspicion leads to alienation and to jealousy. If one does not trust the one whom he claims to love, then he does not love him. Do I respect the values which the other person in the relationship holds sacred? Do I expect the other to change his values in order to please me? Am I marrying one because I can shape him or her into a pale reflection of my own ego, or because I have great respect for the personhood, the selfhood of the other? Do I understand and affirm the other in the fullness of his life, or am I only looking to this one for the sake of my own gratification?

This leads me to say the most important thing I want to say today. Each person must recognize the other person as an end in himself, as a Thou rather than an It. These terms are borrowed from Martin Buber, the contemporary Jewish sage. Many of you know Buber's book and understand what he tells us about man's relationship to the world and to other people. He characterizes the relationship as being twofold: I-Thou and I-It. Each of these relationships involves a different kind of knowledge and in each our response is different. In the I-It relationship we look upon the other person as a thing--an It-- to be manipulated for our own ends. The other person becomes an object which we consume for our own selfish interests. In the I-Thou relationship, the other person is a person like ourselves, with his own interest and integrity. We cannot manipulate the other for our own sake for the moment that we do, the Thou becomes an It.

Buber maintains that the history of the individual and the human race both indicate a progressive augmentation of the world of It. Our age is becoming more and more mechanical and impersonal, and the real crisis of our time is the need to rediscover the personal dimension. When I spoke to you a year ago about Playboy magazine this is what I tried to illustrate. Playboy characterizes the world of It. It glorifies the body. It tells us that we are to treat another as an It, as a playmate, as one to be used, to be manipulated; as one to be enjoyed for gratification, but never, no never, one with whom to be involved or to whom to be committed. We have the glorification of an endless monotony of bared bosoms and bared bodies. We allow ourselves to be depersonalized by looking at the outward signs of what it means to have an attractive body rather than to be a meaningful and attractive person. I believe that Buber is right--that somehow we must discover the reality and depths of genuine interpersonal relationships. To seek sexual pleasure without sexual responsiblity is what J. B. Priestly calls eroticism, and that it is! Nothing worth calling a relationship can be created in this way.

May I suggest, then, that we must honestly examine our motives for wanting premarital sexual relationships? Why are we becoming involved? Am I really there? Is my partner really there? Is this a real relationship? Is there mutual trust and involvement? Are we really seeking a deep and lasting union of two persons, or are we seeking for our own physical satisfaction? Are we treating each other as ends rather than as means? Are we keeping in mind the values that we want to share with the other person so long as we both shall live--trust, decency, truth, love, tenderness--the same values we want our children to hold and uphold?

And what about the sacredness of the sexual act itself? Ought not it be the culmination of the love relationship when both parties can give freely and completely of themselves? I think so, and I believe strongly that it is so. There is an analogy here between the climax of the physical act itself and the act of getting married. Both involve a preliminary period of engagement, of courtship, and certain amount of time that will permit the relationship to bloom in which each person is getting to know with integrity and with increasing intimacy the other person. That man who will not take time, is, psychologically and morally speaking, a fool. The time element is important, and it should not be underestimated by activist people who are always in a hurry! There is something sacred about the intimacies of the close physical relationship just as there is something sacred about the marriage ceremony itself. Time alone allows the development of intimacy and marriage.

The marriage ceremony tries to represent something very important, a covenant between man and woman to love and to cherish as long as they both shall live. It is a sacred event. It is a promise of a new and holy relationship. I believe it to be the most important covenant two people ever make. The promise is of primary importance, and the sex act is one significant aspect of the deeper covenant. But we should never forget that sex is but one of the significant aspects that make marriage meaningful and hopeful. It is the relationship which comes first. If the relationship in marriage is poor, don't ever imagine that sex alone will make the relationship into a good one. The relationship itself is of primary importance, and it is only within the framework of this deeper rela tionship that the physical act takes on a new meaning. This meaning of the physical act of sex comes when each person can give himself to fulfill not himself but the other person. In this sense it is the final culmination of the sacred covenant of marriage.

Now I wish to make myself perfectly clear. I cannot say that premarital sexual relationship is always necessarily bad. In fact, I have attempted not to speak in such theoretical terms this morning. If I were to speak in theoretical terms, someone of you would attempt to cite me statistics, and there are statistics that seem to support both sides of the argument. However, my primary reason for steering in another way comes from my recognition that this is a decision that two individuals will not let me or anyone else decide for them. Two individual persons must decide for themselves, lovingly and privately as persons, as "Thous". They should not easily or quickly assume that they are exceptions to the I-Thou relationship and what it means. But they should know that part of the personal dimension of our humanity lies in the fact that they must decide. They must decide and that is what makes human beings human! There is no eternal Yardstick that can decide every situation. I'm not saying here that whatever a couple decides makes it right.

Chap Tlk

I am saying that I understand that every two individual persons must decide for themselves whether they are enhancing the integrity of their relationship and the sacredness of the physical act itself, or whether they--or one of them--are rationalizing themselves into believing what they want to believe for their own personal satisfaction.

It is my own conviction that there are very great dangers in premarital sexual relationships that can lead to much unhappiness,and that one should be cognizant of the motives and prepared for the consequences. My counseling experience underscores the fact that the consequences of premarital sex are generally unrecognized until later in life. Women usually do not know they are pregnant until a certain length of time has passed after conception. Just so, one does not know the emotional scars that can appear until a period of time after the sex act itself. The broken engagement, the feeling of guilt that cannot be erased, often the disappointment that the sex act was not what it was supposed to be, the inadequacies and inferiorities that seem to come out of a premarital act for many people, are very real possibilities and should not and cannot be ignored.

I think that I have dealt with college students for too long a time to be dumb enough to try to frighten them. I only want to point that the consequences are seldom noticeable immediately and that, in most cases, (and this is what I really want to say this morning; if you remember nothing else about this talk, I hope that you will remember this)-- a delay until after the marriage covenant has been established is not only a sensible, pragmatic device to prevent unnecessary problems but also a genuine acknowledgment between two people who are in love that this is something sacred, well worth waiting for.

It frightens me to think what the values of our society will be for our children's children if we continue the glorification of I-It relationships. The breakdown of authentic I-Thou relationships does very little to give me hope. Where sex was once thought to be dirty, now so many think it to be cheap. I must maintain to you that to treat sex as cheap or easy is just as wrong as to treat sex as dirty. Let us develop a notion of sex as neither degrading or cheap, but as something holy, sacred, and beautiful;as something which can be appreciated fully only in the context of a deeper love between two people.

We have a deep need, a deep hunger for the recognition of the personal qualities of selfhood. Each of us wants to be loved and respected, and trusted. Each of us knows that the only kind of life that makes sense for us is a life in which the I-Thou love relationship is primary. This is the kind of love that is patient, kind; it is not arrogant, or rude. This kind of love does not insist on its own way; it is not irritable, resentful; does not rejoice in wrong, but rejoices in the right. It bears all things, believes all things, hopes all things, endures all things. So faith, hope,love,abide, these three; but the greatest of these is love.

B.   11/22/66   Chapel Talk: Thanksgiving Meditation

Delivered on the Tuesday just before Thanksgiving break (but after the Class of '66 graduated), this chapel talk rails against the narcissism of having too much to eat while others are going hungry. Rev. Asbury's sermons often reveal an impatience with pious Christian inactivity in the face of obvious injustice and need. More poignantly than the sermons within the Cycle, this talk reveals the depth of his personal involvement and passion…and some of toll it took on him.

Thanksgiving Meditation
By Beverly A. Asbury
College of Wooster Chapel
November 22, 1966

Opening Hymn 461   "We Praise Thee, O God"

Some of you don't want to be here today; wish you weren't here. I don't want to be here either; was tempted not to be here. I'm hardly in the proper frame of mind to meditate, to say nothing of being thankful. The reasons for my state are many— and will be left unstated.* So, you ask, why don't we call it off? No, I can't do that. I said I'd do it. I gave my word. And, if you'll pardon the psychological jargon—I'm over-toilet-trained in Puritan ethics.

So, on with the show. Don't look ahead to tonight. Keep it irrelevant, Beverly old boy. Meditate on thanksgiving. God, that's hard. The thing I've always found most difficult to do is create something around an assigned theme, a patriotic day, a religious holiday, or what have you. What can you say? Without being trite? Without sounding like a prayer in a football locker room —or even worse, one over a loudspeaker system before the game?

Thanksgiving, man. Be thankful. Hard to be controversial about that. Your last chapel talk. Well, get with it. Use Malcolm Boyd as a model, <u>Are You Running With Me, Jesus</u>? Write some prayers of your own. Reflect, man. What have you got to say?

Well, here goes.

<u>Lord, it's turkey day, and I'm going to eat too much.</u>
God, upstairs my children are still asleep. There are three of them, two girls and a boy. By each bed is a candy bar. Their rooms are full of toys, some expensive and others a bit worn and old—those are the ones they really love. Soon, a new day starts for them; no school, just play. And then we'll eat that great big bird.
Lord, It's strange! Here all is peaceful. It simply will not enter my mind that men elsewhere are hungry; that ten thousand humans will die today from hunger. Lord, I will watch the Cleveland Browns take on Dallas, but will I hear mothers of children hysterical with despair because they have no food? Lord, I'll carve that bird with white meat for all, dishing it out with cranberries and dressing, but will I hear the fathers of those children cursing <u>me</u> as a <u>rich</u> man, and you, too—a silent God? How would I feel if I had nothing for my children to eat? I know damned well how I'd feel! Lord, I'll pray for peace in Vietnam, end of destruction, but will my conscience hear the one phrase, the one terrible piercing sentence of an African: "You destroy four million people each year by hunger"? Who me? Us?
O Lord God, it's turkey day. I can't pray. I'm too full. Lord, you pray for me and us sinners. Pray for me and mankind. Amen.

Hymn 240   "Lord, From the Depths To Thee I Cried"

John Kennedy spoke a terrible phrase, Lord, when he said that mankind for the first time in history could have enough food to feed all.
That's what he said, Lord. He said it was only a question of the will to help. Lord, he was killed three years ago. But his words! If only he had never said this! I could think today of Pilgrims; I could believe hunger a tragic situation——alas, for two-thirds of mankind. Lord, if only John Kennedy had left me with the frustration that all I can do is give a few dollars a year to Church World Service or CARE. But he did not. Sweet Jesus! Since he spoke that phrase, hunger became a crime. Since only the will to share is required, the simple fact

that we do not share makes me (and you) a criminal.

O Lord, that turkey is a symbol. It's the crime symbol of good people------
our unwillingness to share more than one half of 1% of our Gross National Product
for foreign aid, our collective egotism that we're your special people, our corporate guilt of not killing the demon of hunger. When the judgment day comes and
we are called to account, and we say ½ of 1%, will it be enough?

Now I see it. John Kennedy exposes us as basically inhuman. Take hold of us,
Jesus. Connect us with the lives in the rest of the world. Help us to see the
truth and stop covering it up. But keep us from pessimism; it's our enemy--Kennedy
said all we needed was the will. Give it to us, Lord, whatever it may mean, whatever it may cost, for what we have is surely not Thy kingdom, not now, not in this
world! And it is for that that we ask: Thy kingdom come and free men from hunger.
And Lord, let us never think that we are part of it until we are involved in doing
that ourselves. So be it, Lord. So be it. Amen.

Hymn 424   "Turn Back, O Man"

And now, this benediction:

"Lord,
    Hallowed be Thy name,

                    not ours,

    Thy Kingdom come,

                    not ours,

    Thy will be done,

                    not ours,

    Give us peace with Thee.

        Peace with men,

        Peace with ourselves,

    And free us from all fear. Amen."

                    (adapted from Dag Hammarskjold, Markings)

* This was probably an unfortunate narcisstic thing to say. In committing it to
"print", I am compelled to say: 1) It referred to a personal state, nothing else;
and 2) I was dismayed by the narcisstic reaction of many students who could only
relate it to their concern of the evening ahead, i.e., the "gripe session" with
College officials. My "seriousness" in this presentation seemed to some "unlike"
me. That could only indicate that they had never seen me before in such a "mood"
and/or that I had never before exposed myself to them in such a "mood". Nevertheless, my seriousness in the prayers arose out of my psychological involvement in
what I was saying. From there, you'll have to "psyche" me out. Have a good "game"!
But let this stand, please, for what it is.

C. 12/5/65   What Do We Name God?

Two sermons in the Cycle (#49 and #50) refer to the Name of God. The four sermons that follow (C, D, E, and F) explain the concept.

Second in series
of Advent sermons

Westminster Presbyterian Church
Wooster , Ohio
Rev. Beverly Asbury, Minister
December 5, 1965

WHAT DO WE NAME 'GOD'?
Galatians 4: 4a,b

When the time had fully come, God..... Last week, we discussed what time did to the Law and what time always does to theological formulations. Since "time makes ancient good uncouth", the Church has always been faced with the task of re-examining its doctrinal formulations. This process has always been disquieting to those in the Church who find meaning and content in the familiar forms, and that is so today. Yesterday's Plain-Dealer contained an article about Cleveland Presbytery's action on the proposed "Confession of 1967." The Presbytery appeared to accept the logic of an Elyria pastor who asked:
 "How are you going to reduce timeless truth to a new formula based on modern
 language?"

They accepted this view-point despite a fervent plea by the Rev. Dr. Harry B. Taylor, senior minister of Church of the Covenant. Dr. Taylor urged acceptance of the request for the Presbytery to go on record in favor of a contemporary statement on the Trinity, and said:
 "This is the first time in over 300 years that our church has had a chance to
 speak out on basic, fundamental theology."

I agree with Mr. Taylor even while understanding that this chance to speak threatens many in the church's life. However, they should find some comfort in the fact that the task of reformulation does not fall upon them and is not finally ad-dressed to them. Indeed, they might look upon it with less misgiving if they under-stand that the motivation for theological re-expression comes from the primary desire to refashion men and not the faith. It may do so in the final analysis, but that is not its primary motivation, not what it sets out to do. That is to say, theological expression grows out of the ways men express their faith. Theology reflects on, crit-icizes, and discourses about the life of man and the way he talks about it. It is silly, then, to call theology dangerous--to hold it in suspicion. Theology does not threaten the old forms. Men do, no matter what theology says. But if we would speak to men, theology has to accept that time does make ancient good uncouth and in that light seek new expressions of the faith.

If it is true, then, that theology must begin by taking man into account, it means that it must understand the state of man's mind, his inclinations, what he trusts and relies on. Theology understands that reformulations will not come so long as it confuses truth with formulations of the truth, so long as it confuses its state-ments with "eternal verities". Theology must begin its reflective work on the basis of man's state of life in a time when the ancient formulations sound strange and un-familiar. The work of theology in our day has been defined by the radically secular mood which looks only for tangible and visible reality, which holds that all man's true interests lie solely in this world.

Therein we see the first great work of theology today. "When the time had fully come, God...." This problem, the "God problem" outweighs all others for the contempo-rary Christian. "God" has become more and more unreal for secular man. The very no-tion of "God" seems incredible to him (lacking in credit, in "cash value"), and the secular man who is more or less within the life of the Church has wondered out loud if he knows what he has been talking about. Over twenty years ago Bonhoeffer remin-ded us that the word "God" meant nothing to most men.

Now along comes Bishop Robinson with the honesty of an admission that 300 years after Pascal he has discovered science and calls for a change in the way we imagine or conceptualize "God". Robinson tells us what we have long known: that we shall have to reformulate our faith in "God" as a result of scientific discoveries. This has long been a concern of Bultmann and other Christian thinkers. However, one must recognize that if theologians and ministers have known this for years, they have not done a good job of communicating it to the faithful or else Robinson's book would not have caused such a stir. At least, he communicated something of what we know and something of the task ahead. He prefers to replace images of height (God up there) with images of depth (ground of being), but I, for one, find that such a shift solves some problems only to create a number of others. A Ground of Being may solve a "space" problem, intellectually, but it says nothing to my personal problems of experienced reality.

At least, however, we can see now that knowing "God" is our first direct theological concern, and not the Bible or prayer or anything else. The Bible can be the direct concern only when it is first presupposed that a divine Word comes through it to man, and that is precisely what is under question. It is no wonder then that men today do not read the Bible. They have to believe in the meaning of "God-talk" before it makes any sense to them. You will pardon me for suggesting then in a sermon that departments of religious studies in college and universities might do well to consider requiring courses in theology as prerequisites to courses in Bible. The Biblical scholar can no longer appeal to the "Biblical view" as an assumed theological authority since the question of the revealer is the real one. You don't answer questions about the nature of the revealer, his reality if you will, simply by citing what the Bible says about them. The Bible may retain literary, historical, and cultural values, but that is not here at issue. Knowledge of God is at issue, and it begs the question simply to quote the Bible, for it speaks from faith-to-faith. It makes theological sense to the man who believes already but no theo-logical sense to the secular man who has no belief in God. The danger of churchmen who forever cite the Bible as the answer to the questions of the secular mood is that they will end up talking about faith, their faith and historical faith, but not about the object to which faith is directed, that to which they are responding.

Only if we can talk intelligently, legitimately, meaningfully about the dimension and category of deity, about God and his works, can we speak of other theological issues and problems. The theological question about "God" precedes all others. If the category or concept remains so empty that we cannot talk about it, then other categories and formulations will prove to be unintelligible or impossible.

Well, then how do we go about this job of giving the category meaning in our time? How do we proceed to talk about "God"?

Some hints have been forthcoming from quite a number of contemporary theologians. They stand together in reminding us that we use a word like "God" we are not "Speaking about" something or someone so much as we are "naming". To name is to point, to confess, to locate something in terms of our history. The Hebrews who experienced the Exodus located something in their own history and they pointed to it with the name "YHWH". The Egyptians called it the East Wind, but the Israelites said more-- "It's the Name again." They pointed, located, confessed: "It's the Name, the same Name as the one who got us released from the Pharoah." Names are given by men. If a name is sacred, it is because of the experience which lies behind it. Why do boys fight when nasty things are said about their mothers? "Mother" is a name which points to a person experienced. Names point, locate, confess. We can name something only by using the fund of our memories and meanings which we carry with us as persons and as human beings. That is why men speak of God differently in other lands and cultures. The experience of politics, art, literature, economics, family life all affect the way of speaking, our manner of naming. But the name points not to an object or a concept; rather it points to and locates a disclosed and experienced reality; it expresses conviction.

12-5-65   -3-

As Harvey Cox has reminded us (page 266 of The Secular City), God was named as he was encountered in the world--in creation, tribulation, justice, exile, deliverance, the Israelites said: "There's the Name again." In and through such secular events men get a sense, as Richard Niebuhr has put it, of being aimed at and of being aimed. We live in a field of powers that defines our human existence. We are subject to attacks, solicitations, coercions, persuasions in personal, social, economic, political life. Imagine a person in a drawing. There is a human figure and aimed at him are numerous arrows--the forces playing on his life, the demands, pressures, and expectations. And there are arrows going out from him--the responses and answers he should and/or would give. But he is torn. Every demand in this field of powers cannot be met. We must seek an equilibrium, a principle of conduct that preserves our life, our integrity--and preserves our well-being. When we seek that, we are behaving as religious beings, Neibuhr points out. That is, we are endeavoring so to conduct ourselves as to present an image of what we believe life to be all about. When we sing "We Shall Overcome", we are presenting an image of our purpose. It expresses our integrity in the presence of competing, conflicting, creating, destroying powers. We seek to conduct ourselves on the basis of what we apprehend to be the purpose of life. We conduct ourselves on the basis of our sense not only of being aimed at,but of being aimed. And we get this sense out of the events, the competing, conflicting events of our lives.

Now what this means is that the word "God" will get new or altered meaning or we shall see a new name emerge out of the tension between the history which has gone before us and the events which lie ahead. Naming is remembering and hoping--remembering "God" as Shepherd and hoping to meet Him with another name in urban culture. We cannot conjure up a new name anymore than we arbitrarily discard the old one. Perhaps during this time when ancient names are uncouth we shall have to do without a name for "God", just as Moses did when he was told to go down to Egypt. Perhaps we shall have to declare a moratorium on the use of the word "God" until a new name appears. And it may be all to the good to have no word for now. Then we shall know what we name, the reality, the experience behind the name. We can speak directly and without distraction about purpose, sense of being aimed.

Furthermore, without the word to distract us, we may see that "it is in a functional way that man comes into contact with the reality of God, that God acquires a meaning in history...." (Van Peursen as quoted by Cox, Page 266). Theologians today are telling us this; if we do not have the name, we have functional equivalents. Convictions that function in the same way. We do have deep experiences of power, meaning, value, acceptance, and love which equals answers to questions raised by experiences of human life.

Jim Gustafson has said: "Someone may be embarassed to talk about God, but if he believes that the power of love and life are greater than the abyss of death and evil, if he believes that social institutions can bring life to higher and better qualities rather than merely serve as dikes against chaos, if he is oriented toward life with a cosmic optimism rather than with bitterness and despair, then he is being governed by fundamental convictions that function for him as the knowledge of God did for the traditional Christians." Any man who has those convictions has experienced a meaning and reality in his history, a sense of aim. These experiences give shape to form our humanity, making us the kind of persons we are. Any doctrines or formulation of God will be an elaboration of such an answer experienced in the course of our daily life about God, arising out of experiences of ultimate purpose.

12-5-65   -4-

So, when I say "that's true" to the Gospel, I am not assenting to some proposition that contradicts my reason; I am confessing that it embodies the truth about life and that to deny it is to deny the only premise upon which life can be lived. If I say "That's true", I am pointing to love as the basic law of existence, pointing to the inner connection between truth, justice, and love. When I say "that's true", I am naming an experience of the One beyond the many as a sufferer, a servant whose power consists in just this weakness in the eyes of the world. I am shedding light on what I mean by "God", using the language of conviction to describe and name.

To say this, of course, does not establish the <u>reality</u> of "God". No analysis of man can do that. However, it does establish what I mean, what I name "God". It tells us that God-language is the explication of the answers to the deepest questions about a man's existence. It talks about purpose, of being aimed at and of being aimed, of the power to live creatively and meaningfully.

To try to speak of "God" in this way is to take a risk that we will end up not speaking about "God" but only of an attitude or conviction toward life and the universe. However, that is a risk that we must be prepared to take. If we end up only with the attitude, with the inner sense of purpose, then we shall know that sophisticated humanism is the real alternative to Christian faith. However, if we end up (as I believe we shall) being granted a new name out of the events of the future, we shall again have a plausible and convincing reinterpretation of faith in the God and Father of Jesus Christ.

D.   1/16/66   Man and Reality: Three Stages.

This sermon continues the explanation of The Name of God. It also comments on the theme of God Is Dead found in Sermons #15 and 45.

Westminster Presbyterian Church
Wooster, Ohio
Rev. B everly Asbury, Minister
January 16, 1966

MAN AND REALITY: THREE STAGES
Deuteronomy 10: 1-5, 10-22
Matthew 4: 12-22

TIME exposed the American public in October to the thinking of certain contemporary theologians who declare that "God is dead!" The furor ever since has indicated both the shallowness of some of this "journalistic theology" and the hysteria of "those who have it made" and don't want to bother to think seriously. Well, let's face it! God has died before!

It happened almost before it began, as Paul Lehman and others have pointed out. (Union Seminary Quarterly Review, Nov. 1965 "The Tri-Unity of God" P. 35-49) Scarcely had the Name of God been revealed to those involved in the Exodus than they began to waver in their responses and to pull back in the enterprise. The flesh pots of Egypt seemed at once more luminous and more secure than the mystery of a divine self-disclosure which required the risk of trust. They found it difficult to trust God as a prelude to the promise of insight, clarification, conviction, and, not least, the shape of human life.

Israel was stubborn. Moses goes to the mountain in retreat, alone with the Name of God, preoccupied with the Commandments. Israel at the foot of the mountain declares that "God is dead." Moses in anger smashes the tablets of the Law and the Golden Calf. A careful reading of the story here and in Exodus makes it seem that there was a moment when God took a second look at the wisdom and folly of his self-disclosure of his Name. He indicates he thought of hating and destroying this people who declared his Name dead. B ut He did not. The people lived. They were forgiven, and to them was given a second set of the commandments.

And herein we see a journey. It is a journey as Cox said from "Exodux to Easter", and even more as Lehman has pointed out from "Easter to Pentecost" and from "first Advent to second Advent". In this journey we see, to paraphrase Paul Lehman, God's confidence in the wisdom of the self-disclosure of his Name struggle with man's confidence in God's lack of wisdom in doing it. The result has been to this day a protracted struggle between wrath and fear, withdrawal and doubt, suffering and rebellion, compassion and renewal. Obviously, this still goes on. Men must still engage themselves in a risk of trust as the prelude to clarification, insight and conviction. The movement from acknowledgment of the Name to the freedom of man to name all things in creation is still protracted and intense.

Thus, the struggle is really the same. "God has died before". What is very different is man's changed and changing way of thinking. Cornelis van Peursen, who is professor of Philosophy at the University of Leiden in the Netherlands, indicates three stages in which man has lived. (Student World, No. 1, 1963 "Man and Reality- the History of Human Thought") They overlap and are not clear cut--no sharp end to one and the beginning of another. There will be a fourth, but we cannot know it, he says, because we are only now in the third. Van Peursen presents a model for these three stages, which are really ways of thinking, types of approaches to reality. The first is the stage of myth: the period of primitive society. The second is the stage of ontology: of thinking of being as being, and of the rise of society. The third is the stage of functional thinking: the contemporary way of thinking, the contemporary way of life, in terms of which we have so recently heard it declared that "God is dead". Each stage has its advantages and dangers, but each new stage or way of thinking represents a liberation from the dangers of the stage preceding.

We need to understand these stages if we are to understand what is being said about "God" today. If we would love the Lord with all our mind, we have little alternative to considering our way of thinking about reality, about the Name of God.

In the period or stage of myth, the stage of primitive man, that which is real is an overwhelming force. "God" has as yet no proper identity. The Name has not taken on any concrete shape. Numinous forces are everywhere. There are the "spirits" everywhere. There are the "Gods" --of the mountains, clouds, and streams; of fire, thunder, and lightening. In certain passages of the Old Testament we can get a vivid sense of "haunted nature". The world of nature itself is supernatural. The inner and the outer world are not understood as separate entities. What is true in inner life is true of outer life, and vice versa. We get mythological pictures of men's souls wandering in the world, alone and lost. Nature has a magic force. This is a world of fascination--in it dwell divine forces which relate themselves to society, the clan. This is not our world of astronomy. There is in it none of the scientific knowledge which we now have. And as much as we may occasionally yearn for such a world, as when we attribute a tornado to God, we cannot return to mythical thinking. That 'god' has died. We no longer believe in what insurance men call "acts of God"; we have better explanations.

Furthermore, let us see that such a stage of understanding has a truly demonic element. The danger of myth is magic, which is an effort to master reality. Magic is developed and used in such a stage as an attempt to control powers outside. Such attempts produce a life of anxiety, for you always wonder when your magic will no longer appease the 'gods'. It also produces a dictatorship of medicine men--those who run the temples, who have positions as high priest have powers and privileges not available to other men, have great control over the superstitious masses. The modern magicians are the witch-hunters --the men who find Communists everywhere, who ask that we trust them to cast them out. We see the modern counterpart in those who see a haunted realm, a conspiracy against us --as in those who saw in last November's blackout a work of "devils". We are not yet beyond the pale of myth-bound minds, who look on emerging society as an enemy force. Obviously, technical and social development is hampered and opposed because that would threaten the magic force and power of the practicing priests.

The next stage in man's thinking implies a liberation from the fear of magic. Ontology represents the stage in which the human being puts some distance between himself and the natural world. He no longer sees the world as 'haunted', as occupied by 'spirits. Rather, as Aristotle put it, he now searches for being as being. He overcomes the magical force of myth by the sheer process of human reflection. Man's thinking is evolving. Historical thinking is arising, but it is still over against a background of nature. The divine forces have retired from nature into their own dwelling places. (And in this process no doubt mythical man would declare that the gods of nature are dead.) The 'gods' are not imagined now as aboriginal forces, but are retiring to Olympus; they are no longer divine forces but are becoming the gods. The 'gods become divine and man becomes human. Each to his own. The sacred is separated from the profane; the temple from the market place. Therefore, men as well as gods begin to take a shape of their own. Man and the gods now stand over against each other. Philosophy describes the natural being (man) and metaphysics describes the supernatural beings (the gods). It is no longer a matter THAT something exists, but a matter of WHAT kind of being it is that exists.

Man's thought turns away from magic to analysis. Even the nature of the gods can be analyzed. In this stage of man's thinking he distinguishes between being and high being, nature and supernature, physics and metaphysics, man and God. And God finally is described as the highest being, the first cause, the unmoved mover. Man now has a new type of mastery; it is no longer magic, but reason. It is reason overwhelming the universe. Reason itself becomes a substance, a thing existing in itself.

1-18-66   -3-

And this has a danger too. Reason produces ideas, but then the ideas are confused with substance. Men worship their own ideas as true substance. They confuse their ideas with eternal values. "God" becomes remote, unrelated, static, and without impact on our lives. When you isolate "substances" and begin to think of them as things in themselves, they mean nothing to the life of men. So, what difference does it make? The 'gods' die. Men declare here too that 'god is dead', because this kind of thinking ends up barren speculation.

Thus, man moves into a third stage which is characterized by a functional style of thinking. Again we see man's attempt to escape the dangers of the preceding period Functional thinking does not reflect upon isolated substances. Rather, it is a kind of tool, a tool of concrete human lives, of functioning in a human society.

In a secularized world there is no longer an ontological way of thinking about things. Men do not, in contemporary society, think as the first order of things of higher beings, of metaphysical beings. Men do not, in contemporary society, occupy themselves as the first order of things with how to control the outside entities, the gods of the universe. Instead, in contemporary society, men seek functional ways of making a living, solving problems, overcoming obstacles, preventing destruction, and creating 'great societies'. Architecture uses the motto "form follows function". Functional men do not speak of eternal forms, substances, values, truths. An architect might describe a new chapel as "honest" only if its form expresses its function. He may have no concern for theology, ethos, philosophy; but only for the best functioning of the program. Although we could claim that one does not inevitably rule out the other, we live in a time when "function" seems the uppermost concern.

Perhaps the change in the way of thinking is more clearly illustrated in politics Political life was once controled by the thought of serving eternal ethical and moral values. Man no longer feels that way. Men now feel liberated from such control. Politics now deal with the things at hand. It works out solutions, and what works becomes true. This period is characterized then by a utilitarian, pragmatic, functional approach.

Men now may say that they still believe in 'god' but it is not the 'god' of the preceding period. Fate is no longer considered a factor. We speak of environmental and genetic determination but we surely do not speak of being controlled, as it were, from the outside. Only that which is directly related to us is real. Things are no longer substances. Things exist in and for the sake of what they do with us and what we do with them. Men today are caught up in the power of reality. Nothing high and lofty deters what we seek to do. For example, we scoff at the old and oft-expressed idea that Somebody Up There doesn't want us exploring outer space. The only reality for functional men is that which directly and concretely concerns us. And much of the talk of "spiritual life" only begs the question. It speaks out of another stage.

Therefore, according to a functional way of thinking, reality is that which functions. In other words, a thing becomes a thing to do, an action. The nouns the previous era used become the verbs of this one. Religion becomes a way of behaving. Ethical values are not longer eternal, supernatural values--but ways of organizing and reorganizing societies. Many of the fights that still go on this planet result from confusing functional values with eternal ideologies. Marx saw his system as eternal. He was an ontological thinker. Today the hope of coexistence lies in understanding both Marxism and free enterprise, both democracy and communism not as eternally conflicting value systems but as differing ways of structuring societies for the modern world. How they work will be the final determination in emerging nations.

Let's put it this way. The period of myth saw the main issue to be that something is; the ontological saw it as what is; the functional period sees the issue to be how something is, how it functions. This is seen in the fact that we live in a world that is one huge organization. We are, whether we like it or not, organization men. And so we hear some men today declaring that "God is dead". Which "God"? The ontological "God". The God of another period, another stage of man's thinking.

Now, in this period of functional thinking, there is also great danger. The danger lies in the fact that we may very well concern ourselves only with what works, not why it works, not whether it is good or bad. That's what it means to be an "operator." An "operator" has no values but has an ability to "move" things, to cause things to happen. Perhaps what happens lies on the shady side of "morality", but an operator recognizes no such substance. That is why the "new morality" often appears to be a "no morality". In a society obsessed with organization it can mean that both government and industry end up placing a higher premium on organization than on actual action. That is the danger, and the Church is not immune. How often do you hear it said of a minister that he may be a lousy preacher or a poor pastor but that he is a superb organizer, an "operator"? All he does is organize things, and that is important. "Know-how" becomes more important than doing anything substantial, because substance belongs to another period and way of living. And the danger confronts education. Some men may, pardon me, have concluded that it is unnecessary to put a lot of learning into the mind of the student, or to give higher ethical values, or to bring him into contact with eternal values. No, the student only has to know how to function, how to operate in society. But it's all worthwhile--just think how much you may make in life as a result of 'knowing-how'. And so we may hear future students shift from the line that 'it's not what you know but whom you know' to 'it's not whom you know but how you know'. And if this ever becomes so, we shall be so operational that we shall have lost our identity; we shall be nobodies, who have no idea about the essence of things but lots of ideas about combining them.

All this is said to demonstrate that "god has died before" in man's thought, and men have moved to another way of thinking. In these years, we shall hear it over and over that "God is dead", and something important is being said. The word "God" will not work as a metaphysical entity. The concept doesn't function. It can no longer be used to fill the gaps in our knowledge; these are now filled by new discoveries. We now live in a natural, not a supernatural world. And we are coming increasingly to an operational way of thinking, and the dangers should be obvious to us all. Our task then is one of renewed liberation. We have first to accept our freedom from the previous periods: that is our gain from functional thinking. But we have to be careful now not to replace man by operation, by 'know-how'. Otherwise our identity is lost and man becomes only an operation of organization power.

"God has died before". Our journey continues, and so does the struggle between God's confidence in the wisdom of the self-disclosure of his name and man's confidence in God's lack of wisdom in doing it. Our journey continues from one stage of thinking to another, and we currently travel through a difficult period of transition. And it is still true that men must take the risk of trust as the prelude of clarification, insight, conviction, and not least the shape of human life.

When "God was dead" for the Israelites in the desert, they followed Moses, doing the truth--executing justice and loving the sojourner. When "God is dead" for men in functional society, Christians continue to follow Jesus, seeking to be disciples. We follow him, we are on the move, abandoning old formulations which no longer serve and addressing ourselves to the new issues which are appearing. As Moses led his people to new understanding and responsibility, so we trust that Jesus will lead us to a promised future. To follow him means being participants and not onlookers in changing world of thought and action. It means risking ourselves to live toward new stage in which we are freed from the dangers of dehumanizing operationalism to new hold on a humanizing reality. "God has died before". But the Name of God manifests itself anew, and we here hope for that stage of reality in which men may sing a new song: "I know that my Redeemer lives".

E.   1/23/66   **Where Can God Be Found?**

This sermon continues the explanation of The Name of God.

```
            Westminster Presbyterian Church
                    Wooster, Ohio
            Rev. B everly Asbury, Minister
                  January 23, 1966

                WHERE CAN GOD BE FOUND?
                    Job 23: 1-17
                    John 5: 30-47
```

We live in a period when deity is in eclipse. We are passing through an epochal religious crisis. Our journey of faith in these latter years of the Twentieth Century lacks the vantage of seeing how things will turn out; we only see the old falling apart. The modes of theological thought which held the field until recently (and may still dominate the teaching of religion in our colleges and universities) are not only under strain but on the verge of an utter collapse. The question in this functional stage of man's thought has become: "Can anything be meant by the word God at all?" The novelist John Updike has called it "the ominous hollow noun". And Roger Hazelton has said that "It is as if so much talking about God had only weakened our confidence in all such talk, simply deepening and darkening the very question to which our theology vainly tried to proclaim the answer. Nevertheless;,that is our present situation, and we shall have to face and cope with it as best we can." (Andover Newton Quarterly, Jan., 1966)

Well, those who are coping with it are not providing any too clear and emphatic guidance and direction. Those who are now known as the "death of God boys" have raised the issues which we have to face, the ones we breathe in the air and feel in our bones. However, they have hastily jettisoned the rich tradition of Christendom and have all but ignored the variety of responses given to similar problems in the preceding stages and ages of Christian life. They have often confused the issues as well as raised them, but we can take some comfort from the fact that they have made religion on our campuses now and then as exciting and controversial as the athletic department and administration policy.

Now it is my conviction that God is still, and is bound to remain, the proper subject of both speech and thought. And, if you share that conviction with me, you also share with me the need to say in what sense God is alive, how he can be known, where he can be found. These men, who declare God's death, have been called heretics by some Christians, but they are forcing the church to clear its mind, to be open to new insights, and to move to deeper ideas about both man and God. It is for us to say to them where God can be found and what God has to do with our life and decisions. Their p assionate rebuke to our orthodoxy and complacency puts upon us the burden of searching our hearts and reviewing our <u>lives</u> to see what it is we <u>actually</u> trust.

Where can God be found? What does his Name mean? What difference does it make to you, to me? None can answer in the spur of a moment. One answer has to be avoided--the glib, cheap answer; the answer that one scores as a point won in debate. When I talk to persons who have easy and dogmatic answers about the most profound questions of existence, I wonder if they have any real understanding of the dimensions of the problem. I wonder if they are alive to the real situation and have any comprehension of the issues at stake. I wonder where in their dogmatism and intolerance one can find the compassion and love of their l iving God for those who have doubted and do doubt the meaning of the <u>word</u>, because they have experienced the loss of God.

Then, let us avoid the glib answer as to w here God can be found. If we are convinced that the Name of God is the proper subject of both speech and thought, let us be as thoughtful as we can about it and recognize that what we may say or think

may be transitional, at best. However, that is the nature of man's speech and thought.
The dissolution of old theological modes testifies to that.

In previous times of transition and crisis, historical religions like Christianity have urged men "to remember the days of old". If God cannot be found here and now, perhaps he can be found there and then. The cry, as John Maguire has said, may well be "Go to ancient Bethlehem and find God there, the one whom now nobody knows." (Christianity and Crisis, December 12, 1965) The records back then appear today to be fragmentary, and they are occasionally inconsistent and uncertain. But the "central elements" were clear. We discover there a man who grows up and leaves home, moves actively through the land, is crucified, and yet whose career and afterward is suffused with the authority of supreme victory.

However, there are problems in going back to this man Jesus. Many of those who declare that God is dead go back to him too, although none of them has stated with clarity just why they find Jesus of Nazareth or the Christian tradition important to them. But if they face a problem in explaining why they choose Jesus, we also face great problems in going to him to say where God can be found.

Our creeds have declared that in him the fullness of the Godhead dwelt; that he was the Word made flesh. What an odd Word Jesus was. He was a Word, and words are supposed to speak. However, our records lead us to believe that Jesus spoke little. And when he did speak, he said nothing new. The more I read my Old Testament the more impressed I am with the fact that Jesus knew his Scriptures and that what he said can be found there. Furthermore, his words do not answer our questions about the nature of man and God. What Updike called the "ominous hollow noun" is not filled by anything He says. Indeed, we note with interest that his speech gives little attention to nouns. He has no concern for or with definitions. His speech has a preoccupation with verbs--come, taste, see, love, suffer, become, do. It might be said that he answers questions not with words or ideas but acts. Verbs and not nouns stand at the center of his speech.

We go back then to a man whose speech was unoriginal, unbalanced, and whose relationships with others were filled with enigmatic silences. In his day too, it could have been said that the Word of God was silent. But this man acted. He spoke a universal language of doing rather than words. What he does is his word. He is what he does. We have considered together before that this is really the "definition" of the Name of God given over and over in the Bible; God is as God does. The Hidden God makes his Name known by his actions in history. The Ineffable makes itself known not by becoming articulate but by becoming ambulatory. God is known by the way He functions.

Where can God be found in this man Jesus? Well, see what Jesus does. He heals the sick, relieves the poor, exorcises demons, associates with disreputable persons, frequents questionable places, gives sight to the blind, accepts the sentence of the guilty, suffers on Golgotha, keeps living though declared dead. He does not tell us who God is or where he can be found! He acts it!

This theme is surely struck by the Evangelist of the Fourth Gospel. The Evangelist indicates where we are to look to find God. First, there is the witness of Jesus to himself. The works of Jesus are the works He has seen the Father do; the words he speaks are the words he has heard the Father speak. By his functions, men say--there's You-Know-Who, the Name again. That is, Jesus does not really point to himself but to Another, to One called God, to One known before and Named. Secondly, there is the witness of John. This testimony is not considered essential, but John the Baptizer is seen as a burning, shining light. He witnesses to what is taking place; he points to the action. Thirdly, and more significantly, the Evangelist underlines the works, the acts of Jesus. These acts provide an even more important series of external witnesses to Jesus' mission than do the words of John. The Evan-

1-23-66   -3-

gelist does not here draw out the importance of the miracles of Jesus, perhaps because the earlier verses of the discourse in this chapter dealt with them and perhaps partly because he will deal with them again later. He does however state two salient facts. The works are final, finished, and complete acts--they are not experimental and tentative. And not only are his acts complete, they show the nature of his mission--in them the Father can be known. Thus, the Fourth Gospel suggests that the witness to God can be found in Jesus' acts precisely because men have known the acts of God before. God can be found in present activities because of past activities.

In other words, there the Name again. The God of our Fathers, of Abraham, Isaac, and Jacob; the God of Amos, Elijah, and Jeremiah--the God who acted to redeem his people; there's the Name again. It's You-Know-Who again. The Evangelist understands that all life, in and from the beginning onwards, has borne witness through activity to the Reality Men-Name-God. The witness of John and the Scriptures are only two conspicuous examples. However, we learn here an important lesson for today; the Scriptures should lead men to the Lord, and so to life; for they always point beyond themselves. The Scriptures of themselves do not afford new life to man. Jesus says here that men search the Scriptures for eternal life; "and it is they that bear witness to me; yet you refuse to come to me that you may have life." That seems a more than adequate answer to those who worry about the Confession of 1967 identifying God with Jesus instead of with the Bible. But back to the point. The theme struck here, simply stated, is that the Name of God, The Father, the You-Know-Who can be clearly and decisively known in this man Jesus and what he does.

Nevertheless, we are still faced with the question of what it means that 2000 years ago certain actions were performed. What does it mean that 20 centuries ago, followed by the anguish of man's weeping and waring, that the NAME or Word of God resided in Jesus? Well, it means little and maybe nothing UNLESS the same kind of action is going on right here, right now, and the Name of God can be found in it.... unless men today are so confronted in events that they can and do say "It's the Name again; the same One known by our fathers; the You-Know-Who". That is the issue-- the issue for all who would call themselves Christians.

In the days of Jesus, God forgave. Does he forgive today? Is the forgiveness of sins now experienced?

B ack then, John tells us, things were illumined. Are things made clear for us today, or are they as dark as the existentialists tell us? Do we have enough light to know where to place our next step?

Back in Jesus' acts men could relate what had gone before--the Name again. Do we still have a sense of the past? Do we possess a basis for trust? Do we understand our promises and committments as extensions of the covenanting God's presence? Can we understand today's creative acts apart from a creative power which supports all things? Can we find any key to the present without recalling the days of old, without plunging into the past, without reclaiming the rich variety of response made by faithful men?

For example, one summer in Europe I visited a World Council of Churches workcamp. There was a remarkable espirit de corps among those there. They were living in primitive conditions in the immediate post-war period. They did not take lightly to visitors. They had something we did not have, and I resented it a little. I did not understand how they felt until a couple of years later I helped to lead the first WCC workcamp in the Southern Mountains on an interracial basis. Once participating in this camp we knew and felt something that outsiders, visitors, could not know and feel unless they had experienced it. You know a truth by taking part in it.

And as John Maguire has said, "So it is with God's great charade, his mighty deeds. He moves, acts, becomes ambulatory. And his actions have a distinctive pat-

1-23-66   -4-

tern. It is cruciform in shape, from height to depth, an endless reaching out in
every direction to all men. And that distinctive pattern.....continues in our time."

The action goes on. In every act to relieve suffering, in every act freeing captives, ministering to the poor, bringing light to blindness, lifting vulgarity, defla-
ting stuffiness, preserving privacy and integrity, exchanging love--in all these the
action continues. And here is where God can be found; the place at least where He
has been for me ----in every human action bearing this cruciform pattern.

So do we turn to Jesus, to what is past, searching for and grasping the pattern,
understanding the form. Like the Israelites in the desert huddled together and told
their stories that formed our Old Testament, and like the early Christians who spread
the good news of Jesus from one town to the next, so do we in a time of God's eclipse
tell the old story of Epiphany, of Easter, to keep us alive now. That story reminds
us of who we are, where we came from, and gives us a pattern for understanding where
we shall find God today.

Where can God be found? I offer you no answer, but an invitation. Shuck off
your sophistication. Store away your intellectual stereotypes. And then: taste and
see, come and follow, participate and find.   And we may be found!

F. 1/30/66   Why We Live, How We Live

This sermon concludes the explanation of The Name of God.

Westminster Presbyterian Church
Wooster, Ohio
The Rev. Beverly Asbury, Minister
January 30, 1966

WHY WE LIVE, HOW WE LIVE!
Galatians 5: 13-24

One of the benefits of being called to New York for a consultation is the opportunity for an evening at the theatre. In December my theological and dramatic interests happened to coincide in a play entitled "The Devils." This play was written by
the late John Whiting, who turned to Aldous Huxley's "The Devils of Loudun". Mr.
Whiting turned then to the past to a true story; to a French town in the early 17th
Century, and he produced a play with pertinence for us today. Its pertinence is especially real when men are declaring that the old "god" has died but when the powers of
evil have never been more real. Mr. Whiting has chosen to deal with one of the great
and compelling issues of our time which is marked by both fantastic advances and overwhelming manmade upheavals.

One who preaches Sunday after Sunday knows the difficulties of dealing adequately
with the issues of good and evil. Harvey Cox calls us to celebrate the freedom of
'the secular city', but celebration often comes hard when you face the millions in the
cities who are locked in deprivation and misery. Preachers call for people to live
with joy and thanksgiving, but what can be said meaningfully to those who have known
no love and, therefore, can give no love? Anger and rebellion come more easily in
our inner cities, and with the confrontation of the complexities of dealing with Vietnam, or with racial justice.

It is with real appreciation, therefore, that one saw that in "The Devils" Mr.
Whiting chose to deal with the issue of good and evil despite the overwhelming and in-
hibiting tempo and magnitude of contemporary events. By doing this he has illuminated
for us Christians the issue we must face and speak of if we would claim that the Name
of God is known and functions in our era. This is not to claim that Mr. Whiting is a
Christian speaking for and to Christians. That patently is not so, for John Whiting
said that he did not have a particular religion. He said that he was a christian with
a small 'c', because he had been raised in a society formed by Christian ethics. Nevertheless, Whiting had real affinities personally with certain positions affirmed as
true by Christians. He said that he believed in evil, because he saw evil everywhere.
Thus, he believed in the devil, and he held that if you believe in the devil, you also
believe in God. In order to believe in the reality of evil, you must accept the reality of its opposite. By believing in God, Whiting may have been more honest than
those who stress the uncompromising evil and depravity of our day without ever considering or acknowledging the nature and existence of good. In any case, these beliefs
on his part were not a part of a philosophical system but the result of his own obser-
vations--they were functional beliefs but they had an historical frame of reference.
Man's life did not begin yesterday. Because of the truth previously known, Whiting
was able to say in the events of his time, "There's the devil again", and perhaps less
clearly but just as truly he said, "There's the Name again too." He did not believe in
the essential goodness of man, because he had not experienced man as essentially good.
However, his experience did not produce conclusively that man is evil. Rather, in
"The Devils" he portrays both good and evil as open choices for man.

The chief character in the play, Father Grandier, is a man who can choose for either good or evil. He is a priest, a good pastor to his people, a noted preacher----
a man of eloquence, prophecy, and power. Nevertheless, his vocation does not prevent
him from gratifying his physical desires and needs. He is attracted to more than one
woman in his parish, and his life is hardly marked by poverty, chastity, and obedience.
Father Grandier is a torn man. God is both dead and alive for him in the functions of
his life. He has an almost overwhelming desire to live ardently but possesses an al-

most equally overwhelming need to abuse himself before his conscience. He knows his
capacity for deceit and evil. He sins and repents. He wavers. He seizes love eager-
ly and then rejects it coldly. He acts decisively on occasion and then has no will
for action when confronted with the issue of his own life and death.

Anyone who is a contemporary man and has lived through the morals revolution can
identify with Grandier, at least in part. In him we can see not a priest who has
failed but precisely the same kind of ambiguous quality of human life portrayed by
Graham Greene in The Power and the Glory. We see ourselves---charming but vain, professing faith as we have known it but fundamentally skeptical really--if not totally
doubting, then confused, disturbed, indifferent. Grandier is a modern man, a man at
odds with himself. He is, indeed, the man addressed by Paul Tillich in his theological works, and he is not less than the modern man who speaks of the loss of the experience of God. Grandier appeals to women; he holds the affection of his bishop, who
abhors his sensual exploits and depravity; but he is basically known as a man who has
no clear sense of purpose, no inner peace, no commitment superceding all others.

However, Grandier reveals that he is capable of heroism. The prioress of a convent makes false accusations against him. She has a hump on her back and suffers
terrible memories of childhood. She has a desire for him, and he has unknowingly rejected her by refusing an appointment as the chaplain of her convent. She then
charges that he has possessed her with lewd visions; that he has sent devils to tor-
ment her and her nuns in the convent. This means accusing him of being alligned with
the devil. Grandier will not submit to the hysteria of his accusers or the vicious
prejudice of those who are after him on other grounds. In spite of great feeling of
unworthiness, he will not take an unworthy out.

The play does not make it entirely clear where this reserve and resolve of integrity come from, but the fact that we find it believeable again indicates something
of the ambiguity of our own lives. He refuses to confess to what he did not commit
and to what he does not believe to be possible. And we can find ourselves understanding this, because whatever our personal failings we feel that we too would balk at
this. Grandier again demonstrates that he is a modern man in this. He will not buy
time by naming other victims.

His enemies are unable to break him by torture or death. The torture scenes in
the play seemed quite real to me although one critic indicated that the Broadway production had been tamed so as not to shock American sensibilities. It was nevertheless clear to the audience that integrity has a price tag on it and that the results
are not pretty--in fact just the opposite of the values previously held. Yet Grandier
pays the price and his integrity stands unshaken. And sitting in the audience, you
suffer with him but pull ever so much for his integrity to stand because you have a
deep hope that your own integrity will stand in your own time of testing and truth.
You find Grandier fascinating and perplexing in his sensibility and ambiguity because
you are as he is. And you find some satisfaction in the fact that those who have
hounded and tormented Grandier with the fury of sadists finally break down themselves
into tormented humanity.

This play reinforces the Christian's hatred of bigotry, and it gives a growing
respect for tolerance. Yet, it also manages to remind us that tolerance cannot be
simpleminded, because the motives of men and women are mixed, because each of us has
unappeasable inner conflicts and no small amount of ambiguity. When you are able to
see both sides of a question, when you stop marching somewhere long enough to let
enthusiasm be tempered by skepticism, you are not necessarily immobilized, but you
are impressed by the complex relationships of modern society. Again, this does not
mean that every moral judgment must "die a death of a thousand qualifications", but
it does surely mean no moral judgment can be rendered meaningfully today without
reaching a painful self-awareness.

1-30-66

This would seem to make Paul, for example, guilty of too easy a dichotomy between the flesh and the spirit. However, this is only partly true, because Paul does see, as this play does, that there can be no lasting alliance between the spirit and flesh of man. Between them there is an interminable deadly feud going. That's the issue; we are torn within between what we want to do and what we know we ought to do. Each one of us in this modern era experiences a moral schizophrenia, in which the worth and integrity of the self is at stake. Grandier dramatizes the nature of modern man's battle for a sense of dignity and worth.

The antagonistic forces at work in Grandier are acknowledged by Paul to be present in all men. Paul's expressed need to be freed of the tyranny of the lusts of the flesh find fresh expression in Grandier's plaintive cry to God about his mistress: "O Lord, deliver me from 2 o'clocks on Tuesday afternoons." No man who has confronted himself can deny what Paul seems to classify as sensual passions, violations of brotherly love, and intemperate excesses. And in like manner no Christian man can deny that these things conflict with the habits of mind, the special qualities of relationships, and the principles of conduct which are "the fruits of the Spirit". These are things which are of Jesus Christ, which mark our lives as having encountered the Name of God in him. Apart from these how can men really know our faith, for "faith without (such) works is dead"?

Unfortunately, Christians have often taken this to mean that they should be good --one-dimensionally good! That's really true. It's no simple choice. The Christian man does have a choice; he can choose between good and evil. Both are open! It is up to the person to choose. But that does not and cannot mean that a choice for good does away with the evil in our lives. Some of the greatest evil of our times has been done by those "righteous" men who have so chosen. The Ku Klux Klan has no doubt that it is both right and "righteous", and it has perpetrated unmitigated evil in the name of its race-conscious righteousness, and who could be more "righteous" than the Nazis were in moving "to save the human race." The deadly trouble with such righteousness lies in its emotional and intellectual simplism. The choice is never done once and for all, and the choice is seldom unambiguous. And when a choice is ambiguous, it is painful to make. The choice is not always as clear as Paul portrays it; it may be just as grey and ambiguous and complex as it was in and for Grandier. We spend our lives making this choice --over and over and over, between lesser and greater evils, lesser and greater goods, between the works of the flesh and the fruits of the Spirit. This is how we live!

What Paul does give us is a clue to the making of the choice over and over. He clarifies what the play does not--why Grandier, such a vain and ambiguous man, could be capable of such an act of integrity. He tells us here in Galatians and elsewhere that our integrity, our sense of selfhood and well being, our freedom as Christian men come only as we are willing to suffer, to make the painful choice; to accept the consequences of choosing the good instead of evil. As Paul says there is no law against doing what is right and good, or more nearly right and a greater good than the alternatives. But such a choice will be made only if one is willing to commit himself, and so suffer and endure his ambiguity and the ambiguity and complexity of his choice.

Many modern men are so impressed with the complexities and so objective about them that they are unable to commit themselves. Perhaps a Christian will be marked increasingly in these years not so much by a superior righteousness as by willingness to go ahead and commit himself to positions and actions despite the reservations and ambiguities. That is the freedom given him in Jesus Christ--there is no law against it, however foolish it may seem. We may end up as the play ends up--ambiguous, but we shall know why we have lived--to live as free men for others.

1-30-66

-4-

The knowledge of God, the _why_ we live comes as we give assent to our ambiguity by enduring it, suffering it, choosing the good in it as we see it offered to us. Like Grandier we may not know why we live until we commit ourselves as he did.

This was no easy matter for him. Imprisoned, waiting for a torture he feared he could not bear, denied access to his own church, he was visited by an old priest, Ambrose. At first, it seemed that the old priest would only play the immemorial role of the chaplain who leads the prisoner to accept his fate. But not so. In the presence of an old, more simple and less ambiguous man, Grandier pours out his soul— his tale of shabby infidelities, rejected love, and vain ambition. He tells of his lust for life, and asks what such a man has to offer God. Ambrose tells him simply but truly to offer himself—the only thing he has to offer; offer the very things that have torn his soul open. Commit his pride, his sensual lusts, his beauty, his popularity, himself to God. He need not become what he is not to be accepted by God. He is accepted. Now he is freed to live like it! He can crucify his passions and desires by giving them in the way he acts, and in so doing, God will be known. In the ambiguity of his life, he can choose for good, for wholeness, for integrity— although he will have to suffer. B ut he shall have wholeness; he shall know God.

Grandier speaks with eloquence, about how he created God: "I created him from the light and air, from the dust of the road, from the sweat of my hands, from gold, from filth, from the memory of women's faces, from great rivers, from children, from the works of man, from the past, the present, the future, the unknown. I caused him to be from fear and despair. I gathered in everything from this mighty act, all I have known, seen and experienced. My sin, my presumption, my vanity, my love, my hate, my lust. And last I gave myself and so made God. And he was magnificent. For he is all these things."

Against such, there is no law, and in such may come to us the way and purpose of our living. This then is an invitation! offer yourselves; accept the risk; be willing to suffer your ambiguity for the sake of what is right. Or put it another way: seek first the Kingdom of God and life will come to you.

G. 2/28/65 Metaphor of a Madhouse

Two sermons in particular (this one, G, and the next one, H) deal with eschatology – the future. This sermon is placed here because it introduces the concepts found in H, even though it was delivered chronologically afterward. The reference from Matthew, with which Rev. Asbury closes his sermon, concludes in the familiar affirmation, "Truly, I say to you, as you did it to one of the least of these my brethren, you did it to me."

Westminster Presbyterian Church
Wooster, Ohio
Rev. Beverly Asbury, Minister
February 28, 1965

METAPHOR OF A MADHOUSE
Matthew 25: 31-46

The central theme o f the teaching and preaching of Jesus was the "kingdom of God", or, as Matthew prefers to say, the "kingdom of heaven." Matthew uses "heaven" as a reverent synonym for "God", in accordance with the Jewish practice of not mentioning God's name directly. The Greek meaning of "kingdom" is "sovereignty" or "kingly rule", so we may say that the center of Jesus' teaching lies in what he says about the coming rule of God.

To have this as a central theme of Jesus' teaching does not make it any easier to understand him today or to become his followers. Quite apart from the inner paradox that the kingdom has come and has not yet come, we democratic people are so far removed from "kingly" terminology that we can only partly grasp Jesus' meaning. Yet, this is not really new at all. The years following Jesus' death produced confusion among his followers. Whereas from one point of view the kingdom had already broken into the world with the coming of Christ, from another point of view its complete fulfillment was still in the future. The kingdom was expected to come with power at the end of history with Christ's final coming. The early church expected this to happen in the near future.

Although some parables (Matthew 13) portray the kingdom as a present reality, the parables in chapter 25 place great emphasis upon the eschaton(the end-time,the last things) and upon the arrival (parousia) of Jesus to complete the kingdom. When this final judgment and coming did not materialize, the Church had to revise its theology. Basically, it did this and continues to do this by shifting the frame of reference from history to the individual person. The coming of the end-time and the general resurrection, the kingdom on earth,(the granting of new being, if you will -state of reconciliation) was transformed (or shall we say, transmuted) into a hope for individual, and instanteous salvation of the "soul" at death. In other words, the perspective shifted in eschatology away from the meaning of man in history to man in his individual life in relationship to God. This is not the time to discuss the merits of this shift--only the time to describe it oversimply. This is the time to admit that the Church has reinterpreted the eschatological parables of Jesus to fit personal concerns or else it has abandoned, in fact if not in theory, any concern with eschatology, the end of time.

And it is surely interesting that, in the Church's abandonment of the broad perspective in favor of "personal salvation", others have taken up the eschatological question of our time. On the Beach dealt with a good many of the military aspects of an end-time, and both Dr. Strangelove and Seven Days in May gave good insight into the same problem. The novel, A Canticle for Leibowitz, had more religious overtones, but not even the Church paid much attention to its message. Now, we have before us in this country a good play about the atomic era, and this play can only be described as "secularized eschatology". Perhaps this had to be: the atom is a harbinger of "the last things", but its authority does not come from heaven or hell but from a laboratory. So the age of atomic science is an age of secularized eschatology, and Durrenmatt has written a play about it.

In The Physicists, Durrenmatt examines what may be the gravest problem we face---how to control the fantastic powers of destruction which our scientists have placed at our disposal. He does not exalt or exonerate the physicists. He holds them morally responsible for the danger we face. Here the play agrees more with

2-28-65

scientific opinion itself than with the popular notion in society. The physicists
of the play represent all modern men of knowledge and power. Durrenmatt holds them
responsible, but he does not heap blame upon them. He does not contend that they
could have prevented the three-way divorce between knowledge, morality, and political power, he just confronts us with it!

To present us with this secularized eschatology, Durrenmatt tells a horror story;
he uses the metaphor of a madhouse. He sets the play in a private sanatorium in
Switzerland and then treats us to a mystery story in the science-fiction vein.

One wing of the sanatorium is inhabited by three mad physicists. One believes
that he is Sir Isaac Newton. He wears a periwig and a long robe and fulminates
against the "technicians" who have prostituted his theories of cosmic order by using
them as gadgets. The second physicist believes himself to be Einstein. He is sweet,
plays the fiddle, especially to calm himself down after murdering someone. The third
physicist is called Mobius. He sees visions of King Solomon, who he claims has revealed to him "the principle of universal discovery" and "the understanding of the
force of gravitation." In other words, he has answered all the problems that Newton
and Einstein left unsolved.

As the play progresses from the murder of one nurse to the murder of another,
you see madness revealed as you had never dreamed of it before. Here you feel the
frightening predicament of modern man--can one ever be sure that his discoveries and
contributions won't be perverted? Finally, in the second half of the play, the three
mad scientists reveal themselves and their true interests. Isaac Newton turns out
to be a physicist-agent for what seems like the West. Einstein is revealed as a
physicist-agent for the East. Mobius, who has implied that he is King Solomon, turns
out to be the prototype of the modest creative genius of physics, a man devoted only
to freedom of speculation and uncommitted to any political nationalism. And the Doctor operating the sanatorium discloses that she represents the financial interests
of the world.

Mobius declares that reason demanded this self-incarceration in the madhouse.
Only here "can man be free." "Our knowledge," he cries, "has become a frightening
burden. Our researches are perilous, our discoveries are lethal. For us, the physicists, there is nothing left but to surrender to its reality. It has not kept up
with us. It disintegrates on touching us. We have to take back our knowledge and I
have taken it back." And so they try, those physicists. But the shrewd doctor has
duplicated the copies they destroy. She has set up an international cartel to produce the physicists' discoveries. Their own best intentions are thwarted. Mobius
says sadly and implacably at the end: "What was once thought can never be unthought."
And so does he confront us with the "last things", the "end time".

This is secularized eschatology in a world of monstrous perils and horrifying
responsibilities. The metaphor of a madhouse implies some pretty disenchanted things
about the kind of freedom the two great power systems offer to scientists. Durrenmatt obviously believes that it would be wise for science to declare its independence of time-serving society and to withhold information that will be used for destructive purposes. Yet, at the same time, the playwright does not believe that this
moral decision is possible, for knowledge which exists, or may exist in the future,
is torn from those who possess by those in power or those seeking power.

Durrenmatt does not find the means to personalize or humanize his play. It
presents a thesis. It thinks about an unthinkable hazard. It paints a 'dark picture of "last things." Its eschatology is secular because it does not seek to make
us recoil and take destiny into our own hands. The play offers no solution to the
quandry. It does not lead us to hope and thus to make tenable a humane political
position.

And why should he? Look at contemporary events. France and China stand outside the treaty governing atomic testing. Both seek hydrogen bombs. Within a generation, even the smallest nations will have atomic weapons at their disposal. We seem
to have come to our senses in this country, but too late. The atomic thing· is beyond recall. Durrenmatt says of Jonathan Swift and himself: "He saw the world as it
is, and so do I."

Please, God, no. May that not be the last judgment. Those of us who follow
Jesus have a different eschatology to offer if only we shall grasp it. We can all
too easily abandon the w orld as a madhouse and wait for our personal and individual
salvation. Or we can recognize anew that it was for the world and all men that Jesus
came, l ived, and died. And then we must proceed to work for another "end-time", a
time when all men are one, reconciled to one another. We must proceed to work for
other "last things"--the love and acceptance of men, the affirmation of meaning and
hope in human life.

The story of the Last Judgment may point the way from the madhouse of secular
eschatology. This is not strictly a parable--but a picture. The center of it is
the Son of Man, Jesus. He represents his brothers; he is their spokesman--and his
brothers are his disciples--those w ho follow, those who have a "blik". (Since Matthew paints the picture, it uses sheep and goats--a favorite subject of his--don't
be misled.) There will be a judgment in this picture. The disciples will be measured. And what is the measurement? Very simply, it is service--it lies in whether
one's way of viewing life in Jesus Christ has led inevitably to a way of acting in
life. It tells us that service to man, to our brother is service to our Lord. The
question whether this service has been rendered is decisive in the final judgment.

And that is the Christian hope. It is another form of "secular"eschatology.
It is the hope for the "end-time"--that lovingkindness and compassion may yet produce reconciliation and peace. In Jesus we confess love and compassion to be the
very will and purpose of God himself on earth. To love and to be compassionate stand
central. Whether we render them far outweigh the importance of discussing personal
salvation or the life of the soul. That life is given as we live in Jesus and have
his mind among us here and now. That life is taken from us here and now as we neglect our fellow men for that is a neglect of Christ himself.

We who have witnessed the terrible events of inhumanity in the 20th Century know
full well that man cannot bring the "kingdom of earth". We can profess no optimism
that we possess the power or the will to direct history to its proper goal. However,
we who hold the Christian "blik" do confess that the kingdom is already among us.
And we learn from the New Testament that we are not to sit idly by. We must work to
fulfill our hope, and most, if not all, of that work must be done outside the church.
We must work in law, government, medicine, business, science, and all the branches
of technology. Work we must! In fact, Jesus condemns the sins of omissions: "I tell
you this: anything you did not do for one of these, however humble, you did not do
for me." We can never forget, then, how closely Jesus identified himself with his
people, how "secular" he was, what he hoped for his people. And we can take his parable or picture here not just in terms of personalistic salvation but even primarily
in terms of what he expects his followers to be and do. The escape from a madhouse
lies in what Jesus calls "eternal life", and that must mean reconciliation of men.
It must mean redemption--a buying back into the intended purpose of creation, namely
community. And we can hope for that only as we follow our Lord into giving ourselves
to others.
     "You have my Father's blessing; come, enter and possess the kingdom that has
been ready for you since the world was made. For when I was hungry, you gave me food;
when thirsty, you gave me drink; when I was a stranger, you took me into your home,
when naked you clothed me; when I was ill, you came to my help, when in prison, you
visited me."

H. 11/1/64   An Issue for Christians: The Future History of Mankind

Nuclear Armageddon has receded in immediacy (but not disappeared) during the past 50 years, to be replaced by more diffuse intimidations such as weapons of mass destruction, dirty bombs, threats to buildings and trains and airplanes, public beheadings, and other forms of distributed terrorism. The menace to our humanity is no less genuine.

This sermon, one of two on the subject of eschatology (the other one being Item G above), is actually the finale of a series (Sermons #47 and #48). Somehow, it felt incomplete to include the other two sermons in the Cycle itself without providing access to the powerful ending.

Westminster Presbyterian Church
Wooster, Ohio
Rev. Beverly Asbury, Minister
November 1, 1964

AN ISSUE FOR CHRISTIANS: THE FUTURE HISTORY OF MANKIND
Romans 13: 11-14
I Thessalonians 5: 1-11

One of the conditions of human life at any time is that of being bound by historical circumstances. No one chooses the time and place in which his life will be lived. A person enters a situation which is to a large extent already ordered. We are members of a certain race, a certain nation, a certain class, a certain church. We inherit the rich culture of our civilization, but we also inherit its sin, guilt, and sickness. This has always been the condition of human existence.

However, today as never before, world history has become an inevitable destiny. The general situation has become more acute. To a far greater extent than ever before, human life has been completely woven into the intricate web of world events. We can no longer live within the narrow confines of a town or county, which seldom feel the affect of the events of world history. It is simply not possible to escape the fact that everything that happens today is connected with everything else. An explosion in the remote regions of China now has direct repercussions on our own lives in the towns and cities of America and the Midwest. When we face the questions of war and peace, we discover that this planet has no haven. We no longer are facing the age-old problem of how to control nature--at least, it is not our primary problem Rather, our real problem today is how to control the future history of mankind, because of the decisive power historical events now have over our lives.

In short, the events of history have broken in upon us, and we must reflect anew upon the question of Christian action in history. The events of recent history have questioned some of our most cherished historical ideas. We have lived over 20 years with the thought of a world divided into two hostile and irreconcilable camps, but we find now that many centers of power replace the two. We have nourished the invincible hope that the conflict between the two camps would result in the victory of "freedom"and "democracy" as we Americans define these terms. And now we find a growing sense among our wisest leaders that we must accept long-term negotiation and accommodation with our ideological foes. We have been convinced for years that economic development would engulf the world and bring it to our level of prosperity, but now we find that the gap between the rich and poor na tions is widening; the poor floundering in their freedom toward either dictatorship or revolution. To put it bluntly, then, our popular American view of history no longer fits the harsh facts of 1964, and to cling to it could be fatal--to our society and to the world.

We must shake ourselves loose from the myths of recent history to face reality constructively. We cannot leave such a job to those seeking office. This is an issue for all Christians, an issue where Christians can make a significant contribution to the future of mankind. The very essence of the Christian witness is to find in the place where one is, the historical situation, the calling of God to the service and proclamation of the Word. God has not abandoned history. That is our faith. That is the power of the Christian l ife.

So the Christian lives in history--as it is, but with faith. You can put it this way, the Christian believes that history is a sphere "ruled by divine providence and formed by human confusion." (This definition and several other points are drawn from "Historical Events and Ethical Decisions" by J. Milic Lochman in Theology

11-1-64

<u>Today</u>,July 1964) What we have already said about the last 20 years shows the human confusion and the confusion of human quarrels. Since history takes its form from these confusions, Christians need first of all to have clear grasp of the facts. We must not be too ready to preach. Christians should be slow to claim that their view is <u>the</u> Christian view; truly reluctant to make our political differences into religious positions. Christians above all can caution against making human quarrels into crusades. We are not living in the "end-time , the time when the forces of light and the forces of da rkness are fighting to a decisive close. Rather, we are living in a time of confusion, the time before the "end-time". But it is also the time in which Jesus Christ accepted our human lot, the time in which he dwelt among us. And, thus, we Christians take <u>this</u> time with great seriousness.

Perhaps we should have cared for a time when the lines were less confusing. Yet, our place in history is not a matter of chance. This time is our unique opportunity. We shall have no other time. It is "our" time; the time and actual scene of our concrete responsibility. In this time we must either serve or fall. It is so easy for us to miss this opportunity. We hear voices all around us, longing for the past, limping behind our day. We hear other impatient with the present time, dreaming only of the future. Both miss our concrete opportunities and tasks. You see, it is here, only here and not in any other place, that we perceive God's call and fulfill his commandment.

The New Testament is concerned with recognizing time soberly, seizing it, redeeming it, and acting according to the time and place given to us. The very ethical decisions faced by New Testament Christians were decided in the light of the understanding of God's presence in history. (This is called "eschatology", but we do not have to use the word to get the point. "Eschatology" is not simply history and history is not simply "eschatology") The light of God's presence in history enables us to discern and decipher the signs of the time and to do what is necessary here and now. "....you knowwhat hour it is, how it is full time now for you to wake from sleep..." "For you yourselves know well that the day of the Lord will come like a thief in the night. When people say, 'There is peace and security', then sudden destruction will come upon them... But you are not in darkness, brethren, for that day to surprise you like a thief. For you are all sons of the day....So then let us not sleep...but keep awake." The action of Christians is definitely related to history. We can never be content to repeat what was demanded of people in times past, however, well they responded to the challenge then. We have to fulfill the commandments of the living God here and now. We have to ask ourselves "What are we to be doing here?" in the light of God's rule over the realm of human confusion. There is no substitute for the vocation to reflect clearly on what Christians ought to be doing in the world. Those reflections may not conform to present political thought, and they may produce hostility instead of public favor. The most serious criticism made of my recent sermon on "Our Wealth and the World's Poverty" was that it was "Idealist". I could do nothing but plead "guilty". Guilty, not of Platonic idealism, but of using Jesus as the ideal by which and through which to view the world. Guilty, if that means transcending the accepted political reality to build a new hope for mankind. Guilty, if that means a new understanding of one mankind under God, where each man is responsible for his neighbor. Guilty, if that means a willingness to reflect a Reality beyond the situation of today which produces only apathy and despair. Yes, guilty of Christian idealism if that means willingness to think in new and bold ways about the redemption of the wor ld. Serious commitment to God requires serious reflection about what actions and intentions express God's will and way in highly concrete places and times for specific persons.

A good illustration of this is the question of <u>war</u>. The well-known theory of the "just war", developed in the early centuries of Christendom, has been the classical teaching of the Christian Church about war. Some Christian groups have always

11-1-64

been opposed to this teaching. They have regarded it as a distortion of God's will, and they have held to an absolute pacificism. Other Christians, however, have not had such objections to warfare-in-principle as applied in the past, and Calvinists have stood prominently among them. Yet, these same Christians today clearly feel that the old categories will not apply to our present historical situation. There can be no "just war", no "total victory" in an atomic age where atomic warfare is the negation of all justice. Warfare today constitutes a radical menace to the very existence of mankind. We can no longer simply hand on traditional, classical formulations and decisions relating to war. "...the night is far gone, the day is at hand. Let us then cast off the works of darkness and put on the armor of light; let us conduct ourselves becomingly as in the day......"

Charles A. Wells in his newsletter, Between the Lines, for November 1, 1964, calls to our attention what the scientists are saying. Let me quote what Mr. Wells puts before his readers.

"Our nuclear predicament is clarified in a remarkable declaration by two eminent American nuclear physicists who have had close and authoritative connections with the nation's political and military establishments under both the Democratic Kennedy Administration and the Republican Eisenhower regime. The two spokesmen are Dr. Jerome B. Wiesner(now Dean of the School of Science at the Massachusetts Institute of Technology and former science adviser to President Kennedy) and Dr. Herbert F. York, Chancellor of the University of California at San Diego, formerly the chief scientific adviser to the Dept. of Defense under Eisenhower.

"Their statements, which appear in the October issue of the Scientific American, were also endorsed by Dr. George Kistiakowski, President Eisenhower's chief science adviser. This declaration therefore speaks above all partisan interests. Both Dr. York and Dr. Wiesner—as they stated in the declaration—have full access to all secret and classified materials. Thus their judgments can be accepted as of the highest authority and cannot be ignored except at great peril to ourselves and the rest of the world. This declaration is being largely suppressed and ignored in Washington and in the press, though it is destined to be one of the most important documents of our generation.

"THE INTERNATIONAL TEST BAN is strongly endorsed by these two scientists, the ban now having been enforced for a little over a year........ ......

"A MAJOR CHANGE in military strategy, largely ignored by our military and political leaders, came with the advent of nuclear power, according to the scientists. During World War II England needed to intercept only ten per cent of the German Nazi Air Force to defend her island. For just this much of a loss forced the Germans to give up the Battle of Britain. In only ten attacks the Nazi Air Force would have been wiped out. On the other hand, in warfare by thermonuclear missiles, the scientists explain the situation is quantitatively and qualitatively transformed. It would be easily conceivable for the offensive force to have in its possession weapons enough to exceed the number of targets to the point where failure would be impossible. If ten missiles were fired at each target, the successful delivery of only one warhead against each such target would result in a most effective attack. 'Thus defense against thermonuclear attack is impossible.' It is too easy for an offensive force to launch sufficient missiles to make the attack 100 per cent effective and totally destructive. Both Russia and United States are now in that position several times over.

THE ANTI-MISSILE MISSILES PROGRAM is condemned as futile by the scientists........The offense outran the defense in these developments for the offense designers began to build penetrating mock weapons, decoys, single rockets that eject multiple warheads and other devices that simply overwhelmed the design capabilities of the Nike-Zeus system and compelled it to be abandoned. The scientists therefore reveal that anti-missile missile systems are destined to total failure, although the military-industrial complex is campaigning in Washington for appropriations that will assure the continuation and expansion of the anti-missile programs. ...
....

THE STEADY DECREASE in national security as we become more heavily armed in nuclear weapons is the most significant of all points made by Wiesner and York. "Since shortly after World War II the military power of the U.S. has steadily been increasing. While in the same period the national security of the U. S. has been rapidly and inexorably diminishing." "Early in the 1950's, explain the scientists, 'when we had a strong lead in nuclear weapons power over the U.S.S.R., if the Soviet had launched an attack, four or five million Americans would have died and we would have struck Russia in retaliation, with results in proportion to whatever our atomic lead would have afforded. As we pressed on to ever larget weapons, especially in thermonuclear developments, our capacity to destroy reached the maximum with the Russians following closely behind us. Then should the Soviet have launched an attack we would have lost approximately 50 million dead, again with equal results in Russia from our retaliatory strikes -- plus whatever advantage we had in surplus power.' Now with the U. S and the U.S.S.R. having reached the point of saturation in nuclear weapons, with enormous over-kill capacity, so that each side can repeat the destructive first strikes several hundred times over, Wiesner and York believe that we stand on the threshold of total and absolute futility. 'Should the U.S.S.R. launch such an attack on the U.S. now.... the American casualties would be 100 million or more.' Such casulaty estimates do not include the millions who would suffer lingering radiation illnesses or the long-lasting genetical damage.

"BOTH SIDES in the arms race are thus confronted by the dilemma of steadily increasing military power and steadily decreasing national security. 'It is our considered professional judgment.' continue the physicists, 'That this dilemma has no technical solution.' As the great powers continue to look for solutions in the area of military science and technology, only, the result will be only to worsen the situation. The clearly predictable course of the arms race is a steady open spiral down into oblivion. The scientists continue hopefully, 'We are optimistic, on the other hand, that there is a solution to this dilemma. The nuclear Test Ban, we believe, is truly an important first step to finding a solution in an area where a solution may exist. The next logical step would be the conclusion of a comprehensive test ban which would include the banning of underground tests.' And this is quite possible, the two physicists believe, for they state that 'The great powers came close to an agreement more than once during the long years of negotia tion at Geneva.' They report that the policing and inspection procedures so nearly agreed on in those parlays offer significant precedents, having laid the foundation of mutual confidence for proceeding thereafter to actual disarmament."

Old notions of war are an absurd anachronism in our present situation. We must seek new ways and new formulations. And here an astonishing thing happens to us --- because we take this new situation of human confusion so seriously, the clear message of Jesus speaks to us afresh. His message is not given additional force by the

11-1-64

historical events. Rather, they give us the context in which to recall Jesus' message and commandment from abstract terms to the strong and powerful terms of actual life. We have to love our fellow men in the midst of the human confusion which is history. And this we can do, because in Jesus Christ, we learn that history is not the work of demons but the work of men. It is a human activity. History is the outcome of human confusions, and we must soberly and realistically evaluate its events in order to learn how to reconcile men one to another. Our aim in Jesus Christ is not to conquer but to reconcile. We are not called to judge other men from the viewpoint of our own standards but of his. Our position in history is not absolute for the Christian; Jesus' is. When we know that, we are ready for the genuine encounter and conversation with those who differ with us and are hostile toward us. We stand ready to reconcile and to be reconciled.

In short, when we remember our own human confusion, we see that we do not have to treat those who differ with us as demons or to see history as a conspiracy of demons. We live in the age of cold war, an age full of divisions and tensions. The future history of mankind cannot be considered hopeful if the Church adopts the strategy of the cold war. This is an issue for Christians: to learn in Jesus Christ that the time has come to look at war, even the cold war, from the Christian perspective; to cast out the demonology and to remind the leaders of the human confusion; to reject war and probe the deep anxieties that lead us there; to develop contacts across every barrier and search for peace. For the Christian to accept his place in history from the hands of God is not to take a slogan but to look steadfastly at the relation of Christ to his neighbor and to spell out his social action there. For us, the time is at hand. God remains sovereign, and we live in hope and solemn moral obligation. Let us pray that our sign for the future history of mankind will be one of hope and reconciliation.

I. 11/27/66 Dying of Respectability

From the sermon: "The work of the church, then, is not in happy fellowship but in sacrificial mission." The church can – and should – be a place of happy internal renewal for a community. But the *mission* is outward.

This sermon is included because the final sermon in this collection, namely Item J below, seems to require it as a prelude. This sermon was delivered the week before the final one.

Westminster Presbyterian Church
Wooster, Ohio
Rev. Beverly Asbury, Minister
November 27, 1966

DYING OF RESPECTABILITY
John 15: 18-27

Professor Waldo Beach of Duke Divinity School has written a book on The Christian Life for the adult series of the Southern Presbyterian's Covenant Life Curric-
ulum. The book deserves our study as United Presbyterians, and I wish that it were
a part of our study. In his last chapter, "The Conversion of the Churches to Christianity", Beach speaks of a mythical "First Presbyterian Church", and its truth
obviously applies to many less mythical congregations. Here is what Beach says:

A high virtue honored in the John Calvin Presbyterian Church is social
respectability. The bond of fellowship in this church is "liking", a
mutual attraction in similar cultural tastes and outlooks. Though this
"liking" is called Christian love, it is really quite different from the
agape of the New Testament, the disinterested passionate concern for the
like and the unlike. The church confuses organizational success with
growth in Christian grace and the authentic love of God and neighbor.
"Success" is measured in terms of numbers, budget, and the size of the
church plant. The members are so busy working for the Building Fund that
it never occurs to them that there is no necessary ratio between institutional success and the quality of Christian living; indeed, in some
instances, the ratio may be inverse. The virtues cultivated in the church
are the business and club virtues; adjustability, friendliness, conformity,
an easy tolerance, a sugary niceness, all observed under the sign of a
cross, the symbol of maladjustment and nonconformity, carrying the weight
of One who called his own mission "not to bring peace, but a sword" and
the mission of his disciples to be the salt of the earth.

I don't know Evor Roberts. But one of his admirers a few years ago was a stu-
dent at Wooster who joined our church. I heard all about him from her; her name
was Jean Patterson. Roberts was and is minister of the Swarthmore Presbyterian
Church. On Tuesday (Nov.22) he and his church made the front page of the New York
Times. Now, how about that! The headline said that "Church Asks Pastor to Resign
Over Rights Work and Sermons". You can imagine that the words attracted more than
my attention; like, would you believe that I thought—'there but for the grace of
God and a good congregation....'

Well, anyway, you may want to read the entire account. In fact you should.
The entire story cannot be told here and now. What must be said is that the report
called attention to the fact that 6 years ago the church listed 1850 members and
now lists only 1604. The reason for the drop is not given; it could have resulted
from many factors, but the clear implication is that the blame is placed at Mr.
Roberts' feet, or sermons, or activities—as you would have it. The Session was
concerned that the Church was slowly dying. In six years, the number of pledging
units dropped from 778 to 546. That is enough to make any 'God fearing' trustee
think that the Church is dying. However, the report did indicate that the per capita pledge in the same period had risen from $154 to $207, and that posed a 'thorny
dilemma that defies off-hand or unstudied explanation'. Yet, it was said that if
Dr. Roberts had made 'more frequent references to peace of mind, the joy of salvation, the love of God, the therapy of faith, etc.'....'many of the problems would
never have arisen to the surface of the relationship between pastor and people.'

It would seem that what modern churchmen find least bearable is an act of being "personal". Issues may be "too abstract"; sermons may be "too intellectual; but
to be "too personal" is leveled as the most severe criticism. Don't get too close!

Don't bring feelings to the surface! Keep it "impersonably personal," whatever
that means. In an intensely personal Thanksgiving meditation last week, I found a
dismaying number of students offering the criticism that my "prayers" had been "too
personal". Evor Roberts may have felt the same frustration as I feel. While it
was said of his preaching that it was not "personal" enough, it was obviously so
genuinely personal that it got to some people.

The Church was dying, because he did not refer enough to peace of mind...be-
cause his activities allowed true feelings to come to the surface...because those
feelings said 'either you go or I go' and 250 members went, and pledges dropped
by 222. Because of civil rights activities and too few sermons on 'peace of mind'
and 'joy of salvation', the church was dying.

Does it never occur to 'fashionable churches' that they have accepted the wrong
fashions? Does it never occur to us white, middle-class, Protestants that we may
be dying of social respectability? Does it not stagger us when Christians condemn
the Beattles for saying that they are more 'popular' than Jesus and never let it
dawn that Jesus never won a popularity contest, only a Cross? Have we improved upon our Master? What kind of thinking is it to say that we must not lose pledges or
money because they will enable us to do HIS work--what kind of thinking is that
when we have to become unlike HIM in order to keep those pledges? Jesus chose
twelve poor Jews in Palestine to save all of wealthy America, but we don't want
them. We want peace of mind, not a Cross.

I hope that Evor Roberts turns to John 15 and reads: "If the world hates you,
know that it has hated me before it hated you. If you were of the world, the world
would love its own; but because you are not of the world, but I chose you out of
the world, therefore the world hates you." And this too, "Remember the word that
I said to you, 'A servant is not greater than his master'...." The Swarthmore
Church may die and so may the church-in-general in its present American form, but
Evor Roberts reminds us that if it is to die, it must not be a death of social
respectability. Only if it is a suffering death, the death of a cross, can new
life come forth, a resurrection be granted. The common error of most church people
lies in mistaking the symbol for reality--they only look at the finger that points
the way, and then they prefer to suck it comfortably rather than follow the direction it points.

While the Church does have a legitimate function to serve as a shelter, as a
place of nurture and comfort, that can never be the end pupose for which it exists.
As I have examined my ministry here, I have asked myself carefully if Westminster
Church has been enough of a shelter. A church does have to provide one, because
we cannot be "prophetic" all the time; always "on edge"; forever engaging issues.
The deeper personal dimensions of life often press quite rightly for counsel, assurance, comfort, love, hope. I sincerely hope that in the crises of both life and
death Westminster has provided spiritual solace. But I do not take that to be the
final aim of this church, and I honestly believe that enough other churches are
total shelters that Westminster can and must be different. It must be free to make
a mistake in the opposite direction, and at least provide an alternative to the
patterns of church life prevailing all around us. Jesus says that he chose us out
of the world, and he gives us the clue as to our calling. Ekklesia means not so
much called into the shelter of an organized community but rather called out of
customary attachments and securities, out of the world. To follow Christ meant
venturing out of traditions, out of the 'consensus of opinion', out of any comfortable settling down in the shelter of the anonymous mass.

That is a very threatening notion. Most people hate to be 'out of things',
'out of fashion','out of date', 'out of it', 'out of a job.' When we are 'out',
we seek a shelter as a neurotic defense; instead of being 'out of it', we would almost rather be in trouble. That's a game I've often been tempted to play--it's

called "Where the Action Is". You play by being "hip"; by seeking to accomodate present trends rather than be caught "out of it". It is part of being human to seek security in what we know, in the visible, concrete, tangible or the merely active.

It must be more Christlike to seek to discover one's mission, and to fulfill it, even when it means being "out of it" or going against the stream of fashion and opinion. It may mean going into situation 'whither we would not'. People, instead of being receptive to Christ's teachings to take up a Cross, prefer to be handfed, cured of their ailments with peace of mind and spiritual truth.

Of course, the other side of it lies in the fact that Jesus accepted even such people as those. He would not have rejected the needs of Swarthmore Presbyterians who want Roberts' hide. One of the amazing features of the gospel is the intuitive understanding with which Christ met all those who claim his help on the very level and in the very manner which was adequate and meaningful for them. But one cannot help feeling that even Christ at times inwardly rebelled against this exploitation, against having to give, not at the level at which he was unique and that was closest to his spiritual being, but to bend down to the needs of those who could understand love only in material and physical terms. While Jesus always allowed his 'role' to be determined by the needs of others, he never gave in to a narrow notion of the 'others'. The socially respectable did not command all his time. The needs and fears and ambitions and inclinations of many others and the will of God determined his response. He could never be possessed by those whom he accepted. He could not, would not, be made socially respectable, predictable. Like incarnate love would, he spontaneously jumped every barrier man built.

If we learn anything at all from that, then we should not be surprised to realize that the conflict in the life of the church today is over traditional and the more spontaneous, experimental approaches to its mission. The conflict is no longer between denominations, or even between Western faiths. Those conflicts are boring, to say the least. The conflict can be found in every religious institution.. Yet, for the Church, this is and will continue to be real; whether to settle for the conventional and respectable and die, or to go for the unconventional, for authentic mission, and die as we are---but come again to new life.

The work of the church, then, is not in happy fellowship but in sacrificial mission. We need to know that the place for the church is not the social hall or the church lounge but in the thoroughfares of the world, in the midst of the ambiguity and suffering of our times. As Barbara Ward has said: "The world wonders whether God is dead. But the Christians long since was told the answer: 'If you do not love your neighbor whom you see, how will you love God whom you do not see?'... Christians bent on remarking the face of the earth will discover God both for their neighbors and themselves."

As the Swarthmore Church has made clear, the Church is not always happy about this living and working in the world. The Church often prefers its social respectability, even if it has to change its address or become a new development called "Sacred Shores:, or "Religious Ranch", or "Divinity Dudes", or "Peace of Mind Acres" I prefer another death. If there is to be a coming non-church, then I pray that we shall get there by the way of Jesus, the way of the Cross.

I see that to mean that we need most of all the determination that the love seen in Jesus Christ shall become real among men, whether they recognize the source of it or not. Our task today is not first to baptize but to make the good news known, not to bring people to church but to take its essential power to them; not to induce guilt feelings in the nonbeliever but to help people find the depths in themselves; not to talk theology piously but to express ourselves together as to what good neighborliness means in social, industrial, commercial, educational, and personal life.

If the Church dies, I believe that it will be because the Kingdom is coming. In the meantime, let us expect and accept the fate of Him who went before us. We are his "witnesses", let us then hear his Truth, the marks of His life.

J. 12/4/66 **Safety Last** Last Sermon at Wooster

The title of this sermon, as well as the benediction it conveys, is testimony to the message and actions of someone whose life intersected ours. Does this same benediction apply to our grandchildren? The sermon affirms the principles of a life and confirms the title of this book. The sermon was delivered six months after Wooster's Centennial Class of 1966 graduated.

Westminster Presbyterian Church
Wooster, Ohio
Rev. Beverly A. Asbury, Minister
December 4, 1966

"SAFETY LAST"*
Galatians 3: 21-4:7
II Corinthians 5: 17

Well, it can surely be said (at least in reference to the band) that there
is lots of brass in church on my last Sunday in the pulpit. I appreciate it. It's
loud, and I've learned to like that. This church has what has been called a "shouting' service, and I take that to mean that we know how to celebrate here. I shall
never again be satisfied with less. Deliver me from a quiet church with a quiet
ministry. Perhaps that's why I like the music here. Neither it nor the ministry
have been quiet. Both have been loaded with fireworks, goodies, surprises, shocks.
For example, in the offertory where people so often expect to be left alone in irrelevance, the organ has often shouted out with thanksgiving.

I love it, and I shall miss it. It's a "swinging service'. And it rightly
sets the tone for this last sermon, which is not intended to be maudlin or nostal-
gic. I don't know exactly what it is, but it is not a blast. It's rather free
swinging reflection on what these past four years have been all about and what the
next years ahead mean for us all.

A good many of you, knowing me and having heard, at least, of the South, have
expressed your concern and anxiety about what may lay ahead for me there. You know
I am human enough to feel the same concern. That's natural. We are always anxious
when we don't know exactly what to expect, or know enough to mentally and emotionally anticipate what could happen. But these anxieties are not incapacitating. I
have reminded myself in recent days that the decision to do this was carefully considered and that there were and are good reasons to consider this a "call". In
fact, I never sought it; I had made no effort at all to relocate. Indeed, I had
made a decision to refuse to consider another position that had been offered. (That
happened the same day and a few hours before a phone call came from Vanderbilt
about being considered there.)

In arriving at a decision, considering all the factors both here and there,
finding (as one does) reasons to do both (to stay and to go) and wishing that one
could be both places, I became aware of the unique opportunity before me at Vanderbilt. I have gone into some detail about that before, and I would only add that
one Wooster man who knows both Vanderbilt University and me said that I was "born
for the job". May be! In any case, in accepting the challenge, I knew very well
that I was venturing out of safety. Not that I have been all that safe here! Nor
even that I considered this a 'sure thing'. Simply that I knew that to return South
depended partly on whether the 'time had come'. There are indications that time
has changed the South but recent indications are : Not all that much! Thus, the
anxiety!

There are a good many people in the North but even more in the South who believe that the essence of the Gospel is "faith, hope, and love, and the greatest of
these is the status quo." Anyone who rejects that in action, as well as in word,
in the life of today's church ventures out of safety. Professor Tait called my attention this week to what happened recently to the Reverend John Fry of the First
Presbyterian Church of Chicago, who stirred us up here a bit last Spring. It seems

*This title is borrowed from J.C. Hoekendijk's The Church Inside Out (Westminster
Press, paperback, 1966). So is some sermon content.

that Mr. Fry and his Session, with police cooperation made contact some months ago,
with one of the gangs in the Woodlawn area which the church serves. As a result of
the confidence placed in the church, the gang agreed to check its weapons with the
church. So far as I know, Mr. Fry had the only church vault in the country filled
with guns and various kinds of weapons. At a meeting between the minister, church
officials and the gang, a few weeks ago, there was a raid by the police. The sanctity of First Church was invaded because the police resented the church's role in
the recent elections in which the Daley machine had suffered a setback. Two of the
gang members were arrested and the church was attacked for harboring the weapons.
It did seem that some people would prefer that the weapons stay in dangerous hands
to be used so that the church could condemn them instead of involving itself in the
world and keeping the weapons out of use. The experience there teaches us that the
world really doesn't understand the commitment of the contemporary church to venture
out of the safety of the sanctuary. The core of all religiosity is a safety-first
desire. We want to hold on to old symbols, old ways, familiar patterns. We want
to live through this new time in the categories of the old time. However, the very
Spirit of God cannot, according to his nature, stop doing new things; calling us
new places, forcing us into new patterns and responsibilities. To follow the Spirit,
to be alive to its promptings, is not safety-first, but Safety-Last! That is the
time that has come; the time for Safety-Last! That insight may even be why some of
you have detected a new spirit in me. At least, so far as I am consciously aware
my preaching this Fall has been much more informed by that than by the knowledge
that I am leaving. I have been grasped by the notion again that a Christian must
put safety last.

The very paradigm of that was expressed by Paul in Galatians 4: 4,5: "...When
the time had fully come, God sent forth his Son, born of woman, born under the law,
to redeem those who were under the law, so that we might receive adoption as sons."
That act was anything but 'safety-first'. It was not a religious act, not something
'spiritual'. It was God secularizing himself; becoming incarnate in Man. Can you
call it safe to be born of women? Just consider what that means, especially in the
terms of the ancient world which had no antiseptic hospitals or modern medical knowledge. Safety-last—born under the law; that means God makes hims f in human form
subject to all the limitations of men; to all the conditions of human life; to all
the eventualities of society. A man is subject to disease, pain, anguish, suffering;
a man endures a world of inconsistencies and inconstancies and infidelities. Man
faces a sure and certain death in the world of nature. Perhaps worst of all man
often faces the inhumanity of man. Safety Last! And it was hardly safe for God
to expose himself in this manner. Anyone who exposes himself takes the risk of being misunderstood, rejected, despised, hated, even declared "dead". And this God
did, safety-last, that mankind could be redeemed—bought back to meaning; to the
intention of creation; to faith, hope, and love; to the way of mercy as an original
ordering of reality.

And what does this mean for us, beyond the effect of words? Paul said that
"when anyone is united to Christ, there is a new world; the old order has gone, and
a new order has already begun." That means safety-last. A previous word of Paul's
(II Cor. 5:15) said: "His purpose in dying for all was that men, while still in life,
should cease to live for themselves, and should live for him...." A new life in a
new world can be no safer for us than it was for him. The church is promised a Cross-
road by her Lord, and we need to consider what that means for Westminster Church,
for you, for me.

Safety-last on the Cross-road holds out the prospect of discord, hatred, and
even oppression. But if we are a small flock of sheep which knows itself to be sent
into the midst of wolves, why should we be surprised that we are not safe? This
should be a normal part of the scope of the church, but the older generation (and
that includes all of us as we gradually become a part of it) will have to fade into

the background. The younger generation, always I hope, ready to live more danger-
ously, must be given a generously free hand. To find the rolé of the church on
today's Cross-road, the younger generation must have the chance, or take it, to
break step, to try new ideas without our being annoyed, without pointing fingers
from old 'watchdogs'. Safety-last means that they shall break with not a few of
the patterns of a society to which we have grown so accustomed. Bishop Pike is
quite right in telling us that the church must gear to a new type of society which
can no longer be understood or defined by using the old categories. That fact alone
makes us feel unsafe, insecure. Yet, the grace of such insecurity is that it drives
us to trust in the mercy of God who himself put safety-last.

None of this means that we have to think of the future church purely in terms
of revolution. The end of the establishment-type-thought calls us not away from
the Gospel but back to it. The scurried mobility of our day may disturb our stabil-
ity-type-thinking, but it may recall us to the rich significance of the symbol of
Exodus. In the great church buildings, we have sung "thy tent shall be our home",
and we may now, in Marcel's words, discover ourselves a "barracks people", preparing
living, studying for the uncertain future. There is a new world ahead; the old has
passed.

Of course, the safety-last temptation is not to enter the new time. We may
seek instead to enter that widespread conspiracy which wants to leave everything the
way it is. The clever politics of the ostrich, head in the sand, announces, 'we
don't see anything new'. Or we can fervently mark time and reassure one and all,
'we're progressing nicely, aren't we?' Or we can copy that ingenious invention of
stale intellectual life, namely, getting in a plane, taking off, and setting our
course to land where it is still yesterday. But we can enter the new world if we
dare, if we put safety-last, if we quite deliberately choose tomorrow, as over
against today and yesterday, and see our life as nothing less than a journey, an
exodus.

This is what it means that a new time, a new order has come. We learn in
God's act of love in Jesus Christ to deal freely with the whole of time. We deal
with the past not by forgetting it or ignoring it, not by acting as though it never
existed. Safety-last does not mean forgoing a meaningful sense of history. It
just means dealing with the past in such a way that it cannot exercise power any
more. As you know, any move to the South is still to the "land of the Confederate
Flag." I abhor that flag and have done so ever since I was a boy. It is a despic-
able symbol of a people's commitment to a wrongful past, to a George Wallace who
seeks to lead his people further away from the mainstream of National life. I hope
that it will be in my lifetime that I can in good conscience possess a Confederate
Flag. That day will come only when it no longer exercises power and is no longer
related to segregation and a desire for the old quarter. Then it may become a
true symbol of honor.

The past must be conquered. We as Christians can 'remember it with joy', and
learn from it so surely that the present does not become a dead-end street. The
future must not be a dull repetition of what is past; any man in Christ has died
to the old order and is prepared for the new. Behold, in our time, tomorrow is
already here! And it can turn out to have the open space of freedom which we can
enter with confidence and great expectation. A new order has already begun; it is
of God; and more and more it overpowers the old.

That belief allows us then to put safety last, to engage in the risky venture
of being advantgardist. We proclaim then that in Jesus, people are introduced
into an unprecedented history of free men, a perilous time requiring hazardous
improvization. Each year ahead for me, for you, for Westminster Church is a new

12-4-66   -4-

venture without model or example. Of each year that we count from Jesus Christ,
we can only know that it will be a 'year of our Lord', and that must suffice. Only
the man who is open toward the future in which we shall confront the ultimate realities — only that man is up to date and only he, who has put safety last, will
know the peace which passes understanding.

"We are no better than pots of earthenware to contain this treasure, and this
proves that such transcendent power does not come from us, but is God's alone. Hard-
pressed on every side, we are never hemmed in; bewildered, we are never at our wit's
end; hunted we are never abandoned to our fate; struck down, we are not left to
die. Wherever we go we carry death with us in our body, the death that Jesus died,
that in this body also life may reveal itself, the life that Jesus lives."(II.Cor.
5:7ff). N.E.B.

So be it!

Ω